*A Comprehensive Guide to*

# GOOD ENGLISH

# A Comprehensive Guide to
# GOOD ENGLISH

## GEORGE PHILIP KRAPP

VOLUME II                                    I-Z

FREDERICK UNGAR PUBLISHING CO.
*NEW YORK*

Republished 1962

First published 1927

*Printed in the United States of America*

Library of Congress Catalog Card No. 61-13634

# CONTENTS

# I

**I**, pron., the subject form of the pronoun of the first person, with an objective *me*, and plurals *we, us*.   In dialectal speech **I** is sometimes used for *me*, as in *between you and I*, for *between you and me*, *Let you and I*, for *Let you and me*.   Uses after forms of the verb *to be* are special, as in *It is me*, and in Shelley's line *Be thou me, impetuous one*.   In the vocative also *me* occurs instead of **I**, as in *Dear me, O me imperturbe* (Walt Whitman)   For further discussion, see **her, me**

**Iago**, n., *character in Shakspere*, pronounced (ēah′gō)

**Ian**, n., *man's name*, pronounced (ē′ahn) or (ī′ahn)

**ibidem**, adv., Latin word, *in the same book, passage*, etc.   Pronounced (ĭbī′dĕm) and abbreviated *ib., ibid.*

**ibis**, n., *a kind of bird*, pronounced (ī′bĭs), with a plural *ibises* (ī′bĭsez)

**-ible**, suffix, in adjectives like *flexible, forcible*, etc.   There is no clear distinction in meaning or in pronunciation between the suffixes *-able* and **-ible**.   The form *-able* is the more common and the one which would be used if one were making a new compound of this kind, e. g., *curable, treatable, lightable*, that which may be cured, treated, lighted.   But a number of words occur in which the spelling **-ible** is established and is necessary, and as these words sometimes cause trouble through confusion with words ending in *-able*, a list of those of most frequent occurrence is here given: accessible, admissible, audible, avertible, combustible, comestible, compatible, comprehensible, compressible, contemptible, convertible, corrigible, corruptible, credible, defensible, destructible, digestible, dirigible, divisible, edible, eligible, exhaustible, expansible, expressible, extensible, fallible, feasible, flexible, forcible, fusible, horrible, impressible, indelible, intelligible, invincible, irascible, irresistible, legible, negligible, omissible, ostensible, perceptible, permissible, persuasible, plausible, possible, reducible, reprehensible, repressible, responsible, risible, sensible, submersible, suggestible, susceptible, suppressible, tangible, terrible, vendible, visible.

**-ic, -ical,** suffixes, both forming adjectives, usually of the same, but sometimes of differentiated meaning. The suffix **-ic** is derived from Latin *-icus;* the suffix **-ical** is derived from a late Latin combination *-ic-* and *-alis,* each element being an adjective-forming suffix. The general tendency now in English is in favor of the shorter form **-ic** whenever a choice between the longer and the shorter is possible. In earlier English, adjectives with the ending **-ical** were current which now can have only **-ic,** as, for example, *an heroical epistle,* now only *heroic;* formerly *aristocratical, epidemical,* etc., now only *aristocratic, epidemic,* etc. Many adjectives appear in current English only with the form **-ic,** as in proper adjectives like *Arctic, Asiatic,* etc., and in common adjectives like *athletic, barbaric, chaotic, idiotic, magnetic, scientific,* and many others; and, on the other hand, many appear only with the ending **-ical,** as in *allegorical, astronomical, clerical* (though *a cleric,* n., is current), *critical, dropsical, farcical, genealogical, identical, logical, piratical, surgical, typical,* and many others. No clear principle appears determining the choice of **-ic** in the one of these two groups and **-ical** in the other, that is, *athletical* would seem to be as natural a form as *identical,* and *identic* as *athletic.* The groupings in present use appear to rest upon accidental conventions.

Almost all adjectives in **-ic** form their adverbs like adjectives in **-ical,** that is, in *-ically,* as in *chaotically, idiotically, scientifically,* etc.

In some words both endings occur, with a distinction of meaning, as in the following illustrations:

(1) *comic,* designed to amuse, pertaining to comedy, as in *a comic supplement, comic pictures, a comic actor.*
*comical,* amusing, funny, as in *a comical person, situation, a comical old hat.*

(2) *economic*, pertaining to the science or study of economics, as in *an economic interpretation of history, an economic society. economical*, prudent, saving, as in *an economical housewife, an economical holiday.*

(3) *historic*, noted in history, as in *a historic occasion, the historic Boston Tea Party.*
*historical*, pertaining to the writing of history, as in *a historical scholar, the historical Boston Tea Party*, as contrasted with the legendary.

(4) *optic*, pertaining to the eye, as in *the optic nerve, the optic angle.*
*optical*, visual, as in *an optical illusion, a maker of optical instruments.*

(5) *poetic*, having the quality of poetry, as in *a poetic nature, a poetic impulse.*
*poetical*, in the form or style of poetry as distinguished from prose, as in *a poetical composition* (not the same as *a poetic composition), His interests are poetical.*

(6) *politic*, expedient, prudent, as in *a politic person*, pronounced (pŏl'ĭtĭk)
*political*, pertaining to politics, as in *a political leader*, pronounced (polĭt'ĭkal)

(7) *tragic*, pertaining to tragedy, as in *a tragic actor, the tragic stage.*
*tragical*, fatal, catastrophical, as in *a tragical fate, The death of his father and mother at this time was little short of tragical.* Some speakers and writers, however, might use *tragic* for *tragical.*

Other adjectives in **-ic, -ical** reveal similar differentiations in meaning.

**ice cream,** n., earlier form *iced cream*, which is logically perhaps the better form. But neither logic nor the analogy of *iced tea, iced coffee* is decisive in this case, for usage has placed **ice cream**

beyond question as the correct and only correct form of the word. By the same test *ice water* is correct, but so also is *iced milk*, for usage has given these words their established and fixed forms.

**Ichabod,** n., *man's name*, pronounced (ĭk'abŏd)

**Ich dien,** German phrase, *I serve,* the motto of the Prince of Wales. Pronounced (ĭCH dēn)

**ichneumon,** n., *an animal*, pronounced (ĭknū'mon)

**ichthyosaurus,** n., *prehistoric animal*, pronounced (ĭkthĭōsaw'rus)

**icon,** n., *image*, pronounced (ī'kon) or, somewhat more formally, (ī'kŏn) In the Eastern Church the word is also used to designate a sacred painting or mosaic, neither of these being images in the strict sense of the word.

**idea,** n., *a notion, a mental impression*, pronounced (īdē'a), in some localities (ī'dĭa), in dialectal speech (īdē') Used by some speakers in the phrase *That's the idea* so continually that it becomes a tiresome mannerism.

**idée fixe,** French phrase, *controlling idea, inalterable conviction*, pronounced (ēdā' fēks)

**idem,** pron., Latin word, *the same*, of an author already referred to. Pronounced (ī'dĕm) and abbreviated *id.* The same abbreviation may be used as referring to a word already mentioned, but the unabbreviated form would then be a neuter pronoun with a short initial vowel and would therefore be pronounced (ĭd'ĕm) Ordinarily one is not required to pronounce abbreviations like *ibid., id.,* etc., since they are intended mainly for the eye and not the ear, but when it is necessary in reading to pronounce them, the full forms and not the abbreviations are the ones pronounced. See **viz.**

**identical,** adj., *same*, and as the word means *same*, a phrase like *the identical same person* is tautological and incorrect. Incorrectly used sometimes in the sense *alike*, as in *The two twins were identical*, were very much like each other.

**ides,** n., *eighth day after nones in the Roman calendar*, pronounced (īdz)

**id est,** Latin phrase, *that is*, of explanatory material following. Pronounced (ĭd ĕst) and abbreviated *i. e.*  See **i. e.**

**idiocy,** n., *state of mental weakness*, sometimes incorrectly written *idiotcy*, through the influence of the noun *idiot*.

**idle,** see **idol**

**idle surmise,** trite phrase, bad only because so frequently used.

**idol,** n., *an image*, in connected speech pronounced exactly the same as *idle*.  The attempt to give **idol** a distinctive pronunciation may be useful enough as a phonetic exercise, but it is contrary to the actual practice of untheoretical cultivated speech.

**id omne genus,** Latin phrase, *all that kind*, pronounced (ĭd ŏm'nĭ jē'nus)

**idyll,** n., *a kind of poem*, sometimes spelled *idyl*.  Pronounced (ī'dĭl), with derivatives *idyllic* (īdĭl'ĭk), *idyllist* (ī'dĭlĭst)  A pronunciation with a short initial vowel is less general and less correct.

**i. e.,** phrase, an abbreviation of Latin *id est*, that is, sometimes used to introduce an explanatory or defining phrase following another phrase, and so completely established in English use that the words for which the letters stand are often forgotten and the abbreviation is pronounced (ī ē)  But the proper rendering of the abbreviation in reading is *id est*.  See **idem**  Appropriate only in formalistic writing, as in documents, legal statements, scientific writing, etc., but not to be used in literary or polite style.  See **e. g.**

**if,** conj., incorrectly used sometimes for *whether*, as in *I will write you if I can come or not*, which should be *I will write you whether or not I can come*.  Also used colloquially introducing concessive clauses, as in *He is strong if he is little*, for *He is strong even though he is little*.

**if and when,** conj., often used by writers when one of the two, *if* or *when*, would be adequate, as in the sentence *I shall present these details to you if and when the occasion demands it.* It is not apparent that the addition of *when* to *if* or of *if* to *when* adds anything to the meaning here. The phrase **if and when** has a cumbersome, legalistic sound, not appropriate either to conversation or to literature.

**ignis fatuus,** Latin phrase, *phosphorescent light seen on marshy ground, delusive hope or endeavor,* literally, *fool's fire;* pronounced (ĭg′nĭs făt′ūus)

**ignominy,** n., *disgrace, shame,* pronounced (ĭg′nomĭnĭ), not (ĭgnŏm′ĭnĭ)

**ignotum per ignotius,** Latin phrase, *an explanation more difficult than the thing explained,* literally, *the unknown by the more unknown;* pronounced (ĭgnō′tum per ĭgnō′tĭus)

**I H S,** abbr., the first three letters of the Greek name *Iesous,* Jesus, used as an abbreviation. The letter *H* resembles the Greek capital Ē. The letters are sometimes taken to mean also *Jesus Hominum Salvator,* Jesus Savior of Men, or *In Hoc Signo* (*Vinces*), In this sign (thou shalt conquer), or *In Hac* (*Cruce*) *Salus,* In this (cross) is salvation.

**-ile,** suffix, ordinarily pronounced (-ĭl) in America, as in *agile, reptile,* etc., but (-īl) in England. See **agile, docile, fragile, futile,** etc.

**ilk,** adj., strictly to be used only in the sense *same, identical,* especially in Scotch clan names, as in *Guthrie of that ilk,* meaning Guthrie of that same clan or name, that is, *Guthrie of Guthrie.* Sometimes used incorrectly as though **ilk** were a noun meaning *kind or class of persons,* as in *I can't stand people of that ilk.*

**ill,** adj., distinguished from *sick* in that **ill** usually indicates a slighter degree of unwellness, one's minor ailments being illnesses, unless one is "seriously ill." See **sick**

**I'll, we'll,** colloquial contractions standing either for *I will, we will,* or *I shall, we shall.* Some critics maintain that **I'll, we'll**

can not be contractions of *I shall, we shall,* but the practice of actual usage does not bear them out.

**ill at ease,** phrase, *restless, disturbed,* and idiomatically the noun can not take a possessive modifier before it.   That is, one can not say *John was ill at his ease,* but must say *John was ill at ease.* Without *ill,* however, it is proper to place a possessive before *ease,* and one may say either *John was quite at his ease,* or *John was quite at ease.*

**illegible,** adj., *not plain enough to be read,* to be distinguished from *unreadable,* too dry or dull to be read.

**Illinois,** n., *a state of the United States,* pronounced almost universally (ĭlĭnoi′), sometimes (ĭlĭnoiz′)   If an adjective *Illinoisian* is made, meaning a native of Illinois, the pronunciation is (ĭlĭnoi′yan) or (ĭlĭnoi′zĭan)

**illusory,** adj., *deceptive,* pronounced (ĭlōō′sorĭ)

**illustrate,** v., *provide pictures or examples for.*   Usually stressed on the first syllable, occasionally on the second, but the adjective *illustrative* is always (ĭlŭs′tratĭv)

**illy,** adv., not in good use.   The adverbial form of *ill* is the same as the adjective, as in *to behave ill, to take it ill, ill at ease, it ill becomes you,* etc.

**imbecile,** adj., n., *mentally defective,* pronounced (ĭm′besĭl), in England (ĭm′besēl)   In older English the word could also be used to apply to bodily weakness, but this use is now archaic and practically obsolete.

**imbroglio,** n., Italian word, *complicated situation,* pronounced (ĭm-brōl′yō)

**immanent,** see **imminent**

**immediate,** adj., strictly means *with nothing intervening, nothing between,* therefore, according to logic, not to be compared.   By this reasoning one could not say *our most immediate need, we invited only our more immediate neighbors.*   In actual speech, however, **immediate** does not have only its absolute etymological, logical, or mathematical meaning, but it is used also in the more general sense of *near, approximate,* and it may therefore be employed in phrases that indicate varying degrees of immediacy.

**immediately,** adv., *at once, without delay, with nothing intervening.* Occasionally found in good writers in the sense *as soon as,* but not accepted English in this use. See **directly** The sentence *I came immediately I received your letter* should be *I came as soon as I received your letter* or *I came immediately after I received your letter.*

**immense,** adj., colloquial intensive of approval, as in "*How do you like it?*" "*Oh, it's immense,*" very good. See **great, grand**

**immigrant,** see **emigrant**

**imminent,** adj., *impending, about to happen,* almost always of something unpleasant, as *in imminent danger.* One would not speak of the arrival of a guest as **imminent,** but *expected* or *awaited.* The word *immanent,* inherent, as in *the immanent goodness of the Divine Will,* is often confused in spelling with **imminent,** though in meaning the words are far apart.

**immoral,** see **unmoral**

**impasse,** n., a literary word meaning *deadlock, blind alley,* and pronounced (ĭmpăs′) or (ĭmpahs′) The word is of French origin and may also be pronounced as a French word, approximately (ăṅpahs′)

**imperceptible raising of the eyebrows,** trite phrase, a conventional bit of description often met with in attempts at literary portraits.

**imperium,** n., Latin word, *supreme authority,* pronounced (ĭmpĕr′-ĭum) or (ĭmpē′rĭum)

**imperium in imperio,** Latin phrase, *one supreme authority within another,* pronounced (ĭmpĕr′ĭum ĭn ĭmpĕr′ĭō) or (ĭmpē′rĭum ĭn ĭmpē′rĭō)

**impervious,** adj., *not permitting something to pass through,* or *not open to,* as in *impervious to argument.* The word is incorrectly used in the sense *not affected by*, as in *I am impervious to riding backward*.

**impetus,** n., *force*, *impulse*, pronounced (ĭm'petus), with a plural *impetuses* (ĭm'petusez)

**impious,** adj., *profane*, *irreverent*, pronounced (ĭm'pĭus), not (ĭmpī'us), though the simple adjective is (pī'us) and the noun *impiety* is (ĭmpī'etĭ)

**implacable,** adj., *not to be appeased*, pronounced (ĭmplăk'abl), less commonly (ĭmplā'kabl)

**importune,** v., *press urgently*, pronounced (ĭmpŏrtūn') or (ĭmpŏr'tūn)

**impossible,** adj., colloquial in the sense *difficult to get along with*, as in *an impossible fellow*.  See **possible**

**impress,** v., construed with the preposition *with* in the sense *influence deeply*, as in *He sought to impress the people with a sense of their danger*, and so also in the passive, *The people were impressed with a sense of their danger*.  In the sense merely *to make an impression*, as in *He impresses people favorably*, the construction in the passive would be with *by*, as in *I was not favorably impressed by him*.

**imprimatur,** n., Latin word, *license to print*, literally, *let it be printed;* pronounced (ĭmprĭmā'tur)

**imprimis,** adv., Latin word, *in the first place*, pronounced (ĭmprī'mĭs)

**impromptu,** adj., adv., n., *not prepared beforehand*, pronounced (ĭmprŏmp'tū)  Though of French origin, the word has been completely anglicized.

**improve each shining hour,** trite phrase, originally from one of Isaac Watts's *Divine Songs*.

**improve the occasion, opportunity,** trite phrase, of a stilted, old-fashioned kind.

**improvisatore,** n., Italian word, *improvisator, one who composes ex tempore*, pronounced (ĭmprōvēzahtō'rā), with a plural *improvisatori* (ĭmprōvēzahtō′rē)   Also spelled -*vv*-.   The corresponding feminine is *improvisatrice* (ĭmprōvēzahtrē′chā), *improvisatrici* (ĭmprōvēzahtrē′chē)

**impugn,** v., *challenge, call in question,* pronounced (ĭmpūn′), with an adjective *impugnable* (ĭmpūn′abl) and a noun *impugnment* (ĭmpūn′ment)   But the adjective *inexpugnable*, invincible, not to be called in question, is usually pronounced (ĭnĕkspŭg′nabl), sometimes (ĭnĕkspūn′abl)

**in,** prep., good but not the most general use in the construction *I live in Walnut Street,* for the more common *I live on Walnut Street.*   The phrase *to be all in,* to be exhausted, is slang; *to be in for it,* destined to receive a scolding or punishment, is colloquial; *in with,* familiar with, is also colloquial.

**in, into,** prepositions, after verbs of motion, **in** implying motion within certain limitations of space, as in *The lion paced up and down in his cage,* **into** implying motion from one place to another, as in *He jumped into the water.*   In colloquial speech **in** is often incorrectly used for **into,** as in *He came in the office without knocking,* for *He came into,* etc.

**inadvertence, inadvertency,** n., often confused, but careful style distinguishes them.   The word **inadvertence** means *an act or fault of inattention,* as in *That was an inadvertence;* but **inadvertency** means *the quality or character of being inadvertent,* as in *I did it through inadvertency.*   See **abstinency**

**in a hopeless maze,** trite phrase, being an old-fashioned literary echo.

**inamorato,** n., Italian word, *lover,* pronounced (ĭnahmōrah′tō)

**in a pleasing manner,** trite phrase, so meaningless that it has ceased to be complimentary.

**in articulo mortis,** Latin phrase, *at the point of death,* pronounced (ĭn ahrtĭk′ūlō mŏr′tĭs)

**inasmuch,** conj., *since,* in the somewhat formal phrase *inasmuch as.*   Always written as one word, but never with *as* joined to it.

**in back of,** see **back of**

**in camera,** Latin phrase, *in a private room, not in open court*, pronounced (ĭn kăm′era)

**incarcerate,** v., pedantic word for *imprison*, pronounced (ĭnkahr′serāt)

**incarnate,** adj., *bodily, embodied*, as in *a fiend incarnate*, pronounced (ĭnkahr′nat) Also as a verb, *to give bodily form*, pronounced (ĭnkahr′nāt)

**inchoate,** adj., *just begun*, and therefore by implication not yet developed to its full form. Pronounced (ĭn′kōat), not (ĭnkō′at) Sometimes confused in meaning with *chaotic.*

**inclement weather,** trite phrase, meaning *unfavorable, severe, cold, rainy, stormy*, or any kind of reprehensible weather. The word *inclement* by origin really means *unmerciful*, the negative of *clement* and of the notion that appears in the noun *clemency.* But the phrase has lost all descriptive value, and it lives now only in the style of persons who repeat phrases hallowed by tradition.

**inclination,** n., construed with *to* or *for*, as in *He has a strong inclination to* or *for music.*

**inclusive,** adj., *including*, especially in giving numbers and dates. The phrase *inclusive terms* means with no extras to be added. Pronounced (ĭnklōō′sĭv), not (ĭnklōō′zĭv)

**incog,** adj., colloquial abbreviation of *incognito*, with identity concealed.

**income,** n., *salary or other resources*, pronounced (ĭn′kŭm), not (ĭng′kum)

**incomparable,** adj., *beyond compare*, pronounced (ĭnkŏm′parabl), not (ĭnkompār′abl)

**incongruous,** adj., *discordant*, pronounced (ĭnkŏng′grōŏus), not (ĭnkongrōō′us)

**inconsistence,** n., *an instance of something not consistent*, as in *It is an inconsistence to italicize foreign words sometimes and not at* *others.* To be distinguished from *inconsistency,* the general quality of not being consistent, as in *Inconsistency is not always a vice.* See **abstinency, inadvertence**

**incorrigible,** adj., *not responding to correction,* pronounced (ĭnkŏr'-ĭjĭbl)

**increment,** n., *increase, growth,* pronounced (ĭn'krement), not (ĭng'krement)

**incunabulum,** n., Latin word, *early printed book, early stage of anything,* literally, *swaddling clothes.* Pronounced (ĭnkūnăb'ūlum), but commonly used only in the plural, *incunabula* (ĭnkūnăb'ūla)

**indecorous,** adj., *not proper, unseemly,* pronounced (ĭndĭkŏr'us), less correctly (ĭndĕk'orus)

**indentation,** n., *beginning a line of writing or printing further back from the margin than the rest of the lines.* Also *indention,* though the shorter form is less commonly used than the longer.

**index,** n., with two plurals, *indices* in mathematical and scientific uses, *indexes* referring to the contents of a book.

**index expurgatorius,** Latin phrase, *list of passages to be expunged in books otherwise permitted, list of forbidden things,* pronounced (ĭn'dĕks ĕkspurgatŏr'ĭus)

**index librorum prohibitorum,** Latin phrase, *list of books the use of which is prohibited,* pronounced (ĭn'dĕks lĭbrŏr'um prōhĭbĭtŏr'um)

**Indian,** n., adj., *native of America.* Pronounced (ĭn'dĭn), and pronounced (ĭn'dĭan) only as a formal and artificial exercise.

**indicative,** adj., as a grammatical term pronounced (ĭndĭk'atĭv), but in the sense *giving indication of* usually pronounced (ĭn'dĭkatĭv) But the nouns *indication, indicator* are pronounced (ĭndĭkā'shon), (ĭn'dĭkātor)

**indices,** n., plural of *index,* but ordinarily used only in scientific senses, as in mathematics. Pronounced (ĭn'dĭsēz) The plural of *index,* contents of a book, is usually *indexes,* pronounced (ĭn'dĕkses) See **index**

**indicium,** n., *indication, sign,* pronounced (ĭndĭsh′ĭum), with a plural *indicia,* pronounced (ĭndĭsh′ĭa), as in *Parcels must contain the prescribed indicia as to contents.* A Latin word taken over bodily into English of the formal and official kind.

**indict,** v., *bring a charge against.* Pronounced (ĭndīt′), with related forms *indictable* (ĭndīt′abl), *indictment* (ĭndīt′ment) See **indite, interdict**

**Indies,** n., *place name,* pronounced (ĭn′dĭz), or less commonly (ĭn′dēz) The pronunciation (ĭn′dīez) is artificial and theoretical.

**indisposed,** adj., *not inclined toward, averse to,* but sometimes used as a euphemism to avoid outspoken terms like *sick* or *ill,* as in *The soloist was indisposed and could not sing,* meaning not that the soloist was unwilling, but was unwell. The word usually implies a slight illness, and so also the corresponding noun, *indisposition.*

**indisputable,** adj., *that which can not be controverted,* pronounced (ĭndĭs′pūtabl), not (ĭndĭspūt′abl)

**indissoluble,** adj., *not susceptible of dissolution,* pronounced (ĭndĭs′olubl), not (ĭndĭsŏl′ūbl)

**indite,** v., *to write, to compose,* the same word by origin as *indict,* but *indite* is now used only in rather artificial literary style, as in *to indite an epistle,* to write a letter.

**individual,** n., often overused as a synonym for *person, man.* Strictly, **individual** should mean a single person as distinguished in or from a group. This is one of the words the humorist in language inclines to overwork, as calling a poor man *an impecunious individual* or a person one meets frequently *a ubiquitous individual.* See **Polysyllabic Humor**

**indorse,** see **endorse**

**industry,** n., *application, a particular kind of occupation,* as the mining industry. Pronounced (ĭn′dustrĭ), with an adjective *industrious* (ĭndŭs′trĭus) The pronunciation (ĭndŭs′trĭ) for the noun is frequent, but has not made its way into good use.

**ineligible,** adj., *not fit* (especially for military service), *not qualified for membership,* pronounced (ĭnĕl'ijibl)

**in esse,** Latin phrase, *in actual existence,* the complementary phrase being *in posse.* Pronounced (ĭn ĕs'ĭ)

**inexorable,** adj., *relentless, not to be evaded,* pronounced (ĭnĕg'-zorabl) or (ĭnĕk'sorabl)

**inexpugnable,** see **impugn**

**in extenso,** Latin phrase, *unabridged, in full,* pronounced (ĭn ĕkstĕn'sō)

**in extremis,** Latin phrase, *at the point of death, at the last gasp,* pronounced (ĭn ĕkstrē'mĭs)

**infantile,** adj., *childish, peculiar to children,* as in *infantile paralysis,* pronounced (ĭn'fantĭl), but in England usually (ĭn'fantīl) See **-ile**

**infantine,** adj., *like an infant, innocent,* as in *an infantine expression.* Pronounced (ĭn'fantĭn) or (ĭn'fantīn)

**infectious,** see **contagious**

**infernal,** adj., colloquial intensive, expressing impatience in phrases like *infernal nuisance, infernal weather,* very bad weather, and also as adverb, as in *an infernally long time.*

**inferno,** n., Italian word, *hell,* pronounced (ĭnfĕr'nō)

**infertile,** adj., *thin and unproductive,* of soils, etc., *not capable of reproduction,* of eggs, etc. Pronounced (ĭnfer'tĭl), in England also (ĭnfer'tīl) See **-ile**

**infinitely,** adv., *without limitation,* but in colloquial speech often used as a polite intensive, as in *I am infinitely obliged to you,* greatly obliged to you, like other exaggerated colloquialisms. See **awful, fine, great, terrible, wonderful**

**in flagrante delicto,** Latin phrase, *in the act of committing the offense, red-handed,* pronounced (ĭn flagrăn'tĭ dĭlĭk'tō)

**inflammable,** adj., *easily burned,* pronounced (ĭnflăm'abl), not (ĭnflām'abl)

**inflection,** n., *the grammatical forms of a word, modulation of the* *voice.* The noun corresponds to the verb *inflect*, but it also has a spelling *inflexion*, the different spellings being used with particular application to the several meanings of the word. Theoretically it seems better to keep the spelling *ct* in **inflection**, *deflection, infection, defection,* to agree with the forms *inflect, deflect, infect, defect,* and to use the spelling *x* in words like *flexion, flexible, complexion,* which have cognates *flex, complex.*

**influence,** n., *a power exerted from without,* sometimes political slang in the sense *"pull," bribery.* Pronounced (ĭn'flōŏens), not (ĭnflōŏ'ens), with an adjective *influential* (ĭnflōŏĕn'shal)

**in forma pauperis,** Latin phrase, *as a poor person, not liable to costs,* pronounced (ĭn fŏr'ma paw'perĭs)

**infra,** adv., prep., Latin word, *below, further on,* pronounced (ĭn'fra)

**infra dignitatem,** Latin phrase, *beneath one's dignity,* often abbreviated colloquially to *infra dig.* Pronounced (ĭn'fra dĭgnĭtă'tem)

**Ingelow,** n., *English poetess,* pronounced (ĭn'jelō)

**ingenious,** adj., *skillful, inventive.* To be distinguished from *ingenuous,* candid, simple-minded.

**ingénue,** n., French word, *artless girl,* especially as represented on the stage. Pronounced (ănzhenü')

**ingrain,** adj., *firmly fixed,* originally of a dye, also a participial form *ingrained.* When the words stand immediately before the nouns they modify, they are stressed on the first syllable, as in *ingrain, ingrained carpet,* (ĭn'grān), (ĭn'grānd kahr'pet), *an ingrained habit* (ăn ĭn'grānd hăb'ĭt) In the predicative position the adjective is ordinarily used in a figurative sense and is stressed on the second syllable, as in *This habit has become ingrain, ingrained* (ĭngrān', ĭngrānd') *with him.*

**ingrate,** n., literary for *ungrateful person,* pronounced (ĭn'grāt) or, according to the *New English Dictionary,* (ĭngrāt') The *New English Dictionary* does not record the pronunciation (ĭn'grāt), though that is the one most likely to be heard. The color of the word is slightly melodramatic.

**inhospitable,** adj., *ungracious toward strangers or guests,* pronounced (ĭnhŏs'pĭtabl), not (ĭnhŏspĭt'abl)

**inimitable,** adj., *not to be imitated,* pronounced (ĭnĭm'itabl), not (ĭnĭm'itābl)

**initiate,** v., *to introduce, to start.* Pronounced (ĭnĭsh'ĭāt), with a noun of the same spelling, pronounced (ĭnĭsh'ĭat) The adjective *initiatory* is pronounced (ĭnĭsh'yatŏrĭ), and the noun *initiative* is (ĭnĭsh'yatĭv)

**initio,** adv., Latin word, *at the beginning,* pronounced (ĭnĭsh'ĭō)

**ink,** n., *writing fluid,* pronounced (ĭngk) The attempt to pronounce the word as (ĭnk), and so with other words containing this combination of letters, as in *sink, think,* etc., is theoretical and agrees with no general custom of the speech.

**inlaw,** n., plural *inlaws.* A colloquial term to name those relatives one acquires by marriage.

**in loco parentis,** Latin phrase, *in place of a parent,* pronounced (ĭn lō'kō parĕn'tĭs)

**in medias res,** Latin phrase, *in the thick of it, in the midst,* pronounced (ĭn mē'dĭăs rēz)

**in memoriam,** Latin phrase, *in memory,* pronounced (ĭn mĭmŏr'ĭăm)

**Inness, George,** n. *American painter* (1825–1894), pronounced (ĭn'ĭs) or (ĭn'ĕs)

**innings,** n., slang metaphor derived from baseball in the sense *luck, prosperity,* as in *Things were against him for a long time, but he is having his innings now.* The word **innings** is both singular and plural, as in *the ninth innings, Nine innings were played, The ninth innings was soon over.*

**innocent,** adj., facetious in the sense *unacquainted with, untouched by,* as in *a face innocent of water,* a dirty face. Perhaps polysyllabic humor, but a little more subtle than most humor of this kind. See **Polysyllabic Humor**

**innovation,** n., *a novelty, something just introduced.* The phrase *a new innovation* is a crude pleonasm.

**in nubibus,** Latin phrase, *in the clouds, hazy, vague,* pronounced (ĭn nū'bĭbus)

**innuendo,** n., *a concealed and usually derogatory allusion.* Often misspelled *inuendo.* Pronounced (ĭnūĕn'dō) The plural is *innuendoes.*

**in partibus infidelium,** Latin phrase, *in heretical country,* as of a bishop appointed to an unconverted region. Figuratively, *in unsympathetic surroundings,* and often used in the shortened form *in partibus.* Pronounced (ĭn pahr'tĭbus ĭnfĭdē'lĭum)

**in posse,** Latin phrase, *potential, not realized,* pronounced (ĭn pŏs'ĭ) See **in esse**

**in propria persona,** Latin phrase, *in one's own person,* pronounced (ĭn prō'prĭa persō'na)

**in puris naturalibus,** Latin phrase, *naked,* pronounced (ĭn pū'rĭs nătūrăl'ĭbus)

**inquire,** v., *ask about, seek for.* The form *enquire* may also be used, but is less common than **inquire.** The noun is also *inquirer,* but sometimes *enquirer,* as in the name of a newspaper in Cincinnati.

**inquiry,** n., *question,* pronounced (ĭnkwī'rĭ), not (ĭn'kwĭrĭ), (ĭng'-kwĭrĭ)

**insanitary,** adj., *not conforming to sanitary requirements.* With a variant *unsanitary,* equally correct and of the same meaning.

**insert,** n., *something set in,* pronounced (ĭn'sert) The verb *to insert* is pronounced (ĭnsert')

**inside of,** prep., a low colloquial pleonasm for *inside,* as in *There were four men inside of the house,* which should be *inside the house.* In colloquial use *inside,* **inside of** are used for *within,* as in *He promised to be back inside* or *inside of an hour.*

**insides,** n., colloquial for *stomach,* and sometimes euphemistic for *entrails, guts.* See **gut**

**insignia,** n., *badges, marks,* a plural number; the grammatical singular *insignium* is not in use.

**in situ,** Latin phrase, *in its original place, back in place,* pronounced (ĭn sī'tū)

**insouciance,** n., French word, *carelessness, indifference,* pronounced (ănsōōsĭahns')

**insouciant,** adj., French word, *careless, indifferent,* pronounced (ănsōōsĭahn')

**inspiring sight,** trite phrase, usually employed with little realization of the meaning of *inspiring.*

**install,** v., *to place into position,* as in *to install a furnace,* or *to establish a person in an office,* as in *The president was installed with ceremony.* Sometimes used pompously for *make, build,* as in *The directors voted to install an outdoor basketball court.* The word is appropriate only as applied to some action of importance.

**instanter,** adv., humorous for *instantly, at once,* pronounced (ĭnstăn'ter)

**in statu quo,** Latin phrase, *in the same position as before,* also *in statu quo ante,* pronounced (ĭn stā'tū kwō ăn'tĭ)

**instil,** v., with a variant spelling *instill.* Though the word by origin means to put a liquid into something by drops, its use now is almost always metaphorical, as in *to instil an idea,* to put it into one's mind gradually.

**institution,** n., colloquial in the sense *habit, custom,* as in *Breakfast in bed has never been an institution in our family, Tea on the lawn is quite an institution of* or *in this club.* See **Polysyllabic Humor**

**intaglio,** n., *stone carved like a cameo,* pronounced (ĭntăl'ĭō)

**integer,** n., *a number, a complete thing,* pronounced (ĭn'tejer), with an adjective *integral* (ĭn'tegral), not (ĭntĕg'ral)

**integer vitae,** Latin phrase, *a man of honest life,* pronounced (ĭn'tejer vī'tē)

**intellect,** n., *mind,* not used as a plural except in low colloquial speech, where *intellects* is an occasional name for *mental powers.*

**intelligentzia,** n., *the intellectual class*, especially the self-conscious intellectual class of Russia. Pronounced (ĭntĕlĭjĕnt′sĭa) and also spelled *intelligentsia*. The word has acquired satirical implications from the nature of its content.

**intended,** n., colloquial for *man to whom a girl is engaged*, that is, intended husband. The word is not usually applied to the girl in relation to the man. See **admirer, fiancé**

**inter alia,** Latin phrase, *among other things*, pronounced (ĭn′ter ā′lĭa)

**interdict,** v., *forbid, restrain*, as in *This order interdicts admission to all minors*, or *This order interdicts all minors from attending the theater*. Pronounced (ĭnterdĭkt′) See **indict**

**interest,** n., *advantage, profit, welfare*, and used as a plural in phrases like *in the interests of truth, of regularity, of simplicity*, etc., for the sake of truth, regularity, simplicity, etc.

**interested,** participial adj., *with attention aroused, curious*. Also in the sense *having money invested in*, as in *He is interested in the new real estate development*. In this second sense the negative can not be *uninterested*, but must be *not interested*, or a noun construction, *have no interest*. The stress is on the first syllable, sometimes in low colloquial speech on the third. See **uninterested**

**interesting,** adj., *entertaining, exciting attention*, pronounced (ĭn′terestĭng), or more informally (ĭn′trestĭng) The pronunciation (ĭnterĕst′ĭng) is low colloquial. The noun and verb *interest* are pronounced (ĭn′terest), (ĭn′trest)

**interim,** n., *meantime*, as in the phrase *in the interim*. Also as an adjective, *temporary, intervening*, as in *This is only an interim report*. An abbreviation of the Latin phrase *ad interim*, in the meantime, and pronounced (ĭn′terĭm)

**interment,** n., a pedantic word for *burial*. Pronounced (ĭnter′ment)

**intermezzo,** n., Italian word, *short connecting movement in a musical* *composition, short performance between acts,* pronounced (ĭn'tĕr-mĕd'zō)

**intern,** n., *assistant physician in a hospital.* Also spelled *interne.* Pronounced (ĭntern')

**Internationale,** n., French word, *International Working Men's Association, a socialistic song,* pronounced (ănˇtĕrnăsˇĭonahl')

**internecine,** adj., *deadly, destructive of both parties,* pronounced (ĭnternē'sĭn) or (-sĭn)

**inter nos,** Latin phrase, *among ourselves, confidentially,* pronounced (ĭn'ter nōs)

**interpretative,** adj., *explanatory,* sometimes also in the form *interpretive,* on the basis of the verb *interpret.* But the form **interpretative,** though less euphonious, is the more general usage.

**in terrorem,** Latin phrase, *as a warning,* pronounced (ĭn tĕrŏr'ĕm)

**inter se,** Latin phrase, *among themselves,* pronounced (ĭn'ter sē)

**interstice,** n., *crack, crevice,* pronounced (ĭnter'stĭs), not (ĭn'terstĭs) The plural is *interstices* (ĭnter'stĭsez)

**inter vivos,** Latin phrase, *between the living,* used especially of gifts made during life as distinguished from legacies. Pronounced (ĭn'ter vī'vōs)

**in the words of the poet,** trite phrase, crudely employed to introduce a quotation.

**intimate,** v., *to convey a meaning without direct assertion,* not to be used therefore as a simple synonym for *say.* Pronounced (ĭn'tĭmāt), with an adjective of the same spelling, pronounced (ĭn'timat)

**intituled,** past participle, archaic form of *entitled,* and pronounced (ĭntĭt'ūld)

**in toto,** Latin phrase, *entirely, completely,* pronounced (ĭn tō'tō)

**intrigue,** n., *plot, secret love affair,* pronounced (ĭntrēg') A verb of the same form and pronunciation means *to carry on a plot,* but recently in literary slang it has gained currency in the sense *interest,* as in *This rumor intrigues me greatly, A very intriguing* *plot, I am much intrigued,* borrowed directly from the French meaning of the word.

**introit,** n., *part of the church service,* pronounced (ĭntrō'ĭt)

**invalid,** adj., pronounced (ĭnvăl'ĭd) in the sense *not valid,* but (ĭn'valĭd) in the sense *in bad health.* The word in this second sense is described by the *New English Dictionary* as pronounced (ĭnvăl'ĭd), with the comment that "Webster 1828 [the year of publication of Webster's *American Dictionary*] has *in'valid,* and the pronunciation (given in most Amer. dicts.) is occasionally heard in England also, esp. in attrib. use, as *an invalid sister.*" But later British dictionaries record (ĭn'valĭd) or (ĭn'valēd) without comment. The pronunciation (ĭn'valēd) is rarely heard in America.

**inveigle,** v., *to lead into, to entice,* pronounced (ĭnvē'gl) or (ĭnvā'gl)

**inventory,** n., *list of things,* pronounced (ĭn'ventŏr`ĭ)

**in vino veritas,** Latin phrase, *a drunken man tells the truth,* literally, *truth in wine;* pronounced (ĭn vī'nō vĕr'ĭtăs)

**invite,** n., colloquial and low colloquial for *invitation,* and pronounced (ĭn'vīt)   See **bid**

**iodine,** n., one of the four nonmetallic elements, *bromine, chlorine, fluorine, iodine.* Of these the last is pronounced (ī'ōdĭn), but the others are usually pronounced (brō'mĭn), (klō'rĭn), (flŏŏ'orĭn) The pronunciation (ī'ōdĭn) is occasionally heard.

**iota,** n., *a jot, a very small part,* pronounced (īō'ta)

**Iowa,** n., *name of a state,* pronounced in a variety of ways, (ī'owā), (īō'wa), (ī'owah), but the most general pronunciation is (ī'owa)

**ipecac,** n., colloquial contraction for *ipecacuanha.*

**ipse dixit,** Latin phrase, used as a noun, *dogmatic statement,* as in *I have this on his own ipse dixit,* literally, *he himself said it.* Pronounced (ĭp'sĭ dĭk'sĭt) The word has an English plural, *ipse dixits.*

**ipsissima verba,** Latin phrase, *the very words,* pronounced (ĭpsĭs'ĭma ver'ba) In a different case form, *ipsissimis verbis,* the phrase means *in the very words, in the exact words.* It is incorrectly used in the following sentence in the sense *in the very same words: Now Texas has hastened to fall into line, and has enacted this North Dakota resolve ipsissimis verbis.* What the writer meant to say is that Texas has fallen into line and has passed this North Dakota law in the very same words.

**ipso facto,** Latin phrase, *by that very fact.* Pronounced (ĭp′sō făk′tō)

**irade,** n., *Turkish decree,* pronounced (ĭrahd′)

**irate,** adj., *angry,* but used only in affected literary style. See **Polysyllabic Humor**

**ire,** n., archaic, poetic, or humorous for *anger,* and occasionally used as a verb in newspaper English, as in *Wife's cooking ires husband.*

**Irene,** n., *woman's name,* pronounced (īrēn′), in England usually (īrē′nĭ)

**Irish,** adj., *of Ireland and its people,* current in America as applied to the ordinary white potato, but not in England. In America a distinctive name is needed to keep separate the Irish and the sweet potato. See **murphy**

**Irkutsk,** n., *city in Siberia,* not *Irkootsk* or *Irkoutsk,* by decision of the United States Geographic Board. Pronounced (ĭrkoōtsk′)

**iron,** n., *a metal,* pronounced (īr′n), with an adjective *irony* (īr′nĭ) But the noun *irony* is pronounced (ī′ronĭ)

**Iroquois,** n., *Indian proper name,* pronounced (ĭrokwoi′) or (ĭrokwaw′)

**irrefragable,** adj., *unanswerable, not to be controverted,* pronounced (ĭrĕf′ragabl)

**irrefutable,** adj., *not to be controverted,* pronounced (ĭrĕf′ūtabl), less commonly (ĭrefūt′abl)

**irregardless,** adj., *without regard to.* The word **irregardless** is low colloquial and has never been in good standing. So also *disregardless,* though of course *disregard* is a permissible verb.

**irrelevant,** adj., *not pertinent,* by an easy blunder sometimes made into *irrevelant.*

**irremediable,** adj., *not to be remedied,* pronounced (ĭremē'dĭabl)

**irreparable,** adj., *not to be mended or restored,* pronounced (ĭrĕp'-arabl), not (ĭrepār'abl)

**irrevocable,** adj., *not to be recalled, unalterable,* pronounced (ĭrĕv'-okabl), not (ĭrevōk'abĭ)

**Isaiah,** n., *Biblical proper name,* pronounced (ī'zāa) or (ĭzī'a), but the latter only of the person and book of the Bible.

**Iseult,** n., *character in medieval romance,* pronounced (ĭsōōlt') See **Isolde**

**-ish,** suffix, added to adjectives and nouns, often giving the sense of a slight degree of the quality expressed by the main word, often adding also a shade of contemptuous meaning, as in *sweet-ish, saltish, womanish, mannish, bookish, amateurish, stand-offish,* contrasted with *sweet, salty, womanly, manly, fond of books, of an amateur, aloof.* But this is only a tendency, for many words ending in **-ish** do not have this sense, as *boyish, girlish, wolfish, boorish, foolish;* yet often it will be found that when the minifying or pejorative sense is not added by the suffix **-ish,** it is already present in the main part of the word.

**isinglass,** n., now commonly used to designate thin, transparent sheets of mica, though by etymology the word comes from a Dutch word meaning literally *sturgeon bladder,* and was first applied to a gelatine derived from sturgeon and used for jellies, glue, etc. This latter meaning is still current. The word is pronounced (ī'zĭnglăs) or (ī'zĭngglăs), with of course a variant (-glahs) in the second element. The first element, *isin-,* has nothing to do with German *eisen,* iron, but represents the Dutch word *huysen-,* sturgeon, and the second element, *glass,* stands for Dutch *blas,* bladder, by popular etymology.

**Islam,** n., *Mohammedanism,* pronounced (ĭs'lam) or (ĭz'lam), and so with derivatives *Islamism,* etc.

**isolate,** v., *to set apart*, pronounced (ĭ'solāt) or (ĭs'olāt) So also *isolation*, (īsolā'shon) or (ĭsolā'shon), *isolable*, (ī'solābl) or (ĭs'-olābl) The pronunciation with (ĭ) is less general than the pronunciation with (ī), but it has theoretical justification on its side in that it stands closer to the etymological origins of the word than the pronunciation with (ī) The latter is an anglicized pronunciation, supported perhaps by the analogy of *island* (ī'land), and by compounds like *isosceles* (īsŏs'elēz), *isotherm* (ī'sotherm), etc. See **itinerary**

**Isolde,** n., *character in medieval romance*, pronounced (ĭsŏld') or (ĭsŏl'de) See **Iseult** A great variety of spellings for this character occurs in the manuscripts of the romances, and the modern poets have enjoyed reviving as many of these as possible.

**Israel,** n., *the Jewish people*, pronounced (ĭz'rāĕl), and so also in derivatives, *Israelite, Israelitish*, the first syllable is (ĭz-) The pronunciation with (ĭs-) in these words is a spelling pronunciation not supported by usage. The pronunciation (ĭz'rel) is low colloquial.

**Israelite,** n., *one of the people of Israel*. Sometimes chosen to avoid using the word Jew. See **Hebrew**

**-ist,** suffix, in nouns naming the followers of a creed or policy, as in *an evolutionist, a fundamentalist;* or naming persons with special knowledge or skill, as *an entomologist, an economist, an alienist, a scientist, an artist;* or naming persons who use a thing, as *an organist, a motorist, an autoist, a canoeist, a billiardist*. In all of these uses the suffix is now actively employed, and the originally dignified, somewhat learned associations of the suffix are now often lost in such recent colloquialisms as *baseballist, tonsorialist, manicurist, tobacconist, florist, balloonist, typist*, etc. The attempt to restrict the use of the suffix -ist to learned words runs counter to the very powerful current of customary usage.

**isthmus,** n., *narrow connecting piece of land*, pronounced (ĭsth'mus) or (ĭs'mus)  In connected spoken English the second pronunciation is almost unavoidable.

**it,** pron., used in colloquial and children's English as a vague impersonal, as in *In the newspaper last night it said that the meeting would not be held*, for *The newspaper said* or *stated last night that*, etc.  Slang as a term of reproach, as in *You big it*, or as meaning *a striking example, success*, with more or less scornful implications, as in *She put herself out and certainly she was it, For sheer nerve, I confess you are it*.  This use probably comes from **it** in children's games, the **it** being the person who for the moment is paying some penalty.

**Italian,** adj., *of Italy and its people*, pronounced (ĭtăl'yan), not (ītăl'yan)

**itch,** n., v., often avoided as an inelegant word, as applied to physical sensations, and replaced by *irritation, irritate*, or some other formal word.  But in the figurative sense, as in *I am itching to get at it, My fingers itch to do it for him*, the antipathy toward the word is not felt and these uses are generally current.

**itemize,** v., colloquial in the sense *list item by item*, as in *Please send me an itemized account of my purchases*.  A convenient modernism not current in England.

**itinerary,** n., *route, record of travel*, pronounced (ītĭn'erărĭ) or (ĭtĭn'erărĭ), the latter being the less general.  So also with the adjective *itinerant*, and the infrequently used verb *itinerate*.  See **isolate**

**-itis,** see **appendicitis**

**it's,** phrase, a contraction of *it is*.  The possessive case of *it* is always *its*, never **it's**.  The contraction *'tis* is now archaic or poetic.

**it stands to reason,** trite phrase, objectionable because the use of it so readily becomes a fixed habit.

337

**-ive,** suffix, in words like *active, massive, native, sportive,* etc., pronounced (ĭv), not with the obscure vowel of the first syllable of *about.* See **active, massive, native**

**ivories,** n.. slang for *dice, billiard balls, teeth,* and *piano keys.*

# J

**J,** letter, often written and printed in old texts in the form of the letter *I.* See **I H S**

**jab,** v., not slang, but an abrupt, direct word acquiring its color from its meaning and from its customary use in familiar situations. Literary synonyms would be *thrust, strike,* and words of similar color would be *punch, hit,* and slang words would be *biff, dig,* etc. The question of choice in the use of **jab** is not one of correctness, but of stylistic color. Compare the following two sentences, equally correct, but the first in what might be called a robust style, the second in a restrained style: (1) *She jabbed at it wildly with her umbrella;* (2) *She made vain thrusts at it with her umbrella.* Each style is good in its place, and it is a mistake to suppose that the restrained style is the only good style.

**jabot,** n., *part of woman's dress,* pronounced (zhăbō′)

**jacinth,** n., *a gem,* pronounced (jā′sĭnth) or (jăs′ĭnth)

**jack,** n., colloquial name for *the knave* in a deck of cards.

**jack,** v., slang in the phrase *jack up,* incite, stir up, spur to more vigorous effort.

**jackal,** n., *animal of the same family as the dog,* pronounced (jăk′-awl)

**jackie,** n., colloquial and slang name for *sailor in the American navy.* A diminutive from *bluejacket.*

**Jacobean,** adj., formed from *Jacob,* but pronounced (jăkobē′an) So also *Jacobite* (jăk′obīt)

**jacquerie,** n., French word, *peasant uprising,* pronounced (zhăkerē′)

**Jacques,** n., *French proper name*, pronounced (zhăk), but as a character in Shakspere's *As You Like It* pronounced (jā′kwĭz)

**jaeger,** n., usually in the plural *jaegers, woolen underwear*, from the name of a manufacturer. Pronounced (yā′ger), (yā′gerz)

**Jael,** n., *Biblical character*, pronounced (jā′ĕl)

**Jaffa,** n., *a town in Palestine*, not *Jafa, Joppa, Joppe, Yafa*, or *Yaffa*, by decision of the United States Geographic Board.

**jag,** n., colloquial and dialectal for *a load*, as *a jag of hay.* Also slang, in the figurative sense of a "load" of liquor, *to have a jag on*, meaning *to be drunk.*

**jaguar,** n., *an animal*, pronounced (jăg′war)

**Jahveh,** n., *Jehovah.* The form **Jahveh** is occasionally used as a learned form by Biblical critics, but the customary spelling is *Jehovah.*

**Jairus,** n., *Biblical proper name*, pronounced (jā′ĭrus) or (jāī′rus)

**jamb,** n., *side of a doorway, window*, etc. Pronounced (jăm), indistinguishably from *jam.*

**jamboree,** n., slang for a *feast, celebration.* Pronounced (jămborē′)

**jam satis,** Latin phrase, *already enough*, pronounced (jăm săt′ĭs)

**Jap,** n., colloquial abbreviation for *Japanese.*

**Japan,** n., *the empire of the Japanese.* The United States Geographic Board rejects the variant names *Dai Nippon, Nihon, Niphon, Nipon*, and *Nippon.* None of these variants is extensively used, though *Nipon, Nippon* are sometimes found in poetic or rhetorical writing.

**Japanee,** see **Chinee**

**Japanese,** adj., *of Japan and its people*, pronounced (jăpanēz′), not (jăpanēs′)

**jape,** n., archaic and literary for *jest, joke.* Also used as a verb, and pronounced (jāp) in both uses.

**jar,** n., incorrectly used in the phrase *on the jar* for *ajar*, half open, on the turn. There is no noun **jar** in this sense, and the only current word is *ajar.*

**jar,** v., slang in the sense *annoy, provoke,* as in *Wouldn't that jar you?*

**jardinière,** n., French word, *a stand, pot, etc., for containing growing plants in a room,* pronounced (zhahrdĭnĭär′) The anglicized pronunciation (jahrdĭnēr′) is scarcely in good use.

**jarl,** n., *old Scandinavian tribal leader,* pronounced (yahrl)

**jasmine,** n., *kind of flower,* pronounced (jăs′mĭn), with variants *jasmin, jessamine, jessamin.*

**jaundice,** n., *a disease,* pronounced (jawn′dĭs), (jahn′dĭs), in low colloquial speech (jăn′derz)

**jaunty,** adj., *light and airy,* pronounced (jawn′tĭ) or (jahn′tĭ)

**jaw,** v., slang in the sense *scold.* Also a noun, as in *Don't give me any of your jaw.*

**jawbreaker,** n., colloquial and slang for *a long or hard word.*

**jay,** n., slang for *rustic person, any uncouth person.* See **jaywalker**

**jay bird,** n., colloquial form of the name of the blue jay, ordinarily referred to simply as *a jay.*

**jaywalker,** n., slang for *a person who crosses a city street at an unexpected place,* thus exposing himself to danger from automobiles. See **jay**

**jazz,** n., *a kind of music.* Not a slang word, for, though of recent origin, it has established itself in general use, and the mood and sentiment of the word are inherent in the activity which it names. The etymology of the word is not finally established, but most probably it is an old English dialectal word, and almost certainly not of negro origin. Also used as a verb.

**jean,** n., *a kind of cotton cloth,* but now familiar only in the plural *jeans* (jēnz), as a slang word for *trousers.* In England pronounced (jān)

**Jehu,** n., a humorous or slang word for *a cab or carriage driver,* from II Kings 9:20. But since cab drivers have given way to chauffeurs, the word is now rarely used. See **Jonah** Pronounced (jē′hū)

**jemmy,** n., *burglar's crowbar*, pronounced (jĕm'ĭ), but colloquially also often pronounced (jĭm'ĭ) and sometimes written *jimmy*. The word is in origin a diminutive of *James*, just as *jack*, a hoisting machine, is a diminutive of *Jacob*.

**Jena,** n., *German city and university*, pronounced (yā'na)

**je-ne-sais-quoi,** French phrase, *something indescribable, what-you-may-call-it*, pronounced (zhe ne sā kwah)

**jeopardy,** n., *danger*, a word of the literary, not the colloquial speech. Pronounced (jĕp'ardĭ), with a verb *jeopardize*, to endanger, pronounced (jĕp'ardīz)

**Jephthah,** n., *Biblical character*, pronounced (jĕf'tha)

**Jerome,** n., *man's name*, pronounced (jĕr'om) or (jerōm'), the former as the name of the early church Father.

**jerry,** n., slang for *chamber pot*. See **jordan**

**jessamine,** see **jasmine**

**jettison,** v., *to throw out*, especially of the cargo of a ship to lighten it. Pronounced (jĕt'ĭson) The word is a variant of *jetsam*, current only in the phrase *flotsam and jetsam*, wreckage, derelict materials of any kind. The word *flotsam* is by origin of the same root as the verb *to float*.

**jeu de mots,** French phrase, *play on words*, pronounced (zhŏ de mŏ)

**jeu d'esprit,** French phrase, *witty or humorous trifle*, pronounced (zhŏ dĕsprē')

**jeunesse dorée,** French phrase, *the gilded youth, the idle rich*, pronounced (zhŏnĕs' dōrā')

**Jew,** n., *a Hebrew*, often avoided as being an offensive word, the substitutes being *Hebrew, Israelite*, or some circumlocution. So also *Jewess*.

**jew,** v., colloquial in the phrase *to jew down*, to insist on a reduction of price. The older word in this sense was *cheapen*, but *cheapen* is now used only in figurative senses, as in *Such behavior cheapens a man's reputation*.

**jewelry, jewellery,** n., both spellings being pronounced (jōō'elrĭ)

The usual literary form of the word is **jewelry,** the spelling **jewellery,** parallel to *jeweller,* being a jeweller's and manufacturer's use.

**jibe,** v., colloquial in the sense *to harmonize, to agree,* as in *The two parts of his story don't jibe.* Also construed *jibe in with.*

**jibe,** see **gibe**

**jiffy,** n., colloquial for *a short time.* The etymology of the word is not known.

**jigger,** see **gadget**

**jiggered,** adj., colloquial as a mild oath, as in *Well, I'll be jiggered!*

**Jill,** see **gill**

**Jim Crow,** n., colloquial name for *negro,* especially as an adjective in the phrase *Jim Crow car,* one provided specially for negroes.

**jiminy,** see **Gemini**

**jinn,** n., *a supernatural being in Arabic stories.* Grammatically **jinn** is a plural, but it is commonly used in English as a singular. Sometimes spelled *djinn,* but pronounced (jĭn) The Arabic singular is *jinnee* (jĭnē′), a masculine noun, and the corresponding feminine is **jinneeyeh** (jĭnē′yā) See **genie**

**jinnee,** see **jinn**

**jinneeyeh,** see **jinn**

**jinx,** n., slang for *some power that makes things go wrong,* the opposite of *mascot.* Perhaps from Captain Jinks of the horse marines, who fed his horse on corn and beans. See **horse marines** Colloquial in the phrase *high jinks, to cut up high jinks,* behave boisterously.

**jitneur,** n., slang for *the driver of a jitney.* Made on the analogy of *chauffeur.*

**jitney,** n., slang for *five cents,* or for *an automobile charging a five-cent fare,* and then, by extension, other conveyances carrying passengers. Also used as a verb, *to jitney,* to go by means of a jitney.

**jiu-jiutsi, jiu-jitsu,** see **ju-jutsu**

**Joaquin,** n., *Spanish form of a man's name,* pronounced (wahkēn') or (wawkēn')

**jocose,** adj., *facetious, humorous,* pronounced (jōkōs'), not (jōkōz')

**jocund,** adj., *merry, animated,* pronounced (jŏk'und), but only a literary word.

**Johns Hopkins,** n., *name of a university in Baltimore.* Often incorrectly used in the form *John Hopkins.*

**Johnson, Samuel,** n., *English writer* (1709–1784), author of the *Dictionary* (1755), to be distinguished from Benjamin Jonson, usually referred to as Ben Jonson, dramatist (1573–1637)

**joint,** n., slang for *family, household, establishment in general,* as in *a pretty comfortable sort of joint.* In England **joint** is the customary name for *a roast of meat,* a hot joint being a hot roast and a cold joint a cold leg of lamb, etc.

**join together,** v., a crude pleonasm for *join,* as in *He joined the two ends together.* The word *join* alone expresses the meaning completely. The phrase **join together** occurs in the marriage service, but the archaic English of the services of the church can not be taken as justifying usages in present English. See **connect up**

**jolly,** v., slang in the sense *cajole,* especially in the phrase *to jolly someone along.* Slang also as an adverb, as in *He can jolly well thank his stars it wasn't any worse,* very well, etc.

**Jonah,** n., slang for *a person who brings bad luck.* See **Jehu, jinx**

**jongleur,** n., French word, *wandering minstrel,* especially one of the medieval period. Pronounced (zhŏngler')

**jonquil,** n., *a kind of flower,* pronounced (jŏn'kwĭl), (jŏng'kwĭl), in England also (jŭn'kwĭl), (jŭng'kwĭl)

**Jonson,** see **Johnson**

**jordan,** n., low colloquial for *chamber pot.* See **jerry**

**José,** n., *Spanish name,* pronounced (hōzā')

**journal,** n., etymologically from a word meaning *day,* and a journal should be therefore, literally, a daily. By usage, however, **journal** has come to mean any newspaper or magazine appearing at regular intervals, and it is therefore proper to speak of a weekly journal or a monthly journal.

**joust,** n., a literary and historical word meaning *a combat of knights on horseback.* Also spelled *just,* though less frequently. The pronunciation is usually (jŭst), sometimes (jōōst) Frequently used in the plural, *jousts, justs,* a series of horseback encounters, a tournament.

**Jowett,** n., *English scholar,* pronounced (jō'et)

**jowl,** n., *jawbone, cheek,* pronounced (jowl) Now used of people only in the phrase *cheek by jowl,* very intimate. Still used of pigs' jowls.

**joy ride,** n., slang for *surreptitious ride in an automobile not owned by the persons using it.* By extension, *any irregular pleasure excursion.*

**Juan,** n., *Spanish proper name,* pronounced (hūahn') or as a Spanish word. Or anglicized, as in Bryon's poem *Don Juan,* and pronounced (jōō'an)

**Juarez,** n., *Mexican place name,* pronounced (hwahr'āz)

**jubilee,** n., strictly *a celebration kept every fifty years,* and therefore a phrase like *semicentennial jubilee* is incorrect and tautological. Besides its strict sense, however, the word has a general meaning of *congratulatory celebration,* without reference to a period of time, though this must be characterized as a popular use of the term.

**Judenhetze,** n., German word, *hatred of and persecution of Jews,* pronounced (yōō'denhĕt'se) See **Zeitgeist**

**judicature,** n., *term of office of a judge,* or *a body of judges,* pronounced (jōō'dĭkātūr), not (jōōdĭk'atūr)

**judicious,** adj., *discreet, wise,* as in *He made a very judicious selection from among the candidates.* To be distinguished from *judicial,* pertaining to a judge, *a judicial decision* being a judge's decision, and *a judicial selection* one that a judge might make.

**Jugo-Slavia,** see **Yugoslavia**

**jugular,** adj., *of the neck or throat,* sometimes used alone as the name for the *jugular vein.* Pronounced (jŭg'ūlar), though dictionary authority generally favors (jōōg'ūlar)

**juice,** n., slang for *electricity,* for *whiskey,* especially in the phrase *corn juice,* and for almost anything that supplies vital and motive power.

**ju-jutsu,** n., *Japanese wrestling,* with a variant *jiu-jiutsu,* both pronounced (jōōjŏŏt'sōō) or (jōōjŏŏtsōō'), and another variant *jiujitsu, jujitsu,* pronounced (jōō'jĭtsōō) or (jōōjĭt'sōō)

**Jules,** n., *French proper name,* pronounced (zhōōl) or as a French word.

**julienne,** n., French word, *a term in cookery,* a kind of soup, potatoes, etc. Pronounced (zhōōlĭĕn')

**jumbo,** adj., colloquial for *very large,* from Jumbo the elephant, as in *jumbo peanuts, jumbo pecans, jumbo squab.*

**jump,** v., literary and rare in the sense *harmonize,* as in *This does not jump with his former statement,* agree with; slang in the phrases *jump on,* rebuke, punish, *jump a bill,* depart without paying.

**junker,** n., *monarchistic landholder in Germany,* pronounced (yŏŏng'ker) On the use of capitals, see **Zeitgeist**

**just,** adv., colloquial as a general intensive in the sense *very,* as in *That was just lovely of you,* still more so in a sentence like *I lost my hat and it was just new,* quite new. This latter sentence is characteristic of children's English, and so also a sentence like *I just know it's going to rain,* I know very well, am sure it's going to rain.

**just,** see **joust**

**juvenile,** adj., *youthful, for the young,* usually pronounced (jōō'venĭl), but sometimes (-ĭl), especially when the adjective is used as a noun, as in *a juvenile,* a book for the young. See **-ile**

345

# K

**Kaiser,** n., *the German emperor*, pronounced (kī′zer)

**kale,** n., *a kind of cabbage*, with a variant *kail*.   Slang in the sense *money*.

**kalends,** see **calends**

**Kamchatka,** n., *peninsula in Siberia*, not *Kamtschatka*, by decision of the United States Geographic Board.

**kamerad,** n., *the cry of a German soldier on surrendering during the World War*, now sometimes extended to persons always ready to give up in the face of difficulty.   Pronounced (kahme-rahd′)  See **comrade, Zeitgeist**

**Kamerun,** n., *mountains and river in West Africa*, not *Cameroons*, by decision of the United States Geographic Board.

**kanaka,** n., Polynesian word, *South Sea islander*, pronounced (kăn′aka)

**Kant,** n., *German philosopher*, pronounced (kahnt), or anglicized and pronounced (kănt)

**Karlsruhe,** n., *city in Germany*, not *Carlsruhe*, according to the United States Geographic Board.   Pronounced (kahrlz′rōō′e)

**Katahdin,** n., *a mountain in Maine*, not *Ktaadn*, by decision of the United States Geographic Board.   Pronounced (katah′dn) or (kataw′dn)

**Kattegat,** n., *arm of the North Sea*, not *Cattegat*, by decision of the United States Geographic Board.   Pronounced (kăt′ĭgăt)

**Kavanagh,** n., *family name*, pronounced (kăv′ana) or (kăv′anaw)

**Kearny,** n., *place and family name*, pronounced (kahr′nĭ), sometimes (ker′nĭ), and also spelled *Kearney*.

**keen,** adj., colloquial in the sense *eager*, as in *I'm not very keen about* or *on going to the game*.

**keeps,** n., children's slang in the phrase *for keeps*, for good, permanently.

**keg,** n., *small cask*, with an archaic variant *cag*, current now only dialectally.

**kelson,** n., *line of timber inside a ship.* Also spelled *keelson,* but for both spellings ordinarily pronounced (kĕl′son)

**képi,** n., French word, *a soldier's cap,* pronounced (kĕp′ē)

**keramic,** see **ceramic**

**kerb,** n., also *kirb,* British spellings for American *curb,* in the sense *stone border along a gutter,* etc.

**kerosene,** see **coal oil**

**Keswick,** n., *place in England,* where Wordsworth once lived, pronounced (kĕz′ĭk)

**ketchup,** n., *tomato sauce.* Sometimes spelled *catsup,* but always pronounced (kĕtchup) The spelling *ketchup* is the one commonly used.

**khaki,** n., a *brown cotton material,* pronounced (kah′kĭ), low colloquially often (kă′kĭ)

**khan,** n., *Asiatic ruler,* pronounced (kăn) or (kahn) See **cham**

**Kharkof,** n., *city in Russia.* The United States Geographic Board rejects a number of variant spellings.

**Khartum,** n., *city in Egypt,* not *Khartoum,* by decision of the United States Geographic Board.

**Khayyam, Omar,** n., *Persian poet of the eleventh century,* pronounced (ō′mahr kīyahm′)

**Kiaochow,** n., *a bay and city in China.* The United States Geographic Board rejects a variety of different spellings. Pronounced (kĭow′chō′)

**kibosh,** n., a Yiddish slang word, occurring chiefly in the phrase *put the kibosh on* a person or a plan, make it ineffective, disable it, spoil its chances. Pronounced (kī′bŏsh′)

**kick,** n., slang for *power, strength,* as in *This whisky has lots of kick in it,* or for *objection,* as in *I have no kick against that.*

**kick,** v., colloquial for *object, rebel.* Formerly literary, as in I Sam. 2:29: "Wherefore kick ye at my sacrifice and at mine offering." The phrases *kick the bucket,* die, and *to kick up a row* are slang. In the passive, **kick** is construed with *by,* and *kicked with* is low colloquial and dialectal for *kicked by*, as in *He was kicked with a horse.* So also *hit with*, for *hit by*.

**kid,** n., slang and colloquial for *child*. Also as a verb, *to kid*, meaning *to treat playfully and jokingly.* Though **kid** has the color of slang, the diminutive *kiddy, kiddies* is merely affectionate and familiar. See **cod**

**kidnap,** v., *carry off a person, especially a child.* The second element is a variant of *nab*, and the first a slang word for *child*. The derivative forms double the *p*, that is, *kidnapped*, not *kidnaped*, *kidnapper*, not *kidnaper*.

**Kief,** n., *city in Russia*, not *Kieff*, *Kiev*, or *Kiew*, by decision of the United States Geographic Board. The word is pronounced, however, in at least as many ways as it is spelled, the pronunciation recommended by the Permanent Committee on Geograhical Names being (kē'yĕf) The Committee also favors the spelling *Kiev*.

**kike,** n., slang for *Jew*, usually with contemptuous implications.

**killing,** adj., slang in the sense *very remarkable, highly amusing,* as in *He told us a killing tale about a lost hat and other adventures.*

**kilometer,** n., *a measure of distance, 1,000 meters.* This word is usually pronounced (kĭl'omē'ter), though the analogy of words like *hydrometer, thermometer, speedometer*, etc., would favor the pronunciation (kĭlŏm'eter), and this pronunciation may occasionally be heard. See **hydrometer**

**kiln,** n., *furnace*, especially in phrases like *lime kiln, drying kiln,* etc. The literary pronunciation is (kĭln), but colloquially (kĭl) is the pronunciation commonly heard.

**kilt,** see **burnt**

**kimono,** n., *woman's loose dressing gown*, pronounced (kĭmō'nō), or less formally (kimō'no)

**Kincardine,** n., *Canadian proper name*, pronounced (kĭnkahr'dĭn)

**kinchin,** n., slang for *child*, especially in thieves' argot. From German *kindchen*, little child. See **kid**

**kind,** adj., not to be used in ordinary business correspondence in phrases like *your kind order, your kind attention,* etc., but appropriate in social correspondence and in business correspondence when considerations of special obligation and courtesy are pertinent. The best rule is to use the word only when it is definitely required and not to use it as an epistolary convention.

**kind of,** adv., colloquial in constructions like *I kind of hate to do it, He looks kind of pale.* In Kentucky and Tennessee dialect, also *kindly.* So also *sort of.* The phrase expresses a moderate degree of the word it modifies, as in *I'm kind of busy just now,* rather busy. See **like,** adv.

**kind of a,** in sentences like *What kind of a hat do you want?* Usually regarded as colloquial and unliterary for *What kind of hat do you want?* So also *sort of a,* for *sort of.* But occasional examples will be found in good writers, as in "I do not doubt that the American people know what the war is about and what sort of an outcome they will regard as a realization of their purpose in it" (Woodrow Wilson, Message to Congress, December, 1917)

**kine,** n., archaic and literary plural of *cow,* occasionally surviving in the English of sales' bills and similar inventories.

**kinema,** see **cinema**

**kinsfolk,** n., *family connections.* The word is plural and is construed with a plural verb. The forms *kinsfolks, kinfolks* are not in good use.

**kiosk,** n., Turkish word, *an open pavilion,* pronounced (kĭŏsk′) or (kī′ŏsk)

**kirk,** n., Scotch dialect for *church.*

**Kirkcudbright,** n., *Scotch place name,* pronounced (kĭrkoō′brĭ)

**kirsch,** n., German word, *wild cherry liqueur,* pronounced (kĭrsh)

**Kishenef,** n., *city in Russia.* The United States Geographic Board rejects a number of variant spellings.

**Klondike,** n., *place name in Alaska.* The United States Geographic Board rejects a number of variant spellings, including *Klondyke.*

**knave,** see **jack**

**knickers,** n., colloquial abbreviation for *knickerbocker trousers,* pronounced (nĭk′erz)

**knife,** v., slang, *to betray a fellow worker treacherously,* especially in politics. The figure is from stabbing with a knife.

**knight templar,** n., historically, *a member of a medieval religious order;* in modern times, *member of a society for men.* The modern plural is ordinarily *knights templar, templar* being thus treated as an adjective, like *errant* in *knights errant.* Historically, however, *templar* is a noun, and the older plural is *knights templars,* like *knights hospitallers.* The plural *knight templars* is not in approved use. The plural *knights templars,* though historically justifiable, is not in general use. See **hospitaller**

**knock,** v., slang in the sense *to find fault with.* The noun *knocker* is slang for a person given to knocking.

**knockdown,** n., slang for *introduction,* as in *He gave me a knockdown to his friend.*

**knocked up,** adj., *enceinte.* Not current in cultivated speech. The phrase **knocked up** in the sense *exhausted, worn out,* as in *He was completely knocked up by the long journey,* is current as a general colloquial use in England.

**knock off,** v., colloquial and slang in the sense *to stop,* as in *We knocked off work at twelve o'clock;* so also in the sense *reduce in price,* as in *He knocked off two dollars.*

**knoll,** n., a literary word for *small hill,* pronounced (nōl)

**knot,** n., *a nautical mile.* It is nautical usage to measure the speed of a vessel by knots in terms of an hour. Thus a vessel which is steaming at ten knots is going at the rate of ten nautical miles an hour. But it is not nautical usage to say a vessel is going at ten knots an hour or is making ten knots an hour, for this is tautological. If a vessel is making ten knots, it is going at this rate, and if it keeps the rate for an hour, it will make ten knots in the hour.

**knout,** n., from the Russian word for *whip* or *scourge*. Pronounced (nowt) or (knowt)

**knowledge,** n., *information*, pronounced (nŏl'ĭj), sometimes (nō'lĭj), either as a conscious refinement of speech, affected sometimes by preachers, or as the result of unconscious recollection of the verb *know*.

**Kodiak,** n., *island in Alaska*, not *Kadiak*, by decision of the United States Geographic Board.

**Königsberg,** n., *city in Prussia*. This is the spelling approved by the United States Geographic Board, but the Board does not pass on the pronunciation. See **Goteborg** The pronunciation of **Königsberg** would ordinarily be approximately as in German, that is, (kö'nĭgzbĕrg')

**kopje,** n., Dutch word, *a small hill*, pronounced (kŏp'ĭ)

**koran,** n., *Mohammedan sacred book*, pronounced (korahn') or (kŏr'an)

**kosher,** adj., Hebrew word, applied to food prepared in accordance with Jewish law. Also spelled *cosher, koscher*. Pronounced (kŏsh'er), (kō'sher)

**koumiss,** n., *fermented milk*. Also spelled *kumyss*, and pronounced (kōō'mis) for both spellings.

**kowtow,** n., v., Chinese word for *bow, to bow*, touching the ground with the forehead. Extended to mean *subservience, servility*. Spelled in a variety of ways, but most commonly **kowtow,** pronounced (kowtow')

**kraal,** n., *Hottentot village*, pronounced (krahl)

**kraken,** n., Norwegian word, *mythical sea monster*, pronounced (krah'ken)

**Krakow,** n., *city in Poland*, not *Cracow* or *Krakau*, by decision of the United States Geographic Board. Pronounced (krah'kow)

351

**kreutzer,** n., German word, *a coin of small value*, pronounced (kroit′ser)   See **Zeitgeist**

**kriegspiel,** n., German word, *war game*, pronounced (krēg′shpēl) See **Zeitgeist**

**krone,** n., *Continental European coin*, pronounced (krō′ne)

**Kubla Khan,** n., proper name in one of Coleridge's poems, pronounced (kōō′bla kahn)

**kudos,** n., slang use of a Greek word meaning *glory, credit*, pronounced (kū′dos)

**kultur,** n., *culture*, as defined in Germany in terms of the civilization of a race.   Pronounced (kŏŏltōōr′)   During the World War often used as a scornful designation for German civilization. See **Zeitgeist**

**kursaal,** n., German word, *a building for public use at a health resort*, pronounced (kōōr′sahl′)   See **Zeitgeist**

**kyrie eleison,** Greek phrase, *Lord have mercy*, pronounced (kē′rĭ ĕlā′ĭsŏn)

# L

**laager,** n., Dutch word, *encampment*, pronounced (lah′ger)

**lacker,** see **lacquer**

**lacquer,** n., *a kind of varnish.*   Also spelled *lacker* and pronounced (lăk′er) for both spellings.   Though *lacker* might be preferred on the grounds of simplicity, **lacquer** is the form in general use. The spelling **lacquer** has the advantage of distinguishing the word from the verb *lack*, which is not an important matter, but the real reason for the retention of this spelling is probably that the word is one that pertains to the arts and thus is maintained in an exotic form.

**lacuna,** n., Latin word, *a gap, an omission in a manuscript*, pronounced (lakū′na), with a plural *lacunae* (lakū′nē)

**lady,** n., *a woman distinguished by refinement of manner, birth, sentiment*, etc.   In popular use, extended loosely to any woman,

e. g., *a saleslady, lady clerk,* etc.   The persons thus designated
may or may not be ladies, but where this question is not in point,
it is better to use the general terms *woman, girl,* etc.   Such uses
as *Mr. Smith and lady,* for *Mr. Smith and wife, He was calling
on a lady friend,* for *He was calling on a lady,* are low colloquial.
As a vocative instead of *madam,* **lady** is low colloquial.   For
*lady doctor, lady lawyer,* if a special term is necessary emphasizing
sex, a better form would be *woman doctor, woman lawyer.*

**lager,** adj., German word, *beer,* the full phrase being *lager beer.*
But **lager** is used alone in colloquial speech in the sense of the
full phrase.   Pronounced (lah′ger)

**laissez aller,** French phrase, *absence of constraint, letting things
take their own course,* pronounced (lā′sā ălā′) or (lā′sāz ălā′)

**laissez faire,** French phrase, *abstention from interference with
individual action,* pronounced (lā′sā fār)

**lam,** v., slang for *to strike with a stick, to thrash,* especially in the
language of children.   A strengthened form of this word,
dialectal and slang in its occurrences, is *lambaste.*

**lamentable,** adj., *distressing, regrettable,* pronounced (lăm′entabl),
not (lamĕnt′abl)

**lamp,** n., slang in the sense *eye.*   Also used as a verb, as in *Lamp
this,* Look at this.

**land,** n., low colloquial exclamation of surprise in the expression
*for the land sake,* or *land's sake,* or *my land.*

**landsturm,** n., German word, *German military reserve forces,* pronounced (lahnt′shtŏŏrm‵)   See **Zeitgeist**

**landwehr,** n., German word, *German military reserve forces,* pronounced (lahnt′vār‵)   See **Zeitgeist**

**Language Mutilation.**   This is a supposedly humorous trick of
violently changing the forms of words to make them striking,
as *pictureaskew* for *picturesque, deluscious* for *delicious, splendiferous* for *splendid, slantendicular* for *slanting, episcalopian*
for *episcopalian, muchly* for *much, gust* for *guest,* and so with

many others. It is an easy, but soon becomes a very tiresome substitute for something interesting to say.

**langue d'oc,** French phrase, *medieval French spoken south of the Loire,* pronounced (lahṅ'ge dŏk)

**langue d'oil,** French phrase, *medieval French spoken north of the Loire,* pronounced (lahṅ'ge dŏēl')

**languor,** n., *lassitude,* pronounced (lăng'ger), not (-gwer)  But *languid* is (lăng'gwĭd) and *languish* is (lăng'gwĭsh)

**Lanier,** n., *family name,* especially Sidney Lanier, American poet, pronounced (lănēr')

**Laocoön,** n., *Trojan priest,* pronounced (lāŏk'ōŏn)

**lapis lazuli,** n., *a stone,* pronounced (lăp'ĭs lăz'ūlĭ)

**lapsus calami,** Latin phrase, *slip of the pen,* pronounced (lăp'sus kăl'amī)

**lapsus linguae,** Latin phrase, *slip of the tongue,* pronounced (lăpsus lĭng'gwē)

**larboard,** n., *the left side of a boat or ship,* now usually replaced by the word *port.*  Pronounced (lăr'berd), like *cupboard* (kŭb'erd)

**Lares,** n., *household gods,* usually in the phrase *Lares and Penates,* pronounced (lā'rēz ănd pěnā'tēz)

**large,** adj., occasional literary use in the phrase *by and large,* without minor qualifications, as in *Taking these natives by and large, they are a good lot,* taking them as they come.

**largesse,** n., archaic word for *gift,* pronounced (lahr'jĕs), current chiefly in modern versions of medieval romances.

**lark,** n., colloquial for *an amusing or frolicsome adventure.*

**larrikin,** n., of Australian origin, meaning *a street rowdy, a roughneck,* and current chiefly as an Australianism.

**larrup,** v., colloquial and dialectal for *to beat, thrash.*

**larva,** n., *a grub,* pronounced (lahr'va), with a plural *larvae,* pronounced (lahr'vē)

**larynx,** n., *a part of the throat,* pronounced (lăr'ingks), not (lahr'-)  The adjective is *laryngeal* (lărĭn'jĭal), and *laryngitis* is (lărĭnjī'tis)

**lass,** n., literary and poetic word for *girl*, with a diminutive *lassie*.

**lasso,** n., *long rope with a loop*, pronounced (lăs′ō) or (lăsoo′) Also a verb with the same pronunciations, sometimes used figuratively in the sense merely *to obtain, get possession of*.

**last,** see **first**

**last word,** phrase, colloquial and polite slang in the sense *the most recent thing, the latest fashion*, as in *She wore a hat which was the last word in headgear*.  See **corker, limit**

**later on,** see **on**

**latter,** adj., *that which comes after*, a term complementary to *former*, as in *the latter*, a person mentioned after some other, *the latter part of the evening*, etc.  Constructions like *the latter nineteenth century, his latter life* are elliptical for *the latter part of the nineteenth century, the latter part of his life*, and are literary in tone.

**laudator temporis acti,** Latin phrase, *one who praises the past, a lover of old ways*, pronounced (lawdā′tor tĕm′porĭs ăk′tī)

**laugh,** n., slang in the phrase *have the laugh on, get the laugh on*, secure the advantage over.

**launch,** v., *to send forth, to start the career of something*, pronounced (lawnch) or (lahnch) So also the noun **launch,** a kind of boat.

**laundry,** n., *place where clothing is washed and ironed*, pronounced (lawn′drĭ) or, less generally, (lahn′drĭ) So also in the verb *to launder*.

**Lausanne,** n., *city in Switzerland*, pronounced (lōzahn′)

**lava,** n., *melted volcanic rock*, pronounced (lăv′a) or (lah′va) See **a** (ah), the sound of **a** as in *father*

**law,** interj., low colloquial as an expression of astonishment. In its written form the interjection takes the spelling **law,** though in reality it has nothing to do with the noun **law** and is merely a low colloquial survival of an older pronunciation of the literary exclamation *lo*.  Variant low colloquial forms of **law** are *laws* (lawz), *lawsee* (law′zē), *law sakes, lawk, lawks*.

**lay,** v., present tense of the transitive verb **lay,** *to put, place*, as in *The mason lays one stone upon another.* The past tense is *laid*, and so also the past participle. In low colloquial and dialect speech the forms of **lay,** *laid* are often confused with the forms of *lie*, present tense, *lay*, past tense, *lain*, past participle, meaning *to rest, remain, assume recumbent position*, as in *The sheep lie* (i. e., are lying), or *lay* (i. e., did lie), or *have lain in the shadow of the trees.* See **lie**

**lay off,** v., colloquial for *discharge*, as in *The shop laid off half its force yesterday*, and also for *discontinue*, as in *I think I shall have to lay off skating for a few days.*

**layout,** n., colloquial for *display, plan, general state of preparation for an event*, as in *The whole layout was elaborate and expensive.* Architects and engineers sometimes speak of the layout of a building, of a road to be built, etc., but the more formal term would be *plan, general plan.*

**laze,** v., colloquial for *take things easy, be lazy*, a synonym of *loaf*. The word is a back formation, made into a verb by clipping the ending from the adjective. See **burgle**

**lazzarone,** n., Italian word, *beggar*, pronounced (lăzahrō′nä) or (lădsahrō′nä), with a plural *lazzaroni* (lăzahrō′nē) or (lădsahrō′nē)

**lead to the altar,** trite phrase, a journalistic euphemism and substitute for *to marry.*

**leader,** n., current in England as the equivalent of the American *editorial*, a *leaderette* being a short **leader.**

**leal,** adj., literary synonym for *loyal*. The phrase *the land o' the leal* is from a poem by Lady Nairne, and in the poem the phrase means Heaven, but popularly it is often supposed to mean Scotland, perhaps because the poem is written in Scotch dialect.

**lean and hungry look,** trite phrase, originally from Shakspere's *Julius Caesar*, Act I, Sc. ii.

**leap,** v., with a past tense and past participle *leaped* (lēpt), or less commonly *leapt* (lĕpt) The form *leapt* is preferred in England. In low colloquial speech the past tense is often pronounced (lĕp)

**learn,** v., *to acquire knowledge of a thing.* In low colloquial speech used to mean *teach,* with a personal object, as in *He learned me how to swim,* for *He taught me,* etc., and so also as an archaic survival in writing, as in Tennyson, "Merlin and the Gleam," II, "Mighty the Wizard Who . . . . woke me And learn'd me magic."

**leasing,** n., *lying, deception,* an archaic and Biblical word, pronounced (lēz'ĭng)

**leastways,** adv., low colloquial for *at least.* The form *leastwise* is literary and rare for *at least.*

**leather,** n., slang for *baseball* or *football.*

**leatherhead,** n., slang for *blockhead.*

**leave,** v., past tense, *left,* often incorrectly used for *let* in low colloquial speech, as in *He left go of it just a moment too soon,* for *He let go,* etc.; or *Leave him have it,* for *Let him have it; Leave him be* or *alone,* for *Let him be* or *alone.*

**leaven,** n., *that which makes dough rise and ferment,* but current in this sense now only in the phrase *unleavened bread.* Ordinarily used now only in a figurative sense of something that modifies something else, as in *the leaven of humor.* Also used as a verb, *to leaven,* to lighten, to transform. Pronounced (lĕv'n)

**leeward,** n., *the protected side.* A nautical word and pronounced in accord with nautical tradition as (lū'ard) or (lōō'ard) See **boatswain, larboard**

**left,** v., in the phrase *to get left,* colloquial and slang for *to fail of an expectation.* So also the phrase *over the left, over the left shoulder,* added as a reversal of something just said.

**leg,** n., slang in the phrase *shake a leg,* dance, *shake a nasty leg,* dance well, *pull one's leg,* wheedle something out of one. It is said that some speakers avoid the use of the word **leg** as applied to men and women on the grounds of modesty, substituting *limb* for **leg,** but certainly this would seem to be an excess of modesty.

**leg,** v., colloquial and slang for *walk,* as in *to leg it all the way.*
See **foot**

**legend,** n., *a tale,* usually pronounced (lĕj'ĕnd), occasionally (lē'-
jĕnd), or less formally (lĕj'nd), (lē'jnd)

**leggings,** n., ordinarily used only in the plural, though *a legging,*
like *a stocking,* is possible.  The tendency, however, is to associate **leggings** with *trousers,* and *a legging* seems only little less
absurd than *a trouser.*  The pronunciation is (lĕg'ĭngz), low
colloquially (lĕg'inz), but a variant form *leggins* is sometimes
used in writing and printing.  See **ticking**

**leghorn,** n., *kind of straw for hats* and *a kind of chickens,* pronounced (lĕg'hŏrn), (lĕg'ŏrn), or (lĕg'orn)

**Leibniz, G. W.,** n., *philosopher* (1646–1716), not spelled *Leibnitz.*

**Leipzig,** n., *city in Germany,* not *Leipsic,* according to the decision
of the United States Geographic Board.  Pronounced (līp'zĭg)

**leisure,** n., *freedom from labor,* pronounced (lē'zher) or (lĕzh'er),
and so with *leisured, leisurely,* (lē'zherd), (lē'zherlĭ), or (lĕzh'erd),
(lĕzh'erlĭ)

**leit-motif,** n., German word, *the pervading theme in a musical composition,* pronounced (līt'mōtēf')  Also spelled *leit-motiv,* which
would be the more correct German spelling of the word.  But
the pronunciation is the same for this spelling as for the other.
See **Zeitgeist**

**lemon,** n., slang in the sense *something not desired, the opposite
of a prize, an unattractive person,* a sunkist lemon being a lemon
with good qualities.

**lemonade,** n., *a drink of lemon, water, and sugar.*  Not exactly
a synonym of *lemon squash,* the latter being made with soda
water, the former with plain water.  The *lemon squash* flourishes
chiefly in England.

**length,** n., *linear extent,* in low colloquial speech often pronounced
(lĕnth)  So also with *strength.*  Properly pronounced (lĕngkth),
(strĕngkth)

**lengthways, lengthwise,** adv., of the same meaning and equally correct.

**lengthy,** adj., *notably long or tedious*, usually of speaking or writing. Sometimes stigmatized as an Americanism, but current also in England.

**lenient,** adj., *mild, not severe in judgment*, pronounced (lēn'yent), but the noun *lenity* is pronounced (lĕn'ĭtĭ)

**le roi le veult,** French phrase, *the king's assent to a parliamentary bill*, literally, *The king wills it;* pronounced (le rwah le vŏlt')

**le roi s'avisera,** French phrase, *the king's refusal of assent to a parliamentary bill*, literally, *the king will consider;* pronounced (le rwah sahvē'zerah)

**lese-majesty,** n., *treason*, as an anglicized word pronounced (lēz-măj'estĭ)  As a French word written *lèse-majesté* and pronounced (lāz-mahzhĕstā')

**less,** adj., adv., the comparative degree of *little*, but only in form, not in meaning, the comparative idea corresponding to *little* being expressed by *smaller*.  The meaning of **less** is *fewer, not so much*.  But the comparative *lesser*, as in *the lesser evils of life, the lesser prophets*, is used as a real comparative of *little*, in the sense *smaller*.  The use of *lesser* is restricted, however, to a small number of literary phrases, the usual comparative being *smaller*.  It is of course familiar in certain verses of the Bible, as in *And God made two great lights; the greater light to rule the day, and the lesser light to rule the night*, Gen., chap. 1.  As an adjective, *lesser* occurs frequently in Shakspere.  It is uses like these, however, that keep *lesser* alive as a literary construction.

**let,** v., archaic in the sense *hinder, prevent*, and also as a noun, especially in the phrase *without let or hindrance*.  The word occurs now only in legal use and is not the same word etymologically as the verb *let*, permit, allow.

**let alone,** v., used in the imperative in the sense *not to mention*, *still less, still more*, as in *This is a distinction which few persons would draw under favorable circumstances, let alone such circumstances as pressed so powerfully upon Governor Jay; Cold and fatigue made him cross, let alone the fact that he had had no supper.* This is good idiom, but slightly formal and literary. The more customary phrase would be *not to mention.*

**let in,** v., slang in the sense *involve*, as in *You don't know what you are letting yourself in for*, exposing yourself, committing yourself to.

**let on,** v., colloquial for *to give an intimation or clue*, as in *He never let on that he knew all about it.* Also sometimes, though less frequently, in affirmative constructions, as in *He let on as though he knew all about it.*

**let's,** v., colloquial form of *let us*, as in *Let's go home.* In low colloquial speech, often pronounced (lĕs), and sometimes with a pleonastic pronoun added, as in *Let's us*, or *Less us*, etc.

**let's don't,** verb phrase, colloquial and dialectal for *Let's not*, as in *Let's don't go*, for *Let's not go.* Also sometimes *don't let's*, as in *Don't let's do that*, likewise low colloquial and dialectal.

**lettuce,** n., *a salad plant*, pronounced (lĕt'ĭs) or (lĕt'us)

**levee,** n., *a river embankment*, especially along the lower Mississippi. Also the negro section of a town. Pronounced (lĕv'ĭ) These uses are local or colloquial, but the word has a general literary use also, in the sense *formal reception*, especially one held by a king.

**level,** n., slang in the phrase *on the level*, honest, above board. See **straight, square**

**lever,** n., *a device for lifting weights or forcing things apart*, pronounced (lē'ver) or (lĕv'er), and so also *leverage*, (lē'verĭj) or (lĕv'erĭj)

**lewd,** adj., literary word for *unchaste, indecent.* The word originally meant *lay* as opposed to *cleric, unlearned* as distinguished from *learned*, but this older sense is obsolete.

**lex talionis,** Latin phrase, *law of retaliation, an eye for an eye,* etc., pronounced (lĕks tălĭō′nĭs)

**liable,** adj., *exposed or subject to,* as in *liable to infection.* Often incorrectly used for *likely,* as in *He is liable to be at home at this time,* for *He is likely,* etc.

**liaison,** n., adj., French word, (1) *illicit love affair;* (2) *sounding of an ordinarily silent final consonant in French before a word beginning with a vowel;* (3) *adjective describing a person who serves as an intermediary,* as in *a liaison officer.* Pronounced (lĭä′zn) as an anglicized word, or (lēäzŏń′) as a French word.

**library,** n., *a building for books, a collection of books,* pronounced (lī′brărĭ) or (lī′brĭ), this latter pronunciation being much less general in America than in England. Low colloquially the word is often pronounced (lī′bĕrĭ)  See **February**

**lichen,** n., *small flowerless plant,* pronounced (lī′ken) or (lĭch′en), though neither form of the word is popularly used, growths of this kind being ordinarily spoken of as *moss.*

**lick,** v., slang and juvenile English for *to defeat, beat, thrash,* with added emphasis in the phrase *to lick the stuffing out of.*

**licking,** n., low colloquial and children's English for *punishment, defeat.*

**licks,** n., colloquial for *strokes,* as in *I didn't have time to get in some of my best licks,* points, arguments.

**licorice, liquorice,** n., *a medicine and a candy,* pronounced (lĭk′orĭs), in dialectal English (-ĭsh)  Not the same word as the adjective *lickerish, liquorish,* fond of dainty fare, lascivious; this word is a variant of *lecherous.*

**lid,** n., slang for *hat,* as in the phrase *Pipe the lid,* Look at that hat.

**lie,** v., with a past tense *lay* and a past participle *lain.* In low colloquial and dialectal speech, *laid,* past tense and past participle of *lay,* is commonly used for *lay, lain.* The phrase *lie low,* wait for developments, is slang.  See **lay**

**liege,** adj., archaic and literary, especially in the phrase *liege lord*, feudal sovereign. Pronounced (lēj)

**Liége,** n., *city in Belgium*, pronounced (lēãzh′)

**lieu,** n., in the phrase *in lieu*, instead, pronounced (lū)

**lieutenant,** n., *a navy or army officer*, pronounced (lūtĕn′ant) or (lōōtĕn′ant) In England (lĕftĕn′ant), (leftĕn′ant), and in the navy (letĕn′ant) are recorded as current pronunciations.

**lifer,** n., slang for *prisoner serving lifetime sentence.*

**lift,** n., the current word in England for *elevator*, occasionally heard in America, but only as a Briticism.

**light,** v., meaning (1) *to set fire to, illuminate;* (2) *to descend and settle upon.* In both senses, good English has two forms, equally authorized, for the past tense and past participle, *lighted* or *lit*. In the adjective use of the past participle, *lighted* is preferred, as in *a lighted room.* In this syntax, *lit* would be poetical, as in Matthew Arnold's *over the lit sea's unquiet way.* For *light up*, see **up** The phrase *lit up*, partly intoxicated, is slang.

**lighten,** v., *to emit an electrical discharge in the sky*, as in *It lightens, It lightened, It is lightening.* The noun is *lightning*, which is sometimes improperly used as a verb, as in *It lightnings every minute.*

**lightning bug,** n., colloquial name for *firefly.*

**lightsome,** adj., poetic and literary for *graceful, light.*

**like,** v., dialectal in constructions like *He like to have drowned, I like to have cut my finger*, for *almost drowned, almost cut my finger.* As an impersonal in the sense *please*, as in *It likes me not*, **like** is a literary archaism.

**like,** adv., dialectal as a qualifier in such constructions as *He seemed very gentle like.*

The construction *anything like*, as in *It isn't as big or anything like as big as yours, There is nothing else anything like so interesting to ourselves as ourselves*, is crudely colloquial. The last sentence quoted could be much improved by rephrasing. So also *nothing like* is colloquial in constructions like *It is nothing like as tall as I expected,* for *It is not nearly as tall,* etc.

**like,** conj., in local, colloquial, and dialectal use for *as,* as in *You must do this like I do,* for *You must do this as I do* or *You must do this the way I do.* The construction *It looks like rain, It feels like rain* is a colloquial contraction for *It looks like it would rain,* etc. Because critics of speech have so frequently condemned this construction, careful speakers and writers ordinarily avoid the use of **like** as a conjunction. See **feel, look** Numerous phrases of colloquial color are made with·**like,** as *like anything, like a thousand of bricks, like a house afire, like a shot, like blazes*—not to mention stronger ones.

**like,** prep., correct English, as in *He built a house that looked like a barn, I don't know another like him.* The sentence *Nowhere in that city could a man like he . . . . crack the lash over the backs of governors,* etc., should read *Nowhere in that city could a man such as he was,* or *like him,* etc., since **like** followed by a nominative can not be construed as a preposition but must be a conjunction.

**like a mirror, a silver thread, a silver ribbon,** trite phrases, too crudely obvious and simple.

**likely,** adj., colloquial in the sense *promising,* as in *a likely boy,* or in the sense *good-looking,* as in *a healthy, likely sort of person.*

**likely,** adv., *probably,* as in the sentence *You likely dropped it when you got in.* Though this use of **likely** occurs not infrequently in the speech of educated persons, it is rejected by some critics as a crudity, though in the eyes of these critics the curse seems to be taken off the construction when some qualifying word precedes **likely,** such as *very, more, most,* as in *You very likely,* or *more likely,* or *most likely.* But the distinction here seems very finely drawn.

**like-minded,** adj., *agreeing, harmonious,* sometimes incorrectly given the form *alike-minded.*

**lilac,** n., *a flowering shrub,* pronounced (lī′lak) or (lī′lăk), dialectally (lī′lŏk), (lā′lŏk)

**Lima,** n., as a South American city pronounced (lē′ma), as a place name in the United States pronounced (lī′ma)

**limb,** n., by excess of modesty, euphemistically substituted for *leg.*

**limit,** n., slang for *the last word, the last straw;* an exclamation of astonishment or exasperation, as in *Isn't that the limit!*

**line, lines,** n., crude English in constructions like *He is in the dry-goods line* (that is, *in the dry-goods business*), *He is interested in everything in the athletic line* (for *everything athletic*) So also *along the line, lines,* as in *He gave us a talk along the line of books and reading* (for *about books and reading*), *Our firm has been very conservative and it will continue business along those lines* (for *in the same way* or *spirit*) The phrase *line of goods,* as in *This store carries a very large line of goods,* is commercial. The phrase *in my line, out of my line,* as in *Public speaking is out of my line,* is colloquial English. As a noun, **line** is in general use in *railway line, steamship line, stage line,* and similar phrases.

**linen,** n., *cloth made from the stalk of the flax,* but often used of tablecloths and napkins, even when they are not made of linen, and of men's shirts and collars, which are almost always made of cotton. See **lingerie**

**linen draper,** n., in England *a retail dealer in linens, calicos, and other cloths.* There is no exactly equivalent term in American English, the nearest being *dry-goods merchant.*

**lingerie,** n., French word, *women's underwear,* pronounced (lănzherē′), often used as a euphemistic substitute for the simpler word *underwear.* See **linen**

**lingua franca,** Latin phrase, *mixed jargon,* pronounced (lĭng′gwa frăng′ka) Though originally used of mixtures of French and Latin with other tongues, the term is now often applied to any mixed speech, or, very loosely and colloquially, to any unintelligible and outlandish speech. See **pidgin**

**links,** n., *place where golf is played.* Though plural in form, links can be used as a singular or plural, as in *The club has a fine links, The links were crowded with players.* There is no singular *link.*

**linotype,** n., *kind of machine used in printing,* pronounced (lĭn'-otīp) The word is made from the phrase *line of type,* colloquially *line o' type.*

**lip,** n., slang in the phrase *None of your lip,* None of your impudence.

**liqueur,** n., *a flavored alcoholic drink,* pronounced (lĭker') or (lĭkūr')

**liquor,** v., slang in the phrase *liquor up,* to take a drink of something alcoholic.

**lira,** n., *Italian coin,* pronounced (lē'ra), plural *lire* (lē'rā)

**lissom,** adj., *lithe, agile,* but used now chiefly in the literary phrase *lissom figure,* ordinarily understood in the sense slender and graceful figure. See **buxom**

**list,** v., archaic (1) in the sense *like, be pleasing,* as in *The wind bloweth where it listeth;* (2) and in the sense *listen.* The two words are of different etymological origins.

**listen,** v., slang as a synonym for *sound,* as in *That listens good,* for *That sounds well, promising.* The phrase *listen in* is new but general use in connection with the radio.

**Liszt, Abbé Franz,** n., *pianist* (1811–1886), pronounced (lĭst)

**literae humaniores,** Latin phrase, *polite letters, a university course in this subject,* pronounced (lĭt'erē hūmănĭŏr'ēz)

**literal,** adj., *pertaining to letters,* a literal copy being one faithful even to the letter, and not the same therefore as *verbal,* which means *pertaining to words,* a verbal correction being a correction in wording. One would scarcely speak of a *verbal copy,* since a copy that was not true to the words of the original would scarcely be a copy at all. See **verbal**

**literally,** adj., *with truth to the letter,* as in *He repeated the conversation literally to me,* faithfully, exactly, or *He copied the docu-*

*ment literally*, letter for letter. Sometimes used incorrectly in colloquial speech in the sense *truly, completely*, or with similar intensive meaning, as in *He literally hugged himself for joy* — something he literally could not do; or *The child was literally neglected by its parents*, completely or in effect neglected.

**literatim,** adv., Latin word, *letter for letter*, pronounced (lĭterăt′ĭm)

**lithe,** adj., *flexible, pliant*, pronounced (līdh)

**lithograph,** n., *a picture printed from stone*, pronounced (lĭth′ogrăf); but *lithography* is pronounced (lĭthŏg′rafĭ)

**litterateur,** n., French word, *a man of letters*, pronounced (lĭterahter′)

**little did I think,** trite phrase, of an old-fashioned sentimental melodramatic kind.

**livid,** adj., a somewhat literary word for *a bluish leaden color*, especially in the phrase *a livid bruise*, or as applied to the appearance of the countenance in certain abnormal conditions. The word is often used in conventional descriptions with little realization of its definite meaning. See **lurid**

**Llano Estacado,** n., *a plateau in Texas and New Mexico*, not to be called *Staked Plain*, according to the decision of the United States Geographic Board

**loadstone,** n., *magnetic substance*. Also spelled *lode*. So also *load-, lodestar*.

**loaf,** v., colloquial for *to spend time idly*. Also a noun *loafer*, usually *a disreputable idler*, and an adjective, *loaferish*, disreputably idle in appearance.

**loan,** v., *to lend*. Not as general as *lend*, and avoided by some speakers and writers as a crudity.

**loath,** adj., *disinclined*, as in *I am loath to go*, with a less correct variant *loth*, both pronounced (lōth) To be distinguished from the verb *loathe* (lōdh), to which it is etymologically related.

**lobster,** n., slang as a term of scorn, contempt, *a duffer*.

**lobster palace,** n., slang for *fashionable and gay restaurant*.

**locale,** n., *the scene or place of some happening,* pronounced (lōkahl′) or (lōkăl′), but usually only a literary and written word. The word is French in origin. See **morale**

**locate,** v., colloquial and dialectal in the sense *to settle, to dwell,* as in *Where are you located now?* So also in the sense *remember,* as in *Your face is familiar, but I can't seem to locate you.*

**loco,** adj., slang and dialectal for *demented, frenzied.*

**loco citato,** Latin phrase, *in the passage cited,* pronounced (lō′kō sïtā′tō), and abbreviated *loc. cit.* or *l. c.*

**locum tenens,** Latin phrase, *acting substitute,* literally, *holding the place;* pronounced (lō′kum tē′nĕnz)

**locus,** n., Latin word, *place,* especially in scientific terminology. Pronounced (lō′kus), with a plural *loci* (lō′sī)

**locus classicus,** Latin phrase, *authoritative or most representative passage on a subject,* pronounced (lō′kus klăs′ïkus)

**locus standi,** Latin phrase, *recognized position, credentials,* literally, *place of standing;* pronounced (lō′kus stăn′dī)

**locust,** n., *a winged insect,* pronounced (lō′kust), colloquially (lō′kus), this latter pronunciation being very difficult to avoid in informal or rapid speech.

**loge,** n., French word, *box in a theater,* pronounced (lawzh) or (lōzh)

**loggia,** n., Italian word, *open gallery or arcade,* pronounced (lŏj′a), with a plural *loggie,* pronounced (lŏj′ā)

**logrolling,** n., political slang and colloquial for *combination for mutual benefit,* on the principle of you scratch my back and I'll scratch yours.

**logy,** adj., colloquial and dialectal in the sense *heavy in spirit, not animated, not vivacious.* Pronounced (lō′gĭ)

**loiter,** v., *to linger idly,* but used also of disreputable street walkers. The word is not much used now, perhaps because of associations with this second meaning.

**long,** adj., slang for *to be well provided with, overstocked.* Originally stockbroker's dialect. The contrasting term is *short*. In the phrase *the long green*, slang for *money, bank bills*.

**longevity**, n., *long life*, pronounced (lŏngjĕv'ĭtĭ)

**Longfellow, Henry Wadsworth**, n., *American poet* (1807–1882) The middle name is often mistakenly given as *Wordsworth*.

**long-felt want**, trite phrase, used so much that it has become comic.

**longue haleine**, French phrase, especially in the construction a work or an effort *de longue haleine*, one requiring sustained application, literally, *a long breath*. Pronounced (de lŏngahlān')

**longways, longwise**, adv., possible but infrequent variants of *lengthways, lengthwise*.

**look**, v., formal and literary in constructions like *Look where you will, you will always find slackers*, for the more usual *No matter where you look, Wherever you look*, etc. See **say** Colloquial in constructions like *It looks like rain*. See **feel**

**look a here, looky here**, v., a dialectal survival of *look ye here*.

**-looking**, adj., in compounds like *good-looking, earnest-looking, dissipated-looking*, usually hyphenated. This method of compounding may be regarded as in good colloquial use, but in writing, a phrase like *an excited-looking woman* seems too colloquial to be good literary style.

**loony**, adj., colloquial and slang for *foolish, insane*, a contraction apparently of *lunatic*.

**loquitur**, v., Latin word, (*he, she*, etc.) *speaks*, in stage directions. Pronounced (lŏk'wĭtur)

**lorgnette**, n., *eyeglasses on a long handle to be held in the hand*, pronounced (lŏrnyĕt')

**lorn**, adj., archaic and literary humorous for *desolate, unhappy*, as in *the lorn lass*.

**Los Angeles**, n., *city in California*, pronounced in a variety of ways, but most commonly (lŏs ăn'jeles)

**lose out**, v., sporting slang for *lose*. So also *win out* for *win*. See **up**

368

**lot,** n., colloquial in the sense *considerable number or amount,* as in *a lot of men, I've done a lot of reading on this subject.* The plural form *lots* is low colloquial and dialectal, as in *I've done lots of reading,* etc.   As an adverb, **lot** is also colloquial, as in *I think a lot of that,* a great deal, *Thanks a lot,* and *lots* is low colloquial, as in *I've worried lots about that.*

**lot,** v., dialectal in the sense *plan, intend,* as in *I didn't lot on doing that.*

**loth,** see **loath**

**loud,** adj., colloquial and slang in the sense *striking, vivid* as applied to colors, fashions, and other sensations not received through the ears.   See **scream**

**lough,** n., Scotch and Irish name for *lake,* pronounced (lŏk) or (lŏCH)

**louis-d'or,** n., *a French coin,* no longer current, except in the language of swashbuckling romance.   Pronounced (lōōĭdŏr')

**Louisville,** n., *city in Kentucky,* usually pronounced (lōō'ĭvĭl), sometimes (lōō'ĭsvĭl)

**lounge-lizard,** n., slang for *youth who likes to bask in the sunshine of ladies' favor.*   See **cake-eater, tea-hound**

**lour,** v., *to frown.*   Also spelled *lower,* and always pronounced (low'er)

**Louvain,** n., *Belgian city,* pronounced (lōōvān') or as a French word.

**Louvre,** n., *building in Paris,* pronounced (lōōv'r), or more informally (lōōv)

**love,** v., colloquial in weakened senses, as in *I love strawberries,* like them, *I'd love to go,* want to go, am willing to go, etc., chiefly in the English of women.

**lovely,** adj., in its preciser uses means *beautiful, fair to look upon,* but colloquially the word is current in good use, especially of women, as a general approving intensive, as in *a lovely time, a lovely dinner, lovely seats,* etc.   Not slang, but a part of the necessary conventional vocabulary of daily social intercourse. See **adore, adorable, bully, fine, nice, wonderful**

**low-brow,** see **high-brow**

**lozenge,** n., *small tablet to be dissolved in the mouth.* The form *lozenger* is a popular corruption of **lozenge.**

**lucre,** n., *monetary gain or profit,* as in *He did not do this for lucre but for glory.* Often incorrectly used merely for *money,* especially in the phrase *filthy lucre.* See **Polysyllabic Humor**

**lucus a non lucendo,** Latin phrase, *a paradoxical derivation, an explanation by contraries,* literally, *lucus* [Latin word for *grove*] *is from luceo* [Latin word for *be light*] *because it is not light.* Pronounced (loo'kus ā nŏn loosĕn'dō) The phrase is something of a logical puzzle, and should be used only by those who like and understand such puzzles.

**luggage,** n., the British equivalent for the American *baggage.* But **luggage** is now sometimes used by manufacturers and sellers of trunks, bags, etc., and by fashionable hotel people in America.

**lugubrious,** adj., *mournful,* pronounced (loogoo'brĭus) or (loogū'brĭus) See **Polysyllabic Humor**

**lump,** v., slang in the phrase *If you don't like it, you can lump it,* meaning, you can like it or not, as you please. The word **lump** has no clear meaning in this phrase, but alliteration alone keeps it there.

**lunch,** n., *the name of the midday meal when dinner is the meal of the evening.* Also the name for any light, between-meals repast. For **lunch** as the name of the midday meal, a variant *luncheon* is also used, but commonly only of a large or of a formal midday occasion.

**lunge,** n., colloquial abbreviation of *muskalunge.* See **maski-nonge**

**lunger,** n., slang for *person whose lungs are affected by tuberculosis.*

**lupine,** n., *a plant,* pronounced (loo'pĭn) As an adjective, **lupine,** *pertaining to wolves,* the pronunciation would be (loo'pīn)

**lurid,** adj., *pale, ghastly, tragic, terrible,* especially in the phrase *a lurid light.* Sometimes loosely used of glaring red or smoky light, with the connotation of something ghastly or unnatural. Derived from Latin *luridus,* pale yellow. See **livid**

**lusus naturae,** Latin phrase, *freak of nature,* pronounced (lōō'sus natū'rē)

**luxury,** n., *great comfort,* pronounced (lŭk'shurĭ), less commonly (lŭg'zhurĭ) But in forms like *luxuriance, luxuriate, luxurious* the pronunciation is usually (lŭgzhŏō'rĭans), (lŭgzhŏō'rĭāt), (lŭgzhŏō'rĭus)

**lycée,** n., French word, *French secondary school,* pronounced (lēsā')

**lyceum,** n., *a hall* or *the lectures there given,* pronounced (līsē'um), low colloquially (lī'sĭum) Often used as the name of a theater. The plural is *lyceums.*

**Lycidas,** n., *Greek name,* employed by Milton in one of his shorter poems. Pronounced (lĭs'ĭdas)

**Lyly,** n., *sixteenth-century English writer,* pronounced (lĭl'ĭ)

**lyre,** n., *a musical instrument,* pronounced (līr) But the adjectives *lyric, lyrical* are pronounced (lĭr'ĭk), (lĭr'ĭkal) The noun *lyrist* is (līr'ĭst)

# M

**'m,** n., low colloquial contraction of *ma'am,* as in *Yes, ma'am,* pronounced (yĕsm), and often spelled *yessum* in literary representations of dialect. See **ma'am**

A sound (m), not (ĕm), is also current colloquially and low colloquially as a synonym of *yes.* This sound has no conventional orthographic form and no recognized existence as a word. Nevertheless it has a corresponding negative, (m) being affirmative, with rising inflection, and (m-m) being negative, with rising-falling inflection. Another form of this negative may be represented by (ŭ-ŭ), with rising-falling inflection.

**ma,** n., infantile and colloquial abbreviation of *mamma*. Now generally regarded as rustic or low colloquial. Pronounced (maw), (mah), and in certain regions of the South (mă) Also in the compound *grandma*. The uses of *pa* run parallel to those of **ma.**

**ma'am,** n., a contraction of *madam*, used especially in affirmations or negations, as *Yes, ma'am, No, ma'am*, but mainly in the speech of inferiors addressing superiors, or of clerks and attendants in stores when they address their customers, or sometimes in the speech of young children addressing adults. The forms *Yes, ma'am, No, ma'am* survive more extensively in the South than in the North. So also with *sir*. It is not unusual in the South for adults to address their mother as *Yes, ma'am, No, ma'am*, or their father as *Yes, sir, No, sir*, or in the interrogative, *Ma'am?, Sir?*

The pronunciation of **ma'am** is ordinarily (măm), only very formally (mahm), as in England in addressing the Queen or a royal princess. The pronunciations (mŭm), (ŭm), and (m) are low colloquial. See **'m, madam**

**macabre,** adj., *gruesome*, pronounced (makah'ber)

**macadam,** n., *a kind of road*, pronounced (makăd'am)

**macedoine,** n., *a term in cookery*, pronounced (măsedwahn') as a French word, or anglicized and pronounced (măsedoin')

**Machiavelli,** n., *early Italian writer*, pronounced (măkĭavĕl'ĭ) or as an Italian word. The adjective is *Machiavellian* (măkĭavĕl'ĭan)

**machination,** n., *plotting, trickery*, pronounced (măkinā'shon)

**machine,** n., colloquially used instead of the specific name of a particular kind of machine, especially *an automobile*. In politics *the machine*, the organization, is current usage.

**Mackinac,** n., *the name of a place in Michigan*. Usually pronounced (măk'inaw) and sometimes spelled *Makinaw*. Also spelled *Mackinak* and often pronounced (măk'inăk) A fuller Indian form of the name is sometimes used, most frequently in the form *Michilimackinac*. But the variety of spellings for the name is great, Hodge's *Handbook of American Indians*, I, 857, listing some forty. The *Report of the United States Geographic Board*, p. 204, rejects *Mackinaw* and *Michilimackinac*, and gives only **Mackinac** as the name of the bay, county, island, and strait between Lake Huron and Lake Michigan. But the *United States Postal Guide* gives a post office *Mackinac Island*, and a *Mackinaw* in Illinois and in Michigan. See **mackinaw**

**mackinaw**, n., *a short heavy coat*, from the place at the island in Michigan of the same name. See **Mackinac**

**Macleod**, n., *family name*, pronounced (măklowd′)

**macrocosm**, see **microcosm**

**mad**, adj., colloquial in the sense *angry;* in formal use the word means *distracted, insane.* In the sense *angry*, **mad** is construed with *at* of the person and *about* of the thing, as in *He was very mad at me about the loss of the book* or *for losing the book.*

**madam**, n., as a form of direct address, used only in speaking to a lady with whom one is not acquainted, or as the opening formula, *Dear Madam*, of a circular or general business letter. Sometimes an elderly mother with a married son has the title *Madam* instead of *Mrs.* before her family name, *Madam Price*, as distinguished from her daughter-in-law, *Mrs. Price.* See **ma'am**

**madame**, n., French word, *Mrs.*, pronounced (mahdahm′), with a plural *mesdames*, pronounced (mādahm′)

**mad as a hatter, a hornet, a wet hen**, trite phrases, similes of a crudely popular kind.

**mademoiselle**, n., French word, *Miss, a governess, a teacher of French*, pronounced (mădĕmwahzĕl′), with a plural *mesdemoiselles* (mādĕmwahzĕl′)

**Madrid**, n., as a city in Spain pronounced (madrĭd′) or as a Spanish word; as a place name in the United States pronounced (madrĭd′) or sometimes (măd′rid)

373

**maelstrom,** n., *whirlpool,* pronounced (māl'strom)

**maestro,** n., Italian word, *musical composer, teacher, or conductor,* pronounced (mah'ĕstrō), with a plural *maestri* (mah'ĕstrē)

**magazine,** n., *a storehouse for ammunition, a periodical publication.* In both senses ordinarily pronounced (măgazēn'), but in the second sense sometimes pronounced (măg'azēn)

**Magdalen,** n., as the name of a Biblical character pronounced (măg'dalĭn)   In the name *Magdalen College* (Oxford) and *Magdalene College* (Cambridge) ordinarily pronounced (mawd'lin) The adjective *maudlin* is etymologically the same word. When the name of the Biblical character is given in the form *Mary Magdalene* the word is pronounced (măgdalē'nĭ), but when she is referred to as *the Magdalene* the pronunciation is (măgdalēn')

**Maggiore,** n., *Lake Maggiore,* in northern Italy. The United States Geographic Board rejects the variants *Lac Majeur, Lago Maggiore,* etc., *Lake of Locarno.* Pronounced (mahjō'rē)

**Magi,** n., *the wise men from the East,* a plural of **magus,** seldom used as a singular. The plural is pronounced (mā'jī)

**Magna Charta,** n., *early English charter,* pronounced (măg'na kahr'ta)

**magnesium,** n., *chemical substance,* pronounced (măgnē'sĭum) or (măgnēzh'yum)  So also *magnesia,* (măgnē'sha) or (măgnē'zha)

**Magnificat,** n., Latin word, literally, *(My soul) doth magnify,* the name of a part of the church service.  Pronounced (magnĭf'-ĭkăt)

**magnificent,** adj., current as a colloquial intensive in the general sense *fine, good,* as in *a magnificent performance, magnificent strawberries.*  See **wonderful**

**magnum,** n., Latin word, *large bottle of wine,* pronounced (măg'num)

**Magyar,** adj., n., *Hungarian,* pronounced (mŏd'yar), or anglicized into (măg'yar)

**Maharajah,** n., *Indian prince*, pronounced (mah-arah′ja) Also spelled *Maharaja.* The feminine is *Maharanee* (mah-arah′nĭ)

**mahlstick,** see **maulstick**

**Mahomet,** see **Mohammed**

**mahout,** n., East Indian word, *elephant driver*, pronounced (mahowt′)

**maid, maiden,** n., no longer in general use in the sense *young unmarried woman*, surviving only in literary and poetic style. The word **maid** has taken the specialized sense *servant.*

**mail,** n., by etymology means *bag*, being derived from the French word *male*, bag. In accordance with this etymology, a compound like *mail-bag* is tautological and it is therefore rejected by some critics, the word **mail** alone being preferred in the sense *bag or case of letters*, and the word *post* being used in the specific sense *letters.* According to this latter use, one would *post letters in the mail*, and one would *receive the post*, not the *mail*, when one received one's letters in the morning. The word *postman* is also better usage by this standard than *mail-man* for the person who delivers *the post*, that is, the letters. The obvious answer to all these considerations is that, in America at least, the word **mail** by common custom has been generalized in meaning to apply to the essential part of the postal service, that is, to everything that is transmitted through the service. Thus **mail** may mean *letters*, etc., as in *Has the mail come?*, *Your mail is on the table*, and it is freely compounded to form such words as *mail-man, mail-train, mail-boat, mail-service, mail-delivery, mail-clerk*, and many others. It is also used in various senses as a verb; see **mail,** v. The endeavor to determine present usage with respect to **mail** by an appeal to the ultimate origins of the word is both impracticable and theoretically unsound from the point of view of the history of language. See **post**

**mail,** v., in general use, both in the sense *to send by mail*, as in *The publishers mailed the book to me*, and in the more limited sense *to put in the mail-box, to post*, as in *I must mail this letter* *tonight.* Some speakers object to this latter use and insist on *to post* as the only correct form. The prevailing usage, however, is against them. See **mail, n.**

**mailcarrier,** n., the general term in America, for which the British equivalent is *postman.* See **mail, n.**

**Main,** n., as the name of a German river pronounced (mīn)

**Mainwaring,** n., *family name,* pronounced (măn′erĭng)

**Mainz,** n., *city in Germany,* not *Mayence,* by decision of the United States Geographic Board. Pronounced (mīnts)

**maize,** n., poetic, technical, and literary for *corn, Indian corn.* The word has never been current in general popular use in America.

**make,** n., slang in the phrase *on the make,* grasping, eager for profit, often with the implication of profiting at the expense of one's friends.

**make,** v., employed in many phrases of picturesque color, as in *make up for,* compensate, *make it hot,* pursue relentlessly, *make fun of, make a fool of, make a clean sweep, make head or tail of, make it up with,* become reconciled, etc. Many of these phrases can be translated into different terms, but often only at the expense of idiomatic flavor and vigor. See **jab**

**make night hideous,** trite phrase, adapted from Shakspere's *Hamlet,* Act I, Sc. iv, where it is used seriously, but now possible only humorously.

**malachite,** n., *a mineral,* pronounced (măl′akīt)

**malaise,** n., *feeling of illness,* pronounced (mălāz′) Not general in colloquial use, but a frequent word in the language of physicians.

**malapropos,** adj., adv., *inopportune,* pronounced (mălăpropō′) From French *mal-, apropos.* But the noun *malapropism* is pronounced (mălaprŏp′ĭzm), being derived from the name Mrs. Malaprop, a character in Sheridan's *Rivals.* A malapropism is a confusion between words somewhat similar in form but ludicrously different in meaning, like Mrs. Malaprop's *nice derangement of epitaphs*, for *nice arrangement of epithets*.

**mal de mer,** French phrase, *seasickness*, pronounced (măl de mār)

**male,** n., not ordinarily used to mean merely *man*, except in scientific and medical writing, or sometimes in public announcements, bulletins, and other formal statements. See **female**

**malevolent,** adj., *disposed to think and act with evil intent*, pronounced (mălĕv'olent)

**malfeasance,** n., *official misconduct*, pronounced (mălfē'zans) A technical and legal word.

**malign,** adj., *evil*, pronounced (malīn'), but *malignant* is pronounced (malĭg'nant)

**malinger,** v., *pretend sickness to escape duty*, pronounced (malĭng'-ger)

**Mall,** see **Pall Mall**

**malmsey,** n., *a kind of wine*, frequently referred to in Robin Hood and other tales of romance. Pronounced (mahm'zĭ)

**maltreat,** v., *to abuse*, pronounced (măltrēt'), not (mawltrēt')

**mamma,** n., a somewhat old-fashioned word, now tending to be replaced by *mother*, in the speech of children as well as adults. Pronounced (mamah'), sometimes (mah'ma) The pronunciation (mamă') is limited to certain southern localities. The word *mammy* means an old-fashioned negro woman. See **papa** Various modifications of both of these words are current in familiar colloquial use, such as *mammy, mummy, mom, mum,* etc., *pappy, pap, pop,* etc. See **ma**

**mandamus,** n., Latin word, *command from a superior court to a lower court*, pronounced (măndā'mus)

**mandatary,** n., *one to whom a mandate is intrusted*, especially a commission from the League of Nations to one nation to act for another people not capable of self-government. Thus Great Britain might be a mandatary of certain countries in Asia. This is the proper form for the noun, the form *mandatory* being an adjective, as in *The mandatory government of these provinces is a regrettable necessity.*

**manège,** n., French word, *riding school, movements of a trained horse, horsemanship,* pronounced (mănāzh')

**manes,** n., *spirit of the dead.* A plural number with no singular, and pronounced (mā'nēz) The word is construed as a plural, with a plural verb.

**mangrove,** n., *a kind of tropical tree,* pronounced (măng'grōv), not (măn'grōv)

**maniac,** n., *insane person,* pronounced (mā'nĭăk), but the adjective is *maniacal* (manī'akal)

**manifold,** adv., though a compound of *many* (mĕn'ĭ) and *fold,* pronounced (măn'ĭfōld) The word can also be used as a verb, *to manifold.*

**manly,** adj., as in *manly behavior;* not in good use as an adverb, as in *He spoke very manly,* for *He spoke in a very manly fashion.*

**manner,** n., in the phrase *to the manner born,* fitted by birth to some kind of life or activity. Often mis-etymologized into *manor.* Colloquial in the phrase *not by any manner of means.*

**mannish,** adj., *after the fashion of men,* usually applied contemptuously to women who imitate the manners of men. See -ish

**manoeuvre,** v., *to manipulate, especially for private advantage,* pronounced (manōō'ver), less commonly (manū'ver) A variant spelling *maneuver* has the same pronunciation. Also used as a noun.

**manqué,** adj., French word, *failing of realization,* added after a noun, as in *a novelist manqué,* almost a novelist. Pronounced (mahṅkā')

**manse,** n., *the house of the minister of a parish in Scotland;* by extension, the residence of any Presbyterian minister, less commonly the residence of a minister of some other denomination. A *rectory* is usually the residence of an episcopal clergyman, but *parsonage* is not limited to a particular denomination.

**mantle of snow,** trite phrase, obvious poetic description.

**Maori,** n., *the language and the tribal name of native New Zealanders,* pronounced (mow'rī) or, as anglicized, (māŏr'ĭ)

**maraschino,** n., Italian word, *a kind of liqueur,* often with cherries. Pronounced (mărăskē'nō)

**marble brow,** trite phrase, of an old-fashioned romantic kind.

**marchpane,** n., *confection of almonds and sugar,* with a variant *marzipan* (mahr'zĭpăn)

**Mardi gras,** n., *celebration in New Orleans,* and, by extension, town celebration elsewhere, pronounced (mahr'dĭ grah') or (mahr'dĭ graw')

**mare clausum,** Latin phrase, *a sea under one country's jurisdiction, a closed sea,* pronounced (mā'rĭ klaw'sum)

**mare liberum,** Latin phrase, *sea open to all,* the complementary term being *mare clausum.* Pronounced (mā'rĭ lĭ'berum)

**margarine,** n., *imitation butter,* sometimes called *butterine* or *oleomargarine.* Pronounced (mahr'garĭn), not (mahr'jarĭn); but though this latter pronunciation is less correct etymologically, it is nevertheless the current commercial and popular pronunciation, and it seems bound in time to make its way into general good use.

**marge,** n., poetical and archaic for *margin.*

**marguerite,** n., *kind of daisy,* pronounced (mahrgerēt')

**mariage de convénance,** French phrase, *a marriage made for worldly and practical reasons,* pronounced (mărĭahzh' de kŏn-vānahńs')

**mariner,** n., archaic term for *sailor, seaman,* surviving, however, in legal and literary uses.

**Marlborough,** n., *English proper name,* pronounced in England (mawl'bro), in America, usually brought into closer harmony with the spelling and pronounced (mahrl'boro)

**marque,** n., usually in the phrase *letters of marque,* license to act as a privateer. Pronounced (mahrk)

**marquee,** n., *a large tent,* pronounced (mahrkē′)

**marquis,** n., *a title of nobility.* As an English word, **marquis** is pronounced (mahr′kwis), and it has a variant spelling *marquess.* The corresponding feminine is *marchioness* (mahr′shones) As a French word, **marquis** is pronounced (mahrkē′), and the feminine is *marquise* (mahrkēz′)

**marron glacé,** French phrase, *candied chestnut,* pronounced (măr′ŏn glahsä′)

**Marseillaise,** n., *French national song,* pronounced (mahrselāz′) or as a French word.

**Marseilles,** n., *French city,* pronounced (mahrsālz′)   The French form of the name of this city is *Marseille,* and if this form is used, it would be pronounced as a French word, approximately (mahrsä′y)   Although both the United States Geographic Board and the Permanent Committee on Geographical Names authorize only *Marseille,* the form **Marseilles** is still widely used.

**Marylebone,** n., *place name in London,* locally pronounced (măr′ĭbon)

**marzipan,** see **marchpane**

**Mascagni,** n., *Italian musical composer,* pronounced (mahskahn′yĭ)

**mash,** n., slang, but now old-fashioned slang, for *a conquest in courtship.*   A masher is a professional lady's man.   See **crush**

**maskinonge,** n., *a kind of pike,* pronounced (măskĭnŏnj′)   This is the spelling given by Hodge, *Handbook of American Indians,* as being nearest to the Algonquian origin of the name.   But a great variety of spellings is found, *maskalunge, muskalunge, muskallonge,* etc.   The word is often abbreviated to *lunge* or *longe.*

**masquerade,** n., v., *a disguising costume, to dress in such a costume,* pronounced (măskerād′), not (măskerahd′)

**massage,** n., *kneading and rubbing of the muscles,* pronounced (masahzh′), and also used as a verb.

**Massenet,** n., *French musical composer,* pronounced (măsenā′)

**masseur, masseuse,** n., the former *a man*, the latter, *a woman practitioner of massage.* The masculine is pronounced (mahser'), the feminine, (mahsöz')

**massif,** n., French word, *high mountains in a group*, pronounced (mahsēf')

**massive,** adj., *large and solid*, pronounced (măs'ĭv), not (măs'iv), and not (mah'sĭv), even in the speech of persons who might say (mahst) for *mast.* See **a** (ah), the sound of **a** as in *father*

**master,** n., used as a title with the name of a boy too young to be called Mr., as in *Master Brown* or *Master John Brown.* This title is not used by boys themselves, but by their elders in formal invitations and by newspapers in reports of the doings of fashionable families. See **Miss, mister, mistress**

**mater,** n., Latin word, *mother*, especially as schoolboy's slang. Pronounced (mā'ter)

**materfamilias,** n., Latin word, *mother of a household*, pronounced (mā'terfamĭl'ĭas)

**materialize,** v., colloquial and slightly facetious in the sense *appear, show up*, as in *The promised supplies failed to materialize.*

**materially,** adv., *bodily, not spiritually*, and incorrectly used for *considerably, largely*, in constructions like *His income was materially increased by the sale of his land*, was considerably or greatly increased.

**matériel,** n., French word, *the supplies and equipment available for some undertaking*, the complementary word being *personnel.* Pronounced (matĕrĭĕl') See **personnel**

**mathematics,** n., construed as a singular when it names a branch of knowledge, as in *Mathematics underlies many other sciences;* as a plural when it refers to mathematical processes, as in *The mathematics of this demonstration are very complicated.* See **acoustics**

**matinée,** n., strictly, by etymology, *a morning performance*, but as commonly used, *an afternoon theatrical performance.* A *matinée girl* is an idle girl with a sentimental interest in the stage, especially in the actors.

**matrix,** n., *mould,* pronounced (mā'trĭks), with a plural *matrices* (mā'trĭsēz)

**matronal,** adj., *motherly,* pronounced (mā'tronal) or (matrō'nal)

**mature,** adj., *fully developed,* pronounced (matūr') or (matōōr')

**matutinal,** adj., *pertaining to the morning,* as in *matutinal bath.* Pronounced (matū'tinal) or (mătūtī'nal) See **Polysyllabic Humor**

**Mauch Chunk,** n., *town in Pennsylvania,* pronounced (mawk' chŭngk')

**maulstick,** n., *stick used by painters to steady the hand in painting,* pronounced (mawl'stĭk) Also spelled *mahlstick.*

**Maupassant, Guy de,** n., *French writer* (1850–1893), pronounced (gē de mōpahsahṅ')

**mauvaise honte,** French phrase, *bashfulness,* pronounced (mōvāz' ŏṅt)

**mauvais quart d'heure,** French phrase, *unpleasant experience,* literally, *a bad quarter of an hour;* pronounced (mōvā' kahrder')

**mauvais sujet,** French phrase, *rascal,* pronounced (mōvā' sōōzhā')

**mauve,** n., *a color, pale purple,* pronounced (mōv)

**maxillary,** adj., *pertaining to the jaw,* pronounced (măksĭl'arĭ)

**maximum,** n., *highest point,* with a plural *maxima.*

**may,** see **can**

**maybe,** adv., *perhaps.* Never written *may be* or *may-be* as an adverb, but always as one word. As a verb, as in *it may be,* never written as one word. The adverb **maybe** is more familiar and colloquial in tone than *perhaps.*

**mayhap,** adv., archaic and literary for *maybe.*

**mayonnaise,** n., *a salad dressing,* pronounced (māŏnāz') or (mī-ŏnāz')

**me,** pron., objective case of *I;* see **her** It should be added, however, to what is said under *her,* that constructions like *It* *is me, He is taller than me* are much more prevalent than similar constructions with *her, him, them.* This is well illustrated in a line by Meredith, quoted in *The King's English,* p. 60, *I am she, she me, till death and beyond it.* To write *I am her* would be crudely ungrammatical, and to *write I am she, she I,* would be absurd. Meredith indeed seems to be following a very natural tendency to give the objective form to the pronoun of the first person whenever there is the slightest tendency to objectify the idea expressed by it. Nevertheless the preponderance of theoretical opinion is not on the side either of **me** or of *her, him,* etc., as nominatives, and the degree of recognition one accords to these constructions depends entirely on the degree of authority one grants to popular custom when it comes into conflict with conservative and literary tradition. By the historical rules of grammar such constructions are incorrect. But this test in itself is not decisive, for many uses now in good standing are historically incorrect. The question is whether these particular uses have established themselves as correct beyond debate. The answer to this question must obviously be in the negative, and therefore one must characterize the constructions as still at least dubious.

**mead,** n., literary and poetic for *meadow.*

**meal,** n., *ground grain,* though the word without qualification would usually be understood to mean *corn meal.* Any dry food ground fine might be called a meal, but ordinarily with some qualifying word, like rye meal, oat meal, bone meal, etc. A **meal** is distinguished from a *flour* in being ground less fine and powdery.

**mean,** adj., colloquial in the phrase *to feel mean,* to feel not well, ashamed. Also colloquial in the sense *vicious,* as *a mean horse,* and slang in the sense *skilful, hard to overcome,* as in *Dolan pitches a mean curve.*

**means,** n., (1) *resources, income, wealth;* (2) *process or method by* *which some result is brought about.* In the first of these two uses **means** is regularly construed as a plural, as in *His means do not justify his living on such an extravagant scale.* In the second sense **means** may be construed either as a singular, as in *By this means we were enabled to pass the night in some comfort,* or as a plural, as in *Our means for keeping watch over his expenses were entirely inadequate.* The singular occurs also in the phrase *every other means,* as in *After we had tried every other means, we finally hit upon a plan that worked.* See **pain**

**meantime,** n., especially in the phrase *in the meantime,* in the interval. Always written as one word. A parallel word of the same use and meaning is *meanwhile.*

**measles,** n., plural in form, but usually construed as a singular, as in *Measles is an infectious disease that few children escape.* So also with *mumps, rickets, shingles, smallpox.*

**measly,** adj., slang in the sense *wretched, contemptible,* as in *a measly specimen of humanity.* Though derived from the noun *measles,* the slang adjective is extended in use to a wide variety of applications.

**medicine,** n., *art of healing, a drug,* pronounced (mĕd′isin) in America, sometimes (mĕd′sn) in imitation of a British pronunciation. The derivatives are *medicinal* (medĭs′ĭnal), *medicament* (mĕd′-ĭkament), *medicative* (mĕd′ĭkātĭv)

**medieval,** adj., *of the Middle Ages,* through eye-confusion sometimes mispronounced as though written *medievial.* Sometimes spelled *mediaeval.* Pronounced (mĕdĭē′val) or (mēdĭē′val)

**mediocre,** adj., *of medium quality.* Ordinarily described as pronounced (mē′dĭōker), but quite as often pronounced (mēdĭō′ker) in actual speech.

**medullary,** adj., *with respect to the marrow,* pronounced (medŭl′arĭ)

**meed,** n., archaic and literary for *reward.*

**meet,** adj., archaic and literary for *fitting, proper.* Sometimes used in the tautological phrase *meet and proper.*

384

**meeting,** n., now archaic or humorous in the sense *church,* as in *go to meeting, go-to-meeting clothes.*

**Mekka,** n., *city in Arabia,* not *Mecca* or *Mekkah,* by decision of the United States Geographic Board.

**mélange,** n., French word, *medley,* pronounced (mālahṅzh′)

**mêlée,** n., *tumult, crowd,* pronounced in anglicized fashion (mĕl′ā), low colloquially (mĕ′lē), or as a French word (mālā′)

**melon,** n., slang in the sense *distribution of cash or profits,* especially of trustees or directors when they vote a payment to themselves, usually in the phrase *cut a melon.*

**membranous,** adj., *of the membrane,* pronounced (mĕm′branus), with a variant form *membraneous,* pronounced (mĕmbrā′nĭus) The shorter form is to be preferred on the grounds of economy.

**memento mori,** Latin phrase, *reminder of death,* literally, *think upon death;* pronounced (mĭmĕn′tō mŏr′ī)

**memoir,** n., *a book of personal recollections,* pronounced (mĕm′wahr), less commonly (mē′mwahr) Most frequently used in the plural, *memoirs,* personal recollections.

**memorabilia,** n., Latin word, *memorable things,* pronounced (mĕmorabĭl′ĭa) A corresponding singular is not in use.

**memorandum,** n., *a note for future reference.* Plural *memoranda.* A plural *memorandums* is possible, but is very rarely met with.

**memoria technica,** Latin phrase, *device for helping memory,* pronounced (mĭmŏr′ĭa tĕk′nĭka)

**memorize,** v., *learn by heart.* This sense of the word, which is the only one that has any general currency in American usage, is characterized by the *New English Dictionary* as being peculiar to the United States. In America this use of the word is unquestionable English. The other sense of **memorize,** *to do something in memory of one,* in American use would be expressed by *memorialize, commemorate,* or some more expanded phrase.

**ménage,** n., French word, *household management, domestic establishment,* pronounced (mānahzh′)

**Mendelssohn-Bartholdy, Felix,** n., *German musical composer* (1809–1847), with two *s*'s in **Mendelssohn,** pronounced (mĕn′delson)

**men-folk,** n., *men,* as distinguished from women, with the complementary term *women-folk,* used for women as distinguished from men, as in *The men-folk of the family were always more liberal than the women-folk.* Though these two words are in good use, they always carry with them the implications of a simple, perhaps rustic and dialectal life on the part of the persons whom the words designate.

**mens conscia recti,** Latin phrase, *a good conscience,* literally, *a mind conscious of right;* pronounced (mĕnz kŏn′shĭa rĕk′tī)

**mens sana in corpore sano,** Latin phrase, a *sound mind in a sound body,* pronounced (mĕnz sā′na in cŏr′porĭ sā′nō)

**Mentone,** n., *place in southern France,* pronounced (mĕntō′nĭ)

**menu,** n., *bill of fare.* Usually pronounced in an anglicized fashion as (mĕn′ū) or (mĕn′o͞o) But some speakers avoid anglicizing the word and give it, to the best of their ability, its French pronunciation.

**Mephistopheles,** n., *the devil,* pronounced (mĕfĭstŏf′elēz), with an adjective *Mephistophelean* (mĕfĭstŏfelē′an)

**mercantile,** adj., *commercial,* pronounced (mer′kantĭl) or (mer′-kantīl) See **-ile** The word is formal, therefore appropriately to be applied only to commercial activities of some importance.

**merchant,** n., a more dignified word than *storekeeper* or *dealer,* usually applied to retailers on a large scale, or to wholesalers, especially importers and exporters. In towns, the proprietor of the local dry-goods store is often called a merchant, but not the proprietors of other stores.

**merchant tailor,** n., an archaic survival sometimes used on signs, billheads, and the like for *tailor.* A merchant tailor, as distinct from a journeyman tailor, was one who sold the materials for the making of clothing besides making the clothing. See **costume**

**meringue,** n., *dish made with sugar and beaten egg*, pronounced (mĕră̆ng′)

**Merovingian,** n., *a French dynasty*, pronounced (mĕrōvĭn′jĭan)

**mésalliance,** n., French word, *marriage with a social inferior*, pronounced (māză̆lĭahn̊s′)

**mesdames,** n., plural of *madame.* Used in newspaper reports of social functions. Pronounced (mādahm′) See **madame**

**mesmerism,** n., *hypnotic control*, pronounced (mĕz′merĭzm), *mesmerist* (mĕz′merĭst), and an adjective *mesmeric* (mĕzmĕr′ĭk), and a verb *mesmerize* (mĕz′merīz) From the proper name *Mesmer*, the name of an Austrian physician.

**messieurs,** n., plural of the French word *monsieur*, but commonly used in English, especially business English, to supply the want of an English plural of *Mr.* Ordinarily used in the abbreviated form *Messrs.* The usual pronunciation, whether written **messieurs** or *Messrs.*, is (mĕs′yerz) Sometimes an approximate French pronunciation is used, (mĕsyer′), or a more completely anglicized one, (mĕs′erz) See **monsieur**

**Messrs.,** see **messieurs**

**messuage,** n., *house, buildings, and land*, pronounced (mĕs′wĭj)

**metallurgy,** n., *art of working in metals.* Pronounced (mĕtalur′jĭ) or (mĕtă̆l′urjĭ), and so also the noun, *metallurgist*, pronounced (mĕtalur′jĭst) or (mĕtă̆l′urjĭst) The adjective *metallurgical* is pronounced (mĕtalur′jĭkal)

**metals,** n., *rails of a railway.* Common in British but not frequent in American speech.

**metempsychosis,** n., *migration of souls*, pronounced (mĭtĕmsĭkō′sĭs), with a plural *metempsychoses* (mĭtĕmsĭkō′sēz)

**methinks,** v., archaic and literary for *it seems to me.* The past tense is *methought*, it seemed to me. Frequent in modern imitations of medieval style.

**method in one's madness,** trite phrase, meaning merely that one has a purpose.

**Methusaleh,** n., *a Biblical character*, in low colloquial speech often altered to *Methusalem*, after the analogy of *Jerusalem*.

**métier,** n., French word, *one's strong side or specialty*, pronounced (mā′tǐā)

**mettle,** n., *staying power*, usually in the phrase *put one on his mettle*, with an adjective *mettlesome*, spirited. Though etymologically the same as *metal*, the word **mettle** always has its distinctive spelling.

**meum et tuum,** Latin phrase, *rights of property, the mine and thine*, pronounced (mē′um ĕt tū′um)

**mews,** n., *a stable yard, a cage for hawks*. The word is plural in form but singular in use, *a mews*. The plural would be *mewses*.

**Miami,** n., *name of an Indian tribe*, and, by extension, a geographical term in various sections of the United States. Pronounced (mĭăm′ĭ) Other varieties, such as (mēăm′ĭ), (mēah′mĭ), are not general.

**Michael Angelo,** n., *Italian artist*, pronounced (mī′kl ăn′jelō) The Italian form of the name is Michelagnolo (mē′kĕlănyō′lō), and the French form is *Michel-ange* (mē′kĕl-ahṅzh′)

**Michaelmas,** n., *feast of St. Michael, September 29*, pronounced (mĭk′lmas)

**mickle,** n., Scotch dialect for *much*, and of the same meaning as *muckle*. The saying *Many a mickle makes a muckle* is a popular error, and it should be *Many a little makes a mickle*, or *muckle*.

**microcosm,** n., *the world of man*, as contrasted with *macrocosm*, which means *the world at large in relation to the world of man*.

**microscope,** n., *a magnifying device*, pronounced (mī′kroskōp), with an adjective *microscopic* (mĭkroskŏp′ĭk), and the related nouns *microscopy* (mĭkrŏs′kopĭ), *microscopist* (mĭkrŏs′kopĭst)

**midst,** n., sometimes objected to in phrases like *in our, your, their midst*, for *in the midst of us, of you, of them*. But examples of *in our midst*, etc., have occurred in good writers for the past hundred years, and the construction, though rarely used in spoken language, except facetiously, has sufficient literary authority to counterbalance its lack of logic.

**mien,** n., literary for *appearance, bearing, demeanor.* The word is ordinarily used only in an unfavorable sense, especially in the phrase *a forbidding mien.*

**miff,** n., colloquial and dialectal for *fit of ill-humor.* Also used in the participial form *miffed* as an adjective, as in *He was miffed at something that had been said.*

**mighty,** adv., colloquial as an intensive, as in *mighty glad to see you,* very glad. See **awful, terrible, wonderful**

**mignon,** adj., French word, *small, delicately formed,* pronounced (mēnyŏṅ′)

**milch,** adj., in the compound *milch-cow,* cow giving milk. But the word is archaic and commonly occurs now only in bills of sale, legal statements, and similar printed forms.

**milieu,** n., French word, *environment, social surrounding,* pronounced (mĭlyö′)

**Millet, Jean François,** n., *French painter* (1814–1875), pronounced (zhăṅ frahṅ′swah mēlā′)

**millinery,** n., *women's hats, ribbons,* etc., pronounced (mĭl′ĭnĕrĭ) or (mĭl′ĭnerĭ), the latter being the customary British pronunciation. The term *man milliner* is current only as a jocose word.

**mind,** v., polite colloquialism, as in *"Will you have some tea?"* *"I shouldn't mind,"* i. e., should like to have some. Also familar colloquialism in the sense *take care of,* as in *Mind the baby,* in the sense *obey,* as in *If you don't mind me, I'll punish you,* and in the sense *watch, take heed,* as in *Mind your step, Mind your eye,* i. e., look where you are going.

**mine,** pron., possessive form of the singular first personal pronoun. The form **mine** is used only in the predicative position, as in *This hat is mine.* Archaically it is used before words beginning with a vowel or with *h* unsounded, as in *Mine eyes have seen the glory of the coming of the Lord, Mine host of the Tabard.* See **ours**

**mineralogy,** n., *the science of minerals,* pronounced (mĭnerăl'ojĭ), often mispronounced (mĭnerŏl'ojĭ), under the influence of words like *biology, zoology, theology,* etc.

**minimum,** n., *the smallest amount,* pronounced (mĭn'ĭmŭm), with a plural *minima* (mĭn'ĭma) See **maximum**

**minion,** n., *favorite,* sometimes used rhetorically and bombastically for *follower, supporter,* as in *the minions of the law,* the police, *minions of the king,* soldiers. See **hireling**

**minions of the law,** trite phrase, journalistic and ambitious synonym for *policemen, sheriffs,* etc.

**minister,** n., rarely used of an Episcopal clergyman, but the common term in the Presbyterian and some other churches. The terms **minister** and *pastor* do not belong respectively to any particular denomination, but are used more or less indiscriminately. The designation *parson* is archaic, literary, or slightly facetious. The term *preacher* for **minister,** *pastor* is low colloquial. See **priest, rector**

**minnesinger,** n., German word, *medieval lyric poet,* pronounced (mĭn'esĭng'er) See **Zeitgeist**

**minnow,** n., *small fish,* pronounced (mĭn'ō), dialectally (mĭn'ĭ)

**minute,** n., *a period of time,* pronounced (mĭn'ĭt) The adjective **minute,** of the same etymological origin, is (mīnūt') or (mĭnūt'), meaning *very small* or *very detailed,* as in *He entered into minute particulars.*

**minutia,** n., *a small detail,* pronounced (mĭnū'shĭa) But the word is rarely used in the singular, the customary form being the plural *minutiae,* pronounced (mĭnū'shĭē), less correctly (mĭnū'sha)

**miracle,** n., *a marvel,* pronounced (mĭr'akl), with an adjective *miraculous,* (mĭrăk'ūlus) or (mīrăk'ūlus) The pronunciation (mir'akl) for **miracle** is low colloquial.

**mirage,** n., *visual illusion,* pronounced (mĭrahzh′)   The plural is *mirages* (mĭrahzh′ez)

**misanthrope,** n., *a hater of mankind,* pronounced ⟨mĭs′anthrōp), not (mĭz′anthrōp), with an adjective *misanthropic* (mĭsăn-thrŏp′ĭk) and a noun *misanthropy* (mĭsăn′thropĭ)

**miscellanea,** n., Latin word, *odds and ends, small literary compositions gathered together,* pronounced (mĭselā′nĭa), with no singular form in use corresponding to this plural.

**miscellany,** n., *a mixed collection,* pronounced (mĭs′elanĭ), not (mĭsĕl′anĭ)   Since the noun *miscellany* by itself means a collection, it is tautological and incorrect to speak of *a miscellany collection, a miscellany manuscript, a miscellany volume.*   See **palimpsest**

**mischief,** n., *harm, injury, minor trouble-making,* pronounced (mĭs′chĭf)   The adjective *mischievous* is pronounced (mĭs′chĭvus) dialectally often pronounced (mĭschē′vus) or (mĭschĕv′yus)

**misdoubt,** v., possible but not common synonym for *doubt.*

**mise en scène,** French phrase, *staging of a play, general setting,* pronounced (mēz ahṅ sān)

**miserere,** n., Latin word, *a prayer for mercy,* literally, *be merciful,* from Psalm LI.   Pronounced (mĭzerē′rĭ)   See **misericord**

**misericord,** n., *a seat in a choir stall which provides a support to lean against while one is standing,* a compromise between standing up and sitting down during the services.   From Latin *misericordia,* pity, and pronounced (mĭzĕr′ĭkŏrd)   The word *miserere* is sometimes incorrectly used in this sense.

**misery,** n., dialectal in the sense *a bodily pain,* as in *a misery in the back.*   Frequent in literary transcriptions of negro dialect.

**misfortunate,** adj., a reasonable kind of adjective from the noun *misfortune,* though it has never been an accepted word in the English language.   The form of the adjective in good English is *unfortunate,* though, perversely enough, the language has never had a noun *unfortune.*

391

**misogynist**, n., *one who hates women*, pronounced (mĭsŏj′ĭnĭst)

**misprision**, n., *concealment of knowledge of treason*, etc., pronounced (mĭsprĭzh′n)

**misremember**, v., dialectal for *forget*. So also *disremember*.

**Miss**, n., a shortening of *mistress*, used before the name of an unmarried woman or girl. When no Christian name is given, as in *Miss Brown*, the oldest daughter, unmarried, of the family is ordinarily meant, the younger daughters being designated *Miss Mary Brown*, *Miss Sara Brown*, etc., or more familiarly, in direct address, *Miss Mary*, *Miss Sara*, etc. This is by no means, however, a strict rule of etiquet, and the two forms are used, as convenience requires, for all unmarried women. For the plural two forms are equally correct, *the Misses Brown* and *the Miss Browns*, the former being perhaps the more general. As a form of address, **Miss** not followed by either Christian name or surname is current now only in low colloquial use, or sometimes in business and official English as the equivalent of *madam* for a younger person. As a noun meaning *young girl*, the word **miss** usually has a slightly humorous or satirical color, as in *a pert young miss*. In business English with reference to sizes and styles of clothing, etc., *misses*, as distinguished from *ladies* and *children*, denotes the years between childhood and womanhood. Colloquially and dialectally *Mrs.* is often pronounced (mĭs), in the South (mĭz)

**miss**, v., sometimes with *out*, as in *In copying, he missed out several sentences*, passed over, omitted. But the word **miss** alone is adequate and *out* is an unnecessary encumbrance. See **up**

**missile**, n., *something thrown*, pronounced (mĭs′ĭl) or (mĭs′īl) See **-ile**

**Missouri**, n., pronounced (mĭzŏŏr′ĭ), the pronunciation (mĭzŏŏr′i), that is, with the final vowel like the final vowel of Cuba, being less general and less defensible. See **Cincinnati**

**mister,** n., *a man,* but used only as a word of address. Without a surname or Christian name following, **mister** is used only in low colloquial speech. In good English the surname usually follows the word of address, pronounced (mĭs'ter), but always written or printed in the abbreviated form *Mr.* Before a Christian name alone, as in *Mr. John, Mr. Tom,* the usage is more familiar, or the address of a servant to a master. Though originally a title of honor, the word *Mr.* is now applied to every man on certain occasions, as on the address of a letter. In formal use, as in addressing a letter, the title *Mr.* is omitted when another title precedes the name or follows it, as in *the Rev. Donald Grant,* not *the Rev. Mr. Donald Grant,* although, when the Christian name is omitted, it is permissible to write *the Rev. Mr. Grant.* One would not write, however, *Mr. Postmaster General Brown,* but *Postmaster General Brown.* Nor would one write *Mr. W. H. Brown, Esq.,* but *W. H. Brown, Esq.* When the surname is omitted, one may write or say *Mr. Postmaster General, Mr. President, Mr. Chairman, Mr. Speaker,* but only with official titles, not with professional titles, that is, one would not say *Mr. Doctor, Mr. Professor,* etc.

**mistletoe,** n., *a plant,* pronounced (mĭs'ltō)

**mistress,** n., obsolescent, surviving in a few set phrases, as in *mistress of the situation, her own mistress, mistress of the seas* (poetic and literary), and in the specialized sense of *unmarried living companion of a man.* But a woman school-teacher is not now ordinarily called a *schoolmistress,* though the term *headmistress,* parallel to *headmaster,* is still current. The words *master,* **mistress** for *teacher* are used more in private schools than in the public schools.

**mitrailleuse,** n., French word, *machine gun with many barrels.* Pronounced (mĭtralāz') as an anglicized word, or as a French word (mētrăyōz')

**mitt,** n., *glove,* with a variant form *mitten.* Slang in the sense

393

*hand, boxing glove,* and in the phrase *to get the mitten,* be rejected, especially as a lover.

**mnemonic,** adj., *helping the memory,* pronounced (nemŏn'ĭk)

**mocha,** n., *a kind of coffee,* pronounced (mō'ka)

**moderate,** adj., *not extreme,* pronounced (mŏd'erat), the verb of the same form, *to moderate,* being (mŏd'erāt)

**modish,** adj., archaic and literary for *fashionable.*

**modiste,** n., French word, *dressmaker, milliner,* pronounced (mōdēst')

**modus operandi,** Latin phrase, *manner of procedure,* pronounced (mō'dus ŏperăn'dī)

**modus vivendi,** Latin phrase, *temporary settlement, a working agreement,* pronounced (mō'dus vĭvĕn'dī)

**mog,** v., dialectal for *to move,* as in *to mog off, along.* See **mooch**

**Mogul,** n., *oriental title,* pronounced (mōgŭl')

**Mohammed,** n., *the prophet of Allah.* The derivatives are *Mohammedan, Mohammedanism.* Variant forms *Mahomet, Mahometan,* etc., are also in use but are tending to be replaced by **Mohammed,** etc.

**Mohave,** n., *place name for several regions in Arizona and California,* not to be spelled **Mojave,** by decision of the United States Geographic Board. The pronunciation of the word, however spelled, is (mōhah'vĭ)

**Mohican,** n., a tribe of Indians, pronounced (mōhē'kan) This word is recorded in a great variety of forms, but besides **Mohican** the only ones extensively used are *Mahican* and *Mohegan.* See Hodge, *Handbook of American Indians,* for the many forms of the word.

**moiety,** n., learned and literary word for *half.* Sometimes incorrectly used in the sense *small portion.*

**moire,** n., *a kind of silk fabric,* pronounced (mwahr) A participial adjective form is *moiré* (mwahrā')

**molasses,** n., *sugar syrup,* construed as a singular, as in *This* *molasses is too dark.* The word is of course not thought of either as a singular or as a plural, but as a material name, like *milk, water, bread,* etc.  See **fish, fruit**

**Molière,** n., *French dramatist,* pronounced as an anglicized word, (mōlĭär′) or (mŏlyär′), or as a French word.

**moment,** n., *small space of time,* on the logical side interchangeable with *minute,* n.  Stylistically, however, there may be a choice between the two.  In asking someone to wait, perhaps *Just a moment, please* sounds a little less abrupt than *Just a minute, please.*  This latter phrase may even have a slight threatening color, meaning *I'm not through with you yet, The worst is yet to come,* or it may express a touch of impatience or annoyance.

**momentum,** n., with a technical and mathematical meaning in physics, but as currently employed the word means *the impetus gained by a moving body,* as in *The stone gained in momentum as it came down,* gained in speed and power.  Though not the scientific sense of the word, this second meaning is established in good use.  The plural of **momentum** is *momenta,* used only in scientific writing or speaking.

**monarch of all one surveys,** trite phrase, a roundabout way of saying that one is alone.

**Mondays,** see **afternoons**

**money,** n., *the medium of exchange,* pronounced (mŭn′ĭ), and so also *monetary* (mŭn′etărĭ) and *monetize* (mŭn′etīz)  The plural is *moneys* and the participial adjective is *moneyed* (mŭn′ēd)

**mongrel,** adj., n., *not pure-blooded,* pronounced (mŭng′grel) or (mŏng′grel)

**monkey,** v., colloquial and slang in the sense *meddle, interfere,* as in *Don't monkey with the machinery.*  Pronounced like the noun, (mŭng′kĭ)

**monocle,** n., *single eyeglass,* pronounced (mŏn′okl)

**monopoly,** n., *exclusive possession or privilege.*  The word does not need a qualifier, as in *entire, complete monopoly*, these being tautological and incorrect uses.

**monseigneur**, n., French word, *title of address to princes, bishops*, etc., pronounced (mŏṅsānyer')

**monsieur**, n., French word, *Mr.*, with a plural *messieurs*. The singular is pronounced in an anglicized fashion as (mĕsyö'), or more nearly like the French colloquial pronunciation, (msyö') The plural is pronounced (mĕsyö') See **messieurs**

**monsignore**, n., Italian word, *title for princes, bishops*, etc., pronounced (mŏnsĭnyō'rā)

**Montague**, n., *proper name*, pronounced (mŏn'tagū)

**Montaigne, Michel Eyquem de**, n., *French essayist* (1533–1592), pronounced (mŏntān') or as a French word.

**Montana**, n., *a state in the United States.* Pronounced (mŏntăn'a) by dwellers in the state, and by most other speakers, but occasionally pronounced (mŏntah'na), probably from a half-conscious feeling that the word is Latin or otherwise foreign and therefore should have an (ah) in it.

**Montauk**, n., *place on Long Island*, pronounced (mŏntawk')

**Montesquieu, C. de S.**, n., *French writer* (1689–1755), pronounced (mŏntĕskū') or as a French word, (mŏṅtĕskyö')

**mooch**, v., slang for *to move about slowly and aimlessly.* See **mog**

**moonshine**, n., slang in the sense *illicitly distilled liquor*, and so also *moonshiner*. But perhaps these words have passed out of the slang stage and have become established as useful and accepted terms. Certainly no other words easily take their places.

**mop**, v., slang in the phrase *mop up*, dispose of effectively, as of food, work, profits, business, etc.

**Moqui**, n., *a tribe of Indians*, pronounced (mō'kē)

**morale**, n., *general spirit of a person or a group*, pronounced (morahl'), sometimes (morăl') See **locale**

**morass**, n., literary for *swamp, marsh*, pronounced (morăs')

**moratorium, n.,** Latin word, *an authorized period of delay in the payment of a debt,* pronounced (mŏratŏr′ĭum)

**mordant wit,** trite phrase, a bit of outworn critical terminology.

**more,** adj., often rejected in the sentence *Won't you have some more steak?* and similar phrases on the ground that it is impolite in urging a person to have more food to use a form of phrasing which implies that the person has already had some food. The impropriety supposedly resides in the suggestion of greediness when one says, "Won't you have some more steak?" But as there is such a thing as false modesty, so also there is such a thing as false delicacy and refinement. No reasonable person would ever suppose when a host invites a guest to have more steak that he means to accuse his guest of greediness, and one of the worst forms of bad manners is to seem to see meanings in language which everybody knows are not intended.

**more easily imagined than described,** trite phrase, an evasive substitution for a real description.

**morgue, n.,** *place where bodies of dead persons are held,* pronounced (mŏrg)

**mornings,** see **afternoons**

**morose,** adj., *gloomy, sombre,* pronounced (morōs′), not (morōz′)

**morphadite,** see **hermaphrodite**

**morphine, n.,** *a drug,* with a variant *morphia.*

**morsel, n.,** *mouthful, bit, a small piece,* not appropriately to be used in referring to liquids. See **bit**

**mortgage, n.,** *a claim upon property,* pronounced (mŏr′gĭj) Also used as a verb. The nouns *mortgagor* and *mortgagee* are pronounced (mŏr′gajŏr) and (mŏrgajē′)

**mortise, n.,** *a term in joinery,* also spelled *mortice.*

**mosey, v.,** slang in the sense *to move along aimlessly.* Pronounced (mō′zĭ), and probably derived from *vamose.* See **vamose**

**Moslem, n.,** adj., *Mohammedan,* with a variant *Muslim,* pronounced (mŏz′lem), (mŭz′lĭm)

**mosque,** n., *Mohammedan temple*, pronounced (mŏsk)

**'most,** adv., dialectal for *almost*.

**mot,** n., French word, *a witty saying*, with a plural *mots*, both pronounced (mō); or the plural may be anglicized and pronounced (mōz)

**mother,** see **father**

**mother-in-law,** see **father-in-law**

**motif,** n., French word, *dominant idea in an artistic production*, pronounced (mōtēf′) See **leit-motif**

**motion,** v., *to make a motion.* In good use as a verb, as in *He motioned me aside, He motioned me to a chair,* but perhaps a little crude stylistically, somewhat like *suspicion* as a verb, or *auction.* See **auction**

**motion pictures,** n., in good use, but not so general as *moving pictures.*

**motive,** n., *impelling power or cause*, pronounced (mō′tĭv), low colloquially (mō′tiv)

**mot juste,** French phrase, *the exactly right word*, pronounced (mō zho͞ost)

**motley crew, crowd, throng,** trite phrase, a traditional literary echo.

**motor,** n., v., *an automobile* and *to travel by automobile.* A part for the whole, like *sail* for *ship.* In good use, but not so general as *automobile.* The use as an adjective is more general, as in *motor car, motor truck, motor oil,* etc.

**moujik,** n., *Russian peasant*, pronounced (mo͞o′zhĭk), and sometimes spelled *muzhik.*

**mould,** n., v., (1) *crumbled earth;* (2) *a frame or shape* and *to shape;* (3) *fungous growth.* In all three senses, which correspond to the origins of the word from three different sources, a spelling *mold* is also possible, though not general. Perhaps it occurs more frequently in the first than in the other two senses. The notion that **mould,** *crumbled earth*, comes from **mould,** *fungous growth,* is a bit of erroneous popular science. A *mouldy* *smell* might be merely that of earth, or it might be the very different smell of mould, in the third sense.

**mountain,** n., *elevated land,* pronounced (mown'tĭn), or less formally (mown'tn) The pronunciation (mown'tān) is an artificial spelling pronunciation.

**mouser,** n., *cat good at catching mice,* pronounced (mow'zer) But *mousy,* adj., mouselike, is (mows'ĭ)

**mouth,** n., slang in the sense *impudence.* See **cheek**

**mouthful,** n., slang in the phrase *You've said a mouthful,* I heartily agree with you.

**move,** n., slang in the phrase *get a move on,* to hasten, to start. See **snap**

**movies,** n., colloquial abbreviation for *moving pictures.*

**mow,** n., *grimace,* pronounced (mow) or (mō)

**Mrs.,** n., pronounced (mĭs'iz), but with no written form to correspond to the pronunciation, except the abbreviation **Mrs.** The word was originally an abbreviation of *mistress,* as *Mr.* was an abbreviation of *master,* and formerly it implied certain honorable distinctions. In present use, however, every married woman would be addressed as **Mrs.** on even a slightly formal occasion. The abbreviation may be followed by the woman's surname, as in *Mrs. Rogers,* or by the husband's Christian name (or initials) and surname, as in *Mrs. John Bates Rogers,* or *Mrs. J. B. Rogers,* or by her own Christian name and surname if the woman is a widow, as in *Mrs. Ellen Rogers.* The use of **Mrs.** preceding a husband's title, as in *Mrs. Dr. Rogers, Mrs. Col. James,* is crude style. See **mistress**

**much,** adv., colloquial as an ironic negative, meaning not at all, as in *" Lend me five dollars? " " Not much ! "*

**muchly,** adj., humorous for *much.* See **Language Mutilation**

**muchness,** n., *size, greatness,* but current only in the phrase *much of a muchness,* and then always with facetious implications.

**mucker,** n., slang in the sense *unrefined person, roughneck.*

**muckle,** see **mickle**

**mucus,** n., to be distinguished from *mucous*, the adjective, as in *Mucus is a discharge of the mucous membrane.* The two words are pronounced alike. So also *fungus*, n., is to be distinguished from *fungous*, adj. See **snot**

**muddy,** v., colloquial, and especially children's English in the sense *spatter or cover with mud*, and especially in the phrase *all muddied up.* See **up**

**muff,** n., slang for *an awkward person, a duffer.* Also as a verb, especially in baseball slang, *to fail to catch*, as in *to muff a fly.*

**muffled curses,** trite phrase, a favorite of melodramatic stylists.

**mufti,** n., *plain clothes, dress of an official when off duty*, usually in the phrase *in mufti.* Pronounced (mŭf′tĭ) The word is of Oriental, probably Arabic, origin.

**mugwump,** n., American political slang for *one who rejects association with a political party.*

**Mukden,** n., *city in China*, not *Mookden* or *Moukden*, by decision of the United States Geographic Board. Pronounced (mōŏk′dĕn)

**mullah,** n., Arabic word, *Mohammedan theologian*, pronounced (mŭl′ah) Also spelled *moolah* and pronounced (mōō′lah)

**mullein,** n., *a kind of plant*, pronounced (mŭl′ĭn) The pronunciation (mŭl′ān) is an artificial spelling pronunciation.

**multum in parvo,** Latin phrase, *a great deal in small compass*, pronounced (mŭl′tum ĭn pahr′vō)

**mumps,** n., *a disease*, though plural in form, is usually construed as a singular, as in *Mumps is a disease of childhood.* See **measles**

**Munich,** n., *city in Germany*, pronounced (mū′nĭk) The German form of the name of this city is *München*, which would be pronounced as a German word, (mün′CHen)

**municipal,** adj., *pertaining to a city*, pronounced (mūnĭs′ipal), low colloquially (mūnĭsĭp′al)

**murder,** n., with a variant form *murther*, now obsolete except occasionally in dialect, especially Irish, speech. See **burden**

**murphy**, n., slang for *Irish potato*. See **Irish, spud**

**Muscle Shoals**, n., *a series of rapids in the Tennessee River*, not *Mussel Shoals*, by decision of the United States Geographic Board.

**museum**, n., *a collection of specimens*, pronounced (mūzē′um), not (mū′zĭum) except in low colloquial speech. The *dime museum* of other days was a collection of freaks of nature, the price of admission being ten cents.

**mush**, n., colloquial for *porridge*, especially corn-meal porridge, but in some localities applied also to any of the many other kinds of porridge served at breakfast.

**musicale**, n., *a refined musical entertainment*. Formerly a fashionable word, but not now much used. Pronounced (mūzĭkahl′), sometimes (mūzĭkăl′), or anglicized to (mū′zĭkăl) Words which do not attain to general popular currency, as this word has not done, often do not acquire a definitely settled pronunciation. See **locale, morale**

**musicianly**, adj., in good use as an adjective, as in *a musicianly performance*, but usually rejected as an adverb, as in *He interpreted the sonata eloquently and musicianly*. See **manly**

**muskmelon**, n., a somewhat old-fashioned name for *cantalope*. Also dialectally current in the variant form *mushmelon*.

**musquash**, n., variant name for *muskrat*, according to Hodge, *Handbook of American Indians*, I, 963, used in Canada and northern and western parts of the United States.

**Musset, Louis Charles Alfred de**, n., *French writer* (1810–1857), pronounced (lōō′ĭ shahrl ălfrā′ de müsā′)

**Mussulman**, n., *Mohammedan*, with a plural *Mussulmans*. The last syllable in this word is not the English word *man*, therefore does not take a plural *-men*. See **German**

**mustache**, n., *hair on the upper lip*, also spelled *moustache*. In current pronunciation the word is pronounced (mustăsh′) or (mŭs′tăsh), sometimes (mustahsh′)

**mutatis mutandis,** Latin phrase, *allowing for changes that must be made,* pronounced (mūtăt′ĭs mūtăn′dĭs)

**mutual,** adj., *reciprocal, actions or feelings affecting each of a group with respect to the other or others,* as *a mutual aid society.* Incorrectly used in the sense *common to two or more,* as when an automobile owned by two persons is called *a mutual possession* or a common friend is called *a mutual friend.*

**muzzy,** adj., colloquial for *confused, muddled,* especially from excessive drinking.

**my,** see **mine**

**myrmidon,** n., *follower, pursuer,* especially in the phrase *myrmidons of the law,* officers of the law.   Pronounced (mir′midŏnz)   See **minion**

**myself,** pronoun, sometimes incorrectly used for *I,* as in *Myself and wife were the only ones present,* for *My wife and I,* etc.   It is correctly used in constructions like *I bought myself a hat,* the construction *I bought me a hat* being archaic and dialectal.   See **self**

**myth,** n., *legendary tale,* pronounced (mĭth), sometimes also (mīth)   But *mythic, mythical* always have (mĭth-), and *mythology, mythological, mythologist* are (mĭ-) or (mĭthŏl′ojĭ), (mĭ-) or (mĭthŏlŏj′ĭkal), (mĭ-) or (mĭthŏl′ojist)

# N

**nab,** v., slang for *seize, take,* probably in its origins a thieves' word, but now current in general slang use.

**Nabuchodonosor,** see **Nebuchadnezzar**

**nag,** n., colloquial name for *horse,* especially an old or run-down horse.

**naive,** adj., *natural, artless,* pronounced (nah-ēv′)   The word is of French origin, and in form it is a feminine from a masculine *naif.*   But in English usage **naive** is employed without reference to gender. The use of *naif* for **naive** is a purist affectation. The word **naive** is often written and printed *naïve*. So also the noun *naiveté, naïveté*, pronounced (nah-ēvtā′) For this latter word, anglicized forms also are current, *naïvety* (nah-ēv′ĭtĭ) or *naivety* (nāv′etĭ), but neither of these anglicized forms is widely used.

**Nanking,** n., *a city in China.* The United States Geographic Board rejects a number of variant forms of this name.

**napery,** n., archaic for *table linen*, pronounced (nā′perĭ)

**naphtha,** n., *a distillate from coal*, pronounced (năf′tha), or colloquially (năp′tha) See **diphtheria**

**napoo,** interj., army slang, *Gone! Finished! Done for!*, being the soldier's pronunciation of the French phrase (*Il*) *n'y a plus*, There is no more. Pronounced (nahpōō′)

**narcissus,** n., *a flower*, with a plural *narcissi*, this being a Latin form, or *narcissuses*, or **narcissus**, as in *The narcissus are in full bloom, a bunch of narcissuses, of narcissi*. Of these three plural forms, the form **narcissus** is perhaps most generally used. See **eucalyptus**

**narghile,** n., Persian word, *water pipe for smoking*, pronounced (nahr′gĭlĭ)

**nark,** n., slang for *decoy*, *spy*, especially in thieves' language.

**narwhal,** n., *a sea animal*, pronounced (nahr′whal) or (nahr′wal)

**nasty,** adj., as a description of physical condition, an offensive word not used in polite speech. Figuratively used in colloquial speech in the sense *severe, hard*, as in *a nasty fall, a nasty time of it*, or in the sense *mean, spiteful*, in the phrase *don't be nasty*. The antithesis to **nasty** is *nice*, but **nasty** is a much stronger word than *nice*. The word is more generally used as a colloquial intensive in British than in American speech.

**natheless,** adv., archaic form of *nevertheless*; pronounced (năth′les), used now frequently in modern imitations of medieval romantic style. Also spelled *nathless*.

**native,** adj., *of local growth and origin,* pronounced (nā′tĭv), low colloquially often (nā′tiv)

**nature,** n., *the quality of a thing, the physical world,* pronounced (nā′cher), but sometimes, though usually with special effort, pronounced (nā′tūr)  The adjective *natural,* however, is always (năch′eral) when it is natural, the pronunciation (năt′ŭral) being forced and artificial. The customs of speech always count for more than spelling in determining pronunciation.

**naught,** see **aught**

**nausea,** n., *uneasiness of the stomach,* pronounced (naw′sha), or formally and consciously (naw′sĭa)

**nautch,** n., Hindustani word, *exhibition of professional dancing,* a nautch girl being one who appears in professional dancing. Pronounced (nawch)

**Navajo,** n., *a tribe of Indians,* pronounced (năv′ahō)

**Navesink,** n., *a beach, lights, and river near the entrance to New York Harbor,* not *Neversink,* by decision of the United States Geographic Board.  Pronounced (năv′esĭngk)

**nay,** adv., archaic and literary for *no,* but sometimes used facetiously as a variant of *no.* Frequent in modern imitations of medieval narrative style.

**near by,** adv., colloquial and dialectal for *near,* as in *He lives near by.* Sometimes written *nearby,* though most writers, when they write the word at all, prefer **near by** or *near-by.*

**neath,** prep., archaic and literary for *beneath,* sometimes written *'neath.*

**Nebuchadnezzar,** n., *Biblical character,* pronounced (nĕbōōkădnĕz′ar)  A variant form in the Apocrypha and in the Vulgate is *Nabuchodonosor,* and in Jer. 43:10, etc., *Nebuchadrezzar.* The form **Nebuchadnezzar** is the one customarily used.

**neck,** n., colloquial for *region,* in the phrase *neck of the woods.* On Long Island, **neck** is a common topographical term, as in *Great Neck,* etc.  The phrase *to get it in the neck* is slang.

**neck,** v., slang for *embrace*, a *necking party* being presumably the modern equivalent of the old-fashioned *kissing game*.

**née,** adj., by origin a French past participle, meaning *born*, and added to a married woman's name in giving her maiden name, as in *Mrs. White, née Black*. A bit of society slang found usually in newspaper reports of social events. Pronounced (nā)

**need,** v., archaic and literary in the sense *be necessary*, as in *It needs not that I say*, etc.

**needful,** n., slang for *money*.

**needs,** adv., by origin a genitive singular adverb, surviving now only in the construction *needs must* or *must needs*, of necessity must. Not a plural number of the noun *need*, and therefore a sentence like *Shakspere gave him, when needs were, the center of the stage* is incorrect. The sentence should read *Shakspere gave him, when it was necessary*, etc.

**ne'er-do-well,** n., *shiftless person*, with a variant form *ne'er-do-weel*.

**négligé,** n., *informal dress*, pronounced (nĕglĭzhā′) The word is French in origin and has retained a French pronunciation and spelling as a word in the class of millinery French.

**negotiate,** v., *to confer*, especially about formal business or diplomatic affairs. The word is an ambitious one and should be used only when the circumstances require such a word. It is sometimes used facetiously, as in *He bit off a piece of bread larger than he could negotiate*, could manage. See **Polysyllabic Humor**

**negro,** n., plural *negroes*. The feminine is *negress*, or perhaps more frequently, *negro woman*. Usage varies in the matter of the capitalization of this word. The present tendency seems to be to recognize it as a race name and to capitalize it as one would *European, Malayan, Bushman*, and the like, but see the comments under **Capitalization,** 3, (g) See **nigger**

**neighborhood,** n., *vicinity*. Colloquial but not literary use in the sense *about*, as in *In the neighborhood of a thousand dollars*.

**neither,** conj., pron., pronounced most commonly (nē′dher), but sometimes also (nī'dher)  Both pronunciations are correctly derived historically, and the choice between them is determined entirely by social custom.  As the less usual pronunciation, (nī'dher) is sometimes affected as a refinement of speech.  The pronunciation (nā'dher), also historical, is now dialectal.  See **either**

The proper correlative of **neither** is *nor*, and a sentence like *His words were neither few or well chosen* would ordinarily be regarded as incorrect.  See **nor**

**nemine contradicente,** Latin phrase, *with no one opposing, unanimously,* pronounced (nē'mĭnĭ kŏntradĭsĕn'tĭ)

**nemine dissentiente,** Latin phrase, *with no one dissenting, unanimously,* pronounced (nē'mĭnĭ dĭsĕntĭĕn'tĭ)

**nephew, n.,** *a sister's or a brother's son,* ordinarily pronounced (nĕf'ū) in America, sometimes (nĕv'ū)  The pronunciation (nĕv'ĭ) is dialectal.  The pronunciation (nĕv'ū) is general in England.  The pronunciation (nĕv'ū) is etymologically the more correct, but the American pronunciation (nĕf'ū) has been determined by the spelling, the value of *ph* being usually (f)

**ne plus ultra,** Latin phrase, *point beyond which one may not go;* originally a command, *go no further,* but now commonly used as a noun in the sense *highest achievement, the acme.*  Pronounced (nē plŭs ŭl'tra)

**nerve, n.,** slang and colloquial for *impudence.*  See **cheek, gall**

**nervy, adj.,** slang in the sense *impudent, bold,* sometimes also *brave, courageous.*

**n'est-ce pas,** French phrase, *isn't it so?,* pronounced (nā'se pah)

**nestle among, below the hills,** trite phrase, a bit of conventional description made without keeping the eye on the reality.

**nestling, n.,** *young bird,* pronounced (nĕs'lĭng)  The analogy of the noun *nest* sometimes occasions a pronunciation (nĕst'lĭng), but the *t* is silent in this noun, as it is in the verb *to nestle,* with its present participle, *nestling.*

**nether,** adj., archaic in the sense *lower*, as in *the upper and the nether millstone*, but surviving facetiously in the phrases *nether regions*, a euphemism for *hell*; *nether garments*, polysyllabic humor for *trousers*; *the nether man*, similarly humorous for *legs*.

**neurasthenic,** adj., *pertaining to nervous debility*, pronounced (nūrăsthĕn′ĭk), not (nūrăsthē′nĭk)

**Nevada,** n., usually pronounced (nevăd′a) in the West, often (nevah′da) in the East. To most Americans, however, (nevah′da) seems an artificial pronunciation. See **Montana**

**névé,** n., French word, *snow at the head of a glacier*, pronounced (nĕvā′)

**never,** adv., colloquially used as the equivalent of *not*, as in *He never said a word about that*, *Never mind*, for *Don't mind*, and dialectal in the phrase *Well, I never!*, an exclamation of astonishment, annoyance, etc. See **ever**

**never so,** adv., see **ever**

**new,** adj., unnecessary and stylistically crude in phrases like *a new beginner*, the word *beginner* alone being sufficient.

**newfangled,** adj., *unpleasantly strange and novel*. Usually only in colloquial style, but a good old word, current since Chaucer, and at one time existent in the form *newfangle*, now obsolete.

**New Orleans,** see **Orleans**

**news,** n., *tidings, information*, plural in form but construed as a singular, as in *This news was received with great applause*, *The news of his arrival was withheld from the public*.

**newspaper,** n., *a journal of news*, pronounced (nūz′pā′per) or (nūs′pā′per) The pronunciations (no͞oz′pā′per), (no͞os′pā′per), though in fact widely current in the speech of educated persons, would usually be rejected as incorrect by critics of speech. These pronunciations are too general, however, to be so disposed of, except by persons who are willing to be ruled by theory.

**newsy,** adj., colloquial for *full of news*, as in *a bright, newsy letter*.

**next,** adv., slang in the phrase *get next,* bestir yourself, attend to duty.

**nextly,** adv., archaic and rare for *next,* in the next place.

**Nibelungenlied,** n., *German epic poem,* pronounced (nĭbelōōng'-enlēd), and not spelled *Niebel-.*

**nibs,** n., slang as a mock title of honor, as in *his nibs.*

**nice,** adj., in formal and literary use, *subtle, finely discriminating,* as in *a nice distinction.* In colloquial use, a generally current word in senses like *fine, dainty, pretty, agreeable,* etc. The word is not to be rejected in these senses, since they are established in use and since the language must have words like this for the colloquial purposes of everyday English. See **elegant, fine, grand, great, wonderful**

It is more than doubtful if the use of these generalized terms is a sign of an impoverished vocabulary, as it is often said to be, or is characteristic of the speech only of persons who are incapable of appreciating fine shades of meaning. The truth is that when one of these words is called for, a fine shade of meaning would ordinarily be inappropriate. When an acquaintance inquires politely about one's health, one does not enter into details. What one needs for answering is a vague, generalized term, indicative of a general emotional state, not of an exactly defined idea. The definition of a bore has been given as a person who, when you ask him how he is, tells you. There are many situations in life when it is not necessary to tell anything precisely, when indeed the social situation would be very inadequately met if one did say something precise. It is for these situations that words like **nice,** *fine, great, wonderful,* and their opposites, *awful, terrible, rotten,* etc., provide appropriate expressive terms. That these uses remain on the level of colloquial discourse and do not often pass over into literary use is no condemnation of them. The situations in which they occur are naturally colloquial, and colloquial discourse has a life of its own as necessary and as readily justified as the life of literary expression.

**nicely,** adv., correctly used in constructions like *He is doing nicely,* but incorrectly in *He is nicely, I am nicely.* See **poorly**

**nicht wahr,** German phrase, *isn't it so?*, pronounced (nĭCHt vahr)

**nickel,** n., colloquial for *five-cent piece,* from the metal alloy of which the coin is made. Coins of this material are not current in England, and the word *nickel* as the name of a coin is also not current in England. The participial adjective is *nickeled.*

**nicker,** v., *neigh gently,* used with reference only to horses. The word *snicker* is a variant, but *snicker* usually applies to people.

**Nietzsche, F. W.,** n., *German writer* (1844–1890), pronounced (nē′che)

**nifty,** adj., slang for *stylish, neat.*

**nigger,** n., colloquial for *negro,* usually contemptuous and not used as the ordinary designation for negroes. Among the negroes themselves the preferred terms are *negro, colored person,* or *Afro-American.* See **negro**

**niggertoe,** n., colloquial name for *Brazil nut.*

**nigh,** adj., adv., archaic, poetic, and dialectal for *near,* as in *The day draws nigh, the nigh horse.*

**nightgown,** n., *garment in which women and children sleep at night.* The corresponding man's garment is a *nightshirt.* Neither *nightgown* nor *nightshirt* applies to pyjamas, which differ from gowns and shirts in that they have legs.

**nighty,** n., child's diminutive word for *nightgown.*

**nihil ad rem,** Latin phrase, *irrelevant,* pronounced (nī′hĭl ăd rěm)

**nihilist,** n., *one who opposes all authority,* pronounced (nī′ĭlĭst), and so also the noun *nihilism* (nī′ĭlĭzm)

**nil admirari,** Latin phrase, *not showing surprise or admiration, nonchalance,* pronounced (nĭl ădmĭrä′rī)

**Nippon,** n., *Japanese name for Japan,* sometimes used poetically in English as a synonym for *Japan.* See **Japan**

**nit,** adv., slang for *no*, being probably a corruption of German *nicht*.

**nix,** n., adv., slang for *nothing, no*, being a corruption of German *nichts*.

**no,** n., the word *no*, *denial, negative vote*, with a plural *noes*, not *no's*.

**no,** adj., *not any*, as in *He paid me no money*. Although constructions like this are established beyond question in general use, objection is made to them sometimes that they are illogical, therefore incorrect. For how is it possible to pay no money? Paying implies a payment. On these grounds, the construction is often changed to *not any*, as in *He did not pay me any money*. This of course is also good idiom, though it is not quite parallel to *He paid me no money*. A parallel construction would be *He paid me not any money*, which is manifestly not good English. The truth is that a logical objection based upon an analysis of a phrase which in its entirety is current in good use and satisfactorily intelligible carries no weight. Language is not always constructed on a minutely logical system, nor is it necessary that it should be to be satisfactorily intelligible. When a phrase in current English fails to conform to the demands of logic, it is best to accept it without further question as an idiom. See the definition of **Idiom** in the Introduction. See **not**

**no,** adv., in good use as the equivalent of *not*, as in *He would have me come, whether or no*, whether I wished or not; *It was half-baked eloquence.* . . . . *But half-baked or no, David rose to it greedily* (Mrs. H. Ward, *The History of David Grieve*, I, vii) In colloquial use, also in phrases like *She is no actress*, not meaning *She is not an actress*, but *She is not a good actress*. The phrase *That's no good* is colloquial and slang. See **yes**

**nobby,** adj., slang for *smart, stylish*.

**Nobel,** n., *proper name*, especially with reference to the Swedish Nobel Prize, pronounced (nōbĕl')

**noblesse,** n., French word, *the nobility,* pronounced (nōblĕs′)

**noblesse oblige,** French phrase, *high position entails responsibility,* pronounced (nōblĕs′ ōblēzh′)

**noddle,** n., humorous colloquialism for *head.*

**Noel,** see **Nowel**

**nohow,** adv., low colloquial and dialectal for *in any way, anyhow.*

**nolens volens,** Latin phrase, *willingly or unwillingly,* pronounced (nō′lenz vō′lenz)

**noli me tangere,** Latin phrase, *touch me not,* pronounced (nō′lĭ mē′ tăn′jerĭ)

**nolle prosequi,** Latin phrase, *legal notice of abandonment of suit,* pronounced (nŏl′ĭ prŏs′ekwī)

**nolo episcopari,** Latin phrase, *desire to avoid responsible position,* literally, *I do not want to be made a bishop;* pronounced (nō′lō ĕpĭskopā′rī)

**nomad,** n., *wanderer,* pronounced (nŏm′ad), less correctly (nō′mad) The adjective is *nomadic* (nŏmăd′ĭk)

**nom de guerre,** French phrase, *pseudonym,* pronounced (nŏm de gār′) The phrase literally means *battle name,* name under which one wages one's battles, and it is often used as a facetious synonym for *nom de plume.*

**nom de plume,** French phrase, *pen name, writer's pseudonym,* pronounced (nŏm de plüm′)

**nomenclature,** n., *system of names,* pronounced (nō′menklächer), not (nōmĕn′klacher)

**nonchalant,** adj., *cool, indifferent,* pronounced (nŏn′shalant), with a noun *nonchalance* (nŏn′shalans)

**non compos mentis,** Latin phrase, *not well balanced mentally,* pronounced (nŏn kŏm′pos mĕn′tĭs) Often abbreviated to *non compos.*

**none,** pronoun, by strict etymology *not one,* therefore by this test to be construed only with singular verbs. But usage justifies **none** also as a plural, as in *There were hundreds of people* *on the boat, but none were hurt.* If the singular idea is to be emphasized, the usual form is *not one, not a single one.*

The use of **none** in the sense *no one* is permissible but archaic, as in *None but the brave deserves the fair,* No one but the brave deserves the fair. In modern use] **none** in a sentence like this would be construed as a plural, as in *None but the children were admitted,* or more naturally, *Only the children,* etc. A sentence like *I know very well, none better than I,* etc., is also slightly archaic, the more usual form being, *I know very well, no one better than I,* etc. See **no one**

**non est inventus,** Latin phrase, *he has not been found,* as a legal formula describing a missing person. Pronounced (nŏn ĕst ĭnvĕn′tus)

**non liquet,** Latin phrase, *a verdict which postpones decision,* literally, *it is not clear;* pronounced (nŏn lĭk′wĕt)

**non nobis,** Latin phrase, *a disclaimer of credit,* literally, *not to us,* from Psalm CXV. Pronounced (nŏn nō′bĭs)

**nonpareil,** adj., *without equal,* pronounced (nŏnparĕl′)

**non placet,** Latin phrase, *a negative vote,* literally, *it does not please;* pronounced (nŏn plā′sĕt)

**non possumus,** Latin phrase, *statement of inability, refusal to act or move,* literally, *we can not;* pronounced (nŏn pŏs′ūmus)

**non sequitur,** Latin phrase, *an illogical statement,* literally, *it does not follow;* pronounced (nŏn sĕk′wĭtur)

**nonsuch,** n., *something without parallel,* pronounced (nŏn′sŭch), with a variant *nonesuch* (nŭn′sŭch)

**no one,** pron., *negative indefinite.* Usually written as two words, though the analogy of *anyone, everyone,* and *someone* as pronouns favors *noone.* As the double *o* in this form looks strange, a compromise with a hyphen is sometimes advocated, *no-one.* This has reason on its side, but not custom. See **none**

**nooning,** n., a workman's word for *rest time at noon.*

**noontime,** n., *noon.* As *noon* itself is a designation of time, the addition of *time* is pleonastic.  The compound is occasionally used nevertheless, as also *noonday, noontide.*  Similar tautological compounds are *wintertime, summertime, springtime,* and, in poetry, *eventide.*  These are different from compounds like *dinnertime* in that the first element is in itself an adequate chronological term.

**nor,** conj.  According to most rhetoricians, **nor** should be used as a correlative only after a preceding *neither,* as in *He neither wrote nor spoke.*  But the rule is not invariably followed, and, especially in commands, constructions like *Do not walk nor trespass,* for *Do not walk or trespass,* see **neither,** are in good use, though not the most frequent use.

**nor',** adj., nautical abbreviation of *north,* especially in compounds, as in *nor'wester,* etc.

**normalcy,** n., a word of very rare occurrence which acquired notoriety from its use by President Harding, who was perhaps unaware of the fact that the word was not a customary word in the language.  The more usual noun form corresponding to the adjective *normal* would be *normality.*

**Norsk,** n., adj., a Scandinavian form of the English noun *Norse.*

**nosy,** adj., slang for *inquisitive.*

**not,** adv., often illogically placed, as in *I don't believe it will rain,* which means *I believe it will not rain.*  By the test of use, however, which is decisive in such matters, the illogical construction is better English idiom than the logical.  See **no**

**nota bene,** Latin phrase, *take notice,* literally, *note well;* pronounced (nō'ta bē'nĭ)

**nothing,** n., slang in the phrase *have nothing on,* not be superior, as in *Italy has nothing on California,* is not better than California.

**nothing doing,** interj., slang in the sense of denial, failure, etc., and, like most words of this kind, applied to a great variety of generally similar situations.

**nothing like,** see **like,** adv.

**notions,** n., current in America but not in England in the sense *buttons, threads, needles, pins, and such small wares.* Also in the phrases *notions counter, notions store.*

**notorious,** adj., *well known,* but usually with the implication of unfavorably known. This is always the sense of **notorious** as applied to persons, as in *a notorious character,* and usually the sense of the word in other applications, as in *It is notorious that the inspectors accept bribes.* In the simple sense *well known,* **notorious** would be pedantic for *well known,* as in *It is a notorious fact that many people can not eat strawberries.*

**notwithstanding,** prep., *in spite of,* placed either before or after its object, as in *Notwithstanding all we had done for him,* etc., or *All we had done for him notwithstanding,* etc. But both constructions are cumbersome and formal, and the word is obsolescent and literary.

**nougat,** n., *a sweetmeat,* pronounced (nōō′gah)

**nought,** see **aught**

**nous avons changé tout cela,** French phrase, *we have changed all that,* pronounced (nōōz ăvŏn′ shahṅzhā′ tōō sĕlah′)

**nouveau riche,** French phrase, *a person who has recently become rich,* with implications of ostentatious vulgarity. Pronounced (nōō′vō rēsh)

**nowadays,** adv., written as one word, not hyphenated.

**noways,** adv., dialectal in the sense *in no way, not at all,* as in *I couldn't noways do it.*

**Nowel,** interj., an interjection of joy in Christmas carols, being derived from Latin *natalis* through old French *Noël,* with a variant *Noel,* both pronounced (nōĕl′) The word is not a synonym for *Christmas.*

**nowhere near,** adv., colloquial in constructions like *Dinner is nowhere near ready,* for *Dinner is not nearly ready.*

**noyau,** n., French word, *a kind of liqueur,* pronounced (nwahyō′)

**nuance,** n., French word, *a shading of meaning,* pronounced com-

monly as an English word, (nōō′ahns), or as a French word,
(nüahns′)

**nub**, n., colloquial for *the central idea or point*, of a story or other
matter.

**nuisance**, n., *something offensive or annoying*, pronounced (nū′sans)
or (nōō′sans) The latter pronunciation is sometimes objected
to by theorists, but nevertheless it is widely current among
educated as well as uneducated speakers. See **newspaper**

**numb**, adj., *without sensation*, pronounced (nŭm), and in the
comparative, as in *The older we get the number our senses become*,
pronounced (nŭm′er), with a superlative *numbest* (nŭm′est)

**number**, n., slang in the phrase *to have one's number*, to see through
one, as in *You can't fool me. I've got your number.* Slang also
in *back number*, old-fashioned.

**nunc dimittis**, Latin phrase, (*Lord*) *now lettest thou* (*thy servant*)
*depart*, a part of the church service, often used as a general
expression of resignation. Pronounced (nŭnk dĭmĭt′ĭs)

**nuncio**, n., *a papal messenger*, pronounced (nŭn′shĭō), with a
plural *nuncios* (nŭn′shĭōz)

**nuptials**, n., *wedding*, a plural without a singular, as in *The nuptials
were celebrated in the presence of a large assembly of friends.* A
poetic and literary word, often used ambitiously in newspaper
and other journalistic writing. Pronounced (nŭp′shalz)

**Nuremberg**, n., *city in Germany*, not *Nurnberg* or *Nürnberg*, by
decision of the United States Geographic Board. The Permanent Committee on Geographical Names prefers *Nürnberg*.

**nut**, n., slang in the sense *head, crazy person*, as in *off his nut*, out
of his head, *a nut*, a crazy person.

**nutty**, adj., slang in the sense *crazy*.

**nymph**, n., poetic term for *maiden*, pronounced (nĭmf) In
classical mythology a nymph was a semidivine maiden who
inhabited the sea, rivers, fountains, hills, woods, and other
secluded places.

# O

**o** (ŏ) as in *not*. The quality of this so-called "short o" in American speech is in some respects open to question. It is ordinarily described as a sound like the vowel of *fall*, only shorter. In reality the sound actually heard in words like *not, got, hot, bottom, body, robber, cotton*, etc., is a vowel closer to the vowel of *father*, only shorter. The American "short o" is therefore really a short (ah), not a short (aw) sound. In some localities, however, especially in eastern New England, words like *hot, got*, etc., are pronounced with a short (aw) sound, and in certain words, for example, *dog, log, soft, moss, froth*, etc., this sound may occur in any region, and is in fact more general than the short (ah) sound. The pronunciation (dahg), for example, is much less general than the pronunciation (dawg) for *dog*. Custom in the use of these vowels varies a great deal with individuals and localities, and as a special exercise a useful collection could be made of words having the short (aw) sound and of others having the short (ah) sound, words like *coffee, chocolate, Boston*, etc. The question of propriety is not of great importance in this matter, since the pronunciations of both types are in good current use.

**O, oh,** interj., in direct address or as an exclamation of surprise, pain, joy, etc. The form **O** is always used before a vocative name, as in *O John, come here, O Great Jehovah*, and also as an exclamation when not separated by punctuation from what follows, as in *O dear me! O no! O just once more*. When a comma follows the exclamation, or when it stands alone, the form **oh** is used, as in *Oh, I didn't know you were here, Oh, give me about a dozen*. Standing alone the exclamation is followed by an exclamation point, **Oh!** The form **O** is always written with a capital, but **oh** follows the usual rules of capitalization, that is, it takes a capital only at the beginning of a sentence or of a direct quotation, or of a line of verse. When **Oh** is followed by an exclamation point, the next word begins with a capital as the beginning of a new sentence.

**o',** prep., abbreviated form of *of* and regularly current in *four o'clock*, etc.; sometimes colloquially in other phrases, as in *man-o'-war, cat-o'-nine-tails, o' nights*.

**oak,** see **sport,** v.

**oaken,** adj., archaic and poetic, as in *The old oaken bucket*, for *oak*. The ending *-en* in adjectives shows a progressive tendency to disappear, and though one still says *a wooden bucket*, one would now say *an oak bucket*, omitting the ending *-en* as in many other adjectives that formerly had it.

**oar,** v., poetic or dialectal in the sense *row*, as in *to oar a boat*.

**oarlock,** n., *appliance for holding an oar in place*, with an equivalent *rowlock*, both equally correct and in good use.

**oasis,** n., *fertile place in a desert*, usually pronounced (ōā′sis), with a plural *oases* (ōā′sēz), though the word is sometimes stressed on the first syllable instead of the second.

**oats,** n., *a kind of grain*, with no corresponding singular. If one wanted to refer to a single grain, one would speak of it as *a grain of oats*, or to a single plant, as *an oat plant*. The use of *oat* in compounds and as adjective is general, as in *oatmeal, oatcake, oat grass*, but the form *oaten* is archaic. See **oaken**

**obbligato,** n., *a term in music*. Pronounced (ŏblĭgah′tō), with a plural *obbligatos*, and not spelled *obligato*.

**obdurate,** adj., *unyielding*, pronounced (ŏb′dūrat), less commonly (ŏbdū′rat), with a noun *obduracy* (ŏb′dūrasĭ), (ŏbdū′rasĭ)

**obeisance,** n., *bow*, as in *make obeisance*, pronounced (ōbā′sans) The original sense *bow* is now archaic and the word has taken the derived sense *homage, obedience*, as in *to pay obeisance*, or *do, make obeisance*, do homage, show respect.

**obese,** adj., learned word for *fat, corpulent*, pronounced (ōbēs′), with a noun *obesity* (ōbēs′ĭtĭ)

**obiit,** v., Latin word, *died*, on tombstone inscriptions, with date of death. Pronounced (ŏb'ĭit)

**oblige,** v., old-fashioned at the end of a letter, as in *and oblige, Yours very truly.* Replaced now simply by *I am.* Colloquial in the sense *play, sing, perform*, as in *Mr. Brown will now oblige with a song.* Related forms are *obligate* (ŏb'lĭgāt), *obligatory*, adj., *required*, pronounced (oblĭg'atŏrĭ) The two nouns *obligee, obligor* are pronounced (ŏblĭjē') and (ŏb'lĭgŏr)

**oblique,** adj., *slanting*, usually pronounced (ōblēk'), sometimes (ōblĭk'), with a noun *obliquity* (ŏblĭk'wĭtĭ)

**oblivious,** adj., *having forgotten*, as in *We talked for a while, but soon he took up a book and was straightway oblivious of my presence.* Often incorrectly used in the sense *unobservant, unaware*, as in *He entered the room hurriedly, oblivious of the fact that the number on the door was 34, not 24.* The proper construction is *oblivious of*, not *oblivious to*.

**obloquy,** n., *bad reputation, detraction*, pronounced (ŏb'lokwĭ)

**oboe,** see **hautboy**

**obscurantist,** n., *wilfully ignorant person*, pronounced (ŏbskūr'antist), not (ŏbskūrăn'tist) So also *obscurantism* (ŏbskūr'antĭzm)

**obsequies,** n., used only in the plural, with the meaning *funeral, funeral rites.* It is therefore incorrect to speak of *funeral obsequies.* A very formal word, often abused in ambitious journalistic writing. Pronounced (ŏb'sĭkwĭz)

**obsequious,** adj., *too eager to please*, pronounced (ŏbsē'kwĭus)

**obstreperous,** adj., *noisy.* See **Polysyllabic Humor**

**obtain,** v., literary in the sense *to be in vogue, to be the custom*, as in *The method, which now obtains, of electing all officers by ballot*, etc. The word **obtain** is often used ambitiously when the simple word *get* would do as well, as in *Milk is hard to obtain in the mountains.*

**occasion,** n., *opportunity, event*, pronounced (okā'zhn) Theoretical speakers sometimes try to pronounce this word with an (s), but they succeed in doing so only by destroying the word as it exists in real speech.

**occident,** n., especially *The Occident,* literary for *The West,* as a term antithetic to the generally current *The Orient.* Pronounced (ŏk′sident)

**occult,** see **abject**

**occupancy,** n., *state of occupying or being occupied,* pronounced (ŏk′ūpansĭ)

**ocean,** n., *large body of salt water,* pronounced (ō′shn), but the adjective is *oceanic* (ōshĭăn′ĭk) or (ōsĭăn′ĭk) The pronunciation (ō′sĭan) for **ocean** is not current in natural speech, being only a theoretical spelling pronunciation.

**ocelot,** n., *an animal,* pronounced (ō′selot)

**ochre,** n., *a pigment,* pronounced (ō′ker)

**octopus,** n., *a mollusc with eight arms,* often used metaphorically to name some all-embracing destructive power. Pronounced (ŏk′topus), or less generally (ŏktō′pus)

**octoroon,** n., *a person of mixed blood,* with a less correct variant *octaroon.*

**octroi,** n., French word, *duty or tax paid on goods brought into a town,* pronounced (ŏktrwah′)

**ocular,** adj., *apparent to the eyes, an ocular demonstration* being one that begets belief through seeing the thing itself. The word has nothing to do with hearing, the equivalent term for hearing being *auricular.* Pronounced (ŏk′ūlar)

**oculist,** see **optician**

**odds,** n., construed as a singular in *What's the odds?,* meaning *What difference does it make?* But it may be a plural also, especially in the sense *advantage,* as in *The odds are all in his favor.*

**odeum,** n., *building, especially for musical performances,* the plural being *odeums, odea,* often used as a name for a theater. Pro-

nounced (ōdē′um), (ōdē′a), like *museum* (mūzē′um), low colloquially (ō′dĭum)   A variant form is *odeon* (ōdē′on), this representing a Greek nominative, and **odeum** a Latin nominative.
As the name of a theater in Paris the proper form is
*Odéon.*

**odium,** n., *dislike, disapproval,* pronounced (ō′dĭum)   The word
is formal and would be used only of persons, usually of persons
in somewhat important public positions.

**odor,** n., *smell,* pleasant or unpleasant.   But often specialized in
the sense *unpleasant smell,* as a euphemistic substitute for the
unrefined words *stench, stink,* as in *There is an odor in the ice box,
the odors of cooking, emit an odor* (of an animal)   If a pleasant
odor is meant, an appropriate adjective usually precedes.

**odoriferous,** adj., *bearing odors.*   Usually poetic or facetious.   See
**Polysyllabic Humor**

**odorous,** adj., usually poetic in the sense *grateful to the sense of
smell,* as in *odorous breezes,* but sometimes colloquially and facetiously used as a synonym for *malodorous,* as in *an odorous baby.*

**Odyssey,** n., *Homer's poem,* pronounced (ŏd′ĭsĭ)

**oe** (ē)   This spelling was formerly more general than at present,
especially in words of Greek origin.   Thus *economy* was formerly
written *oeconomy.*   Many of these *oe*-spellings have been simplified to *e,* but usage still varies in some words, as in *foetus*
or *fetus, foetid* or *fetid,* and other words, especially proper names,
regularly retain the spelling **oe,** as in *Oedipus.*   A reasonable
general principle would be to replace **oe** by *e* in the interests of
simplicity whenever it is practicable, that is, whenever usage
makes it possible to do so.

**oecumenical,** adj., *world wide,* especially in the phrase *oecumenical
council,* of the church.   Pronounced (ēkūměn′ĭkal) or (ĕkūměn′-
ĭkal), and also written *ecumenical,* although conservative ecclesiastical tradition tends to preserve the spelling **oecumenical.**

**Oedipus,** n., *Greek proper name,* pronounced (ē′dipus) or (ĕd′ipus)

**oesophagus,** n., *gullet*, pronounced (ēsŏf′agus), and sometimes, though less generally, spelled *esophagus*.

**of,** prep., in good use in the construction known as the genitive of definition, as in *a man by the name of Smith, the city of New York*, although the word has no logical value in such phrases. Incorrectly and pleonastically used in constructions like *The question of whether it is or is not legal for women to vote is settled*, for *The question whether*, etc., or *The legality of the question of women's voting is settled*.

In telling time, **of** is used colloquially for *to, before*, as in *five minutes of three*. See **o'**

In constructions like *It would take two of him to make a man*, two like him, the stylistic color is colloquial and mildly facetious.

**of,** v., weakened form of *have*, in verb phrases like *could have gone, would have told*, etc., pronounced (kŏŏd ŭv gawn), (wŏŏd ŭv tōld) But though generally heard in all colloquial English, the word in written English is never **of** but always *have*, unless the color of dialect speech is to be indicated.

**off,** adj., slang in the senses *mad, delirious*, as in *He's a little off; not holding*, as in *The lecture is off for tonight; improper*, as in *off color*, and as an adverb in the interjection *Come off*, Stop, I don't believe you, etc. See **on**

**officiate,** v., *to serve in office*, pronounced (ofĭsh′ĭāt) The pronunciation (ofĭs′ĭāt) is theoretical and has no currency in general practice. See **enunciate**

**offish,** adj., colloquial, meaning *distant, stiff*. See **-ish, stand-offish**

**off of,** prep., dialectal for *from*, as in *I bought this off of a friend of mine, I got it off of a pedlar*.

**oft,** adv., archaic and poetical for *often*, surviving in combination with past participles, as in *an oft-repeated tale, an oft-rehearsed part, an oft-told story*, or present participles, as in *oft-recurring attacks*, and in the phrase *many a time and oft*.

**often,** adv., regularly pronounced (aw'fn), the pronunciation (awf'ten) occurring only dialectally or in artificially precise speech. Sometimes, in singing, the *t* in *often* is pronounced, but ordinarily it is silent, as in *soften, listen,* etc.

**oftentimes,** adv., now rarely used in speech, but occasionally found in archaic and literary style as a synonym for *often.* Also written *ofttimes.*

**ogle,** v., *make eyes,* pronounced (ō'gl) Chiefly literary, the customary term being *to make eyes.*

**oh,** see **O, oh**

**Ohnet, Georges,** n., *French writer,* pronounced (zhŏrzh ŏnā')

**old,** adj., colloquial as a term of endearment, as in *old man, old woman, old chap,* and as an approving intensive, as in *a high old time, a fine old fellow, the grand old man,* or the opposite, as in *the old Nick, the old Harry, the old boy,* the devil, *the old man,* one's unregenerate nature.

**olden,** adj., archaic and poetic for *old.* See **oaken**

**Old Sol,** trite phrase, often used as a stylistic substitute when the simple word *sun* would do as well.

**oleaginous,** adj., *oily,* pronounced (ōlĭăj'inus) Chiefly in scientific and learned use, the customary word being *oily.*

**oleomargarine,** see **margarine**

**olfactory,** adj., *pertaining to the sense of smell,* especially in the phrase *olfactory nerves.* Pronounced (ŏlfăk'torĭ) See **Polysyllabic Humor**

**oligarchy,** n., *a state governed by a few persons,* pronounced (ŏlĭgahr'kĭ), with an adjective *oligarchical* (ŏlĭgahr'kĭkal) An *oligarch* (ŏl'ĭgahrk) would be one of the persons who governs an oligarchy.

**olio,** n., Spanish word, *mixed dish, a medley,* pronounced (ō'lĭŏ)

**olla-podrida,** n., Spanish word, *a mixed dish, a medley,* the same as *olio.* Pronounced (ŏl'a-pŏdrē'da)

**Omaha,** n., *city in Nebraska,* pronounced (ō'mahaw) or (ō'mahah)   There is a tendency to regard the latter as the more refined pronunciation, as in *Chicago, hurrah,* and other words with the same sounds.   See **hurrah**

**omega,** n., pronounced (ōmē'ga) or (ō'mĭga), less commonly (ōmĕg'a)   Literally, the last letter of the Greek alphabet, but used metaphorically of any last thing.

**omelette,** n., *eggs whipped and fried,* pronounced (ŏm'let), with a variant spelling *omelet.*   The word is trisyllabic only in artificial pronunciation.

**omnibus,** see **bus**

**omnifarious,** adj., *of all sorts,* but used only in the spirit of polysyllabic humor.   Pronounced (ŏmnĭfā'rĭus)

**omnipotent,** adj., *all-powerful,* pronounced (ŏmnĭp'otent)

**omniscient,** adj., *all-knowing,* therefore incorrectly used in the phrase *the omniscient eye of God,* but correctly in *the omniscient mind of God.*   Pronounced (ŏmnĭsh'ent)

**omnium gatherum,** Latin phrase, *large mixed meeting,* literally *gathering of all,* the word *gatherum* being an imitation Latin word made from the English verb *gather.*   Pronounced (ŏm'nĭum gădh'erum)

**omnivorous,** adj., *all-devouring,* pronounced (ŏmnĭv'orus)

**on,** adv., frequently added pleonastically to verbs and adverbs, as in *He continued on for about an hour, I will discuss this later on, He takes up that point further on.*   For *continue on, later on,* the simple words *continue* and *later* are better style, and for *further on* either *hereafter* or *later* would be better.   Slang in the phrase *Are you on?*, Do you understand?, Will you join us?   See **off, up**

**once in a way,** phrase, in colloquial use in the sense *now and then, occasionally but not as a regular thing,* as in *It's all right to put up with such treatment once in a way, but there are limits to one's endurance.*

**on dit,** French phrase, *one says, it is said,* pronounced (ŏṅ dē')

**one,** pron., impersonal pronoun, and, according to rule, to be followed only by the same pronoun in the same sentence, as in *If one wishes to keep one's teeth, one must take care of them.* But this is stylistically stilted, and, in general, constructions with several impersonal **one's** can be improved by rephrasing. The sentence just given might better run, *To keep one's teeth, it is necessary to take care of them,* or *Care is necessary for the preservation of the teeth.*

In constructions like *That is a good trick, but I know a better one,* the phrasing is improved stylistically by omitting **one,** and very frequently **one** can be omitted in similar constructions to advantage.

**one another,** see **each other**

**one-horse,** adj., colloquial for *unimportant, undeveloped.*

**Oneida,** n., *city in New York,* pronounced (ōnī′da)

**oneself,** pron., reflexive and emphatic form of *one,* as in *One might do that for another, but not for oneself.* Sometimes written *one's self,* but the simpler compound is more customary and preferable. The form *one's self* can be used when *self* has the value of a separate word, as in *It is difficult to know one's self, One never knows one's self,* different in meaning from *One never knows oneself.*

**one-time,** adj., occasional literary use in the sense *former,* as in *a one-time friend of mine.* See **quondam, sometime**

**only,** adv., adj., to be placed carefully in the sentence in the position which will make clear what word it modifies. A sentence like *He only walked as far as the door* might mean *Only he walked,* etc., or *He only walked* (that is, didn't run), or *He walked only as far as the door.* In colloquial speech, **only** sometimes has the value *but, except that,* as in *I'd like to come, only I haven't time.* The use of **only** as an adjective meaning *fine, excellent* often in the superlative, is slang, as in *He's my onliest player.*

**onomatopoeia,** n., *harmony between the sound of a word and the* *thing it names,* pronounced (ŏnŏmătopē'a) or (ŏnomătopē'a) The adjective has two forms, *onomatopoeic* (ŏnomătopē'ĭk) and *onomatopoetic* (ŏnomătopōĕt'ĭk)

**Onondaga,** n., *city in New York,* pronounced (ŏnŏndaw'ga)

**on to,** prep., generally written and printed as two words, though *onto* occurs occasionally and has the support of the analogy of *into, unto,* and also the support of the feeling of a distinct need for a compound preposition *onto.* But printers, publishers, and rhetoricians for the most part do not countenance *onto* and insist on printing or writing as two words.

**onus,** n., *the responsibility for anything,* with no plural. Pronounced (ō'nus) The word is learned, being the Latin word **onus** taken over into English without modification. Compare the word **bonus,** which, however, has become a genuinely popular English word.

**ōō** as in *root.* The value of **oo** is definitely established in some words as (ōō), as in *boot, mood,* etc., in others as (ŏŏ), as in *good, stood,* etc., and in still others as (ŭ), as in *blood, flood.* Some words with the spelling **oo** vary in pronunciation between (ōō) and (ŏŏ) in the speech of different persons, as, for example, *broom, coop, Cooper, hoof, hoop, roof, room, root, soon, soot.* No dogmatic rule can be given for the use of (ōō) or (ŏŏ) in these words. The word *soot* is pronounced (sōōt) or (sŏŏt), and dialectally (sŭt), and (rōōt) and (rŏŏt), (hōōp) and (hŏŏp), (cōōp) and (cŏŏp), (hōōf) and (hŏŏf), and so with various other words, are both current in good use as pronunciations of *root, hoop, coop, hoof,* etc. See **o** (ŏ) as in *not*

**opal,** n., *a gem,* pronounced (ō'pal), the pronunciation (ō'păl) being artificial and determined by the spelling.

**opera,** n., *stage performance combining music and acting,* an *opera house* being a place where operas are given. Sometimes incorrectly used merely as a synonym for *theater.* Pronounced (ŏp'era), dialectally (ŏp'rĭ) See **opus**

**operative,** adj., *functioning,* pronounced (ŏp'eratĭv), low colloquially (ŏp'erātĭv)  The word is also used as a noun, meaning *artisan, workman,* especially of mill and factory workers.

**O Pip,** abbr., slang for *observation post.*

**opponent,** n., *adversary,* pronounced (opō'nent), low colloquially often (ŏp'onent)

**optic,** adj., *pertaining to the eye,* as in *optic nerve,* to be distinguished from *optical,* visual, as in *an optical illusion,* an illusion of vision. See **-ic, -ical**  The word **optic** as a noun, meaning *eye,* is humor of the polysyllabic variety.

**optician,** n., *one who makes or sells eyeglasses and other optical goods,* to be distinguished from *oculist, one who specializes in the defects and diseases of the eye.*

**optics,** see **acoustics**

**opus,** n., Latin word, *a work,* usually of musical compositions with a number attached, as in *opus 4.* Pronounced (ō'pus), and abbreviated *op.*  The Latin plural of **opus** is *opera,* but the plural is not commonly used in this sense.  See **opera**

**opus magnum,** Latin phrase, *chief or important work.*  Also in the form *magnum opus.*  Pronounced (ō'pus măg'num)

**-or, -our.**  The spelling **-our** in words like *honour, colour, humour, ardour* is peculiar to British usage, all of these and similar spellings being replaced by **-or** in American spelling.  Some publishers in America, however, follow the British spellings, especially in a few formal words, like *honour, Saviour.*  It should be noted that all words are not spelled **-our** in British spelling which have **-or** in American spelling.  British usage, indeed, is quite unsystematic, and special lists of **-our** and **-or** words must be learned in order to follow the British customs faithfully, *captor, doctor, donor, tenor,* and many others, for example, being spelled the same way in England and America.  The spelling **-our** supposedly appears in words derived from Latin through an Old French form, but it is often difficult to tell whether or not a modern word of this type had an Old French original.  The spelling **-or** in British spelling appears in nouns of agency from verbs of Latin origin, as in *instructor, detector, protector*, as well as in other words of Latin origin.  The American custom has simplicity and economy in its favor.

**oral**, adj., *pertaining to the mouth*, as in *oral hygiene*, or *spoken*, as in *an oral communication*.  The word *verbal* is commonly used as a synonym for **oral**, as in *a verbal communication, a verbal contract*, spoken, not written, *verbal evidence*.  According to the strict etymology of *verbal*, this seems a little loose, but common usage perhaps justifies it.  See **verbal**

**orange**, n., *a fruit*, pronounced (ŏr'ĭnj) or (ŏr'inj), less commonly (ahr'ĭnj), (ahr'inj)  The pronunciation (ŏr'inj) is rejected by some students of speech, but is nevertheless widely current among cultivated speakers.

**orchestra**, n., *a group of instrumental players*, pronounced (ŏr'-kestra), not (orkĕs'tra), except low colloquially.  But the adjective *orchestral* is pronounced (ŏrkĕs'tral), not (ŏr'kestral)

**orchid**, n., *a plant*, pronounced (ŏr'kĭd), with a variant form *orchis* (ŏr'kĭs)

**order**, n., slang in the phrase *a tall order*, something hard to do, perhaps from the language of the restaurant, where an order is what one asks to have brought to one.

**organum**, n., Latin word, *system of thought or logic*, as in Bacon's work, *Novum Organum*.  Pronounced (ŏr'ganum)  A synonymous term is *organon* (ŏr'ganon), a Greek word of which **organum** is a Latin adaptation.

**orgy**, n., *wild celebration*, pronounced (ŏr'jĭ), plural *orgies* (ŏr'jēz)  A rhetorical or facetious word.

**Orion**, n., *a constellation*, pronounced (ōrī'on)

**orison**, n., archaic and literary for *prayer*.  Pronounced (ŏr'ĭzn)

**Orleans**, n., *proper name*, in the United States, especially in *New Orleans*, pronounced (nū ŏr'lĭanz) or (nū ŏr'lanz), low colloquially (nū ŏrlēnz′) As a French proper name the word would be pronounced in the French fashion.

**ornery,** adj., low colloquial and dialectal corruption of *ordinary,* used in the sense *contemptible, disreputable,* especially in the phrase *an ornery cuss.*

**orthography,** n., etymologically means *correct or proper spelling,* therefore from the etymological point of view it would be improper to speak of *correct* and *incorrect orthography.* General usage, however, has given the word in English the meaning merely of *spelling, any mode of spelling,* and it is therefore permissible to speak of good and bad, correct and incorrect orthography.

**osier,** n., *a plant,* pronounced (ō′zher)

**Oslo,** n., *city in Norway,* formerly called *Christiania.* Pronounced (ō′slō) or as a Norwegian word. The spelling *Kristiania* is rejected by the United States Geographic Board.

**Ossining,** n., *place in New York,* pronounced (ŏs′ĭnĭng) Formerly known as *Sing Sing.*

**ostler,** see **hostler**

**other,** pron., construed with *than,* not *but,* in sentences like *We have no other prospect than this* or *We have no prospect other than this.* When **other** is omitted, *but* is correct, as in *We have no prospect but this.*

**otiose,** adj., *not needed, not useful,* pronounced (ōshĭōs′), but the adjective is not widely used and is familiar to most persons only as a reading word.

**otium cum dignitate,** Latin phrase, *ease or leisure with dignity,* pronounced (ō′shĭum kŭm dĭgnĭtā′tĭ)

**otto,** see **attar**

**Ottoman,** n., *a Turkish subject,* with a plural *Ottomans.* The syllable *man* is not etymologically the English word *man.* See **German, Mussulman**

**ought,** n., dialectal for *nought,* especially in children's speech.

**ought,** v., colloquial in the sense *to be in need of*, as in *This ax ought to have a new handle.* See **had ought**

**Ouida,** n., *pen name of Louise de la Ramée*, pronounced (o͞oē′da) or (wē′da)

**our,** pron., avoided now in modern correspondence style in expressions like *our Mr. Brown*, i. e., our agent, salesman, representative, etc., Mr. Brown. Usually the context makes the pronoun **our** unnecessary, but if it does not, it is better style to state Mr. Brown's position and title explicitly.

**ourself,** pron., compounded of *our*, plural, and *self*, singular. Used only when *we* refers to a single person, as in royal or editorial style.

**ousel,** see **ouzel**

**outdoors,** adv., the same as *out of doors*, the latter being slightly more formal.

**out loud,** see **aloud**

**outré,** adj., French word, *eccentric, unconventional in a high degree.* A fine word, often affected in a journalistic style of speaking and writing. Pronounced (o͞otrā′)

**outside,** prep., colloquial and dialectal in the sense *except*, as in *There was no one present outside my immediate family.* Also in the sense *more than*, as in *He won't be gone outside three weeks.* See **inside**

**ouzel,** n., *a bird*, pronounced (o͞o′zl), with a variant spelling *ousel*, pronounced the same.

**oven,** n., *place for baking*, pronounced (ŭv′n), in spite of the discrepancy between spelling and pronunciation.

**over,** adv., colloquial in the sense *more than*, as ın *We walked over fifteen miles.*

**overly,** adv., colloquial and dialectal for *very, extremely*, as in *I'm not overly fond of that fellow.*

**overnight,** adv., a compound word, as in *He learned Greek overnight.* Compounded in the same way as *today, tomorrow,* *tonight.* The word does not mean *during the night,* but the interval between one day and the next, as in *I'll consider it overnight,* until tomorrow.

**overt,** adj., *revealed, open,* pronounced (ōvert′) The complementary term is *covert.* See **covert**

**overweening,** adj., properly refers to a quality of the mind, *arrogant, presumptuous,* as in *an overweening self-confidence.* Incorrectly used therefore in *the Bagdad Railway, which played such an overweening part in the pan-Germanic scheme of expansion,* from a newspaper editorial.

**over with,** adv., colloquial in the sense *over, done,* as in *I am glad that is over with,* for *I am glad that is over.* See **done with**

**own,** n., colloquial in the phrase *to be on one's own,* to be acting independently.

**oyez,** interj., the cry of a public officer to command attention. Also spelled *oyes,* and sometimes *o yes,* as though it were the two words *o* and *yes.* By origin, a French word meaning *hear, listen,* and pronounced (ōyĕs′), sometimes (ōyēz′)

# P

**pa,** see **ma**

**pace,** Latin word, used as a preposition, in the sense *with all respect to, with the approval of,* and employed in expressing a contrary opinion. Literally, a case form of the word *pax,* peace. Pronounced (pā′sĭ)

**pachisi,** n., *name of a game,* from the Hindi word for twenty-five. Pronounced (pachē′zē) The word is current in various colloquial forms, *parchesi, parchisi, parcheese,* etc., but etymologically **pachisi** is the most correct form.

**pachydermatous,** adj., *thick-skinned.* A technical term in zoölogy, but also used figuratively in humorous expressions of the polysyllabic type. Pronounced (păkĭder′matus) See **Polysyllabic Humor**

**packing,** adv., colloquial in the phrase *send one packing,* dismiss without ceremony.

**pacifist,** n., *an opponent of all war.* A fuller and etymologically more correct form *pacificist* is sometimes advocated, but **pacifist** has definitely established itself in usage.

**pact,** n., *agreement, compact.* A favorite newspaper word, rarely spoken and rarely used in good literary style.   See **ban**

**pad,** v., slang in the phrase *pad it,* go on foot.   See **hoof**

**Paddy,** n., colloquial synonym for *Irishman.*

**Paderewski, Ignace J.,** n., *pianist and composer* (1860–), pronounced (pădĕrĕv′skĭ)

**padrone,** n., Italian word, *employer of a group of workmen,* pronounced (pahdrō′nā), with a plural *padroni,* pronounced (pahdrō′nē)

**paean,** n., *a song,* specifically a song of thanksgiving or triumph. As this meaning is contained in the word itself, it is tautological to speak of a *paean of thanksgiving,* or *a paean of triumph,* and in learned use such phrases would not occur.   In less careful usage, however, **paean** is used merely as a synonym of *song,* as in *a paean of praise, of joy,* good phrases to avoid.   Pronounced (pēan)

**pageant,** n., *spectacular exhibition,* pronounced (păj′nt), with a related noun *pageantry* (păj′ntrĭ)   A pageant is usually illustrative of some historical event, but not necessarily so.   It may be merely picturesque.

**Pagliacci,** n., *name of an Italian opera,* pronounced (pahlĭah′chĭ)

**pail,** see **bucket**

**pain,** n., slang in the sense *annoyance, disgust,* in the sentence *You give me a pain.*   In the plural number, *pains* means *effort, endeavor,* as in *That is what he got for his pains.*   In this use *pains* is usually construed as a plural, as in *His pains were rewarded by ingratitude,* but it can also be used as a singular, as in *Much pains has been taken to secure a favorable hearing* *of this petition.* This latter construction, however, seems not altogether satisfactory, and instead a construction like *Great pains* or *many pains have been taken,* etc., in most instances would be preferred. See **means**

**paint,** v., slang in the phrase *paint things, the town red,* celebrate riotously.

**pair,** n., *a set of two,* with a plural *pairs;* in dialectal speech often with a plural *pair,* as in *two pair on a side,* for *two pairs on a side.* In standard use one would not speak of *four pair of shoes,* but *four pairs of shoes.*

**pajamas,** see **pyjamas**

**pal,** n., colloquial for *comrade, companion.* By origin the word is slang, but it has lost a great deal of its slang coloring, though it has scarcely passed out of the region of the colloquial.

**palaeography,** n., *study of ancient inscriptions and writing,* pronounced (pālĕŏg′rafĭ), and so (pālē-) in other words with the first element *palae-,* as in *palaeobotany, palaeolithic, palaeontology, palaeozoic.*

**palatial residence,** trite phrase, high style for *house, dwelling.*

**palette,** n., *painter's board for colors,* pronounced (păl′et) Like many words in connection with the arts, **palette** is by origin a French word, but it has been completely anglicized in everything except spelling.

**palfrey,** n., archaic and romantic literary word for *lady's saddle horse.* Pronounced (pawl′frĭ) and used chiefly in modern imitations of medieval romantic narrative.

**palimpsest,** n., *parchment on which the original writing has been erased and which has been used again for writing.* The word is not used as an adjective in phrases like *palimpsest manuscript,* the word **palimpsest** itself implying a manuscript, and one specifically of the kind defined. This is the learned use of the word, and, since the word is a learned word, it seems reasonable to require that, if used at all, it should be used with respect for its learned associations. Pronounced (păl'ĭmpsĕst), incorrectly (palĭmp'sest) See **miscellany**

**pallet**, n., archaic and literary for *bed*, usually of a poor and humble kind. Pronounced (păl'et)

**Pall Mall**, n., *a street in London*, pronounced (pĕl mĕl') The *Mall* in Central Park, New York City, is pronounced (măl) The adverb *pell-mell* is not etymologically of the same origin.

**palm**, n., *a tree*, pronounced (pahm), dialectally (păm), and so also *palmer* (pahm'er), *palmist* (pahm'ĭst), *palmy* (pahm'ĭ), but palmetto (pălmĕt'ō), *palmar* (păl'mar), of the palm of the hand, *palmaceous* (pălmā'shus), of the palm tree. See **calm**

**palpable**, adj., *tangible, apparent*, pronounced (păl'pabl) The word literally means *something that may be touched*, then, by extension, something as evident as though it were verifiable by the physical senses, something clearly demonstrable, as in *a palpable falsehood*. The word is one, however, that should be used carefully and not too freely.

**palpitate**, v., *flutter*, pronounced (păl'pitāt), not (pawl'pitāt)

**palsy**, n., *a disease*, pronounced (pawl'zĭ), not (păl'zĭ)

**palter**, v., *hesitate, compromise with*, as in the phrase *palter with the truth*. Pronounced (pawl'ter) The word is not current in colloquial use, but has a slight literary flavor.

**paltry**, adj., *mean, insignificant*, pronounced (pawl'trĭ)

**Pamela**, n., *woman's name*, pronounced (păm'ela) or (pamē'la)

**pampas**, n., *the treeless plains of South America*. The form pampas is a plural, but the singular *pampa* is not in use. Pronounced (păm'paz), not (păm'pas) or (pahm'pas)

**panacea**, n., *a remedy that cures all, a universal remedy*. The phrase *universal panacea* is therefore tautological and incorrect. Pronounced (pănasē'a)

**Panama**, n., *place name in Central America*, pronounced (păn'-amaw), (păn'amah), or (pănamaw'), (pănamah') The pronunciation with final (aw) is the older traditional pronunciation, but the pronunciation with final (ah) is now often considered the more refined. See **Chicago, Omaha**

**pancreas,** n., *a bodily organ*, pronounced (păn'krĭas)

**panegyric,** n., *eulogy*, pronounced (pănejĭr'ĭk), not (pănejī'rĭk) The noun *panegyrist*, one who eulogizes, is pronounced (panĕj'-ĭrĭst) or (păn'ejĭrĭst)

**panorama,** n., *extended view*, pronounced (pănorah'ma) or (pănorăm'a) The word is Greek in its etymological origins, and the pronunciation with (ah) may be called the learned, the pronunciation with (ă) the popular or anglicized pronunciation. The anglicized pronunciation is probably numerically the more general.

**pants,** n., colloquial and low colloquial abbreviation of *pantaloons*. The more general word in good English is *trousers*. The term *breeches* usually applies to a garment that does not cover the whole leg, as in *riding breeches, knee breeches*. The word **pants** is construed as a plural, as in *His pants were too long*, and it has no corresponding singular. See **breeches**

**pap,** n., slang in the sense *obviously deceptive talk*, as in *You don't expect me to believe such pap*, that is, the kind of talk that might deceive infants. Dialectal as a variant of *papa*.

**papa,** n., a somewhat old-fashioned word whose history runs parallel to that of *mamma*. See **mamma** The tendency now is to replace this word by *father*, or in more familiar use by *daddy*. Two pronunciations are current, (papah') and (pah'pa), the former being commonly regarded as the more refined. The abbreviations *pap* (păp) and *pop* (pŏp) occur only on the very familiar or on the dialectal level.

**papier-mâché,** n., a French word meaning *chewed paper*, and applied to paper pulp moulded into shapes and then hardened. Pronounced (păp'yā măshā'), but sometimes the phrase is half-anglicized into *paper-mâché* (pā'per măshā')

**papist,** n., pronounced (pā'pist), and so also *papistry* (pā'pĭstrĭ), but *papistical* (papĭs'tĭkal) The word **papist** usually carries with it some hostile implications, the more colorless term being *Roman Catholic*. The term is not now commonly used, but has something of the archaic color of a word pertaining to the religious controversies of the seventeenth and eighteenth centuries.

**papyrus,** n., *Egyptian plant*, pronounced (papī'rus) The plural is *papyri*, pronounced (papī'rī) As this plant was used to make the writing material of the ancient Egyptians, the name **papyrus** also came to mean *a manuscript written on papyrus*. See **eucalyptus**

**par,** n., colloquial figure of speech in *below par*, not in one's usual health. The associations of the word are chiefly commercial, and for that reason it would be avoided in writing of an intentional literary coloring.

**parachute,** n., *a device used to retard falling from a height*, pronounced (păr'asho͞ot) The word is a made-up word, coined by a French aeronaut from two classical elements, like *bicycle*, *automobile*, *aeroplane*, all of which also English owes to French.

**paradigm,** n., *a set of inflections in grammar*, pronounced (păr'-adĭm), or less frequently (păr'adīm) The silent *g* in this word is accounted for by its French origin, as in *condign* (kondīn'), *consign* (konsīn'), etc.

**paraffin,** n., *a distillate from shale, wood*, etc., pronounced (păr'-afĭn) A variant spelling also occurs, *paraffine*, and a pronunciation (păr'afēn), perhaps after the analogy of *gasoline, kerosene*, but the spelling and pronunciation as first given are to be preferred and are the ones in use in chemistry.

**parakeet,** n., *a kind of parrot*, pronounced (păr'akēt), with a variant *paroquet* (păr'okĕt) The word is of French origin, but is not pronounced with a silent final consonant.

**parallelepiped,** n., *a solid contained by parallelograms*, with a variant of the same meaning, *parallelepipedon*. Pronounced (păra-lelĕp'ĭpĕd), (păralĕlepĭp'edon), less correctly (păralĕlepī'ped), (păralĕlepī'pedon) The form *parallelepipedon* is the Greek form of the word, of which **parallelepiped** is an anglicized version. The spellings *parallelopiped, parallelopipedon* sometimes occur, under the influence of the analogy of *parallelogram*, but they are less correct etymologically than the spellings **parallelepiped, parallelepipedon,** the elements of the compound being the word *parallel*+the Greek preposition *epi,* upon,+Greek *pedon,* ground. By the test of etymology, the spellings *parallelipiped, parallelipipedon* are also incorrect. It must be said, however, that though the pronunciations (păralĕlepī'ped), (păralĕlepī'pedon) are less correct from the etymological point of view, they are nevertheless widely current, even in the use of professional mathematicians. The analogy of the noun *pipe* seems to have affected the pronunciation of these words, though they have no connection either in meaning or in origin with *pipe.*

**paramour,** n., *illicit lover,* especially in literary newspaper style. An adverb also occurs in the form *par amour,* in the way of love, in modern imitations of medieval romantic style.

**parasite,** n., *sycophant, plant or animal living upon another,* pronounced (păr'asīt), with an adjective *parasitic* (părasĭt'ĭk)

**parcel post,** n., *postal service for packages,* colloquially also called *parcels post,* though the form used in the *United States Postal Guide* is only **parcel post.**

**pard,** n., archaic for *leopard,* and slang abbreviation for *partner,* from a pronunciation of the latter as (pahrd'ner)

**parent,** n., *a father or mother,* pronounced (păr'ent), not (pā'rent), except in an artificially precise pronunciation which attempts to regulate pronunciation by spelling.

**parental roof-tree,** trite phrase, ambitious synonym for *father's house.*

**par excellence,** French phrase, *preeminently, representatively,* pronounced (pahr ĕkselahńs')

**parfleche,** n., *a hide stretched and dried,* pronounced (pahr'flĕsh)

The word naturally does not come within the circle of the daily needs of many persons, but it occurs frequently in early descriptions of frontier life and is a useful technical term when it is needed.

**pariah,** n., *social outcast,* pronounced (păr'ĭah), not (parī'a) In India the word designates one of the definitely recognized religious castes of the country, the "untouchables," but elsewhere it is a rhetorical and literary word of vague meaning but strong feeling.

**pari passu,** Latin phrase, *with equal pace, at the same time, equally,* pronounced (pā'rī păs'ū)

**parishioner,** n., *dweller in a parish,* pronounced (parĭsh'oner), not (păr'ĭshoner), though the noun from which it is derived is *parish* (păr'ĭsh)

**park,** v., now in general use in the phrase *to park an automobile,* to bring and leave an automobile at a place of rest. Probably from the military use of **park,** to arrange wagons, artillery, etc., compactly. Slang in the sense *coming to a stop, waiting,* as applied to persons.

**parliament,** n., *a deliberative assembly,* pronounced (pahr'lament), and so also *parliamentary* (pahrlamĕn'tarĭ) The pronunciation (pahr'lĭament) is theoretical and not actually current in speech. It is a spelling pronunciation, resulting from the theory that pronunciation should be made to conform to spelling even to the extent of violating actual practice—an untenable theory.

**parlor,** n. As ordinarily used the word means *the best room in the house,* entered often only on state occasions. As such rooms exist now only in old-fashioned houses, the word is going out of use. Instead of **parlor** the more customary word for the general assembly room of the house is now *living room,* or the slightly less formal *sitting room,* and **parlor** on the other hand has taken special senses, especially as applied to public rooms, as in *beauty parlor, the parlors of a hotel,* and, as an extreme, a sign formerly exhibited on upper Seventh Avenue in New York, *horseshoeing parlors*. The term *parlor boarder* in America is used only facetiously of one supposed to be the landlady's favorite among her guests, but in England *parlor boarder* was the name formerly for a boarding school pupil who lived in the principal's family. The word has fallen into disuse in England, probably with the practice. For the spelling *parlour*, see **-or, -our**  See **drawing-room**

**parlous,** adj., archaic and facetious for *disconcerting, intimidating, distressing,* affected by modern imitators of medieval romantic style.

**parochial,** adj., *pertaining to a parish, provincial,* pronounced (parō′kĭal), not (parō′shĭal) or (parō′chĭal)

**parquet,** n., as part of a theater, pronounced as a French word, (pahrkā′); as a name for floors made from wooden blocks, anglicized and pronounced (pahr′kĭt), sometimes (pahrkĕt′)  The nouns *parqueting, parquetry* are (pahr′ketĭng), (pahr′ketrĭ)

**parson,** see **minister**

**parsonage,** see **manse**

**part,** v., construed with *from* in the sense *take leave of, depart from,* and with *with* in the sense *surrender, give up,* as in *I hate to part with this old pipe.*

**partake of,** v., ostentatious and affected for *eat,* as in *The guests partook of an elaborate repast.* A favorite euphemism in ambitious journalistic style.

**parti,** n., French word, *a person considered as a possibility in marriage,* pronounced (pahrtē′)

**partial,** adj., stilted for *fond of,* as in *I am very partial to peas,* I like peas. The word has a better literary use in the sense *biased partisan,* as in *The judge should never be partial in his decisions.*

**partially,** adv., *not wholly or completely,* but usually readily and advantageously replaced by the simpler word *partly,* as in *The* *roast was only partially consumed*, more simply *The roast was only partly eaten* or *used*.

**parti pris,** French phrase, *partiality, prejudice,* pronounced (pahrtē' prē')

**partisan,** n., *a narrow supporter of a party, one who places party above everything,* as in *a partisan of fanatic severity.* The noun is often used as an attributive, especially in the phrase *partisan spirit.* Pronounced (pahrtĭzăn') or (pahr'tizan), (pahr'tizn), the latter being the pronunciations likely to occur when the word is used in attributive position. Another word of the same form, also spelled *partizan,* and pronounced (pahr'tĭzn), meaning *a long-handled spear,* is now obsolete, except as it is occasionally restored by historians in descriptions of chivalric feats of arms.

**partner,** n., *a sharer,* in dialect speech often *pardner,* with an abbreviation *pard.*

**partridge,** n., *a bird,* pronounced (pahr'trĭj), in old-fashioned dialect (păt'rĭj), (păt'rĭch) The precise difference between a partridge and a quail is a question for the ornithologist, not the linguist, but it may be pointed out that popular usage does not make a scientific distinction in the way in which it employs these two terms. See **huckleberry**

**parturiunt montes, nascetur ridiculus mus,** Latin phrase, *great effort but small result, much fuss but little feathers,* literally, *the mountains labor, an absurd mouse is brought forth;* pronounced (pahrtū'rĭunt mŏn'tēz, năsē'tur rīdĭk'ūlus mŭs)

**party,** n., in good English means *a group of persons holding an opinion,* as in *a political party,* or *a person in a legal action,* as in *the party of the first part,* or *a social gathering.* In low colloquial English, and sometimes humorously, it is often used as the equivalent merely of *person,* as in *a disagreeable old party, The party I have in mind won't accept these terms.* In the sense *social entertainment,* **party** has somewhat the color of a children's word.

**parvenu,** n., French word, *upstart, new-rich,* pronounced as an English word, (pahr′venōō), or as a French word, (pahrvenü′)

**pas,** n., French word, *precedence,* as in *give the pas to, dispute the pas with,* etc. Pronounced (pah)

**paschal,** adj., *pertaining to Easter,* pronounced (păs′kal), reflecting in the pronunciation of *ch* as (k) the Greek origins of the word.

**pas de deux,** French phrase, *dance for two,* pronounced (pah de dō)

**pasear,** n., Spanish word, *a walk, a promenade,* current locally in the Southwest, and also used as a verb. Pronounced (pah′sĭahr)

**pasha,** n., *Turkish title,* pronounced (pashah′) or (pah′sha)

**passé,** adj., French word, *past the prime, out of fashion,* pronounced (păsā′)

**pas seul,** French phrase, *dance for one, action in which one person takes the prominent part,* pronounced (pah söl)

**passim,** adv., Latin word, *here and there,* pronounced (păs′ĭm)

**passing,** adj., archaic and literary as an intensive, like *surpassing,* as in *passing fair,* very beautiful, *passing rich,* very rich. The word occurs now chiefly in modern imitations of medieval narrative style, though still remembered in Goldsmith's line, *passing rich with forty pounds a year.*

**pastel,** n., *material for color in drawing,* pronounced (păstĕl′) or (păs′tel) The word is of Italian origin through French, the pronunciation (păstĕl′) representing a French pronunciation, (păs′tel) an anglicized pronunciation.

**pastorium,** n., *a parsonage.* This word is said to have been coined by M. B. Wharton, who published a book in 1898 entitled *Pictures from a Pastorium* and who was at the time pastor of a Baptist church in Norfolk, Virginia. It was intended to take the place of *parsonage, rectory,* and *manse,* and to "name the place where pastors take their seat." The word was formed on the analogy of *auditorium.* The word has gained a certain degree of currency, especially in Baptist churches in the South, but any person who uses it should do so with full realization that it is a new, and in the opinion of many people a laughable word. The pious wish expressed by the inventor of the word has not yet been realized:

> "God speed the day when every fold
> Shall cheerful raise the needed sum
> And build their pastor, young or old,
> A sweet and snug Pastorium."

**pasty,** n., *meat pie of venison,* etc., pronounced (pahs′tĭ) or (păs′tĭ) The word is not colloquially current in America, though familia: to all readers of Robin Hood and other romantic tales. To be distinguished from the adjective *pasty,* of the character of paste, pronounced (pās′tĭ), and to be distinguished also from *pastry* (pās′trĭ)

**pate,** n., archaic and facetious for *head.* The origin of the word is not known, but the head has always inspired the creative linguist to fashion new names for it, and it is not surprising that the history of some of these words is obscure. A later generation may be puzzled to know how *coco* or *bean* came to mean head, and compare French *tête,* head, from the Latin word for *shell.*

**paté,** n., French word, *pie, patty,* pronounced (pătā′)

**paté de foie gras,** French phrase, *pie, patty of fatted goose liver,* pronounced (pătā′ de fwah grah)

**patent,** n., adj., v., usually pronounced (pā′tnt) as an adjective in the sense *open, apparent, obvious,* as in *It must be patent to the densest observation,* but (păt′nt) in all other uses, as in *to patent an invention, to take out a patent, patent leather,* etc. The word in all these uses is of the same etymological origin.

**pathos,** n., *feeling of sadness, melancholy,* etc., pronounced (pā′thŏs) with an adjective *pathetic* (pathĕt′ĭk) The pronunciation (păth′ŏs) also occurs, but is much less general than (pā′thŏs)

**patois,** n., *rustic dialect,* pronounced (păt′wah) or (pătwah′), the latter reflecting more nearly the French origins of the word.

**patriot,** n., *a lover of his country*, with the prevailing pronunciation (pā′trĭot), rarely (păt′rĭot) So also *patriotic, patronage, patronize,* although the pronunciation (păt-) is probably more frequent in these words than it is in **patriot.**

**patron,** n., somewhat ostentatious commercial English for *customer*, in sentences like *Our patrons can always be sure of fair treatment.* Pronounced (pā′tron) or (păt′ron), and so also with *patronage, patroness, patronize,* though the pronunciation with (pā-) is much the more general in all of these words.

**pawky,** adj., Scotch dialect for *sly, arch*, especially as descriptive of a kind of humor, and not infrequently met with in the literary dialect of some modern critics.

**pawpaw,** n., *name of a tree and its fruit*, pronounced (paw′paw) Also spelled *papaw*, and recorded in the books on pronunciation as pronounced in various ways. But in the regions in which the pawpaw grows and in which there is frequent and natural occasion for pronouncing the word, the only current pronunciation is (paw′paw)

**pax Romana,** Latin phrase, *peace maintained within the Roman empire*, pronounced (păks rōmā′na) The phrase is varied by the substitution of the names of other countries for **Romana,** as in *pax Britannica,* etc.

**pax vobis,** Latin phrase, *peace to you*, pronounced (păks vō′bĭs) Also *pax vobiscum*, of the same meaning, pronounced (păks vōbĭs′kum)

**peach,** n., slang as a general synonym for something approved or desirable, as in *a peach of a day, This bat is a peach*, etc. Also an adjective *peachy*, fine, excellent. See **bird**

**peach,** v., slang in the sense *turn informer on*, especially in relation to an accomplice. The same word etymologically as *impeach*, but bad association has corrupted **peach** and brought it to the level of slang.

**peasant,** n., *rustic person*, pronounced (pĕz′nt), and so also *peas-*

*antry* (pĕz′ntrĭ)   Though the word etymologically means merely *dweller in the country* (in contrast, for example, to *citizen*) and therefore might seem reasonably to be equated with the word *farmer*, the word *peasant* nevertheless has never been applied to tillers of the soil in America, no matter how humble, and always carries with it implications of European rustic life, the life often of an impoverished and oppressed country people. It is chiefly, therefore, a literary word in America.

**pecan,** n., *a kind of nut,* usually pronounced (pēkahn′), sometimes (pē′kahn), and still less frequently (pēkăn′)

**peccavi,** n., Latin word, *confession of fault,* usually in the phrase *to cry peccavi,* literally, *I have sinned;* pronounced (pĕkā′vī)

**pecker,** n., slang in the sense *nose,* especially in the phrase *keep your pecker up,* don't lose courage, don't give up, like the phrase *to keep a stiff upper lip.*

**peckish,** adj., slang in the sense *hungry,* as in *I feel a bit peckish myself.*

**pectoral,** adj., *pertaining to the chest,* pronounced (pĕk′toral), not (pĕktŏr′al)

**pecuniary,** adj., *of money,* as in *pecuniary aid,* aid through the supplying of money, *pecuniary embarrassment,* caused by money, usually the lack of it, *pecuniary reward,* reward in money.   The word *financial* is sometimes incorrectly used for **pecuniary.** The word *finance* means the *management of money,* not specifically *money* itself.   The phrase *financial aid* should therefore mean aid in the management of one's finances, a kind of aid which might be quite different from pecuniary aid.   To be in financial difficulty would be in difficulty over the management of one's business affairs, and only facetiously could one speak of a person short of cash as being in financial difficulties.

**pedagogue,** n., *school-teacher,* especially a man teacher, but usually with an attempt at humor.   See **Polysyllabic Humor**   This noun is pronounced (pĕd′agŏg)   The nouns *pedagogy, pedagogics*

443

are pronounced (pĕdagō′jĭ), (pĕdagō′jĭks), or (pĕdagŏj′ĭ), (pĕda-gŏj′ĭks) The *New English Dictionary* also records (pĕdagŏg′ĭ), (pĕdagŏg′ĭks), but this pronunciation, not given in Michaelis-Jones, *A Phonetic Dictionary of the English Language*, is very rare, if it occurs at all in America.

**peddle,** v., *to sell things from a pack or wagon, to go from house to house selling things.* Usually considered not a very dignified word, though it survives on the colloquial level in certain phrases, as in *to peddle milk, to peddle meat, to peddle papers*, merely in the sense *to carry about and deliver*, without any contemptuous or disrespectful implications. See **pedlar**

**peddler,** see **pedlar**

**pedicel,** n., *term in botany*, pronounced (pĕd′ĭsel), with a variant *pedicle* (pĕd′ĭkl)

**pedlar,** n., *man who travels about with a pack or wagon selling things.* The form **pedlar** is the old and original spelling of the noun, from which later a verb *to peddle* was formed. From this verb was then derived a new form of the noun, *peddler*, now probably as generally current as the older noun **pedlar.** The form *peddler* has analogy in its favor, for though there are many nouns of agency ending in *-er* in English, *butcher, baker*, and *candlestick-maker*, there is little besides its history to support a spelling like **pedlar.** But it seems that in this instance history should count for a good deal.

**peeler,** n., slang for *a policeman*, from Sir Robert Peel. See **bobby, cop** Policemen for some reason appeal to the slang-making imagination, and slang terms to name them are consequently numerous.

**peeper,** n., colloquial name for *frog*, the kind that peeps in the spring.

**peeve,** v., slang for *annoy, vex*, usually in the passive, as in *Now don't be peeved at what I'm going to say.* Probably a back formation from *peevish*. See **burgle**

**peignoir,** n., French word, *woman's dressing gown,* pronounced (pānwahr')

**Peirce,** n., *family name,* with a variant spelling *Pierce,* and sometimes *Pearse.* The name is pronounced sometimes (pērs), riming with *fierce,* and sometimes (pers), riming with *verse.* The two pronunciations are both regular phonetic developments from the older Middle English forms of this name, but the pronunciation (pers) is the less general.

**Peixoto,** n., *family name,* pronounced (pāshō'to)

**pekoe,** n., *a kind of tea,* pronounced (pē'kō) or (pĕk'ō)

**pelf,** n., literary for *money,* usually with implications of contempt, as of ill-gotten gains, tainted money.

**pell-mell,** see **Pall Mall**

**pellucid,** adj., literary word for *translucent,* pronounced (pĕlōō'sĭd)

**penal,** adj., *punitive,* pronounced (pē'nal), and so *penalize* (pē'nalīz), but *penalty* is pronounced (pĕn'altĭ)

**Penates,** see **Lares**

**penchant,** n., French word, *inclination, liking for,* pronounced (pahn'shahn)

**pendant,** n., *ornament attached to a neck chain,* with a less usual spelling *pendent,* this latter word being ordinarily the spelling for an adjective and **pendant** for a noun.

**pendent,** adj., *hanging, overhanging, awaiting decision,* with a less frequent spelling *pendant.*

**pendente lite,** Latin phrase, *with the case still unsettled,* pronounced (pĕndĕn'tĭ lī'tĭ)

**penny,** n., a kind of generic word for *a coin of small value,* but specifically in England a bronze coin of the value of $\frac{1}{12}$ of a shilling, in America a cent. Since American coinage is based on the decimal system, *cent,* from Latin *centum,* hundred, is the proper term for the coin of smallest value, **penny** being used only as a colloquial survival of the older English use. The plural of **penny** is *pence* with reference to a sum of value, as in

*It costs seven pence*, but *pennies* with reference to coins, as in
*He laid seven pennies in a row.*

**pent**, adj., literary for *confined, restrained*, though the phrase
*pent up*, as in *all his pent-up energy*, etc., is still current in general spoken use.

**pentstemon**, n., *name of a plant*, pronounced (pĕntstē′mon), and
often incorrectly heard as though spelled *penstemon.*

**penult**, n., *next to last*, pronounced (pē′nult) or (pĭnŭlt′), but
*penultimate* is always (pĭnŭl′tĭmat) The most common use
of the word is in designating the syllables of a word, the **penult**
being the next to the last syllable, and the *antepenult* the syllable before the next to the last syllable.

**penury**, n., *poverty*, pronounced (pĕn′ūrĭ), but *penurious* (pĭnū′-
rĭus)

**peony**, n., *a plant and flower*, pronounced (pē′onĭ), dialectally
(pī′nĭ)

**people**, n., sometimes used colloquially in the sense *family*, as
in *My people won't let me go*, and in low colloquial use as a word
of address to a mixed group, as in *Say, people, what do you think?*

**pep**, n., slang in the sense *vigor, vitality.* Probably a contraction
of *pepsin*, the digestive principle that produces vitality, or
perhaps of *pepper.* See **bounce, kick**

**Pepys, Samuel**, n., *author of "Pepys's Diary"* (1632–1703) Perhaps
the most general pronunciation of this name is (pĕps), but
(pēps) is also frequently heard, and sometimes (pĕp′ĭs) How
Pepys himself pronounced his name is not definitely known.

**per**, prep., Latin word, frequently used in phrases like *per annum,
per diem, per cent.* Some rhetoricians make the rule that **per**
should be used only with other Latin words and therefore regard
*five cents per yard, five dollars per day*, etc., as incorrect. These
latter constructions might very well, or better, be *five cents
a yard, five dollars a day*, but the constructions with **per** are too
common in business and commercial English to be set aside

as incorrect. The construction *per your letter of yesterday,* in accordance with your letter, etc., is crude commercial style.

**peradventure,** adv., archaic and literary for *perhaps.* The word has another archaic use in the sense *doubt,* a noun, and this also occasionally appears in literary use in the phrase *beyond peradventure,* without or beyond doubt, and sometimes tautologically and incorrectly in the phrase *beyond peradventure of a doubt.*

**per annum,** Latin phrase, *for or by the year,* pronounced (per ăn′um)

**per caput,** Latin phrase, *a head, by the head,* pronounced (per kăp′ut) Sometimes incorrectly given *per capita* (per kăp′ĭta), a plural, meaning *(counting) by heads.*

**per cent,** Latin phrase, the word *cent.* being an abbreviation of Latin *centum.* For this reason, some rhetoricians maintain that it must be followed by a period. General usage, however, justifies **per cent** both with and without a period.

**perchance,** adv., archaic and literary for *perhaps.*

**per contra,** Latin phrase, *on the other hand,* pronounced (per kŏn′-tra)

**per diem,** Latin phrase, *for or by the day,* pronounced (per dī′ĕm)

**Perdita,** n., *character in Shakspere,* pronounced (per′dĭta)

**père,** n., French word, *the father,* added to a name to distinguish the senior from the junior, the father from the son, as in *Dumas père,* the elder Dumas, *Dumas fils,* the younger Dumas. Pronounced (pār), and *fils* is pronounced (fēs)

**peremptory,** adj., *imperious, not permitting of delay,* pronounced (pĕr′ĕmtŏrĭ), very frequently also, but less correctly, (perĕm′-torĭ)

**perfect,** adj., sometimes said by theorists from the nature of its meaning not to permit of comparison, *more perfect, most perfect* therefore being illogicalities. In good general use, however, **perfect** does not mean an absolute state of perfection, as a philosophic idea, but perfect as things in the world are perfect,

447

that is, more or less perfect.  It is therefore permissible from the point of view both of logic and of usage to speak of things as more or less perfect, most or least perfect.  See **full**

**perfect in every detail,** trite phrase, objectionable also because it usually is not true.

**perfume,** n., *odor,* pronounced (per′fūm), but as a verb (perfūm′) A similar distinction of stress characterizes many nouns and verbs of the same spelling form, e. g., *conduct,* (kŏn′dŭkt), noun, and (kondŭkt′), verb; *contract,* (kŏn′trăkt), noun, and (kontrăkt′), verb; *transfer,* (trăns′fer), noun, and (trănsfer′), verb, etc.

**peril,** v., in journalistic English, as in *Inspection Indicates Water Shortage Perils City,* often used for *imperil.*  But *imperil* also is a somewhat literary word, the more customary term being *endanger.*

**perimeter,** n., *inclosing outline,* pronounced (perĭm′eter)

**periphery,** n., *boundary line of a figure,* usually a circle, pronounced (perĭf′erĭ)

**perk,** n., slang abbreviation of *perquisite,* "something on the side," the "pickings" of an official position.

**perk,** v., colloquial in the sense *become more active, animated,* as in *He began to perk up at once.*  See **chirk**

**permeate,** v., *pervade, penetrate in all parts,* and therefore not correctly to be supplemented by modifiers, as in the phrase *permeated all through.*  The word *permeated* alone expresses the idea.

**per mille,** Latin phrase, *in each thousand,* pronounced (per mĭl′ĭ)

**pernickety,** adj., colloquial and dialectal for *fastidious.*

**perpend,** v., *think about, consider,* but only facetiously.  See **Polysyllabic Humor**

**per procurationem,** Latin phrase, *by proxy,* pronounced (per prŏkūrāshĭō′nĕm) and abbreviated *p. proc., p. pro.,* or *p. p.*

**per saltum,** Latin phrase, *at a bound, all at once,* pronounced (per săl′tum)

**per se,** Latin phrase, *in itself,* pronounced (per sē)

**Persia,** n., *a country of Asia,* pronounced (per'zha) or (per'sha) So also with the adjective *Persian,* though (per'zhn) seems much more general than (per'shn) Though statistical evidence is not available, one may say with some conviction that (per'zha) is also more general than (per'sha)

**persiflage,** n., *raillery,* pronounced (persĭflahzh') The word is of French origin and in the pronunciation of the final syllable follows French pronunciation. Sometimes it is anglicized, however, though not frequently, and pronounced (per'siflāj) See **camouflage**

**persona grata,** Latin phrase, *a person who is welcome,* especially of a diplomatic envoy. Also *persona non grata,* a person not welcome. Pronounced (persō'na grā'ta), (persō'na nŏn grā'ta)

**personality,** n., *state or quality as a person,* to be distinguished from *personalty* (per'sonaltĭ), personal property.

**personnel,** n., *staff of persons in a business or organization,* pronounced (personĕl') A favorite word now with organizers, social agents, and efficiency managers, and often incorrectly spelled *personel.* See **matériel**

**perspicuity,** n., *clearness,* as in *perspicuity of style,* clearness of expression. To be distinguished from *perspicacity,* insight, penetration, as in *His erudition was equaled only by his perspicacity.* Both are learned words, and anyone who ventures to use them should do so only with a full realization of their learned meanings.

**pesky,** adj., colloquial and dialectal for *vexatious, annoying.* Probably by origin a phonetic variant of *pest.*

**pestle,** n., *a device for pounding,* especially in a mortar, pronounced (pĕs'l)

**peter,** v., colloquial and slang in the phrase *peter out,* come to an end, give out. The origin of the phrase is not known with certainty, though probably it came from the language of mining and may ultimately have had something to do with the Greek

449

word *petra*, rock, a word which appears in *saltpeter*, *petrify*, *petroleum*, and other English words.

**petit**, adj., French word, *small, daintily formed*, often also as a term of endearment. Pronounced (pĕtē′), with a plural *petits*, pronounced in the same way, and a feminine *petite*, plural *petites*, both pronounced (pĕtēt′)   See **petite**

**petite**, adj., feminine of the French adjective *petit*, small, pronounced (pĕtēt′)   Although **petite** is not thought of as being feminine in its uses in English, it is nevertheless ordinarily applied only to women, not merely in the sense *small*, but *small and animated, sprightly*. This word has become almost completely anglicized, at least in meaning.

**petitio principii**, Latin phrase, *begging the question*, pronounced (pĭtĭsh′ĭō prĭnsĭp′ĭī)

**petit maître**, French phrase, *coxcomb, dandy*, pronounced (pĕtē′ mā′tr)

**petit souper**, French phrase, *small supper for intimate friends*, pronounced (pĕtē′ sōōpā′)

**petits pois**, French phrase, *peas of small size*, pronounced (pĕtē′ pwah)

**petits soins**, French phrase, *small attentions*, pronounced (pĕtē′ swăṅ)

**petit verre**, French phrase, *glass of liqueur*, literally, *a small glass;* pronounced (pĕtē′ vĕr′)

**petrel**, n., *kind of bird*, pronounced (pĕt′rel)

**Petrograd**, n., *Russian city*, formerly St. Petersburg.   Pronounced (pyātrōgrahd′), but often anglicized into (pĕt′rōgrăd)   This city is now known as *Leningrad*.

**petrol**, n., the usual equivalent in England for the American *gasoline*.   Pronounced (pĕt′rŏl), (pĕt′rōl)

**Petruchio**, n., *character in Shakspere*, pronounced (petrōō′chĭō) or (petrōō′kĭō)

**pettifogger**, n., contemptuous term for *a lawyer or other person* *active in a small way about small matters.* A good ancient word, but no more beautiful than the idea it expresses. Even time has not availed to elevate the word.

**ph,** the current spelling for the sound (f) in many words of Greek origin, as in *phaeton, phalanx, pharmacy,* etc., sometimes borrowed directly from Greek, sometimes through a Latin mediary. Some tendency exists to replace this spelling by (f), and it is open to any person with a passion for reform to spell *photograph* as *fotograf, philosophy* as *filosofy, phenomenon* as *fenomenon,* etc.; but until such spellings are more widely used than they are at present, they must still be counted as reforms, desirable perhaps, but not yet realized.

**phalanx,** n., *a formation for battle,* especially in the records of Greek and Roman history. Pronounced (fā′lăngks) or (făl′-ăngks)

**phantasy,** see **fantasy**

**Pharaoh,** n., *Egyptian ruler,* pronounced (fā′rō), less correctly as a trisyllable, (fā′rāō)

**pharmaceutic,** adj., *pertaining to pharmacy,* pronounced (fahr-masū′tĭk)

**phenomenal,** adj., in its strict sense, a philosophical term, but loosely and colloquially used sometimes as a synonym for *remarkable, extraordinary,* as in *The growth of this city has been phenomenal.* This is not a use which anyone interested in maintaining the values of speech would be willing to encourage. The words *remarkable, extraordinary* are adequate, and it is not necessary to abuse a technical word like **phenomenal** to express the meaning of them.

**phenomenon,** n., a learned word, with a plural *phenomena.* The plural *phenomena* is often incorrectly used as a singular, as in *This tendency gives the consideration of such a phenomena as the I. W. W. a dual nature.* This sentence is a good illustration of ambitious, therefore bad writing. Except in its philosophical uses, **phenomenon** can with advantage almost always be replaced by a simpler word, such as *fact, occurrence, happening.* All that the sentence quoted says is that the I. W. W. suggests two thoughts.

**phial,** n., *small bottle,* pronounced (fī'al), with a variant *vial* (vī'al) Neither form of the word is now generally current in popular speech, though both survive in the language of physicians and druggists.

**philanthropy,** n., *the practice of doing things beneficial to others,* usually on a large scale. Pronounced (fĭlăn'thropĭ), with a related noun *philanthropist* (fĭlăn'thropĭst) But the adjective *philanthropic* is pronounced (fĭlanthrŏp'ĭk)

**Philippi,** n., *a city,* pronounced (fĭlĭp'ī)

**Philistine,** n., *a race of people,* pronounced (fĭlĭs'tĭn), (fĭl'ĭstĭn), or (fĭl'ĭstīn) Originally a race of people mentioned in the Bible as the enemies of the Hebrews, but, by extension, now sometimes applied to any persons who are regarded as outsiders, as barbarians and enemies of culture.

**philology,** n., *science of the past,* especially as revealed in language. Pronounced (fĭlŏl'ojĭ), with a related noun *philologist* (fĭlŏl'ojĭst) But the adjective *philological* is pronounced (fĭlolŏj'ĭkal)

**philosophy,** n., *the study of wisdom,* pronounced (fĭlŏs'ofĭ), but *·philosophical* is pronounced (fĭlosŏf'ĭkal), not (fĭlozŏf'ĭkal)

**philtre,** n., *love potion,* pronounced (fĭl'ter) Not etymologically the same as *filter,* material through which liquid is strained.

**phiz,** n., slang for *face,* being an abbreviation of *physiognomy.*

**phlegm,** n., *mucus,* pronounced (flĕm), but the adjective *phlegmatic* is pronounced (flĕgmăt'ĭk)

**Phoebus,** n., *sun god,* pronounced (fē'bus)

**phoenix,** n., *fabulous bird,* supposed periodically to rise again from its own ashes after it has been burned, and hence various metaphorical applications of this notion.

**Phoenix,** n., *capital of Arizona,* and a place name elsewhere in the

United States, not to be spelled *Phenix*, by decision of the United States Geographic Board.

**phone,** n., v., colloquial abbreviation of *telephone.*

**phonetic,** adj., *pertaining to speech sounds,* pronounced (fŏnĕt'ĭk), but *phonetician* is pronounced (fŏnetĭsh'n)

**phonetics,** n., *the science of speech sounds.* The word *phonics,* pronounced (fŏn'ĭks) or sometimes (fō'nĭks), is occasionally used in similar senses, especially as the study of speech sounds is applied practically in the teaching of correct sound production to elementary students.

**photo,** n., colloquial abbreviation of *photograph.*

**photograph,** n., *a picture taken with a camera,* pronounced (fō'tō-grăf), but the related nouns *photographer, photography* are pronounced (fotŏg'rafer), (fotŏg'rafĭ), and the adjective *photographic* is pronounced (fōtogrăf'ĭk)

**phthisis,** n., *pulmonary consumption,* pronounced (thī'sĭs), but the adjective *phthisical* is pronounced (tĭz'ĭkl)

**physic,** n., in careful use, means *the medical art or profession,* as in the title *doctor of physic.* Colloquially the word is used in the sense *medicine,* as in *He is always taking physic of some kind or other,* especially laxative medicine. See **physique**

**physics,** see **acoustics**

**physiognomy,** n., pronounced (fĭzĭŏg'nomĭ) or (fĭzĭŏn'omĭ) The word means *face, features of the face,* and is ordinarily used with facetious intent. See **Polysyllabic Humor**

**physiology,** n., *the science of living things on their physical side,* pronounced (fĭzĭŏl'ojĭ), with a corresponding adjective *physiological,* pronounced (fĭzĭolŏj'ĭkl)

**physique,** n., *body, bodily structure,* pronounced (fĭzēk'), and of the same etymological origin as *physic.*

**pia mater,** Latin phrase, *a part of the brain, wits, understanding,* literally, *tender mother;* pronounced (pī'a mā'ter)

**pianist,** n., *one who plays the piano,* especially a professional player, pronounced (pĭăn'ĭst) or (pē'anĭst) The word is adapted from French *pianiste*, of the same meaning, but the form *pianiste* is sometimes used in English specifically for a woman player, as though the French noun were feminine. In reality, however, French *pianiste* may refer to either a man or woman pianist. The word *pianiste* is pronounced (pēanēst') See **artiste**

**piano,** n., *a musical instrument*, ordinarily pronounced (pĭăn'ō), sometimes and very formally (pēah'nō) The pronunciation (pĭăn'o) verges on the low colloquial, and (pīăn'o) is distinctly low colloquial and dialectal. See **yellow**

**pianoforte,** n., the full name for *piano*, but used now only in historical or formal writing. Pronounced (pĭăn'ōfŏr'tĭ)

**piazza,** n., now become slightly old-fashioned as the name for *the porch of a house*. So also *verandah* tends to be replaced by the simpler word *porch*. Both **piazza** and *verandah* suggest the elaborate scrollwork architecture of the past generation. As the anglicized word meaning *porch*, **piazza** is pronounced (pĭăz'a) As an Italian word meaning *square, market place*, it is pronounced (pĭaht'sah) See **verandah**

**pibroch,** n., *a kind of bagpipe music*, pronounced (pē'brŏk) or (pē'brŏCH) A Scotch word current only in Scotch connections.

**picayune,** n., originally *a Spanish coin of small value*, now colloquial in phrases like *don't care a picayune, don't give a picayune*. Also as a colloquial adjective in *picayunish*, of something small in conception and execution.

**pick-a-back,** adv., *way a child is carried on the back*, with a variant *pig-a-back*. Perhaps from *pig on back*.

**pickelhaube,** n., German word, *helmet*, pronounced (pĭk'elhow'be) See **Zeitgeist**

**pickled,** adj., slang in the sense *drunk*. See **soused**

**picture,** n., colloquial in the sense *moving picture*, and technical as a verb in the sense *to make into a moving picture*, as in *to picture* *a story*. Colloquially used also as a strong term of approval, as in *She was a perfect picture*, as beautiful as things can be made only in a picture. A *picture hat* is a lady's large hat such as is often seen in old pictures.

**pidgin,** adj., a Chinese corruption of the word *business*, in the phrase *pidgin English*, and not related to the noun *pigeon*. Current in a variety of spellings, *pigeon, pidjin, pidjun, pidgeon*, but the simplest and best spelling is **pidgin.** The word is sometimes extended to apply to any kind of popular mixed dialect. See **lingua franca**

**pie,** n., in England ordinarily means meat covered with pastry and baked, in America fruit similarly prepared. But both uses are current in both countries, the difference being one of proportions in the extent of their use. See **tart**

**piece,** n., dialectal in the sense *distance*, as in *I'll go a short piece with you*, for *I'll go a short distance* or *way with you*.

**pièce-de-résistance,** n., French phrase, *chief dish of a meal, most important part*, of a meal or anything else. Pronounced (pĭās' de rāzēstahńs')

**pied à terre,** French phrase, *resting or abiding place*, pronounced (pĭād' ah tĕr')

**Pierce,** see **Peirce**

**Pierrot,** n., *a character in pantomime*, pronounced (pĭĕr'ō) or (pĭerō'), with a corresponding feminine *Pierrette* (pĭerĕt') Also written as common nouns without capitals. The word is of French origin, and, though it has long been current in English, it has not been anglicized.

**piffle,** n., slang for *silly talk*. Also used as a verb, and as an adjective *piffling*, as in *piffling talk*.

**pigeon,** n., colloquial and slang in the sense *victim, one who is plucked*. Pronounced (pĭj'n)

**pike,** see **huckleberry**

**piker,** n., slang name for *tramp*, or for one who makes a living by going about and selling stocks, bonds, etc., wherever he can find a buyer—a peripatetic rather than a settled business man. The term usually carries with it a strong contemptuous coloring.

**pile,** n., slang in the sense *fortune,* as in *He has made his pile and retired.*

**pill,** n., slang in the sense *uninteresting, disagreeable person,* or as applied to *baseball or other ball used in a game.*

**pill box,** n., slang as the name for *a small round hat, a small house,* etc.

**pillow,** n., *headrest,* correctly pronounced (pĭl′ō), low colloquially (pĭl′o) or indistinguishably from *pillar.*

**pin,** n., slang for *leg,* as in *to knock one off his pins,* to throw him down, *not very steady on one's pins,* a bit wobbly.

**pince-nez,** n., French word, *eyeglass held on the nose by a spring,* literally, *pinch nose;* pronounced (păns̃ nā)

**pincers,** n., *a tool for grasping things.* Used only in the plural. The pronunciation is (pĭn′serz), dialectally (pĭnch′erz), through confusion with the verb *to pinch.*

**Pinchot,** n., *family name,* pronounced (pĭn′shō)

**Pinero,** n., *English dramatist,* pronounced (pĭnĕr′ō)

**pinochle,** n., *a game of cards,* with the variant spellings *pinocle, penuchle.* Pronounced (pē′nŏkl), (pĭn′ŏkl)

**pinxit,** v., Latin word, *(he) painted it,* as an artist's signature. Pronounced (pĭngk′sĭt), with a plural *pinxerunt,* pronounced (pĭngksē′runt)

**pipe,** v., slang in the sense *see, look at,* as in *Pipe the lid,* Look at that hat.

**pippin,** n., *a kind of apple,* and slang as a general term of approval, as in *He is a pippin,* etc.

**piquant,** adj., *spicy,* pronounced (pē′knt), and the noun *piquancy* is (pē′knsĭ) The word is of French origin, but in the pronunciations given, it has been pretty completely anglicized. It may be restored, however, to its French form, in which case it would be pronounced as a French word.

**pique,** n., v., *vexation, pettishness, to cause these feelings,* pronounced (pēk)

**piqué,** n., *kind of cloth,* pronounced (pēka′)

**piquet,** n., a card game, pronounced (pĭkĕt′)

**pis aller,** French phrase, *last resource, nothing better to do,* literally, *pis,* worse, *aller,* to go. Pronounced (pēz ălā′)

**Piscataqua,** n., *New England geographical name,* pronounced (pĭskăt′akwaw)

**Pisgah,** n., *Biblical name,* pronounced (pĭz′ga)

**piss-ant,** n., colloquial and dialectal for *pismire* (pĭs′mīr), a name for the ant.

**pistachio,** n., *a nut,* pronounced (pĭstah′shĭō) or (pĭstā′shĭō)

**pistil,** n., *a term in botany,* pronounced (pĭs′tĭl)

**pistol,** n., *a firearm,* pronounced (pĭs′tl), the second syllable containing a syllabic vowel only in a very slow and formal pronunciation.

**pistole,** n., *a coin,* pronounced (pĭstōl′) A necessary word for anyone who would write a tale of buried treasure.

**piteous,** adj., archaic and literary for *pitiful.*

**pitiable,** adj., *calling for pity,* usually as combined with contempt, as in *a pitiable display of ignorance,* and to be distinguished from *pitiful,* moving, distressing, as in *a pitiful sight*

**pitiful,** see **pitiable**

**Pittsburgh,** n., *city in Pennsylvania,* not *Pittsburg,* according to the decision of the United States Geographic Board.

**pituitary,** adj., *pertaining to phlegm or mucus,* pronounced (pĭtū′itărĭ)

**placable,** adj., *mild-tempered,* pronounced (plăk′abl), more commonly used with a negative prefix *im-.* See **implacable**

**placate,** v., *to satisfy, to soothe hostile or ruffled feelings.* The word is not of frequent use in America, and perhaps is still less generally used in England. Critics of speech in England often reject it as an Americanism. "A very firm stand," say the authors of *The King's English*, p. 24, "ought to be made against *placate, transpire,* and *antagonize,* all of which have English patrons," the ground of objection of the authors of *The King's English* being merely that the words are Americanisms. The word **placate** has been in existence at least three hundred years, and undoubtedly it first came into existence on British soil.

**place,** n., in low colloquial and dialectal use often combined with *any, some* as the equivalent of *anywhere, somewhere,* as in *I can't find it any place, I saw it some place,* for *I can't find it anywhere, I saw it somewhere.*

**place aux dames,** French phrase, *ladies first!,* literally, *place for the ladies;* pronounced (plahs ō dahm)

**placer,** n., *a gravel bank,* ordinarily used only in the phrase *placer mining* and pronounced (plăs'er) The word is of American Spanish origins and is not merely the English word *place* with an ending *-er.*

**placid,** adj., *peaceful, serene,* pronounced (plăs'ĭd)

**plague,** n., colloquially used as an imprecation, as in *Plague take it.* The adjective *plaguy* (plā'gĭ) is also colloquial in the sense *very,* as in *a plaguy hard time.*

**plaid,** n., pronounced (plăd), but (plād) in Scotland. Originally the word meant *a shawl* or *rug,* but later was extended merely to the design woven into the shawl or rug.

**plain sailing,** noun phrase, used in the sense *free from obstructions or perplexities.* The original form of the phrase was *plane sailing,* an easy method of navigation on the theory that a ship is moving on a plane. This original sense, however, has been lost, and the general sense merely of easy sailing survives.

**plait,** n., v., *hair, straw, etc., woven into a strand, to weave thus.* Pronounced (plăt) and sometimes spelled *plat.* The same word etymologically as *pleat,* a fold of cloth, especially in dressmaking, but the two forms have become differentiated both in spelling and in meaning.

**plank down,** v., slang for *lay down, place down, pay,* as in *I had to plank down $10 for that.*

**plan on,** v., crudely colloquial for *plan,* as in *We planned on reaching the town by night,* for *We planned to reach,* etc. See **connect up, continue on, refer back**

**plant,** n., slang in the sense *something intentionally brought into a situation,* especially in the early part of a play, for the purpose of using it later to incriminate a person or to develop a plot.

**plant,** v., colloquial in the sense *strike a blow,* as in *to plant one in his right eye.*

**plantain,** n., *a weed,* pronounced (plăn′tn), or more formally (plăn′tĭn)

**plantation,** n., in colonial times meant a *settlement,* of any kind, both in the North and in the South. Later the word became specialized in the South in the sense *a large farm,* as in a *cotton, tobacco, sugar plantation.* But with the passing of the Old South, the word is now tending to fall into disuse, or to take on merely sentimental or historical meanings.

**plaque,** n., *ornamental plate, tablet,* etc., pronounced (plahk) or (plăk)

**plash,** n., v., a variant of *splash,* but much less commonly used than *splash.*

**plat,** n., *a dish served,* pronounced (plah), usually in restaurant English. The word is of French origin, and has not been anglicized in pronunciation. The plural would be *plats,* pronounced the same as the singular, or anglicized to (plahz)

**plat de jour,** French phrase, *the special dish of the day in a restaurant,* pronounced (plah de zhoōr′)

**platter,** n., *a large flat dish,* designated as archaic in the *New English Dictionary,* but generally current in America, especially in the word *meat platter.*

459

**plead**, v., with a past tense and past participle *pleaded*. A past tense and past participle *pled* occurs occasionally in good colloquial use, but frequently only in dialect speech.

**please**, v., incorrectly construed with *at*, as in *I was much pleased at his record*, for *I was much pleased with his record*. See **angry**

**plebeian**, adj., *popular, of low social standing*, pronounced (plĭbē′an) or (plēbē′an)

**plebiscite**, n., *direct vote of the people*, pronounced (plĕb′ĭsĭt), not (plĕbĭs′ĭt)

**Pleiads, Pleiades**, n., *a constellation*, pronounced (plē′yădz), (plē′yadēz), or (plī′ads), (plī′adēz)

**plenary**, adj., *complete*, as in *plenary powers, plenary indulgence.* Pronounced (plē′narĭ) or less generally (plĕn′arĭ)

**plenteous**, adj., archaic and literary for *plentiful*. See **beauteous, piteous**

**plenty**, n., *abundance*, but in colloquial use often employed as an adjective, *abundant*, as in *Deer are not plenty in this region.* As a noun, **plenty** is not preceded by the indefinite article, except in low colloquial use, in constructions like "*Will you have some tea?*" "*No, I have a plenty*," for *I have plenty*. The construction *We have plenty time* is a colloquial ellipsis for *plenty of time.* Also as adverb, e. g., *plenty good enough*, **plenty** is colloquial.

**pleural**, adj., *of the pleura*, as in *pleural pneumonia*, pneumonia combined with pleurisy. Sometimes mistaken for *plural*, plural pneumonia, according to this misunderstanding, being double pneumonia, that is, in both lungs.

**pliant**, adj., *easily bent or influenced*, with a variant *pliable*, of the same meaning.

**plover**, n., *a bird*, pronounced (plŭv′er)

**plow**, n., *to prepare the soil for planting*, with a variant spelling *plough*. Both spellings are correct historically, but **plow** is to be preferred on the grounds of simplicity.

**pluck**, n., colloquial in the sense *courage*, from the use of the word meaning the heart, liver, and lungs of an animal as used for food, these being regarded as the seat of courage.

**pluck,** v., slang in the sense *refuse to pass*, in an examination. More generally used in this sense in England than in America, the usual American equivalent being *flunk*.

**plug,** n., slang for *a decrepit horse*.

**plug hat,** n., slang for *a man's tall silk hat*, but the slang of other days, as the tall silk hat is the hat of other days.

**plumb,** adv., dialectal as a general intensive, as in *I'm plumb tired out, plumb crazy*.

**plump,** adj., *well-rounded*, often used as a euphemistic substitute for *fat*.

**plunder,** n., colloquial for *household goods*. Not now very general, but formerly in wide use in the United States. Probably of Dutch origin.

**plunge,** v., slang in the sense *gamble or speculate wildly*. From this is derived a slang noun *plunger*, reckless gambler or speculator.

**poetaster,** n., *minor poet*, pronounced (pō'etăster) The word has nothing to do etymologically with the verb *taste*, the element *-aster* in the compound being a Latin suffix expressing contempt.

**poignant,** adj., *penetrating, sharp*, pronounced (poin'ant), and a noun *poignancy* (poin'ansĭ), less generally (poin'yant), (poin'yansĭ)

**poilu,** n., French word, *French soldier*, literally, *hairy (one)*; pronounced (pwah'lōō) or (pwahlü')

**pointer,** n., colloquial and slang for *hint, suggestion*.

**poisson,** n., French word, *fish*, pronounced (pwahsŏṅ') The word belongs to the general class of restaurant French and occurs chiefly on hotel bills of fare.

**poke,** n., obsolescent word for *bag*, surviving generally in the proverb *a pig in a poke*, and occasionally in localities as a dialectal use.

**polenta,** n., Italian word, *porridge of corn meal,* etc., pronounced (pōlĕn′tah)

**Polish,** adj., *of Poland,* pronounced (pōl′ĭsh) But the verb of the same form, though not the same etymology, *to polish,* is (pŏl′ĭsh)

**politics,** see **acoustics**

**polony,** see **bologna**

**poltroon,** n., literary word for *coward.*

**polygamy,** n., *the custom of marrying more than one wife,* pronounced (polĭg′amĭ), with a related adjective *polygamous* (polĭg′amus)

**Polysyllabic Humor.** This is the device of using an ornate and elaborate term instead of a normally appropriate simple term, as calling a red nose *a sanguinary proboscis,* or speaking of clothes as *habiliments,* or of one's home as *a domicile,* or of the sense of smell as *olfactory nerves,* or of the *nigritude* of something black. This is an easy and cheap device which very soon grows tiresome. See **Language Mutilation**

**pomace,** n., *apples crushed for cider-making, the leavings after the juice is extracted,* pronounced (pŭm′ĭs), but in dialectal use often made into a singular *pummy,* with a plural *pummies.*

**pomade,** n., *ointment,* pronounced (pōmahd′) or (pōmād′), with a variant *pomatum,* pronounced (pōmah′tum) or (pōmā′tum)

**pomegranate,** n., *a fruit,* pronounced (pŏm′grănat) or (pŭm′-grănat)

**pommel,** n., *part of a saddle,* pronounced (pŭm′el)

**pone,** n., southern local name for a form of corn bread, but not current except in the South.

**pons asinorum,** Latin phrase, the Euclidean proposition, I, 5, as something difficult for beginners; by extension, any difficult task that tests one's abilities, literally, *bridge of asses.* Pronounced (pŏnz′ ăsĭnŏr′um)

**pony,** n., slang for *a literal translation,* used as a students' help. See **trot**

**poor but honest,** trite phrase, an ancient and supercilious description of virtue.

**poorly,** adv., low colloquial and dialectal as an adjective in the sense *sick, unwell,* as in *He has been poorly for a long time,* for *He has been feeling poorly* or *unwell,* etc. See **nicely**

**pop,** n., colloquial name for *effervescent beverage,* and also colloquial as abbreviation of *popular,* popular concert.

**pop,** v., slang in *pop the question,* propose marriage; colloquial in *pop in, pop out,* come, go unexpectedly.

**popover,** n., colloquial name for *a light, very puffy kind of muffin.*

**poppycock,** n., slang for *nonsense, foolishness.*

**porcelain,** n., *china,* pronounced (pŏrs′ln), more formally (pŏrs′lĭn), but (pŏrs′lān) only in artificial pronunciation. There is no difference of meaning in *china* and *porcelain,* the former being a simple, the latter an elaborate word for the same thing.

**pork barrel,** n., slang for *spoils of political office.*

**porpoise,** n., *a salt-water mammal,* pronounced (pŏr′pus)

**porte-cochère,** n., French word, *porch under which carriages stop to take or discharge passengers,* pronounced (pŏrt kōshār′)

**portière,** n., French word, *hanging for a doorway,* pronounced (pŏrtĭär′), not (pŏr′tĭer)

**Porto Rico,** n., *island in the West Indies,* not *Puerto Rico,* by decision of the United States Geographic Board.

**poseur,** n., French word, *a person who assumes poses,* pronounced (pōzer′)

**posse,** n., Latin word, *a party of police,* pronounced (pŏs′ĭ) The word is very generally current and familiar, but is nevertheless still pronounced as two syllables, not anglicized as one.

**posse comitatus,** Latin phrase, *a body of citizens summoned to suppress riot,* etc., pronounced (pŏs′ĭ kŏmĭtä′tus)

**possible,** adj., *tolerable as a person to associate or deal with,* as in

*Is she at all possible?*, a bit of refined conversational slang. The predicate adjective **possible**, and so also *impossible*, is not correctly to be completed by an infinitive except when the subject is the impersonal *it*. The sentence *Nothing like this is possible to happen* should be *Nothing like this can happen*, or *It is impossible for anything like this to happen.* See **impossible**

**possum**, n., colloquial aphetic form of *opossum*, also written *'possum*.

**post**, n., v., *delivery of letters and the letters themselves*, as in "*Has the post come?*" "*Yes, you had a very light post today. It is on your study table.*" Also as a verb, *Please post this letter for me.* These uses are more generally current in England than America, the word *mail* being ordinarily used in America as a noun, adjective, and verb. See **mail**

**postal**, adj., n., by origin an adjective, meaning *pertaining to, connected with the post office*, but by extension used as a noun, *postal card*, as in *Please send me a postal when you arrive.* The process is the same as that by which *nickel* comes to mean *five-cent piece*. Objection is sometimes made to the word *postal card*, which is rejected in favor of *post card;* but *postal card* is the official name in the United States, and logically and linguistically there is little to choose between *post card* and *postal card.* See **-al**

**posted**, adj., colloquial for *informed*, especially in the construction *I'll keep you posted.*

**poste restante**, French phrase, *hold until called for*, as direction on a letter. Pronounced (pōst rĕstahṅt')

**post hoc, ergo propter hoc**, Latin phrase, *after this, therefore on account of this*, with reference to those who confuse sequence with consequence. Pronounced (pōst hŏk, er'gō prŏp'ter hŏk)

**posthumous**, adj., *born after the father's death*, or *published after the author's death*, pronounced (pŏs'tūmus)

**postman**, see **mailcarrier**

**post meridiem,** Latin phrase, *after noon,* pronounced (pōst merĭd'-ĭĕm) Abbreviated *P. M.* or *p. m.*

**post mortem,** Latin phrase, *after death,* pronounced (pōst mŏr'tĕm)

**pot,** n., colloquial and slang in the phrase *go to pot,* go to ruin, and slang in *pot of money,* large sum of money, a fortune.

**potage,** n., French word, *soup,* pronounced (pōtahzh') Current in English in the general class of restaurant French.

**pother,** n., literary for *confusion, agitation,* in the phrases *make* or *raise* or *be in a pother.* Also in exclamations, as in *Such a pother!* Pronounced (pŏdh'er) or (pŭdh'er) The etymology is unknown, and the word is probably unrelated to *bother.*

**potter,** v., colloquial for *to occupy oneself aimlessly and triflingly,* usually *to potter around.* A variant *putter* occurs.

**Poughkeepsie,** n., *city in New York,* pronounced (pōkĭp'sĭ)

**pound,** v., slang in the phrase *pound one's ear,* go to sleep, to sleep.

**pourboire,** n., French word, *a tip,* pronounced (pōōrbwahr')

**pourparler,** n., French word, *a conference for discussion,* a diplomatic term, with a plural *pourparlers,* both pronounced (pōōrpahrlā')

**pour prendre congé,** French phrase, *to take leave,* pronounced (pōōr prahṅ'dr kŏṅzhā'), and abbreviated *p. p. c.*

**power,** n., local and dialectal in the sense *quantity, large amount,* as in *There was a power of people there, He does a power of work in a morning.*

**Powhatan,** n., *Indian and place name,* pronounced (powhatăn')

**powwow,** n., humorous and contemptuous for *conference, meeting,* from an Indian word which was not humorous to the Indians. But the English word is colored by the attitude of the colonial English toward the Indians' powwows.

**pox,** n., low colloquial and vulgar as a synonym for *syphilis.* The word is used also as an interjection or oath, as in *A pox on you!,* in the literary style of swashbuckling romance. See **clap, smallpox**

**practicable,** adj., *susceptible of being put into practice,* as in *a practicable solution;* to be distinguished from *practical,* which means *active, not theoretical,* as in *practical men, a practical farmer, a practical suggestion.* A practical joke consists in practicing some trick on a person, as in removing a chair as he is about to sit down, a kind of joke that calls for no wit or intelligence.

**prairie oyster,** n., slang and humorous for *raw egg swallowed whole.* The humor is like that exemplified in *marblehead turkey,* codfish, *Welsh rabbit,* toasted cheese.

**pram,** n., British colloquial slang abbreviation for *perambulator,* baby carriage.

**prandial,** adj., *pertaining to dinner.* The word is heavy humorous, occurring chiefly in phrases like *postprandial eloquence,* after-dinner speeches. See **Polysyllabic Humor**

**praties,** n., Irish dialectal corruption of *potatoes.*

**pray,** v., elliptical for *I pray* as a polite formula, equivalent to *please,* as in *Pray let me hear from you, Where are you going, pray?* This usage seems a bit archaic and literary now, the customary word being *please.*

**pre-,** prefix, *before,* and used freely as a compositional element with nouns, verbs, and adjectives, as in *precaution, predispose, prenatal,* etc. In most of these compounds, both elements are of Latin origin and the combination of them is often very old. New compounds are sometimes made, however, in which the second element is not a Latin word, as in *pre-war,* e. g., *We can never return to pre-war wages, pre-view,* of pictures, etc., exhibited to small groups before they are shown to the public, *pre-iced,* of fruit cooled before it is placed in refrigerator cars for shipping. To the classical scholar, hybrids like *pre-war, pre-view, pre-iced* seem barbarous, but the speaker or writer who looks at language only from the practical side often finds them very convenient. The main objection to such compounds is not that they are badly formed, but that they may seem too ingenious or technical. They often have a shade of slightly humorous color, as in *I always enjoy a pre-breakfast smoke.*

The adjective *pre-school*, before the age for school, is an invention in the recent lingo of pedagogy. When compounds with **pre-** are new and the first element is distinctly felt, it is usually separated from the second element by a hyphen. See **Hybrids**

**preachment,** n., *obtrusive moralizing*, as when a story-teller stops to insert a moral digression. The word may be described as a literary colloquialism, that is, a literary word which a writer would use only at a half-serious, half-playful moment.

**prebend,** n., *an ecclesiastical term*, pronounced (prĕb'end) So also *prebendary* (prĕb'endărĭ) The terms are not in general use in America and now are chiefly of historical significance.

**precedence,** n., *priority*, as in *Studies take precedence over sports*, pronounced (prēsēd'ens), not (prē'sedens) But the noun *precedent* is pronounced (prĕs'edent), not (prēsēd'ent)

**preciosity,** n., *overrefinement in the use of words*, pronounced (prĕsh-ĭŏs'itĭ)

**precious,** n., colloquial in the sense *fine*, with ironical implications, as in *A precious lot of studying you will do.* Also as an adverb, as in *He will take precious good care*, etc., very good care, *Precious little he knows*, etc., very little he knows.

**précis,** n., French word, *summary, abstract*, pronounced (prĕs'ē)

**predilection,** n., *liking*, construed with *for* and pronounced (prĕd'ĭlĕkshon) or (prēdĭlĕk'shon)

**prefer,** v., not to be followed by *than* unless *rather* precedes. Thus the sentence *He preferred to live poor and honest than to die rich and dishonored* should be *He preferred to live poor and honest rather than*, etc., or *He preferred to live poor and honest to dying rich and dishonored.* The derivatives are *preferring*, *preferred*.

**preference,** n., *choice*, pronounced (prĕf'erens), and so also *preferable* (prĕf'erabl), though the verb is *prefer* (prĭfer'), and the noun *preferment* is (prĭfer'ment)

**prelate,** n., *ecclesiastical officer*, pronounced (prĕl'at), not (prē'lat) or (prē'lăt), though (prĕl'ăt) might excusably occur in very formal pronunciation.

**prelude,** n., *an introductory performance*, pronounced (prĕl'ūd), sometimes (prē'lūd)

**premature,** adj., *too early, overhasty*, pronounced (prĕm'atūr) or (prē'matūr)

**première,** n., French word, *first appearance*, pronounced (prĕmĭār')

**premise,** n., as a term in logic, etc., pronounced (prĕm'ĭs) The verb **premise,** *to state beforehand*, is pronounced (prĭmīz') The term in logic is sometimes spelled *premiss*. The word *premises*, a house and surroundings, is a plural that has no corresponding singular.

**prentice,** n., archaic abbreviation of *apprentice*, surviving now in the phrase *try one's prentice hand at*, make an effort at something in which one has no special skill.

**prepense,** adj., *deliberate*, placed after its noun and current chiefly in the phrase *malice prepense and aforethought*. Pronounced (prĭpĕns')

**Prepositions at the end of sentences.** The rule as commonly given is that sentences must not end with prepositions. It should be noted first of all, however, that whatever justification this rule has is rhetorical and not grammatical. The rhetorical reason for not ending a sentence with a preposition is that stylistically the effect is weak, that the final position in a sentence is emphatic and should be utilized for a significant word. Some of the repugnance to ending a sentence with a preposition may arise from low colloquial constructions like *Where is he at?*, *Where are you going to?*, in which *at* and *to*, however, are not prepositions but adverbs, and in standard English would be omitted altogether as pleonastic. Nor is *of* a preposition in a sentence such as *I don't like to be made a fool of*, but again an adverb. The sentence just quoted is markedly colloquial, and crudely colloquial in tone. It is an extension of the phrase *to make a fool of a person*, but in formal style it would be much improved by recasting, e. g., *I don't like to be treated as though I were a fool.*

The only clauses or sentences which frequently end with prepositions are relative subordinate clauses, as in *He owns the house which he lives in* or *He owns the house he lives in.* This latter sentence with the relative omitted is distinctly more colloquial in tone than the one with the relative expressed, and when the relative is omitted the preposition must come at the end. No other word order is idiomatic. Sentences of this type are quite correct, the question of their use being dependent upon their appropriateness to the general situation. The sentence *He owns the house which he lives in* is again more colloquial than *He owns the house in which he lives.* Many writers prefer this last syntactical expression as being more formally literary, but in conversation both of the other two constructions, with the preposition at the end, are customary, and perhaps they are the most general usage even in writing.

The fear of ending sentences with prepositions sometimes leads writers into omitting prepositions which are necessary, as in *This is a statement the truth of which I am convinced*, which should be *This is a statement the truth of which I am convinced of,* or *This is a statement of the truth of which I am convinced;* another example is the sentence *The reservation might jeopardize a procedure, the great usefulness of which all League members are convinced,* in which the same correction must be made. The sentence *She had disgraced them all and had made Amherst an impossible place for her daughter to live* requires *in* at the end to complete it. Here *in* is a necessary part of the verb, and it was omitted merely because the writer had some vague recollection in mind of the foolish rule that sentences must not end with prepositions.

**presage,** n., *a foreshadowing*, pronounced (prĕs'ĭj), but **presage,** v., *to foreshadow*, is pronounced (prĭsāj')

**present,** v., *to give*, followed either by the word for the thing given as a direct object, the receiver being construed with *to*, as in *They presented ten dollars to him*, or by the receiver as direct object, the thing given being construed with *with*, as in *They presented him with ten dollars*. This latter construction may also be passive, as in *He was presented with ten dollars*.

**presentation,** n., *the act of giving*, pronounced (prĕzĕntā'shon), less commonly (prēzĕntā'shon)

**prestige,** n., *reputation, standing*, pronounced (prĕstēzh'), in accordance with the French origins of the word. But the word is sometimes, though less generally, anglicized and pronounced (prĕs'tĭj)

**pretend,** v., correctly used in a sentence like *He pretends to be an expert*, makes pretensions to being, but incorrectly used in a sentence like *This is not an expensive material as it is often pretended to be*, for *as it is often said to be*, or in the active, *This is not as expensive a material as it pretends to be*, for *This is not as expensive material as the manufacturers pretend that it is*. Only a person can make pretensions, and therefore **pretend** must have a personal subject. See **claim**

**pretense,** n., *make-believe*, pronounced (prĭtĕns'), not (prē'tĕns)

**pretty,** adj., adv., colloquial in the sense *rather, somewhat*, as in *I feel pretty well*. Often used ironically, as in *Here's a pretty mess*. The slang abbreviation *P. D. Q.* stands for *pretty d—n quick*. Pronounced (prĭt'ĭ), with an adverb *prettily* (prĭt'ĭlĭ)

**preventive,** adj., n., *serving to prevent*, as in *preventive treatment*, in medicine, treatment which forestalls disease. A measure of this kind is a **preventive**. The adjective **preventive** is formed like the adjective *inventive*, the adjective and noun *corrective*, etc. A variant form is *preventative*, with the same uses and meanings, formed like *talkative, preservative*, etc. Of these two forms, one is not more correct than the other, but **preventive** has brevity in its favor.

**previous,** adj., slang in the sense *impatient, presuming,* as in *Now don't get too previous,* wait until I am ready.

**Pribilof,** n., *islands in Bering Sea, Alaska,* not *Prybiloff,* nor to be known as *Fur Seal,* according to the decision of the United States Geographic Board.

**price,** n., slang in the phrase *what price,* as a taunting allusion to a failure, as in *What price the brotherhood of man?* Chiefly British.

**priceless,** adj., slang in the sense *extremely amusing or agreeable;* in British slang used in season and out, but heard in America only as an echo of British use.

**prie-dieu,** n., French word, *a prayer desk before which one kneels,* pronounced (prē dyö′)

**priest,** n., ordinarily understood to mean *a Roman Catholic ecclesiastic,* but applied also sometimes to Anglican or Episcopal clergymen, and also to heathen religious ministers, as in *a Druidic priest, the priests of the Aztec church,* etc.

**prima donna,** n., *opera singer,* literally, *first lady.* Pronounced (prē′mah dŏn′ah), with a plural *prime donne,* pronounced (prē′mā dŏn′ā), or an anglicized plural *prima donnas,* pronounced (prī′ma dŏn′az)

**prima facie,** Latin phrase, *at first view, at first consideration,* pronounced (prī′ma fā′shĭē)

**primate,** n., (1) *archbishop of a province,* pronounced (prī′mat), with a plural *primates,* pronounced (prī′mats); (2) *one of the highest order of mammals,* including man, monkeys, etc., pronounced (prī′mat), with a plural *primates,* pronounced as a Latin word, (prīmā′tēz)

**primer,** n., *elementary schoolbook,* pronounced (prĭm′er) in America, (prĭm′er) or (prī′mer) in England.

**primo,** adv., Latin word, *in the first place,* pronounced (prī′mō)

471

**primus inter pares,** Latin phrase, *one who represents or speaks for a group of equals,* literally, *first among equals;* pronounced (prī′mus ĭn′ter pā′rēz)

**princess, n.,** *noble lady,* pronounced (prĭn′sĕs), but when a name immediately follows, pronounced (prĭn′ses), (prĭn′sĭs), as in *Princess Mary* (prĭn′ses mā′rĭ), (prĭn′sĭs mā′rĭ) The formality of the word, as well as the spelling with double final consonant, tends to preserve a fairly full pronunciation in the second syllable.

**principal, adj., n.,** by origin an adjective, and so most commonly used, as in *the principal occupations.* Also as a noun, meaning the principal person, as in *the principal of a school.* To be distinguished from *principle,* by origin a noun and used only as a noun, as in *The principle of this machine is simple,* the rule or fundamental manner of construction.

**prior to, prep.,** stiff and formal for *before,* as in *He always drinks a glass of milk prior to retiring,* before he goes to bed.

**pristine, adj.,** *early, primitive,* pronounced (prĭs′tĭn) or (prĭs′tīn)

**privy, n.,** archaic and dialectal for *outhouse.* As an adjective, as in *He was privy to all these matters,* knew about them, the use is obsolescent, the customary modern expression being *He was informed of, in touch with, aware of,* etc.

**prize, v.,** *to force open or up.* Also spelled *prise.* Colloquially and dialectally changed to *pry,* as in *He pried the door open with a crowbar.*

**pro, n.,** slang for *a professional.* Pronounced (prō), with a plural *pros* (prōz) The word belongs to the slang of sport, especially baseball, boxing, and football.

**probity, n.,** *straightforwardness, honesty,* pronounced (prŏb′ĭtĭ)

**proboscis, n.,** pedantic word for *trunk, snout,* or humorously *nose.* Pronounced (prōbŏs′ĭs) See **Polysyllabic Humor**

**process, n.,** *a method or procedure,* pronounced (prŏs′ĕs) or (prō′-sĕs), the latter being more general in England than in America.

Also used as a verb, *to process* a thing being to put it through a process, as when cloth is processed to make it waterproof.

**procès verbal,** French phrase, *report, minutes of a meeting,* pronounced (prō′sĕs vĕrbahl′)

**procrastinate, procrastinator, procrastination,** v., n., see **Polysyllabic Humor,** the simpler words being *delay, put off,* and similar terms.

**prodigy,** n., *a marvel,* pronounced (prŏd′ĭjĭ)

**produce,** v., *to bring forth, to yield,* pronounced (prodūs′) or (prodōōs′) But the noun, *the yield, that which is produced,* is pronounced (prŏd′ūs), (prŏd′ōōs), incorrectly (prō′dūs), (prō′dōōs)

**professor,** n., strictly an official title in universities or colleges given through appointment by governing boards. Often used freely, however, like *Colonel,* as a kind of title by courtesy, especially as applied to music teachers, or teachers of dancing, fencing, palmistry, and other popular arts and sciences. The abbreviation *prof* is familiar colloquial, like *doc* for *doctor.*

**profile,** n., *outline,* pronounced (prō′fēl) or (prō′fīl) The pronunciation (prō′fēl) gives the word a shade of foreign quality, but (prō′fīl) is the anglicized pronunciation. A pronunciation (prō′fĭl), see **agile,** does not occur, probably because the word is always felt to be somewhat learned or artistic, not popular.

**profiteer,** n., a recent but now well-established word for *one who takes excessive profits when he has the consumer at his mercy.*

**pro forma,** Latin phrase, *as a matter of form, for form's sake,* pronounced (prō fŏr′ma)

**prog,** n., slang for *food.*

**program,** n., *a statement of events,* also spelled *programme.* Pronounced (prō′grăm), not (prō′gram), although this latter pronunciation is in accord with a necessary tendency in the anglicization of French words with an original stress on the final syllable. If this word is to have only a stress on the first syllable, almost necessarily the second syllable must become as in (prō′gram) Only academic authority prevents (prō′gram) from becoming an accepted pronunciation of the word, but the objection to this pronunciation is still strong enough to be of some consequence.

**progress,** n., *advancement,* usually pronounced (prŏg′res), sometimes (prō′gres), and as a verb (progrĕs′) The pronunciation (prō′gres) for the noun would seem to most speakers a little old-fashioned.

**pro hac vice,** Latin phrase, *for this occasion,* pronounced (prō hăk vī′sĭ)

**prohibited,** part. adj., construed with *from,* as in *He is prohibited from making an appeal,* not *against.* But one would say *The judge issued a prohibition against making an appeal.*

**project,** n., *an undertaking,* pronounced (prŏj′ĕkt), though the verb *project* is pronounced (projĕkt′) See **perfume**

**proletariat,** n., *the common people,* pronounced (prōletā′rĭăt), with a variant spelling *proletariate,* pronounced the same.

**promenade,** n., *a formal walk, a going up and down in a public place,* pronounced (prŏmenād′), or with a slight feeling as for a foreign word, (prŏmenahd′) Also used as a verb, *to promenade,* with the same pronunciations.

**pronunciamento,** n., *a manifesto, a decree,* pronounced (pronŭn-shĭamĕn′tō) or (pronŭnsĭamĕn′tō), with a plural *pronunciamentos.* The Spanish original of this word is *pronunciamiento,* but the form **pronunciamento** is established in English usage. The Spanish word was employed usually with reference to the manifestos or decrees of a party just assuming power, that is, of insurgents, and something of this color the English word still retains.

**pronunciation,** see **enunciate**

**propaganda,** n., *an association or a plan for spreading a particular doctrine,* as in *to organize a propaganda against smoking.* Incorrectly used in the sense *doctrine* or *teaching,* as in *This propaganda was believed by thousands of people.* The noun *propa-*

*gandist* means *one active in spreading a particular doctrine.* The word is singular and is not derived from a Latin neuter plural. The plural is *propagandas.*

**properly,** adv., colloquial as an intensive, as in *He thrashed the boy good and properly,* severely, or still more colloquially, *good and proper.*

**prophesy,** v., *to foretell,* pronounced (prŏf'esī), the noun being *prophecy* (prŏf'esĭ)

**propitiate,** v., *appease,* pronounced (prōpĭsh'ĭāt), and so *propitious* (prōpĭsh'us), *propitiatory* (prōpĭsh'atŏrĭ)  The noun *propitiation* is (prōpĭshĭā'shon) or (prōpĭsĭā'shon)

**proportion,** n., *one part in relation to another part,* as in *A large proportion of the people own their own land.* The word is not to be used merely as a high-sounding substitute for *part,* as in *A proportion of his speech was devoted to the tariff,* though one might say *A large proportion of his speech* or *The larger proportion of his speech,* etc.  But *A large part* or *The larger part of his speech,* etc., is simpler, and, being simpler, is better.  The word **proportion** has definite mathematical meanings, as in *The proportion of landowners to renters is small,* or in the phrase *out of all proportion,* so great as to be out of proper relation, and to these meanings the word might be well restricted.

**proportional,** adj., *with due respect to proportions.* This is the customary form of the adjective, though *proportionate* is also used in the same way, with the two corresponding adverbs *proportionally* and *proportionately.* The adjective *proportionable* and the adverb *proportionably* have also been employed in the same senses, but these forms are now tending to fall into disuse.

**proposition,** n., a learned and technical term, as in geometry, but often incorrectly used in crude English in the general sense *enterprise, concern,* as in *The factory was not a paying proposition.*

**pro rata,** Latin phrase, *proportionally,* pronounced (prō rā'ta)

**prosit,** interj., Latin word, expression of good will in drinking one's health, literally, *may it do you good;* pronounced (prō'sĭt)

**prostrate,** adj., *prone,* pronounced (prŏs'trāt), but (prŏstrāt') for the verb.  See **perfume**

**pro tanto,** Latin phrase, *to that extent,* pronounced (prō tăn'tō)

**protean,** adj., *taking many shapes,* pronounced (prō'tĭan)

**protégé,** n., French word, *one who is under the protection of another,* pronounced (prōtezhā') or (prō'tezhā)

**protein,** see **casein**

**pro tempore,** Latin phrase, *for the time, temporary,* pronounced (prō tĕm'porĭ), and abbreviated *pro tem.* and so pronounced colloquially.

**Protestant,** adj., ordinarily understood to apply to all Christian churches not Orthodox or Roman Catholic, though members of the Anglican and Episcopal church sometimes reject the term Protestant as applying to them, maintaining that they are of the true and original church, not the protesting parts of it.

**proud,** adv., slang in the phrase *do oneself proud,* act creditably or magnanimously.

**proud possessor,** trite phrase, once slightly humorous, but even this quality has evaporated.

**proven,** v., past participle of *prove,* especially in legal use, as in the verdict *Not proven.*  Ordinarily, however, in good English the past participle, like the past tense, is *proved.*

**Provençal,** adj., *pertaining to Provence,* a region of France.  Pronounced (prōvahṅsahl')

**provided,** conj., *on the condition that,* as in *I will serve, provided you can't find anyone else.*  The form *providing* is also used in the same way, and though it is less general and more recent than **provided,** usage has now gone a long way toward making it correct.  In most instances it will be found that when **provided** is used, the simpler word *if* will more satisfactorily answer the purpose.  The conjunction **provided** is appropriate only in formal statements in which a provision is distinctly made, as in *I will accept this office provided I am not required to serve more than one year.*

**provost,** n., *an official,* especially of a college or university, pronounced (prŏv'ŏst) or (prō'vŏst)  The pronunciation (provō') is limited to specialized military uses.

**proximity,** n., *closeness, nearness.*  The word is ultimately derived from a Latin superlative, meaning *nearest,* and on this ground it is sometimes said that the English word should not take a modifier, as in *The house lies in close proximity to the town.* But the word **proximity** in English has come to mean merely nearness, and certainly there may be degrees of nearness.

**Prussia,** n., *province of Germany,* pronounced (prŭsh'a), low colloquially (prōō'sha)  So also *Prussian, Prussic,* also spelled *prussic.*

**pry,** see **prize**

**ps,** spelling, in words beginning with *pseud-, psy-,* usually pronounced (s), but in England also (ps), as in *pseudonym, psychical,* etc., (sū'donĭm), (sī'kĭkl), (psū'donĭm), (psī'kĭkl), etc.

**psalmist,** n., *author of the psalms,* pronounced (sahm'ist)  But *psalmody* is (săl'modĭ) and *psalter* is (sawl'ter)

**psychiatry,** n., *the science of mental healing.*  Pronounced (sīkī'atrĭ) or (psī-), a *psychiatrist,* (sīkī'atrĭst) or (psī-), being a practioner of psychiatry.  A term in the fashionable psychology of the day which, like *psychosis, psycho-analysis,* etc., should be used circumspectly.

**psychological moment,** trite phrase, commonly used to mean *at exactly the right moment, the appropriate moment,* or *the nick of time.*  This meaning is historically not correct, the word *moment* in this phrase having had originally the sense *momentum,* the whole phrase meaning therefore *the mental impulses conditioning an action.*  The main objection to the use of **psychological moment** now, however, lies, not in the unfaithfulness of the modern use to the historical origins of the phrase, but in the fact that the phrase has become trite and almost meaningless through much repetition.

**ptarmigan**, n., *a kind of grouse*, pronounced (tahr′mĭgan)

**pterodactyl**, n., *prehistoric animal*, pronounced (tĕrodăk′tĭl)

**Ptolemaic**, adj., formed from the noun *Ptolemy*, and current usually in the phrase *Ptolemaic system, Ptolemaic astronomy*, pronounced (tŏlemā′ĭk)

**ptomaine**, n., especially in the phrase *ptomaine poisoning*, poisoning caused by ptomaine.   Pronounced (tō′mān)

**pub**, n., British colloquial abbreviation for *public house*, place where alcoholic drinks are sold.

**public school**, n., in England *a large endowed school*, like Eton and Harrow, attended by children of the well-to-do classes, preparatory to the university.   In America free, tax-supported schools from the kindergarten through the high school.

**Puccini**, n., *Italian musical composer*, pronounced (pōōchē′nē)

**puerile**, adj., *childish*, pronounced (pū′erĭl) or (pū′erīl)   See **-ile**

**puisne**, adj., the same word as *puny* and pronounced the same, (pū′nĭ)   The form **puisne**, from French *puis né*, survives only in legal uses.

**puissant**, adj., an archaic word meaning *mighty*.   Pronounced (pū′ĭsnt)

**pull**, n., slang for *influence, power*, especially when indirectly exercised, as in *He got his job through pull.*   See **push**

**pulmonary**, adj., *pertaining to the lungs*, pronounced (pŭl′monărĭ), not (pōŏl′monărĭ)

**pumice**, n., *a kind of lava for polishing*, etc.   Usually in the combination *pumice stone*, and colloquially often abbreviated to *pummy stone*.

**pumpkin**, n., *a vegetable*, colloquially and dialectally pronounced (pŭng′kĭn), but in careful use pronounced (pŭmp′kĭn)   A still more informal pronunciation would be (pŭng′kn)

**punch,** n., slang for *vigor*, as in *He still has lots of punch in him.*

**punk,** adj., slang for *poor, worthless, unentertaining.*

**pupil,** see **student**

**purée,** n., French word, *a thick soup,* pronounced (pūrā')

**purlieu,** n., *suburb,* usually in the plural *purlieus,* pronounced (pur'lūz)

**purport,** n., *general or apparent meaning,* pronounced (pur'pört), the corresponding verb being (purpört')

**pur sang,** French phrase, *of pure blood, unqualified,* pronounced (pür sahń')

**purslane,** n., *a plant,* dialectally and colloquially pronounced (pŭs'lĭ), and sometimes written, usually humorously, as *pusley.*

**purulent,** adj., *containing or discharging pus,* pronounced (pūr'ŏŏlent)

**push,** n., slang in the sense *group, company,* as in *The judge fined the whole push.* Also slang in the sense *vigor, enterprise,* as in *If you can't get what you want by push, try pull.* See **pull**

**pushcart pedlar,** see **costermonger**

**pussyfoot,** v., *to tread lightly,* slang term applied to a person who moves about gingerly and silently, with the implication of prying into other people's business.

**put,** v., in most uses pronounced (pŏŏt), but (pŭt) as a term in golf or in throwing a stone or weight. In this second sense, sometimes spelled *putt.* The word in these various senses is of a single etymological origin.

**put case,** see **case**

**put in,** v., colloquial in the sense *spend,* as in *We put in a couple weeks camping.*

**put over,** v., slang in the phrase *put it over,* succeed in doing, securing, etc.

**puttee,** n., *bandage for the leg,* pronounced (pŭt'ĭ)

**pygmy,** n., *dwarf,* pronounced (pĭg'mĭ), and less correctly spelled *pigmy.*

**pyjamas,** n., *nightdress,* pronounced (pĭjah'maz), sometimes spelled *pajamas.* Sometimes pronounced (pĭjăm'az), but usually felt as in some way a foreign word, therefore as appropriately having an (ah) in it. The word is in fact borrowed from Persian. See **nightgown**

**Pyrrhic,** adj., usually in the phrase *Pyrrhic victory,* a victory which is virtually a defeat, from the victory of Pyrrhus at Asculum. Pronounced (pĭr'ĭk)

**python,** n., *large snake,* pronounced (pī'thon), or more formally (pī'thŏn)

## Q

**qua,** adv., Latin word, *in the capacity of,* as in *He spoke not* qua *judge, but* qua *friend.* Pronounced (kwā)

**quad,** n., colloquial abbreviation of *quadrangle,* especially in college and university communities.

**Quadragesima,** n., *first Sunday in Lent,* pronounced (kwŏdra-jĕs'ĭma), and so also (-jĕsima) in other similar compounds.

**quadratics,** see **acoustics**

**quadrille,** n., *a kind of dance,* pronounced (kwadrĭl') or (kadrĭl'), in the latter way much less frequently than in the former.

**quaere,** Latin word, *question,* often appended or prefixed to a doubtful statement. Pronounced (kwē'rĭ)

**quaff,** v., poetic for *drink,* pronounced (kwahf) Other pronunciations, like (kwăf), (kwŏf), are due to the fact that the word is not spoken often enough to establish it in an aural form, being familiar to most persons only as an eye-word.

**quagmire,** n., *swamp,* pronounced (kwŏg'mīr)

**Quai d'Orsay,** French phrase, *headquarters of the French foreign department,* pronounced (kā dŏrsā')

**quake,** n., colloquial abbreviation of *earthquake.*

**qualitative,** adj., *with respect to quality,* especially as a term in chemistry. The form *qualitive* is incorrect.

**qualm,** n., *squeamishness, misgiving,* pronounced (kwahm), with a corresponding adjective, *qualmish,* pronounced (kwahm′ĭsh)

**quandary,** n., *state of perplexity,* pronounced (kwŏn′darĭ) or (kwŏndā′rĭ), the second pronunciation being much less general in America than the first. Michaelis and Jones, *A Phonetic Dictionary of the English Language,* also give (kwŏndā′rĭ) as the exceptional pronunciation in England, although the *New English Dictionary* gives this pronunciation the first place.

**quand même,** French phrase, *all the same, nevertheless,* pronounced (kahṅ mām)

**quantitative,** adj., *with respect to quantity,* pronounced (kwŏn′-tĭtātīv) The form *quantitive* is less general. See **preventive**

**quantum libet,** Latin phrase, *as much as desired,* pronounced (kwăn′tum) or (kwŏn′tum lĭb′ĕt) and abbreviated *q. l.*

**quantum placet,** Latin phrase, *as much as desired,* pronounced (kwăn′tum) or (kwŏn′tum plā′sĕt) and abbreviated *q. p.*

**quantum sufficit,** Latin phrase, *as much as suffices,* pronounced (kwăn′tum) or (kwŏn′tum sŭf′ĭsĭt) and abbreviated *quant. suff.* or *q. s.*

**quart,** n., as a term of measure pronounced (kwŏrt); as a term in fencing pronounced (kahrt) In this second sense, also spelled *quarte,* likewise pronounced (kahrt)

**quarter,** n., colloquial for *twenty-five cent piece,* being a contraction of *a quarter of a dollar.*

**quash,** v., *annul,* pronounced (kwawsh), although the analogy of *squash* would lead one to expect (kwahsh) The pronunciation of *a* after *qu,* however, does not follow a single rule.

**quasi,** adv., Latin word, a qualifying term used as a kind of prefix, meaning *nearly, not really but seemingly,* as in *charitable and quasi-charitable institutions.* Pronounced (kwā′sī)

**quatrain,** n., *stanza of four lines,* pronounced (kwŏt′rān) or (kwŏt′-rĭn), the former being a slow and formal pronunciation, the latter the usual pronunciation of connected speech.

481

**quay,** n., *landing place for ships*, pronounced (kē) The noun *quayage*, fees for landing at a quay, is pronounced (kē′ĭj)

**quean,** n., archaic and literary for *bold girl or woman*. The word occurs now only in modern imitations of older style, especially in historical novels, and it would be pronounced as though spelled *queen*, of the same etymological origin.

**queer,** v., slang in the sense *cause to work unsatisfactorily*, literally and figuratively, as in *A little water in it will queer gasoline, He has queered the whole situation by his abruptness.*

**quell,** v., literary for *put down, crush.* The word is scarcely ever heard in daily spoken use, but it is a favorite word with journalistic writers in phrases like *quell an insurrection, quell a disturbance,* etc.

**quencher,** n., slang for *a cooling drink.*

**quenelle,** n., French word, *fish or meat ball*, pronounced (kwĕnĕl′) anglicized or (kĕnĕl′) as a French word. The word belongs to the general class of restaurant French.

**querulous,** adj., *full of complaints, fault-finding,* pronounced (kwĕr′ o͝olus)

**quest,** n., literary for *search, inquiry*, kept alive by *the quest of the holy grail* and similar phrases.

**question,** n., v., in general use both as noun, as in *I asked him a question*, and as verb, as in *I questioned him.* But on the second use, see **auction**

**questionnaire,** n., *a set of questions*, pronounced (kĕstĭŏnār′) or (kwĕs′tĭŏnār), or still further anglicized to (kwĕs′chonār) The word is French in origin, hence the pronunciation (kĕstĭŏnār′)

**queue,** n., *a braid of hair, persons or vehicles standing in a line,* pronounced (kū) The word is the same etymologically as *cue,* as in *to give one the cue, billiard player's cue,* but the meanings have been differentiated with the spellings. Literally the word means *tail.*

**quickly,** see **hastily**

**quid,** n., British slang for *a sovereign,* £ 1, with a plural of the same form. In the sense *chew of tobacco,* **quid** is a variant of *cud.*

**quid pro quo,** Latin phrase, *a return for what is given, done, etc., tit for tat,* pronounced (kwĭd prō kwō)

**quiet,** n., slang in the phrase *on the quiet,* secretly.

**quieten,** v., dialectal for *to quiet or to become quiet.* Although the verb has the support of other verbs in *-en* formed from adjectives, like *soften, harden, liven,* etc., the word **quieten** has not become general usage A similar verb occasionally heard, but likewise not in general use, is *brisken.*

**quietus,** n., *release, final disposition,* pronounced (kwīē'tus) A learned word, kept alive by a passage in *Hamlet.*

**Quincy,** n., as a place in Massachusetts pronounced (kwĭn'zĭ); as a place in Illinois and fourteen other states pronounced (kwĭn'sĭ) As a family name, as in John Quincy Adams, **Quincy** is usually pronounced (kwĭn'zĭ) in New England, and elsewhere (kwĭn'sĭ)

**quinine,** n., *a drug,* with a variety of pronunciations in acceptable use, (kwī'nīn), (kĭnēn'), (kĭnīn'), (kwĭnīn') Of these the one first given is the most generally used, but the other pronunciations have their hearty advocates. The word is of Peruvian origin, and the appeal to etymology is of no avail in deciding the pronunciation of the word in its English uses.

**quinsy,** n., *a disease of the throat,* pronounced (kwĭn'zĭ)

**quintet,** n., *set of five,* with a variant spelling *quintette.* Pronounced (kwĭntĕt') for both spellings.

**Quirinal,** n., *Italian court,* pronounced (kwĭr'ĭnal)

**quirt,** n., local western name for a *riding whip,* pronounced (kwirt)

**quit,** v., dialectal in the sense *stop, discontinue,* as in *quit teasing, quit fooling, quit work,* and in the exclamation *Quit it!* Archaic in the sense *conduct,* usually with reflexive object, as in *quit yourselves like men* or *quit you like men.*

**quite,** adv., *altogether, entirely,* as in *Are you quite ready?* Colloquially used as a mild intensive, *very*, as in *It was really quite warm today*. The constructions *quite a few, quite a little, quite some distance* are low colloquial and dialectal. If the word **quite** is used in its original sense *altogether, entirely*, it may be qualified by *almost*, as in *almost quite over the road*, almost entirely over the road, in *Pilgrim's Progress*. But the word is not frequently used in this sense nowadays, and a sentence like *His second chapter was almost quite as interesting as his first* has one word too many. It should read either *His second chapter was almost* or *was quite as interesting as his first*. In the sense *altogether, entirely*, the word **quite** is sometimes used when *still* would be more appropriate, as in *He lost his father when he was quite a child, When quite a boy at school he came under the influence of a distinguished theologian*.

**Quito,** n., *city in South America*, pronounced (kē'tō)

**quits,** adj., in good use in the phrase *to be quits*, as in *We are quits now*, even, have settled all scores. The origin of the -*s* in **quits** is not clear, but pretty certainly it has nothing to do with the *s* of the plural of nouns. Perhaps the word is an abbreviation of medieval Latin *quittus*, a variant of Latin *quietus*.

**quitter,** n., slang for *shirker*.

**qui vive,** French phrase, occurring in English especially in the expression *on the qui vive*, on the watch, on the alert. Pronounced (kē vēv)

**Quixote,** n., the name of a character in a novel by Cervantes, with an adjective *quixotic*. Pronounced (kwĭx'ot), (kwĭxŏt'ĭc) The Spanish pronunciation of **Quixote,** (kēhō'tĭ), is now less commonly used than the anglicized pronunciation, and the adjective *quixotic* would never have the Spanish pronunciation.

**quoad,** Latin word, *as regards*, **quoad hoc,** *as regards this*, pronounced (kwō'ăd hŏk)

**quod,** n., slang for *prison*, as in *to be in quod, out of quod*.

**quod erat demonstrandum,** Latin phrase, *which was to be proved* *or demonstrated,* pronounced (kwŏd ĕr'ăt dĕmonstrăn'dum) Abbreviated *Q. E. D.*

**quod vide,** Latin phrase, *which see,* in cross-references in books, documents, etc. Pronounced (kwŏd vī'dĭ) and abbreviated *q. v.*

**quoit,** n., *iron ring,* used in the game of quoits. Pronounced (koit) or (kwoit), dialectally *quait* (kwāt)

**quondam,** adj., occasional literary use for *former,* as in *a quondam friend of mine.* The word is brought over literally from Latin, and is sometimes translated as *one-time, sometime,* as in *a one-time* or *sometime friend of mine.* Pronounced (kwŏn'dam)

**quota,** n., Latin word, *share or amount to be received, contributed, etc.,* pronounced (kwō'ta)

**quote,** n., colloquial abbreviation for *quotation,* and also for *quotation mark.* In the latter sense, usually a plural, *quotes,* meaning the pair of marks inclosing a quotation, " ", sometimes called *double quotes,* as distinguished from *single quotes,* ' '.

**quote,** see **cite**

**quoth,** v., archaic for *said,* with a proper name or personal pronoun following, as in *quoth I, quoth he, quoth the judge.* The verb survives now only in imitations of older style, especially in historical novels.

**quotient,** n., *a term in arithmetic,* pronounced (kwō'shnt)

# R

**r** (r) One of the troublesome sounds of the language, the trouble being occasioned by the question whether one should or should not "pronounce one's *r's.*" The question does not apply to all **r's,** however, but only to **r** final, as in *mar,* and to **r** before a consonant, as in *mark.* The question is, should such words be pronounced (mahr), (mahrk), or (mah), (mahk)? In answer, one must say first that both pronunciations are current in good use, and therefore by the test of usage both pronunciations are correct. The question of choice between them, when such question arises, is consequently not a question of correctness but of preference. The pronunciations (mah), (mahk) for *mar*, *mark* are characteristic of the eastern and the southern types of American pronunciation, but elsewhere the pronunciations (mahr), (mahrk) prevail. If by natural custom one has a pronunciation of this latter type and wishes to alter it to one of the eastern and southern type, this is a perfectly legitimate thing to do, the wisdom of it depending upon the circumstances. And of course it is just as proper for a speaker who does not pronounce his r's to change his speech to accord with the northern and western custom. The presence of the **r** in spelling is a slight but not important argument in favor of the pronunciation with the **r** sounded. It is best frankly to recognize two definitely established types of pronunciation with respect to **r** and to make one's decisions accordingly.

**rabbet**, n., *a term in carpentry*, indistinguishable in pronunciation from *rabbit*, an animal. Sometimes spelled *rebate*, but pronounced as though written **rabbet**. The form *rebate* is the more correct etymologically, but less general in use. The two words *rabbit*, and **rabbet** are etymologically not related.

**rabbit**, n., *a dish of cheese and other ingredients*, *Welsh rabbit*. Often incorrectly etymologized as *rarebit* and so pronounced. See **prairie oyster** Phrases of this kind seem to have arisen originally as jokes, the joke consisting in giving a simple and familiar food the name of a more luxurious and exotic food, as, for example, calling codfish *Marblehead turkey*.

**Rabelais**, n., *early French writer*, pronounced (răblā′), (răbelā′), or (răb′lā), (răb′elā), or as a French word. The adjective *Rabelaisian* is (răbelā′zhĭan)

**rabies**, n., *hydrophobia*, pronounced (răb′ĭēz) or (rā′bĭēz)

**Rachmaninoff**, n., *musical composer*, pronounced (rahCHmah′nēnŏf)

**racial**, see **-al**

**rack**, n., *storm clouds, destruction*, now only a literary word, especially in the *rack of the storm*, but surviving popularly in the alliterative phrase *rack and ruin*, ruin and destruction. The word is a variant of the root that appears in *wreck*, and it is sometimes spelled *wrack*.

**racket,** n., *bat for playing tennis*, also spelled *racquet*, pronounced (răk′et), (răk′ĭt) In the plural, *rackets, racquets*, the word is the name of a game played with a racket and ball.

**raconteur,** n., French word, *teller of anecdotes*, pronounced (răkŏṅter′), with a corresponding feminine, not frequently used, *raconteuse*, pronounced (răkŏṅtöz′)

**racoon,** see **coon**

**racquet,** see **racket**

**radiotrician,** n., a new word for *one skilled in the mechanics of the radio.* Formed on the analogy of *electrician.* Sometimes given in the form *radiotician*, but there is no apparent analogy which would make *radiotician* seem a reasonable form for the word to take.

**radish,** n., *a plant and its root*, pronounced (răd′ĭsh), dialectally (rĕd′ĭsh)

**radius,** n., *a geometrical term*, pronounced (rā′dĭŭs), with a plural *radii*, pronounced (rā′dĭī) A plural *radiuses* also occurs, but the word is usually technical and takes the learned plural *radii* more appropriately than the popular anglicized form.

**raft,** n., dialectal for *large number*, as in *a whole raft of people*, perhaps by origin a figure from the notion of **raft** as a large collection of logs bound together.

**rag,** v., slang for *noisy and rough joking.* Also used as a noun in similar slang senses, and in the slang phrase *chew the rag*, talk noisily and disputatiously. See **glad rags**

**ragout,** n., *a stew*, pronounced (răgōō′) The word belongs to the general class of what may be described as restaurant French.

**Rahway,** n., *town in New Jersey*, pronounced (raw′wā)

**raillery,** n., *banter*, pronounced (rā′lerĭ) or (răl′erĭ) The latter pronunciation occurs not infrequently in cultivated speech, though some authorities do not record it.

**railroad,** n., with a synonymous term *railway.*   In Great Britain the usual word is *railway,* but **railroad** is probably more general in America as applied to long-distance steam roads.   For short and occasional tracks of rails for running handcars, trucks, etc., *railway* would be used in America.

**raiment,** n., poetic and archaic for *clothing,* pronounced (rā'ment), the pronunciation (rā'ĭment) being a spelling pronunciation arising from the infrequency of the use of the word as a spoken word.

**raise,** n., colloquial for *increase,* as in *a raise in salary.*   The manner of formation of this noun from a verb is exceptional only in that nouns are not frequently made from intransitive verbs, though they are very often made from transitive verbs. But this is nevertheless the probable reason why **raise** as a noun has not passed into general good use.

**raise,** v., low colloquial and dialectal in the sense *rear, bring up,* as in *I didn't raise my boy to be a soldier.*   See **rise** Slang in the phrases *raise Cain, raise a rumpus, raise Ned,* and various stronger terms for *behave uproariously;* also slang in *raise the wind,* raise money.

**raison d'être,** French phrase, *explanation or cause of a thing,* pronounced (rā'zŏṅ dā'tr)

**raj,** n., *sovereignty or rule,* pronounced (rahj), and to be distinguished from *rajah,* prince or king.

**rajah,** n., *East Indian prince or king,* pronounced (rah'ja)

**Raleigh, Sir Walter,** n., *English explorer and writer* (1552–1618) According to the *Dictionary of National Biography,* a more correct spelling of the name would be *Ralegh,* but **Raleigh** is customary.   As a modern proper name **Raleigh** is usually pronounced (raw'lĭ), sometimes (rǎl'ĭ)

**ramekin,** n., *small baking dish,* pronounced (rǎm'ekĭn), with a variant spelling *ramequin*, the latter reflecting the French origin of the word.

**Rameses,** n., *Egyptian name*, pronounced (răm'esēz)

**rampage,** n., facetious in the phrase *on the rampage*, from the verb *ramp*, originally applied to animals standing on their hind legs with forelegs in the air. Similar humorous words are *rampant*, *rampageous*.

**ranch,** n., formerly applied only to *a cattle ranch*, especially one on a large scale. Now extended to *chicken ranch*, *fruit ranch*, and almost any kind of farm, even one of a few acres. Limited in use to the West, but on the whole a disappearing word and suggesting now the romance of the departed West. See **plantation**

**range,** n., western usage for *grazing grounds*.

**rangy,** adj., of a horse or a man, *long, slender, and muscular*. Chiefly western usage.

**ranz-des-vaches,** French phrase, *Swiss herdsman's melody*, pronounced (rahns dā vahsh')

**Raphael,** n., *Italian painter*, pronounced (răf'ïel), not (rā'fïel)

**Rapidan,** n., *river in Virginia*, pronounced (răpïdăn')

**rapidly,** see **hastily**

**rapine,** n., *plundering, robbery*, pronounced (răp'ĭn), not (rā'pīn) The word is oratorical and rhetorical, current chiefly in ambitious journalistic style.

**rapprochement,** n., French word, *harmonious relations*, usually as a diplomatic term. Pronounced (răprŏshmahn')

**rara avis,** Latin phrase, *something rarely met with*, literally, *a rare bird;* pronounced (rā'ra ā'vĭs)

**rare,** adj., *not well done*, especially of meat. Not generally current in England, the equivalent term there being *underdone*. The opposite of **rare** is *well done*.

**rarebit,** see **rabbit**

**rase,** v., *to level to the ground*, pronounced (rāz), not (rās) See **raze**

**Rasselas,** n., *name of a character in a book by Dr. Johnson,* pronounced (răs'elas)

**rate,** n., *local or municipal assessment,* usually in the plural. The word is more generally used in this sense in England than in America, the American equivalent being *town or city taxes.*

**rathe,** adj., archaic and poetic for *early blooming,* as in *the rathe primrose.* Pronounced (rādh)

**rather,** adv., colloquial as a strong affirmative, as in *"Do you know him?" "Rather!"* —with the implication of knowing him too well. Usually pronounced (rădh'er), rarely (rah'dher)

**rathskeller,** n., *eating and drinking place,* pronounced (rahts'-kĕler) The word is by origin German, and it has not commonly been anglicized in pronunciation. See **Zeitgeist**

**ratio,** n., *term in mathematics,* pronounced (rā'shĭō) or (rā'shō) The noun *ratiocination* is pronounced (rătĭōsĭnā'shon), and *rational* is (răsh'onal)

**ration,** n., *a regular allowance, especially of food,* pronounced (rā'shon) or (răsh'on), the latter being the more general and the established pronunciation in military uses.

**rationale,** n., Latin word, *raison d'être,* pronounced (răshonā'lĭ), less correctly (răshonāl') See **locale, morale,** these being French words.

**ratline,** n., *small rope in a ship's rigging,* but usually in the plural, *ratlines,* with a variant *ratlin, ratlins* and another *ratling, ratlings.* The etymology of the word is unknown, and both the form *rat-* and the form *-line* are probably due to popular etymology.

**rats,** n., slang exclamation, *nonsense,* or varied shades of scornful and contemptuous feeling. Now a bit archaic as slang, belonging to the same period as *How'd you like to be the ice man?* and *I should smile!*

**rattle,** v., slang in the sense *disconcert.*

**ratty,** adj., slang in the sense *shabby, worn,* as in *This dress looks pretty ratty.*

**raucous,** adj., *hoarse, rough,* pronounced (raw'kus), not (raw'shus)

**ravel,** v., with two opposite meanings: (1) *to complicate, entangle;* (2) *to disentangle, to separate into threads.* The words **ravel** and *unravel* may therefore have the same meaning. In the sense *disentangle, fray,* the form of the verb is often *ravel out.* In the sense *complicate,* **ravel** is commonly used only in the past participle, as in *the raveled skein of life.*

**raven,** v., *seek prey,* but usually only in the present participle, as in *ravening beasts, I am ravening,* fiercely hungry. Pronounced (răv'en), and so also the adjective *ravenous* (răv'enus) The noun *ravin* (răv'in) is a literary variant of *rapine,* meaning *plunder, booty.*

**raven hair, locks,** trite phrases, survivals from an old-fashioned pompous poetical diction.

**ravishing,** adj., colloquial intensive for a variety of approving senses, as in *a ravishing hat, a ravishing time,* etc. See **elegant, fine, great, wonderful**

**raw,** adj., colloquial in the sense *inconsiderate, unjust,* as in *I call that a raw deal.*

**raze,** v., *destroy,* especially in the phrase *raze to the ground,* with a variant spelling *rase.* Not etymologically the same word as *raise,* though indistinguishable from it in pronunciation. The word is chiefly literary, the customary expression being *tear down, destroy.*

**re,** prep., the ablative case of the Latin word *res,* and used commonly in legal and business documents as a heading, as in *Re the new building,* with respect to, concerning the new building; sometimes used also in connected discourse, as in *The discussion re the new building was animated.* Not good style, however, as a substitute for *concerning, about,* in ordinary discourse.

**re-,** prefix with the primary sense of *repetition, again, return to,* and a part of many words in which this meaning as a separate element is no longer clearly felt, as in *recommend, recognize,* etc. In such words, the prefix is usually pronounced (rĕ-) or (rĭ-) When a new compound is made, with the sense of the prefix clearly in mind, as in *re-collect*, collect again, as distinguished from *recollect*, remember, *re-condition*, to put into good condition again, the prefix is pronounced (rē-), and is usually followed by a hyphen, though the hyphen may be omitted, especially when there is no danger of confusing the new compound with an old one. Thus one would write *recreation* (rĕkrĭā′shon), but *re-creation* (rēkrĭā′shon) A word like *recast* (rēkăst′), however, would be written without a hyphen. The hyphen is also used to avoid an awkward combination of letters, as in *re-echo* (rēĕk′ō)

**reaction,** n., recent colloquial usage in the sense *response*, as in *What was his reaction to your question?*, meaning How did he take your question? This seems to be a figure taken from chemistry, as when one chemical substance is said to react upon another, meaning, merely, produce changes in it. As applied to mental states, in the sense opinion, response, answer, impression, **reaction** is a pedagogic and academic word, now popular in these circles.

**Reading,** n., *place name in England and America*, pronounced (rĕd′ĭng)

**real,** adv., dialectal and low colloquial in the sense *very*, as in *He isn't feeling real well.* The standard form of the adverb is *really*, as in *Is it really true?*

**realize,** v., colloquial and commercial in the sense *receive, obtain*, as in *He realized twenty-five thousand dollars by the sale of this property.*

**realtor,** n., *real estate broker*. A coined word adopted by the National Association of Real Estate Boards in 1916 for the use of its members only. The word was made on the analogy of words of Latin origin, like *doctor, debtor, creditor, inventor*, etc., but the analogy was not complete, most words in *-or* having as their first elements words derived from verbs, whereas the first element of **realtor** is an adjective.  See **Hybrids**

**Réaumur,** French word, *name of a man,* and used in a system of measuring temperature, pronounced (rā′ōmūr) or (rāōmür′)

**rebate,** see **rabbet**

**recalcitrant,** adj., *refractory,* pronounced (rĭkăl′sĭtrant) The word is learned; therefore, if used at all, should be used only with the accepted learned pronunciation.

**receipt,** see **recipe**

**recess,** n., according to dictionary authority, stressed only on the second syllable, both in the sense *period of intermission* and in the sense *niche, alcove, indented place.*  In good colloquial use, however, frequently stressed on the first syllable, especially in the sense *period of intermission.*

**réchauffé,** part. adj., n., French word, *warmed up, a rehash,* pronounced (rāshōfā′)

**recherché,** adj., French word, *notably good and choice,* pronounced (rĕshārshā′), or anglicized, (rĭshār′shā)

**recipe,** n., pronounced (rĕs′ĭpē), incorrectly (rĭsēp′) on the analogy of the synonymous word *receipt.*  There is no distinction of meaning between *receipt* and *recipe* in the sense *directions for cooking, baking,* etc.

**reciprocal,** adj., *mutual, in return,* pronounced (rĭsĭp′rokal), with a noun *reciprocity* (rĕsĭprŏs′ĭtĭ)

**recitative,** n., *declamatory singing,* pronounced (rĕsĭtatēv′)

**reck,** v., literary for *care, heed,* as in phrases like *little he recks, what recks it him,* concerns him, *what recks he of mercy,* cares about mercy.

**reckon,** v., *to calculate or count up.*  In colloquial and dialectal, especially southern use, the word frequently occurs in the sense *think, suppose.*  See **calculate, figure**

**réclame,** n., French word, *art of securing notoriety,* pronounced (rāklahm′)

**recluse,** n., *hermit, retiring person,* pronounced (rĭklōōs'), not (rĕk'lōōs)

**recognizance,** see **cognizance**

**recognize,** v., *to know again,* pronounced (rĕk'ognĭz), the pronunciation (rĕk'onĭz) being low colloquial and dialectal, or, at best, very informal. See **cognizance**

**recommend to,** v., cannot be taken as indicating a preference between two possibilities, as in *Physicians recommend coddled eggs to boiled ones,* for *Physicians recommend coddled eggs in preference to* (or *as better than*) *boiled ones.* The phrase *recommend to* means *advise to use,* etc., as in *Physicians recommend coddled eggs to all their patients.*

**recondite,** adj., *abstruse,* pronounced (rĕk'ondĭt), less commonly (rĭkŏn'dĭt)

**reconnaissance,** n., *exploratory survey,* pronounced (rĭkŏn'ĭsans) The word occurs chiefly in military uses, and though of French origin it has been anglicized in pronunciation.

**reconnoitre,** v., *investigate, make reconnaissance,* pronounced (rĕkonoi'ter)

**recreant,** adj., n., literary for *cowardly, unfaithful,* and as a name for such a person. Pronounced (rĕk'rĭant)

**rector,** n., the ordinary term in the United States for an Episcopal clergyman having charge of a congregation. In England the word has a more precise official meaning. See **minister, vicar**

**rectory,** see **manse**

**recuperate,** v., *recover health,* pronounced (rĭkū'perāt), though also frequently, but less correctly, (rĭkōō'perāt)

**recusant,** n., *one who refuses compliance,* pronounced (rĭkū'zant), not (rĕk'ūzant) So also the noun *recusancy* is pronounced (rĭkū'zansĭ) The word has a special sense in English history as designating persons who refused to attend the services of the Anglican church.

**red,** adj., colloquial in the phrases *not to have, not to care a red cent;*

*to see things red*, to be angry.  As a noun, *a red* is colloquial for an anarchist, a follower of the red flag, or sometimes even for any radical.

**rede,** v., archaic for *advise*, but surviving in the phrase *rede a riddle*, interpret it, sometimes incorrectly given as *read a riddle*.

**redolent,** adj., *having the smell of*, as in *redolent of cooking*, pronounced (rĕd'olent)  The term usually implies a strong and disagreeable odor.

**redress,** v., n., *to put right*, and as a noun *compensation*, both pronounced (rĭdrĕs')  As a new compound, *to dress again*, as in to *re-dress a wound*, pronounced (rē-drĕs')  See **re-**

**reduce,** v., colloquial in the sense *reduce weight by dieting*, as in *I can't eat any potatoes, I am reducing now.*

**reductio ad absurdum,** Latin phrase, *proving something false by showing that it leads to an absurdity*, pronounced (rĭdŭk'tĭō ăd ăbsur'dum)

**reeve,** v., nautical term for *threading a rope or some other object through a ring*, with a past tense *rove* or *reeved.*

**referable,** adj., *susceptible of being referred*, pronounced (rĕf'erabl), often incorrectly (rĭfer'able) from the analogy of the verb *to refer* (rĭfer')

**refer back,** v., a crude pleonasm for *refer*, this word alone being sufficient.  See **connect up**

**referee,** n., v., as a noun, *an umpire;* as a verb, *to act as umpire.* The verb is sometimes questioned, but it is in good use.

**reflex,** n., adj., *something reactive, responsive*, pronounced (rē'flĕks)

**refulgent,** adj., literary for *shining, very bright*, pronounced (rĭfŭl'jent)

**refuse,** v., n., adj., as a verb pronounced (rĭfūz') in the sense *deny a request*, but (rēfūz') in the sense *fuse again*.  As a noun, *rejected or worthless material*, and as an adjective pronounced (rĕf'ūz)  The noun *refusal* is pronounced (rĭfūz'al)

**regardless,** adj., *not heeding or considering*, but also used as an adverb in low colloquial speech, or humorous imitations of it, as in *He spent his money regardless*, recklessly. Through confusion with *irrespective*, and incorrectly, *irregardless* is sometimes used.

**regards,** v., correctly used, but in rather stilted commercial style, in the phrase *as regards*, as in *The firm is in good condition as regards its credit*, so far as its credit is concerned. Somewhat similar is the phrase *with regard*, and the present participle *regarding*, as in *Regarding its credit, the firm is in good condition*. It is incorrect, however, to say *with regards*, this being a mixture of *as regards* and *with regard*. Sentences containing *as regards* can usually be improved by simplifying. Thus the sentence given above would be better *The credit of the firm is in good condition*.

**régie,** n., French word, *state monopoly*, pronounced (rāzhē′)

**regime,** n., *system or organization of things*, pronounced (rĕzhēm′), and also written as a French word, *régime*.

**register,** v., *to express by expression of face*, a meaning derived from the technical vocabulary of the moving pictures and still felt to be on the border between slang and colloquialism.

**regular,** adj., a colloquial intensive meaning *thorough*, as in *He's a regular genius at word-coining*, and in the phrase *regular fellow*, good companion.

**Reichstag,** n., *German deliberative body*, pronounced (rīCHs′tahg), not (rīshs′tahg) or (rīsh′tahg)  On the capitalization of German nouns, see **Zeitgeist**

**Reims,** n., *city in France*, not *Rheims*, according to the decision of the United States Geographic Board. The anglicized form **Reims** is pronounced (rīmz) or (rēmz)  The French spelling is *Rheims*, pronounced (răṅs)

**relation,** n., *kinsman, kinswoman*, with a synonym *relative*. Both **relation**(s) and *relative*(s) are in good use, with perhaps a slight preference in favor of *relative*(s)  One objection to **relation**(s) is that it suggests the idea of friendly or cordial relations, as in *The relations between them are strained*, whereas *relative(s)* implies merely the idea of being related.

**relevé**, n., French word, *the course following the entrée in a dinner*, pronounced (rĕlĕvā´)

**reliable**, adj., *that which may be depended on*. There can be no question that **reliable** is now in good general use, as in *reliable information, a reliable person*, but echoes of many battles over this word which took place in the last generation are still to be heard. The objections to the word **reliable** were based on the assertion that the word is not properly formed. As we can not *rely a person*, but only *rely on a person*, so the adjective should not be **reliable**, but *rely-on-able*, like *come-at-able*. The logic of this objection is sound, but in answer it may be said that if the word had been made *rely-on-able*, quite certainly it would not have passed into general use as extensively as **reliable** has done; and second, that **reliable**, whatever the defects of the manner of its formation, has established itself in the general custom of the language. It is now too late to object to **reliable**, too late because futile. And if **reliable** were rejected because it ought to be *rely-on-able*, *dependable* also would have to go because it should be *depend-on-able*, and *dispensable* because it should be *dispense-with-able*, and *indispensable* for *indispense-with-able*, and *disposable* for *dispose-of-able*, and *unaccountable* for *unaccount-for-able*. See **-ible**

**relict**, n., *widow*, chiefly in legal use. Pronounced (rĕl´ĭkt)

**religious**, n., *a member of a monastic order*, as in *Any indication of the lives and characters of pre-Reformation religious is previous*, Gasquet, *Monastic Life*, p. 121. This use of **religious** as a noun is not very general, is indeed somewhat technical ecclesiastical use, but it is well established.

**reliquiae**, n., Latin word, *remains, relics*, pronounced (rĭlĭk´wĭē)

**reluct**, v., *to show reluctance*. A rare and artificial literary word, being a back formation from the noun *reluctance*, like *enthuse* from *enthusiasm*. See **burgle**

**remedial,** adj., *curative, corrective,* pronounced (rĭmē′dĭal), and to be distinguished from *remediable,* that which may be cured or corrected, pronounced (rĭmē′dĭabl)

**reminisce,** v., *to recall.* A back formation from the noun *reminiscence,* fairly widely current in careless colloquial use, but employed by careful speakers and writers only facetiously. See **burgle**

**remit,** v., usually a transitive verb, as in *to remit a punishment, to remit a thousand dollars,* but in business English also used as an intransitive in the sense *send a check for,* as in *Please let me know the amount and I will remit.* The word is also sometimes an intransitive in the sense *slacken, grow less,* as in *After several hours, the pain began to remit.*

**remonstrate,** v., *protest,* pronounced (rĭmŏn′strāt), not (rĕm′onstrāt), although this latter pronunciation may be heard now and then from cultivated speakers and has the analogy of *demonstrate* (dĕm′onstrāt) in its favor.

**renaissance,** n., *the revival of learning,* and any similar revival. This is the French form of the word, and it is usually pronounced (rĭnā′sens) or as in French, approximately (rĕnāsahńs′) The word is often anglicized as *renascence,* pronounced (rĭnăs′ens) or (rĭnā′sens), and in the interests of simplicity this anglicized form is certainly much to be preferred.

**Renan,** n., *French writer,* pronounced (rĭnăn′) or (rĕnahń′)

**rencontre,** n., French word, *a meeting,* usually hostile, pronounced (rahńkŏń′tr)

**rencounter,** n., archaic and literary for *encounter.* See **rencontre**

**rend,** v., archaic and literary for *split, tear,* but surviving in *heart-rending,* low colloquially often *heart-rendering.* The past tense and past participle of **rend** is *rent.*

**render a selection,** trite phrase, from the language of routine newspaper reporting.

**rendezvous,** n., *appointment or place of appointment,* pronounced (rŏn′dĭvōō) or (rĕn′dĭvōō), the former being closer to the pronunciation of the French original, the latter a more completely anglicized pronunciation of the word.

**renege,** v., *to revoke.* A colloquial term in card playing, pronounced (rĭnēg′), dialectally (rĭnĭg′)

**Rensellaer,** n., *family name,* pronounced (rĕn′seler)

**rep,** n., *a cloth material,* with variants *repp, reps* (rĕps)

**rep,** n., slang for *disreputable person,* being an abbreviation of *disreputable.*

**reparable,** adj., *susceptible of being restored or made good,* as of injury, loss, etc., pronounced (rĕp′arabl), and to be distinguished from *repairable,* which is used only in the literal sense of that which may be repaired. The word **reparable** is more frequently used in the negative, *irreparable,* pronounced (ĭrĕp′arabl), than in the positive form.

**repartee,** n., *a witty answer, a return thrust,* pronounced (rĕpartē′) Sometimes incorrectly pronounced (rĕp′artā) on the supposition that the final *ee* is similar to the final *ee* in *matinée* and other French words. The word **repartee** is of French origin, but the French form of the word would be *repartie,* not *repartée.*

**repeat,** v., should not be used in the pleonastic phrase *repeat again,* since **repeat** alone means to say or do again.

**repertoire,** n., pronounced (rĕp′ertwahr) This word means *a stock of pieces at the command of a performer or company,* and is to be distinguished from *repertory,* which means *a store of information or facts,* as in *The dictionary is a great repertory of facts.* But occasionally *repertory* is used as an anglicized form of **repertoire.**

**replete with interest,** trite phrase, of a stiff literary kind.

**replica,** n., *a copy or duplicate of a work of art;* strictly, one made by the artist himself, that is, a repetition, but loosely used of any copy or facsimile. Pronounced (rĕp′lĭka)

**répondez s'il vous plaît,** French phrase, *please answer*, pronounced (räpŏn'dā sēl vōō plä')

**Repplier,** n., *American writer*, pronounced (rĕplēr')

**reptile,** n., *snake*, pronounced (rĕp'tĭl) or (rĕp'tīl)   See **-ile**

**reputable,** adj., *having good reputation*, pronounced (rĕp'ūtabl), incorrectly (rĭpūt'abl) under the influence of the verb *repute* (rĭpūt')

**requiem,** n., *funeral chant*, pronounced (rē'kwĭem) or (rĕk'wĭem)

**requiescat in pace,** Latin phrase, *may (he, she) rest in peace*, pronounced (rĕkwĭĕs'kăt ĭn pā'sĭ)   The plural is *requiescant in pace* (rĕkwĭĕs'kănt ĭn pā'sĭ)

**requisite,** adj., n., *needed, the thing needed*, pronounced (rĕk'wĭzĭt)

**reredos,** n., *ornamental screen above an altar*, pronounced as a dissyllable, (rēr'dŏs)

**res angusta domi,** Latin phrase, *the poverty or simplicity of home*, pronounced (rēz ănggŭs'ta dō'mī)

**research,** n., *scientific investigation*, pronounced (rĭserch')   The pronunciation (rēserch') is sometimes used, but would more appropriately mean *search again*.   See **re-**

**reservoir,** n., *storage place for liquids*, pronounced (rĕz'ervwahr), dialectally (rĕz'ervoier), (rĕz'evoier)   As the word is current in general popular use, there exists a strong tendency to anglicize it, and a natural anglicized pronunciation would be (rĕz'evoier)   At present, however, this pronunciation has not made its way into standard cultivated use.

**reside,** v., a formal word for *live*, often ostentatiously used when the simpler word would be more appropriate.   See **residence**

**residence,** n., formal word for *house, home*, and often used when the simpler words would be more appropriate.   The word sometimes has official uses, as in *the residence*, the official dwelling of a governor, etc.

**residenter,** n., low colloquial and humorous for *resident*, especially in the phrase *an old residenter*.

**residential,** adj., *of residences,* pronounced (rĕzĭdĕn'shal), also *residentiary* (rĕzĭdĕn'sharĭ) Although the adjective forms *residental, residentary* are properly formed and perhaps the ones that the language might be expected to adopt, they are nevertheless not in current use and never have been.

**resign,** v., usually construed with *from,* as in *After two months he resigned from the presidency.* In England the object would follow the verb directly, *he resigned the presidency.* This latter usage is also current in America.

**resilience,** n., *power of recovery,* pronounced (rĭzĭl'ĭens), not (rĭsĭl'ĭens)

**resin,** n., *an exudation from plants.* The word *rosin* is a variant of the same word, but *rosin* usually means a solidified **resin,** especially from pine trees, **resin** being the generalized term and the one from which derivatives are made, e. g., *resinous, resiniferous, resinol.*

**res judicata,** Latin phrase, *something already passed upon,* literally, *a thing judged;* pronounced (rēz jōōdĭkā'ta)

**resolve,** v., usually intransitive in the sense *come to the resolution,* and a sentence like *This experience resolved me to learn the language of the country as quickly as possible,* with the verb used transitively, is colloquial, or perhaps verging on the low colloquial. See **determine**

**resound,** v., *to ring with, be filled with,* pronounced (rĭzownd'), and so also the adjective *resounding* (rĭzownd'ĭng)

**resource,** n., *supply, stock to draw upon,* pronounced (rĭsôrs'), with a plural (rĭsôrs'ez) Low colloquially often pronounced (rē'sôrs), (rē'sôrsez)

**respectively,** adv., *each in relation to his own situation.* The word should be used only when it is necessary to keep two sets of statements apart in their proper relations, as in *Mr. Smith and Mr. Jones were elected respectively secretary and president,* that is, Mr. Smith was elected secretary and Mr. Jones president, which would be the simpler and less pedantic way of expressing the meaning. It is incorrect to use **respectively** merely in the sense *individually, each,* as in *All the clerks have respectively three weeks' vacation.* In a sentence like this, **respectively** is not needed at all. "The simple fact is," says Fowler, *Tract No. IX,* Society for Pure English, p. 26, "that *respective(ly)* are words seldom needed, but which a pretentious writer will drag in at every opportunity for the air of thoroughness and precision they are supposed to give to a sentence."

**respite,** n., *delay,* pronounced (rĕs'pĭt), and so also the verb, *to respite.* The analogy of the word *spite* (spīt) often affects the pronunciation of this word in low colloquial speech, causing it to be pronounced (respīt'), especially in the verb.

**restaurant,** n., *public eating place,* pronounced (rĕs'tarant), or more colloquially (rĕs'trant) The pronunciation (rĕs'tarawnt) is a partial attempt at a French pronunciation.

**restive,** adj., *restless, fretting.* An older form *restiff* is no longer in use, and **restive** also shows signs of obsolescence, with *restless* taking its place.

**resume,** v., usually active and transitive, as in *They resumed the fight,* they continued the fight, but occasionally in literary use employed as though it were a passive, as in *The fight began in the house and resumed on the sidewalk,* was continued.

**résumé,** n., French word, *summary statement,* pronounced (rāzōōmā')

**retch,** v., *the motion of vomiting,* pronounced (rēch) or (rĕch) Not etymologically the same word as the verb *to reach.*

**retire,** v., formal, and often unnecessarily formal for *go to bed.*

**retribution,** n., *recompense for evil,* pronounced (rĕtrĭbū'shon), with an adjective *retributive* (rĭtrĭb'ūtĭv)

**retrospect,** n., *backward view,* pronounced (rĕt'rōspĕkt), not (rē'trōspĕkt)

**retroussé,** adj., French word, *turned up,* of a nose, pronounced (rĕtrōōsā')

**reveille,** n., *a morning signal.* The word is of French origin, but it has been more or less anglicized and is used in a variety of pronunciations. The one least general and nearest to the French is (revāl′y) In the United States army service it is pronounced (rĕvelē′) or (rĕv′elē) In Great Britain the current pronunciation is (revĕl′ĭ)

**revenue,** n., *income,* especially of a state. The current pronunciation is (rĕv′enū), but formerly (revĕn′ū) also occurred and still survives in legal and parliamentary usage in England.

**Reverend,** adj., as a title usually abbreviated, *Rev.,* and used with the given name, or initial, as well as the surname following, as in *Rev. John Smith,* or *the Rev. John Smith,* but low colloquial with only the surname, as in *Rev. Smith,* or *the Rev. Smith.* Not used in direct address, as *Professor* or *Doctor* may be.

**reverent,** adj., *showing respect, esteem,* as in *reverent silence,* respectful, worshipful silence. To be distinguished from **reverend,** deserving or eliciting reverence, as in *a man of very reverend aspect,* one who by his appearance causes others to be reverent.

**revolt,** n., v., pronounced (rĭvōlt′), rarely (rĭvŏlt′) In the sense *feel revulsion,* **revolt,** v., is construed with *at, against,* or *from,* as in *Even a savage would revolt at,* or *against,* or *from such an action.* In the sense *rise against,* **revolt** is construed with *against* or *from,* as in *His subjects revolted from* or *against his iron rule,* or *were in revolt from* or *against,* etc.

**revue,** n., French word, *a loosely constructed theatrical performance,* pronounced (rĕvü′), but also anglicized sometimes in spelling and pronunciation to *review.*

**Revue des Deux Mondes,** n., *name of a French journal,* pronounced (rĕvü′ dā dö mŏnd), that is, approximately as a French phrase.

**Reykjavik,** n., *city in Iceland,* pronounced (rāk′yahvēk) The United States Geographic Board rejects other variant spellings.

**Reynard,** n., traditional name for *the fox,* pronounced (rĕn′ard) This is the French form of the name, and the one most commonly used, but it appears also in other characteristic forms in most of the languages of Europe.

**rez de chausée,** French phrase, *the ground floor, au rez de chausée,* on the ground floor, pronounced (ō rä de shōsä′)

**Rheims,** see **Reims**

**Rhenish,** adj., *pertaining to the Rhine,* pronounced (rĕn′ĭsh)

**rheumatics,** n., colloquial for *rheumatism,* pronounced (rŏōmăt′-ĭks), and *rheumatism,* (rŏō′matĭzm)

**rheumatiz,** n., dialectal for *rheumatism,* and probably more current in literary than in actually spoken dialects.

**rhino,** n., slang for *money,* pronounced (rī′nō), and one of an infinite number of slang terms for this stimulating notion.

**rhinoceros,** n., with the same form for singular and plural, and with a colloquial abbreviation *rhino,* plural *rhinos,* pronounced (rī′nō), (rī′nōz) A plural *rhinoceroses* sometimes occurs, likewise a learned form *rhinocerotes* (rīnŏserō′tēz), but the most frequently used plural is **rhinoceros.**

**rhyme,** n., *a term in versification,* with a variant *rime.* The spelling *rime* is the older and closer to the etymological origin of the word, but **rhyme** is the prevailing literary form of the word. Under the influence of theories of spelling reform, however, *rime* is becoming more widely used and would ordinarily be accepted now as a correct spelling.

**Rhys,** n., *family name,* pronounced (rēs)

**rhythm,** n., *arrangement of sounds,* pronounced (rĭdh′m), rarely (rĭth′m) The adjective form is *rhythmic, rhythmical,* pronounced (rĭdh′mĭk), (rĭdh′mĭkal), less commonly (rĭth-) The form *rhythmic* is poetic, oratorical, and literary, *rhythmical* being the more literally descriptive of the two terms.

**ribald,** adj., *irreverent, jeering,* pronounced (rĭb′ald)

**riband,** n., occasional but obsolescent spelling of *ribbon.*

**ribbons,** n., slang for *reins,* in the phrases *take the ribbons, handle the ribbons,* for *to drive a horse* or *horses.*

**Richelieu, Cardinal,** n., *French statesman* (1584–1642), usually pronounced (rĭsh'elo͞o), that is, partly anglicized, though of course it may be pronounced as a French word.

**riches,** n., *wealth.* Etymologically a singular and so construed sometimes, but ordinarily taken as a plural, as in *Riches are not always a blessing, Riches take to themselves wings and fly away.* See **alms**

**rickets,** see **measles**

**ricochet,** v., *to glance or skip along,* pronounced (rĭkōshā') The word is of French origin and has not been anglicized in pronunciation.

**rid,** v., dialectal in the sense *to make tidy,* as in *to rid up a room.* Also current dialectally in the form *red.*

**rifle,** n., dialectal name for *a scythe sharpener, a whetstone.*

**rig,** n., colloquial for *equipage, horse and wagon,* or almost any kind of "outfit." Also *jigmarig, thingamarig,* etc. See **gadget** Also current in the sense *a prank, a trick, a joke,* but more general in this sense in England than in America.

**Riga,** n., *name of a city,* pronounced (rē'ga)

**right,** adv., dialectal in the phrases *right off,* at once, without hesitation, *right smart,* in considerable numbers, *right glad,* very glad, *right down sorry,* very sorry. Colloquial in the sense *straight, at once,* as in *He walked right into the water,* and *sane,* as in *He isn't quite right.* Colloquial also in the phrase *right along,* as in *He has been doing that right along,* persistently, continually, and in *right away,* at once.

The two forms of the adverb are **right** and *rightly,* the latter being slightly more formal than **right.** Thus one may say *You have answered right* or *rightly, Did I understand you right* or *rightly? You have spelled the word right* or *rightly.* See **aright**

**righteous,** adj., *good, just,* pronounced (rī'chŭs), only affectedly (rī'tĭŭs) See **beauteous** The word usually implies a self-conscious goodness and is used chiefly in the compound *self-righteous.*

**right-hand side,** n., colloquial for *right side.* So also *left-hand side.*

**rigid,** adj., *stiff, unyielding,* to be distinguished from *rigorous,* harsh, stern, severe. One speaks of a pole, a leg or arm as being *rigid* when it is fixed and stiff, but phrases like *a rigid economy, a very rigid bringing up* are usually incorrect for *a rigorous economy, a rigorous bringing up.*

**rigmarole,** n., a colloquial and satirical term for *a long string of words.*

**rigor,** n., in the sense *severity* pronounced (rĭg′or), but as a medical term meaning *chill, shivering,* etc., usually pronounced (rī′gor), especially in the Latin phrase *rigor mortis* (rī′gor mŏr′tĭs), the stiffening of the body after death.

**rigorous,** see **rigid**

**rigsdag,** n., Danish word, *the Danish parliament,* pronounced (rēgz′dahg) The Swedish parliament is the *riksdag,* pronounced (rēks′dahg)

**Riis,** n., *family name,* pronounced (rēs)

**rile,** v., colloquial and dialectal for *to anger, vex,* and sometimes spelled *roil,* after an older fashion, though always pronounced (rīl) Also an adjective *riley* (rī′lĭ), often spelled *roily.*

**rime,** n., literary and archaic for *hoarfrost.* See also **rhyme**

**ring,** n., colloquial in the sense *a controlling body of self-interested persons.* Slang in the phrase *make rings around,* greatly surpass, as in *He can make rings around me at tennis,* and also in the sense *telephone call,* as in *I'll give you a ring at noon.*

**ring,** v., slang in the phrase *ring one in,* to find a place for on a program, etc. The past tense of **ring** is ordinarily *rang,* sometimes *rung.* The past participle is always *rung.*

**rinse,** v., *to cleanse with water.* Pronounced (rĭns), dialectally (rĕnch) by confusion with *wrench.* A pronunciation (rĭnz) is also current in good use.

**rip,** n., slang for *disreputable person or horse.* See **rep**

**Ripon,** n., *English town and cathedral,* pronounced (rĭp′on)

**ripper,** n., slang for *first-rate person or thing.*

**ripping,** adj., slang as a general intensive of approval, *fine, splendid,* etc. More generally used in England than in America, the common equivalent term in America being *great.*

**rise,** n., *ascent, increase,* as in *a rise in salary.* Pronounced (rīz), the same as the verb. By theorists sometimes pronounced (rīs) to distinguish the noun from the verb. As a synonym for *increase,* **rise** is somewhat colloquial. In the sense *response, retort,* as in *I mentioned the matter to him, but never got a rise out of him,* the word is slang, being a figure taken from trout fishing.

**rise,** v., the correct form of the verb to use in speaking of bread as it becomes light through the action of yeast. In popular dialects, confusion exists between the intransitive **rise** and *raise,* the latter being always intransitive and often incorrectly used for the former, as in *My bread didn't raise, Raise up.*

**risqué,** adj., French word, *doubtfully proper,* pronounced (rĭskā′)

**ritzy,** adj., slang for *smart, fashionable,* from the name the Ritz-Carlton and other fashionable Ritz hotels.

**rive,** v., literary for *split, cleave,* with a past tense *rived* and a past participle *riven,* pronounced (rīv), (rīvd), (rĭv′n), as in the phrase *the riven oak.*

**Riviera,** n., *French geographical name,* pronounced (rĭvyĕr′a)

**roast,** n., v., slang in the sense *banter, chaff,* or also in stronger senses, *reprehend, rebuke scathingly.* The figure is obviously that of language being warm enough to roast its victim.

**roasting ears,** n., *sugar corn.* But **roasting ears** is now passing out of use, perhaps because roasting is no longer a common way of preparing corn.

**robe,** n., poetic and literary for *dress, long and flowing garment,* but restored to general use in the compound *bath-robe.*

**Robert College,** n., *college in Constantinople,* not *Roberts.*

**robust,** adj., *vigorous,* pronounced (rōbŭst′), not (rō′bŭst)

**rocker,** n., colloquial for *rocking-chair.*

**rocks,** n., *money,* one of the innumerable slang terms for this idea.

**rocky,** adj., slang for *not well,* "*seedy.*"

**rodeo,** n., *a riding exhibition,* pronounced (rōdā′ō), (rōdē′o), and colloquially often (rō′dĭō) This last pronunciation is etymologically incorrect, the word having been taken over from Spanish in the West and Southwest. As the word becomes anglicized, however, it is probable that the pronunciation (rō′dĭō) will gain in frequency and respectability.

**rogue,** n., *rascal,* pronounced (rōg), and *roguery* (rō′gerĭ), *roguish* (rō′gĭsh)

**roi fainéant,** French phrase, *figurehead,* literally, *idle king;* pronounced (rwah fānāahṅ′)

**roil,** see **rile**

**rôle,** n., *actor's part,* pronounced (rōl) The word is French in origin, and though very generally used, and often without any realization that it is a French word, nevertheless in writing and printing the word still ordinarily takes the French circumflex accent over the vowel.

**romance,** adj., v., n., in all uses pronounced (rōmăns′), not (rō′măns) Though this latter pronunciation is in accord with English analogies, and though **romance** has been a current word in English since the Middle English period, nevertheless the anglicized pronunciation (rō′măns) has not made its way into good usage.

**romaunt,** n., archaic and literary for *romance,* a tale of chivalry. Pronounced (rōmahnt′), and current now only in artificial imitations of medieval style.

**Romish,** adj., a hostile or opprobrious adjective designating the Roman Catholic church, having taken this color by usage, though by origin the suffix in **Romish** would be no more significant than the suffix in *English,* *Spanish,* etc. In common nouns, however, the suffix *-ish* may have a derogatory sense. See **-ish**

**romp,** v., slang in the phrase *romp past, in, home,* to win in a race without effort.

**rondeau,** n., *a short stanzaic poem,* pronounced (rŏn′dō) or (rŏndō′), with a variant *rondel* (rŏn′del)

**rondel,** see **rondeau**

**rood,** n., archaic and literary for *cross,* kept alive by modern imitations of medieval narrative style.

**rookie,** n., army slang for *recruit.*

**Roosevelt,** n., *family name,* pronounced (rō′zevĕlt), (rōz′vĕlt), less correctly (rōō′zevĕlt), (rōōz′vĕlt)

**rooster,** n., colloquial term in America for *the male of the domestic fowl,* corresponding to the feminine *hen.* The word **rooster** is not current in England, the customary equivalent there being *cock,* which is also the literary word in both England and America. The word *cockerel* means a young cock.

**root,** v., slang in the sense *to support by applause, by yelling,* etc. Also a slang noun *rooter,* one who applauds and encourages another, especially a player in an athletic game.

**Roquefort,** n., *a kind of cheese,* pronounced (rŏk′fŏr) The word is of French origin, but it has not been completely anglicized.

**Rosalind,** n., *woman's name,* pronounced (rŏz′alĭnd) or (rŏz′alīnd) The rimes in Shakspere indicate this latter pronunciation for the character in *As You Like It.*

**roseate,** adj., *rose-colored,* pronounced (rō′zĭat), less correctly (rō′zīat)

**rosin,** see **resin**

**roster,** n., *list showing assignments of military duty,* pronounced (rŏs′ter) or (rōs′ter)

**rot,** n., slang for *nonsense,* often *tommy rot.*

**rot,** v., a bit of melodramatic journalistic rhetoric in the phrase *to rot in jail.* Any man who is imprisoned always *rots in jail* in the language of the journalist who thinks the imprisonment is unjust.

**Rothschild,** n., *family name,* pronounced (rŏths′chĭld), (rŏs′chĭld) Though of German origin, as an English name the word is not pronounced (rōt′shĭlt), but is anglicized.

**rôti,** n., French word, *roast,* as a course of a dinner, pronounced (rōtē′)

**rotten,** adj., slang for *poor, bad, disagreeable,* as in *rotten weather, a rotten headache.*

**rotter,** n., slang for *an objectionable person.* Chiefly current in England.

**roturier,** n., French word, *a frequenter of city streets and public resorts, a "rounder,"* pronounced (rōtōorēā′)

**roué,** n., French word, *dissipated person, rake,* pronounced (rōōā′)

**Rouen,** n., *French town and cathedral,* pronounced (rōōahn′)

**rouge,** n., *colored powder,* pronounced (rōōzh), but also a noun, meaning *touchdown* in Eton football, and pronounced (rōōj)

**rouge-et-noir,** n., French word, *a card game,* literally, *red and black;* pronounced (rōōzh ā nwahr)

**rough,** adj., colloquial in the sense *bad, severe,* as in *rough luck, rough on one, have a rough time, rough on rats,* and slang in *roughhouse,* n., v., rowdy behavior. Slang also in the phrase *treat 'em rough,* be stern, severe.

**roughneck,** n., slang for *unmannerly person, rowdy.* See **thug** The image suggested by **roughneck** is not apparent, as it is, for example, in *rubberneck,* but perhaps a **roughneck** is a collarless and necktieless person, that is, a person who does not observe the simple conventionalities.

**round,** adv., prep., as in the phrases *the wheels go round, take one round the town, go a long way round, not enough food to go round.* In these constructions *around* is sometimes incorrectly used for **round.** See **around**

**rounder,** n., slang for *man about town, dissolute person.*

**roundhouse,** n., *circular shed for engines.* The equivalent term in England is *engine shed.*

**roup,** n., *a poultry disease,* pronounced (roop)

**Rousseau, J.-J.,** n., *French writer* (1712–1778), pronounced (rooso′)

**rout,** v., in good use in the phrase *rout one out,* drag out, force to come out, literally or figuratively, as in *They routed me out of bed at six o'clock.* Also used of swine *routing up* the ground in search of food. This verb has a variant form *root,* as in *They rooted me out of bed at six o'clock,* and both go back in Anglo-Saxon to the noun meaning *root,* the verbal meanings being derived from the notion of dragging things up by the root.

**route,** n., *a road or itinerary,* pronounced (root), except in certain specialized uses, in which the pronunciation (rowt) prevails. This latter pronunciation is general in military and railroad use, also colloquially and dialectally of a delivery route, as in *a milk route, a paper route, a mailcarrier's route,* and occurs also in the noun used as a verb.

**row,** n., colloquial for *disturbance, commotion.* Also as a verb *to row,* scold, and a noun *rowing* (row′ing), a scolding. Pronounced (row)

**rowlock,** n., *appliance for holding the oars,* pronounced (rŭl′ŏk) See **oarlock**

**Rubaiyat,** n., *poem by Omar Khayyam,* pronounced (roo′bīyaht), or anglicized to (roo′bīyăt)

**rubberneck,** n., slang for *staring, inquisitive person,* or for persons on a sightseeing expedition. Also used as a verb, *to rubberneck,* to stare.

**rubbers,** n., colloquial name for *overshoes.* In children's English *rubber* is also used in the sense *eraser,* a piece of rubber for erasing ink and lead marks. See **galosh**

**Rubens, Peter Paul,** n., *painter* (1577–1640), not to be spelled *Reubens.*

**ruche,** n., *frill,* pronounced (roosh) The pronunciation (sh) reflects the French origin of the word as a term in the general class of millinery French.

**rucksack,** n., German word, *shoulder knapsack,* pronounced (rŏok'-sahk)

**ruction,** n., slang for *dispute, row, disturbance.*

**rugger,** n., colloquial and slang for *Rugby football.*

**ruin,** n., *downfall,* pronounced (rōo'ĭn), low colloquially (rōon) Also a verb, *to ruin,* as in *You have ruined your dress with those peach stains.* This last usage is questioned by some stylists, who maintain that **ruin** as a verb applies only to financial and business matters, as in *He ruined himself by making too many investments.* The generalized use of **ruin** in the sense *destroy, spoil* is too prevalent, however, to be disregarded.

**ruination,** n., colloquial and humorous for *ruin,* as in *That automobile will be the ruination of him.*

**rum,** n., strictly a particular kind of alcoholic beverage, but in the loose language of oratory often employed as a synonym for all alcoholic drinks, especially when helped by alliteration, as in *Rum, Rome, and Rebellion.*

**rum,** adj., slang for *strange, queer,* as in *a rum go,* a strange happening, *a rum time,* a good time. Perhaps etymologically the same as **rum,** n., and both of gipsy origin. Also in the form *rummy.*

**rumpus,** n., slang for *uproar.*

**run,** n., local and dialectal, especially in the South and Southwest, in the sense *a small stream.* See **branch, brook, creek**

**run,** v., colloquial in the sense *conduct, manage,* as in *to run a newspaper, to run a fruit stand;* or *to run for an office,* be candidate; *to run for it,* escape by running, as in *The rain came up so quick, we had to run for it; to run in,* arrest; *to run to,* amount to, as in *The attendance usually runs to about fifty; to run the show,* manage it, and in various other verb and noun phrases with **run.**

**runt,** n., originally *an ox of a small breed,* but now colloquially applied to persons of undersize and as a term of contempt.

**rus in urbe,** Latin phrase, *country within the town,* pronounced (rŭs ĭn ur'bĭ)

**rusé,** adj., French word, *tricky*, with a feminine *rusée*, both pronounced (rüzā')

**Russ,** n., archaic for *Russian.*

**Russia,** n., pronounced (rŭsh'a), the adjective *Russian* being (rŭsh'n), low colloquially (roo͞'sha), (roo͞'shn) The words are made trisyllables only in a conscious and unnatural pronunciation.

**rustle,** v., slang in the sense *move*, as in *to rustle freight*, transfer freight from cars to wagons, etc., the figure implied being that of moving so rapidly as to cause a rustle. Pronounced (rŭs'l)

**ruth,** n., archaic and literary for *pity*, pronounced (roo͞th)

# S

**Sabaoth,** n., from a Hebrew word meaning *host*, in the phrase *Lord God of Sabaoth*, Lord of hosts. Not the same as *Sabbath*. Pronounced (săb'āŏth)

**Sabbath,** n., not by strict etymology the name of a day of the week, but by common usage now, and for several centuries, employed as a synonym for *Sunday*, and therefore capitalized like the names of the days of the week.

**sabot,** n., *wooden shoe*, pronounced (săb'ō) or (săbō') From this is made the noun *sabotage* (săb'otij), wilful destructiveness, especially by workingmen during a labor dispute.

**sac,** n., a form of the word *sack*, used in the specialized sense of *a bag of membrane in a living body*, and employed only in technical medical and scientific writing.

**saccharin,** n., *sweet substance chemically produced from coal tar.* The adjective form is *saccharine*, sugary, literally and metaphorically. The noun is pronounced (săk'arĭn), the adjective (săk'arēn) or (săk'arīn), the pronunciation (săk'arēn) being the more general.

**sacerdotal,** adj., *priestly*, pronounced (săserdō'tal), not (săkerdō'tal)

**sachem,** n., *Indian chief,* pronounced (săch'em) or (sā'chem), but not (săk'em), (sā'kem)

**sachet,** n., *small bag for perfumed powder,* pronounced (săshā') or (săsh'ā)

**sack,** n., v., colloquial in the sense *discharge,* as in *to give, to get the sack, to sack a person.* The construction is old and perhaps originated from the time when a servant on being discharged was given a sack or bag in which to carry with him all his earthly possessions.

**Saco,** n., *place name in Maine,* pronounced (saw'kō)

**sacrifice,** n., v., *an offering, to offer,* both pronounced (săk'rĭfīs), not (săk'rĭfīs) A pronunciation (săk'rĭfīz) was formerly prescribed for the verb, but is now seldom heard. See **rise,** n.

**sacrilegious,** adj., *not respectful of sacred things,* pronounced (săkrilē'jus), not (săkrilĭj'us) The incorrect pronunciation is caused by unconscious memory of the word *religious.*

**sad,** adj., colloquial and a bit provincial in the sense *doughy* as applied to cake, bread, etc. The word is the same in this sense as the word **sad,** *melancholy,* and though the meaning *doughy, heavy* probably stands nearer to the original value of **sad,** the word is now used chiefly as applied to mental states. The compound *sadiron* contains the word **sad** in the sense *heavy.*

**sad to relate,** trite phrase, usually ironical in intent.

**safety,** n., colloquial abbreviation for *safety razor,* or formerly for a *safety bicycle,* but since all bicycles are now *safeties,* i. e., low-wheeled bicycles, the term **safety** as applied to a bicycle has become obsolete.

**saga,** n., *Icelandic heroic tale,* pronounced (sah'ga) The word is sometimes extended from its original use to apply to any long narrative dealing with simple life on a large scale.

**Sahara,** n., *desert in Africa,* pronounced (sahăr'a) or (sahah'ra)

**sahib,** n., title of address used by natives in India in addressing a European, from an Arabic word meaning *friend.* Pronounced (sah'ĭb), with a corresponding feminine *memsahib* (mĕm'sah'ĭb) The words are used alone as words of address, or are appended as a title to a name, as in *Jones Sahib,* Mr. Jones.

**said,** see **say**

**sail into,** v., colloquial and slang in the sense *abuse, scold,* as in *The owner sailed into us without delay.*

**Saint Gaudens,** n., *American sculptor,* pronounced (sānt gaw'denz)

**Saint-Saëns,** n., *French composer,* pronounced (săṅ sahṅs)

**Sakhalin,** n., *island in Okhotsk Sea,* not *Sachalin* or *Saghalien,* according to the decision of the United States Geographic Board.

**salaam,** n., *Oriental salutation,* pronounced (salahm')

**salame,** n., Italian word, *sausage with garlic and strong seasoning,* pronounced (sălah'mĭ)

**salariat,** n., a humorous learned word for *the salaried class,* formed on the analogy of *proletariat,* pronounced (salār'ĭat)

**salary,** n., *periodical compensation paid to a person who is not a workingman,* the compensation of the latter being *wages.* As **salary** is relatively a pretentious word, it should be used only when the amount of the compensation justifies it.   See **emolument, wages**

**saline,** adj., *salty,* pronounced (sā'līn)   A learned, scientific, and technical word, the words *salt, salty* being the words employed in general use.

**saliva,** n., *spittle,* pronounced (salĭ'va), with an adjective *salivary* (săl'ĭvărĭ)   Although **saliva** is really a technical and learned term, it is now preferred to the native and popular term *spittle,* which has come to seem old-fashioned, or to *spit,* which is low colloquial.   See **spit**

**salle-à-manger,** n., French word, *dining room,* pronounced (săl ah mahṅzhā')

**salle-d'attente,** n., French word, *waiting room,* pronounced (săl dătahṅt')

**salmon,** n., *a kind of fish.* Pronounced (săm'on), with the *l* silent. The word is the same in the plural as in the singular, except that a plural *salmons* is used as a scientific term to denote different species of **salmon.** The proper name **Salmon** is sometimes pronounced (săl'mon), but the pronunciation of family names is always determined by family traditions, which often differ from the customary pronunciations of common nouns.

**salon,** n., French word, *reception room, the Salon,* exhibition of pictures in Paris. Pronounced (săl'ŏṅ)

**Saloniki,** n., *a city and gulf in Turkey,* not *Salaniki, Salonica, Salonika, Selanik, Selonica,* or *Thessalonica,* by decision of the United States Geographic Board. Pronounced (sălonē'kē) or (sălonĭ'kĭ) The Permanent Committee on Geographical Names recommends the form *Salonika,* pronounced (sahlŏnē'ka)

**salutary,** adj., *beneficial, wholesome,* pronounced (săl'ūtărĭ), the nouns *salutation* (sălūtā'shon) and *salutatory* (saloo'tatŏrĭ) being of the same origin.

**salvage,** n., *rescue of property,* usually at sea, but sometimes extended to the rescue of property from a fire, etc., on land; also the property thus rescued, and also as a verb, *to salvage.* Pronounced (săl'văj), (săl'vĭj) The spelling **salvage** sometimes occurs as a picturesque archaism for *savage,* uncivilized person, but *savage* is a word of different etymological origin.

**salve,** v., pronounced (sălv) in the sense *to save a ship or its cargo from loss at sea,* otherwise with the *l* silent. The pronunciation (săv) is the usual pronunciation, the pronunciation (sahv) being much less general. The same applies to **salve,** n., *an ointment.* See **a** (ah), the sound of **a** as in *father*

**salver,** n., *tray,* pronounced (săl'ver)

**same,** adj., often used in crude English like a personal pronoun, as in *Your order has been received and we shall give the same our careful attention.* Stylistically it is much better to say simply *We shall give it,* etc. This use of **same** is one of the old-fashioned stilted customs of business correspondence that business is outgrowing.

**same as,** adj., as in *Is your inspector the same as mine?* This construction can not be used as an adverbial conjunction in careful speech. The sentence *He died the same as he had lived* must be *He died as he had lived,* or *He died in the same manner as that in which he had lived.* Nor can *same* be followed directly by a *that*-clause without *as.* The sentence *Editors refer to it in the same scornful manner that a New York reporter talks about the crossroads correspondent of a county-seat weekly* must read *Editors refer to it in the same scornful manner as that in which,* etc., and *I read it in the same mood that I pored over my geography in the fifth grade* must be *I read it in the same mood as that in which I pored over my geography in the fifth grade.*

**samite,** n., archaic name for *a kind of cloth,* as in Tennyson's *clothed in white samite.* Pronounced (săm′ĭt)

**samurai,** n., *a member of a Japanese social class,* the plural being the same. Pronounced (săm′ōōrī)

**sanatorium,** n., *a place for invalids.* There is also a word *sanitarium* of the same meaning, but *sanitorium* is an incorrect blending of the two.

**Sancho Panza,** n., *character in "Don Quixote,"* pronounced (săng′kō păn′za) or as a Spanish word.

**sand,** n., slang for *courage, firmness.* See grit

**Sand, George,** n., *assumed name of Madame Dudevant, a French writer* (1804–1876) The first name is in the English form, not the French form *Georges.* The last name is pronounced as in English, (sănd), or as in French, (sahṅd)

**Sandys,** n., *family name,* pronounced (săndz)

**sang-froid,** n., French word, *coolness, unperturbedness,* literally, *cold blood;* pronounced (sahṅfrwah′)

**sanhedrim,** n., *a Jewish council,* pronounced (săn′ĭdrĭm) Etymologically, a more correct form would be *sanhedrin,* but the form with final *-m* has been established in English for several centuries.

**San Jose,** n., *city in California*, pronounced (săn hōzā′)  There is also a San Jose in Illinois, New Mexico, and Texas, all presumably pronounced in the same way.  Not written *José*.

**sans,** prep., archaic and literary for *without*, pronounced (sănz), commonly used in modern versions of romantic medieval narratives.

**sans-culotte,** n., French word, *a Republican of the lower classes in the French Revolution, a popular radical*, pronounced (sahṅ külŏt′)

**sans façon,** French phrase, *outspokenly, unceremoniously*, pronounced (sahṅ făsŏṅ′)

**sans gêne,** French phrase, *at ease, unconstrainedly*, pronounced (sahṅ zhān′)

**Sanskrit,** n., *ancient language of India*.  Also written *Sanscrit*, but **Sanskrit** is preferred as closer etymologically to the original.

**sans peur et sans reproche,** French phrase, *without fear and without reproach*, descriptive of a chivalrous character.  Pronounced (sahṅ per ā sahṅ rĕprōsh′)

**sans phrase,** French phrase, *without circumlocution*, pronounced (sahṅ frahz′)

**Saône,** n., *European river*, pronounced (sōn)

**saphead,** n., slang for *foolish person*.

**sapient,** adj., an ironical word for *wise*, pronounced (sā′pĭĕnt) or (săp′ĭĕnt)

**sappy,** adj., slang for *foolish and sentimental*.

**Sarajevo,** see **Serajevo**

**sarsaparilla,** n., *a kind of herb, a drink flavored with sarsaparilla*.  Dialectally pronounced (săs′aparĭla), but (sahr′saparĭla) in standard speech.  Often abbreviated colloquially to *sas*.

**sashay,** v., slang for *to move to and fro*.  A mispronunciation of French *chassé*.

**sass,** n., v., low colloquial and dialectal variant of *sauce*, impudent speech, to speak impudently. Also an adjective *sassy*, a variant of *saucy*.

**sate,** v., archaic form of the past tense of *sit*, pronounced (săt) or (sāt)

**satiety,** n., *the condition of being full*, pronounced (satī'ĕtĭ) But *satiate, insatiable* are (sā'shĭăt), (ĭnsā'shabl)

**satisfied,** adj., colloquial and dialectal in the sense *convinced, sure*, as in *I'm satisfied he is the man who took my pocketbook.*

**satis superque,** Latin phrase, *enough and too much*, pronounced (săt'ĭs sūper'kwĭ)

**satrap,** n., *ancient Persian governor*, pronounced (sā'trăp)

**satyr,** n., *half-human woodland creature*, pronounced (săt'er)

**sauce,** n., (1) *a liquid preparation to be eaten with other foods*, especially meats and puddings; (2) *stewed fruits*, especially *apple sauce*. In this second sense **sauce** passes readily into the dialectal, as when a dish of stewed pears is called **sauce.** But **sauce** as applied to apples, cranberries, rhubarb is in good use. In the meaning *vegetables*, **sauce** is dialectal, and now largely extinct dialectal. The phrase *garden sauce* survives humorously, but *long sauce* for beets, carrots, and parsnips, and *short sauce* for potatoes, turnips, onions, etc., belong only to the humor of the past. See **sass**

**sauté,** adj., French word, *usually of vegetables, fried in a pan*, with a plural *sautés* and a feminine *sautée, sautées*, all pronounced (sōtā'), though the plural may be anglicized and pronounced (sōtāz')

**sauve qui peut,** French phrase, *every man for himself*, literally, *save (himself) who can;* pronounced (sōv kē pö)

**savant,** n., *scholar*, especially a scholarly scientist. Pronounced (săv'ŏn), the word being French in origin.

**save,** prep., archaic and literary for *but, except*, as in *I've lost all my pencils save one*, which would now be more naturally *but one*, or *Everybody has had breakfast save me*, more naturally, *except me*, or *I am ready save that I can't find my hat*, except that, etc.

**save,** conj., archaic and literary for *unless, but*, as in *You got no mercy save you pleased his fancy*, unless you pleased his fancy, *whence all had fled save he*, but he (or of course more naturally, *except him*)

**savoir faire,** French phrase, *tact, social adaptability*, pronounced (săv'wahr fār)

**savoir vivre,** French phrase, *at home in good society*, pronounced (săv'wahr vē'vr)

**savvy,** v., slang for *to know*, being merely an anglicized pronunciation of the second person plural of the imperative of the French verb, *savoir*, to know.

**sawbones,** n., disrespectful slang for *surgeon*.

**Sawney,** n., contemptuous term for *Scotchman*.

**saw the light of day,** trite phrase, for the simpler *was born*, which is much to be preferred.

**saxophone,** n., *a wind instrument*, with a variant *saxhorn*, the element *sax-* being from the name of the inventor.

**say,** n., colloquial in the sense *chance to talk*, as in *Each man had his say*.

**say, said,** v., low colloquial when followed immediately by an infinitive, as in *He said to tell you not to come*, for *He said I should tell you*, etc., or *He said that you were not to come*, or *He asked me to tell you*, etc. The phrase *says I*, often printed *sez I*, is dialectal. The use of **say** in sentences like *Say what you will, I shall always think he was innocent* is formal and literary for the more usual *No matter what you say, I don't care what you say*, etc. See **look** The use of **said** as an adjective, meaning *aforesaid, already mentioned*, as in *the said cars being all provided with tires and accessories, the said small boy having two large apples in his hands*, is either commercial and legal in tone or facetiously literary. As a literary device this use of **said**

is easily overworked.  As a persistent sentence-beginner, as in *Say, let's take a walk,* **say** is low colloquial, though it may also be poetical, as in *Oh, say, can you see by the dawn's early light.* Similar unnecessary sentence-beginners are *listen, well, why.*

**say-so,** n., colloquial and dialectal for *a person's mere word,* as in *I wouldn't believe it on his say-so,* usually with scornful implications.

**sbirro,** n., Italian word, *policeman,* pronounced (zbĭr'ō), with a plural *sbirri,* pronounced (zbĭr'ē)

**scab,** n., *a workman who refuses to join in an organized labor movement.*  Not slang, but best described as one of the technical terms of labor controversy.  In England also called a *blackleg.*

**scabies,** n., *the itch,* pronounced (skā'bĭēz)  The adjective *scabrous* is pronounced (skā'brus), often used metaphorically as a critical adjective of disapproval.

**scallion,** n., *a kind of onion,* pronounced (skăl'yon), with a variant *shalot,* *shallot* (shalŏt'), both being derived ultimately from the noun *Ascalon.*  It seems, therefore, that the Lady of Shallot and the lowly scallion are indebted to the same source for their name.

**scallop,** n., *a shellfish,* and *an edging like the edge of a scallop shell.* Also written *scollop,* though **scallop** is the more common spelling. The usual pronunciation, however, is (skŏl'op), in accord with the rejected spelling.  The pronunciation (skăl'op) is rarely used.

**scallywag,** n., slang for *scamp,* with a variant *scalawag.*

**scaly tribe,** trite phrase, old-fashioned rhetorical variation for *fish.*

**scant,** adj., *small, slight,* as in *The motion was received with scant applause, dressed in scant attire.*  This is artificial literary style, for though *scanty* as an adjective is good current English, **scant** is not, except in one or two phrases, such as *scant of breath* (kept alive perhaps by the line in *Hamlet, He is fat and scant of breath*), *with scant courtesy.*  As a verb, *to scant,* skimp, provide grudgingly, the word is but rarely used.

521

**scarce,** adv., but only in poetry, as in *You'd scarce expect one of my age,* the customary prose form being *scarcely.*

**scarcely,** adv., incorrectly followed by *than,* as in *Scarcely had she gone than several friends came in,* for *Scarcely had she gone when,* etc.  See **hardly**

**scared,** adj., dialectal for *afraid,* as in *I'd be scared* or *a-scared to do that.*  The pronunciation (skērd), represented in dialect stories by the spelling *skeered,* is dialectal, and so also (skärt), represented in dialect stories by the spelling *scairt.*  The standard sense of *scare,* **scared** is *frighten, frightened.*

**scarf,** n., *neckpiece or necktie.*  The plural is *scarves* or *scarfs.*

**scary,** adj., dialectal for *terrifying,* often pronounced as though written *skeery.*

**scavenger,** n., *person or animal that removes refuse,* pronounced (skăv′enjer)  The verb is *scavenge,* by an abbreviation of the noun, as though a verb *butch* were made from the noun *butcher.*  The verb *butch* is not good English, but *scavenge* is in standard use.  See **broking, burgle, butching**

**scenario,** n., *outline contents of a play or opera,* pronounced (senā′-rĭō), (senăr′ĭō), or (shānā′rĭō)  Of these three pronunciations the second is probably the most general and the third the most literary.  In the manufacture of moving pictures the pronunciation (senăr′ĭō) is almost universally used.

**scenery,** n., *landscape, view in general.*  The word has no plural except in low colloquial uses like *This was one of the finest sceneries I ever saw.*  If a plural is used, it must be *scenes, views,* or some similar word.

**scenic,** adj., *strikingly picturesque,* pronounced (sē′nĭk) or (sĕn′ĭk), with (sē′nĭk) the more general, perhaps through the influence of *scene, scenery.*

**schedule,** n., *table or list of details*  pronounced (skĕd′ūl), in England (shĕd′ūl)

**schedule,** v., *to make or to place something in a schedule.*  In colloquial style often used merely as a synonym of *expect, arrange for*, as in *Supper is scheduled for six o'clock, He is scheduled for a visit with us in September*.   See **book, slate**

**Scheldt,** n., *river in Holland*, pronounced (skĕlt)

**Schenectady,** n., *city in New York*, pronounced (skenĕk′tadĭ)

**scherzo,** n., *a term in music*, pronounced (skĕrt′sō)

**schism,** n., *a splitting or separation*, especially in a church.   Pronounced (sĭz′m), with an adjective *schismatic* (sĭzmăt′ĭk)

**schist,** n., *a kind of rock*, pronounced (shĭst)

**Schley,** n., *American family name*, pronounced (slī)

**Schoharie,** n., *town in New York*, pronounced (skōhăr′ĭ)

**scholar,** see **student**

**schoolma'am,** n., facetious or satirical name for *a woman schoolteacher*.   Often spelled *schoolmarm*.

**schooner,** n., *a ship*, pronounced (skōōn′er)   Slang in the sense *a tall glass of beer*.

**schottische,** n., *a kind of dance*, pronounced (shŏt′ĭsh) or (shŏtēsh′)

**Schouler,** n., *American historian*, pronounced (skōō′ler)

**Schuyler,** n., *family name*, pronounced (skī′ler)

**Schuylkill,** n., *river in Pennsylvania*, pronounced (skōōl′kĭl)

**scilicet,** adv., Latin word, *that is to say*, introducing an explanatory word or phrase.   Pronounced (sī′lĭsĭt), and abbreviated *sc.* or *scil.*

**scimetar,** n., *a sword*, also spelled *scimitar*.   Pronounced (sĭm′etar)

**scintilla,** n., *shred, spark*, usually in the phrase *not a scintilla of evidence*.   Pronounced (sĭntĭl′a)

**scintillate,** v., *sparkle*, pronounced (sĭn′tilāt), usually in the trite phrase *a scintillating wit*.

**scion,** n., ,*young branch*, pronounced (sī′on)   A poetic, literary, or horticultural word.

**scissors,** n., *instrument for cutting*, used as either a singular or a plural, as in *A scissors was lying on the table, The scissors were very sharp*.   A corresponding singular form *scissor* does not occur. But **scissors** are usually referred to as *a pair of scissors* when it is necessary to refer definitely to one.

**Sclav,** see **Slav**

**sclerosis,** n., *hardening of tissue*, pronounced (sklĕrō'sĭs)

**sconce,** n., archaic and jocular word for *head*, pronounced (skŏns)

**scone,** n., *a kind of small cake*, pronounced (skōn), with a variant *scon*, pronounced (skŏn)

**scoop,** n., slang in the sense *an advantage or profit unshared by others*, especially in newspaper reporting.

**scoot,** v., slang, meaning *dart, shoot off, move rapidly*, and as an exclamation, *Begone!*

**scorcher,** n., slang for *a hot day, a stinging remark, a blow, a speedy bicycle rider.*

**Scotch,** adj., n., with the variants *Scottish* and *Scots*. Of these three words **Scotch** is much the most general. The form *Scottish* is dignified and literary, as in *Scottish literature, the Scottish character*. The form *Scots* occurs chiefly in Scottish use, as in *a Scotsman, a Scotswoman*. The word *Scot* for a native of Scotland is usually facetious or poetic. But the common word is **Scotch,** as in *Scotch mist, Scotch whiskey, a Scotch marriage*, etc.

**scout,** n., colloquial in the sense *fellow*, especially in the phrase *a good scout, good old scout*. Colloquial also as a verb, as in *to scout around for food*, hunt up something to eat. In this latter use the word is probably not the same etymologically as **scout,** *one who reconnoitres, to reconnoitre.*

**scran,** n., slang for *food, victuals*, and in the phrase *Bad scran to you*, Bad luck to you.

**scrap,** n., v., slang for *a fight, to fight*, with a noun *scrapper*, fighter.

**scream,** see **screamer**

**screamer,** n., slang for *something exceptionally fine*. First current in the early nineteenth century, later shortened to *scream*. See **loud**

**screen**, n., v., colloquial for *moving picture*, *to make into a moving picture*. Often used in journalistic English to provide a synonym for *moving picture*.

**screw**, n., slang in the sense *miserly person*, and also in the phrase *a screw loose*, mentally unbalanced. In the past participle *screwed* is slang for *drunk*.

**scrimmage**, n., colloquial for a *confused struggle,.row*, with a variant *scrummage* in English Rugby football.

**scrouge**, v., slang or dialectal for *to crowd, to crouch*.

**scrummage**, see **scrimmage**

**scrumptious**, adj., humorous and slang for *fine, good, excellent*, etc.

**scull**, n., *an oar*, the word for the bony structure of the head being *skull*.

**sculp**, v., a colloquial or jocular word for *to sculpture*.

**sculpsit**, v., Latin word, (*he, she*) *carved* (*it*), a sculptor's signature. Pronounced (skŭlp′sĭt), with a plural *sculpserunt* (skŭlpsē′rŭnt)

**sculpture**, v., *to carve*, especially in stone. The verb *to sculpture* is not very generally used, the activity of the sculptor being usually spoken of as carving, chiseling, or modeling. The adjective use of the past participle, as in *a sculptured figure*, is more general than the use of **sculpture** as a verb. See **sculp**

**scunner**, n., dialectal in the sense *dislike*, as in *He took a scunner to him*.

**scup**, n., v., New York children's dialect for *a swing, to swing*.

**Scylla**, n., especially in the phrase *Scylla and Charybdis*, the danger of running into the opposite peril by avoiding one, from an incident in Homer, *Odyssey* xii. Pronounced (sĭla and karĭb′dis)

**seamstress**, n., *a sewing woman*, pronounced (sēm′stres), with an obsolescent variant *sempstress*, pronounced (sĕm′stres)

**séance**, n., French word, *a sitting or meeting of a society*, especially for spiritualistic experiments, pronounced (sā′ahns)

**search**, v., slang in the general sense of **denial**, as in *You can search me*, I don't know, from the idea probably of not having anything about one that would imply any connection with the subject under discussion.

**second,** n., *sixtieth part of a minute,* but used also as a colloquial exaggeration for any short but undefined period of time, as in *I'll be with you in a second*—perhaps in five minutes.

**secretive,** adj., *uncommunicative,* pronounced (sē'krĭtĭv) or (sĭkrē'tĭv)

**secundo,** adv., Latin word, *secondly,* pronounced (sĭkŭn'dō)

**secundum artem,** Latin phrase, *skilfully, professionally,* pronounced (sĭkŭn'dŭm ahr'tĕm)

**secundum naturam,** Latin phrase, *naturally, not artfully,* pronounced (sĭkŭn'dŭm natū'răm)

**sedan,** n., formerly *a kind of portable chair,* now *a kind of automobile,* pronounced (sĭdăn')

**see,** v., colloquial and slang in the sense *bribe,* as in *You will have to see the inspector if you want these men to go back to work.* See **square**

**seedy,** adj., colloquial for *shabby,* with reference to physical appearance; *unwell,* with reference to state of health.

**seem,** v., colloquial in the construction *I can't seem to get the hang of this,* for *It seems I can't get the hang of this, I can't seem to make him understand,* for *It seems that I can't,* etc., or *It seems as though I couldn't,* etc.

**seep,** v., *to ooze through.* Good English in the United States, but current only dialectally in England.

**seething mass of humanity,** trite phrase, ambitious and rhetorical.

**seiche,** n., *high and unexpected wave on a lake,* pronounced (sāsh)

**Seidlitz,** n., *Seidlitz powder,* pronounced (sĕd'lĭts), from the name of a place.

**seigneur,** n., French word, *lord,* pronounced as an anglicized word, (sēnyer'), or as a French word, (sänyer') Also spelled *seignior, signior,* pronounced (sänyŏr'), (sĭnyŏr'), or with accent on the first syllable. See **señor, signor**

**seismic,** adj., *of earthquakes,* pronounced (sīz'mĭk), and so with the derivatives *seismograph, seismology,* (sīz'mōgrăf), (sīzmŏl'ojĭ)

**seldom,** adv., *infrequently,* not to be construed with *ever,* as in *I seldom ever go to church,* for *I seldom go to church,* or *I hardly ever go to church,* or *I seldom, if ever, go to church,* although this last sentence means something slightly different. The construction *seldom or ever* is incorrect for *seldom or never* or *seldom if ever.*

**selection,** n., crude colloquialism in a sentence like *She played a selection on the piano.* If what is played is worth mentioning at all, it should be designated by its proper title.

**self,** pron., low colloquial as an equivalent of *myself, yourself,* etc., as in *my wife, children, and self, Please accept our thanks to Mr. Jones and self,* thanks to Mr. Jones and you. *Make your check payable to self,* payable to yourself, is a good banking usage.

**sell,** v., slang in the sense *dupe, take in,* as in the exclamation *Sold again!,* Fooled again. Also a noun, as in *What a sell!,* What a disappointment! In recent use the verb **sell** has developed a slang sense *to present so persuasively as to induce someone to accept what is presented,* not necessarily for an immediate return in money. Thus a person who should rewrite the story of the Bible popularly and entertainingly might be said to have sold the Bible; or a person seeking a position in putting his best foot forward is trying to sell himself.

**selvage,** n., *edging of cloth,* also *selvedge,* both pronounced (sĕl'vĭj)

**semioccasionally,** adv., facetious and slang for *now and then, rarely.*

**send-off,** n., colloquial for *demonstration, good-by celebration.*

**senile,** adj., *characteristic of old age,* pronounced (sĕn'ĭl) or (sē'nĭl) The noun is *senility* (sĭnĭl'ĭtĭ) See **-ile**

**seniores priores,** Latin phrase, *elders first,* pronounced (sēnĭŏr'ēz prīŏr'ēz)

**señor,** n., Spanish word, *a gentleman,* also used as a title of address

527

like *Mr.* The corresponding feminines are *señora*, a married lady, Mrs., and *señorita*, an unmarried lady, Miss. The words are pronounced (sĕnyŏr'), (sĕnyŏr'a), (sĕnyorē'ta) See **seigneur, signor**

**sensual**, adj., *not intellectual, licentious*, pronounced (sĕn'sūal) or (sĕn'shōŏal)

**sentient**, adj., *capable of feeling*, pronounced (sĕn'shĭent) or (sĕn'shent)

**sepal**, n., *part of a plant*, pronounced (sē'pal) or (sĕp'al)

**septicaemia**, n., *blood-poisoning*, pronounced (sĕptĭsē'mĭa)

**sepulcher**, n., *tomb*, pronounced (sĕp'ulker), with an adjective *sepulchral* (sepŭl'kral)

**Sequence of Tenses.** The sequence of tenses in English is dependent very largely upon the shade of meaning to be conveyed, more so than upon fixed grammatical rules. The tense of the verb in a subordinate clause is not always the same as the tense of the verb in the main clause, although in simple situations they would be the same. Thus one would write *He says he has two more dogs at home* (the whole situation being thought of as in the present), or *He said he had two more dogs at home* (the whole situation being thought of as in the past) But one might also write *He says he had two more dogs at home* (did have, but no longer has), or in answer to the question *What did he say?* one might write *He said he has two more dogs at home* (still has them) The only rule that can be given for the sequence of tenses is to employ the tense form which adequately expresses the meaning intended. No grammatical rule of correctness forbids the use of any tense form in a subordinate clause which is required for the expression of the thought, no matter what the tense form in the main clause may be.

A perfect infinitive is used only when the action expressed is completed at a time preceding that of the verb in the principal clause, as in *I should like to have heard him* (desire expressed now to have heard him at some preceding time) Otherwise the present infinitive is used, as in *I should have liked to hear him,* and the construction *I should have liked to have heard him* is incorrect. See **Digest of Grammatical Rules,** §19

**seraglio,** n., *harem,* pronounced (sĭrahl′yō)

**Serajevo,** n., *city in Yugo-Slavia.* The United States Geographic Board rejects other variants, including *Sarajevo.* Pronounced (sĕrah-yā′vō)

**seraph,** n., *an order of the angels,* with a plural *seraphim, seraphs.* An older singular *seraphin* is now obsolete. Pronounced (sĕr′af), (sĕr′afĭm), with an adjective *seraphic* (sĭrăf′ĭk)

**Serbian,** adj., n., now the current form, *pertaining to, a native of Serbia.* The older forms, *Servia, Servian,* which prevailed before 1914, were etymologically less correct than *Serbia,* **Serbian,** and perhaps were influenced by the English word *serve,* or it may be by the *v* in *Slav.* Also *Serb* for a native of Serbia. The United States Geographic Board authorizes only *Serbia* for the noun.

**serbon,** n., *a school which trains for good service.* This is a word proposed by the American Board of Applied Christianity as the name for a school of religious education. It is a mongrel word made by combining Latin *servio,* I serve, and French *bon,* good, and it is meant to designate a school which trains for good service. Perhaps the French word *Sorbonne,* the name of a university in Paris, also influenced the formation of the word. The word has not gained currency, and it is doubtful if it ever will or should. Crude mechanical coinages of this kind may perhaps be permissible as humorous fancies, but for serious uses better methods of word formation are available. Scholarly standards are not always a final test of good use, but when one has a free hand, as in the coinage of a new word, there is no reason why scholarly traditions should not be respected. See **Hybrids**

**sere,** adj., literary and poetic for *dried, withered.*

**sergeant,** n., *an officer,* pronounced (sahrh′jnt)   A spelling with *j* survives in a few official names in England.

**seriatim,** adv., Latin word, *successively, in a sequence,* pronounced (sĕrĭā′tĭm)

**series,** n., *a number of things in a sequence.*   The plural is the same, both pronounced (sĭr′ēz), or very formally (sĭr′ĭēz)

**serpent,** n., literary and archaic word for *snake,* as in the story of the temptation of Eve.

**servant,** n., usually applies to a woman or girl in domestic service, though of course not restricted to this use.   As applying to a domestic servant, the word **servant** is frequently avoided as being too obviously descriptive of a lower social class, and some other term, often *maid,* or a specialized term such as *cook, laundress,* etc., is used instead.   In public advertisements, for example, one does not advertise for a servant, but for a house-worker, a maid, a waitress, a nurse, etc., nor does one apply the word **servant** to domestic helpers in addressing them personally.

**serviette,** n., *table napkin,* pronounced (servĭĕt′)   The word is not in general use, pertaining chiefly to the language of waiters and servants, the customary word being *napkin.*

**servile,** adj., *menial, obsequious,* pronounced (ser′vĭl) or (ser′vīl)   See **-ile**

**sesame,** n., *magic word,* in the phrase *open sesame.*   Pronounced (sĕs′amĭ)

**set,** v., *to put down, to place,* with an object, often incorrectly used for *sit.*   Thus *to set* should mean *to put down,* as in *He set his burden on the ground; to sit* should mean *to take a seat,* as in *I will sit near the door.*   The proper form with reference to a garment is **set,** as in *This coat sets well,* as also of flower buds about to set for fruit.   With reference to hens, the form **set** is used when it is a causative, that is, one sets a hen when one places it on eggs to hatch.   But a hen which is in the mood to be set wants to sit, and when it is set, it is properly described as a *sitting hen*. In colloquial and dialectal use, however, set is often used for *sit*, as in *This hen wants to set, A setting hen never lays*. In the sense *to occupy a seat*, especially on horseback, the proper form is *sit*, as in *He was so weak he could scarcely sit his horse, He sits his horse well*.

**settle,** v., colloquial in the sense of paying an ordinary bill, as in *You get your breakfast and I will settle the bill.* Also *settle up*. The simpler word *pay* would be better here, leaving **settle** for more elaborate transactions, as in *His business accounts were complicated and difficult to settle*.

**sew,** v., *join with needle and thread*, with a past tense *sewed* (sōd) and a past participle *sewed* (sōd), less frequently *sewn* (sōn) The parts of the verb *sow*, to scatter seed, are *sowed* for the past tense and *sowed* or *sown* for the past participle.

**sewage,** n., *the matter contained in a sewer*. Not to be misused for *sewerage*, the system of draining by means of sewers. The words are properly used in the sentence *The sewage is carried away by an elaborate sewerage*.

**shabby,** adj., *seedy, contemptible*. "A word that has crept into conversation and low writing; but ought not to be admitted into the language," says Dr. Johnson. But what should we do now without **shabby?** The word **shabby** is etymologically well derived, being from an Anglo-Saxon word from which, or from a closely related form of which, the modern English word *scab* is also derived.

**shackle,** n., *bond for the ankle or wrist*, often in the plural *shackles*. Also as a verb *to shackle*. In all its uses the word **shackle** is now archaic, literary, or poetic and is often an affected ambitious word in journalistic style, as in *the shackles of convention, to throw off the shackles of civilization*, etc. See **fetters, gyves**

**shad,** n., *kind of fish*, with a plural the same, as in *Shad are delicious but bony*. The plurals of most fishes are the same as the

531

singulars, and when the plural form *shads* is used it would mean not a number of individual shad, but different varieties or species of shad.   See **salmon**

**shaddock,** see **grapefruit**

**shagbark,** n., local and dialectal for *a kind of hickory nut.*   So also *shellbark.*

**shake,** v., low colloquial and dialectal for *shake hands.*   As a formula of introduction, *shake hands* is low colloquial, as in *Shake hands with Mr. Smith,* meaning *Let me introduce Mr. Smith to you.*   Slang in the sense *abandon, get rid of.*

**shakes,** n., slang in the phrase *no great shakes,* does not amount to much, and dialectal for *chills and fever,* as in *to have the shakes.*

**Shakspere,** n., *dramatist.*   Other spellings of this name are also used, especially *Shakespeare* and *Shakspeare,* but since no one knows just how Shakspere himself spelled the name, it seems permissible to prefer the shortest and the simplest spelling for use nowadays.

**shall** and **will,** v., the great bugaboo of the English language. The difficulty in the use of **shall** and **will** arises from the fact that colloquial practice, even good colloquial practice, does not closely accord with the prescriptions of grammarians, rhetoricians, and lexicographers.   In the rules of the grammarians, **shall** is to be used in the first person, singular and plural, to express futurity, and **will** in the second and third.   When **will** is used in the first person it expresses some other shade of thought than simple futurity, such as willingness, resolution, as in *"Will you have this man for your husband?" "I will."*   On the other hand, **shall** in the second and third persons expresses compulsion, determination, and other shades of thought, as in *You shall take this money, whether you want to or not.*   These rules hold with fair consistency in formal and literary English, but in general colloquial use **will** is very commonly employed in the first person to express futurity, as in *I will be in town tomorrow and* *will come to see you at ten o'clock*, as well as in the second and third, and **shall** is used only in the specialized senses of compulsion, determination, etc.

"In the first person," says the *New English Dictionary*, "*shall* has, from the early Middle English period, been the normal auxiliary for expressing mere futurity, without any adventitious notion. . . . . To use *will* in these cases is now a mark of Scottish, Irish, provincial, or extra-British idiom." If Scottish, Irish, American, and all non-British use is excepted, this limits **shall** as the "normal auxiliary" for expressing futurity in the first person to a relatively small area.

The prescriptions for the use of **shall, will** are of importance mainly in literary style. In spoken language the abbreviation '*ll* would ordinarily be used, and as this abbreviation may stand for either **shall** or **will,** there is no way of telling whether *I'll, you'll, he'll* contains the one or the other of these forms, nor in actual speech is there any implication or feeling that '*ll* stands for one or the other of the words.

Although the use of **shall** and **will** according to the grammarian's rules of correctness is of some importance for literary style, it must be said that this importance is easily exaggerated. The highly subtilized rules which are sometimes given may be too subtle to be practicable and are rarely necessary to clearness of expression. It often results also that in the effort to live up to an elaborate set of rules, a writer succeeds merely in becoming artificial and unidiomatic. It is a healthy impulse to rebel against a too great elaboration of the mere machinery of language, that is, to insist that the mechanism of language shall satisfy a clearly perceived need in expression. See **should**

**shalot,** see **scallion**

**sham,** n., *something not the real thing, a trick, imposture.* First appears in slang about 1677, but long since accepted into the general vocabulary of the language. A **pillow sham** is a somewhat old-fashioned name for a covering for a pillowcase or pillow slip. The word is also used as a verb, as in *to sham sleep*, pretend to be asleep.

**shamefaced,** adj., *bashful*. The original form of this word was *shamefast*, but this original form has passed out of use.

**shammy,** see **chamois**

**shanty,** n., colloquial for *hut*. The etymology of the word has been much debated but never definitely determined. Not the same word as **shanty,** *sailors' song*. See **chanty**

**shape,** n., colloquial for *condition*, as in *He had been sick and was not in very good shape for traveling.*

**shaps,** see **chaparajos**

**shark,** n., slang in the sense *remarkably skilful, capable*, as in *He is a shark at billiards.*

**shaveling,** n., a term of contempt for *a hypocritical time-server*, originally applied to priests because of their tonsure. Now somewhat literary and archaic.

**shaver,** n., colloquial and slightly humorous for *small boy, a little fellow.*

**Shawangunk,** n., *mountains in New York*, pronounced (shŏn'gŭm)

**shay,** n., obsolescent and dialectal for *chaise*.

**she,** see **he**

**shebang,** n., slang for *hut*, and sometimes facetious for a larger establishment.

**sheeny,** n., slang for *Jew*, probably derived from the syllable *Schön-*, frequent as the first syllable in Jewish compound names, as in *Schönthal, Schönfeld*, etc.

**sheepskin,** n., colloquial and slang for *diploma*.

**sheer,** adj., of fabrics, *fine, diaphanous*. Not used in this sense in England, but only in the sense *mere*, as in *sheer nonsense*, or *perpendicular*, as in *a sheer descent*.

**sheik,** n., *Arab chief*, with a variant *sheikh*, both pronounced (shēk) or (shāk)   Recent slang in the sense *man attractive to women*.

shekel, n., *a Jewish weight and coin*, pronounced (shĕk′el) Slang in the sense *money, coins*, as in *to rake in the shekels*, to win much money.

sheldrake, n., *a kind of duck*, with a possible *shelduck* (shĕl′dŭk) as a corresponding feminine, though sheldrake is ordinarily used for both.

shell, v., slang in the phrase *shell out*, pay.

Shelley, Percy Bysshe, n., *English poet* (1792–1822), not spelled *Shelly*. The middle name is pronounced (bĭsh)

shewbread, n., *ceremonial loaves in the Jewish temple*. The spelling *shew-* is an archaic survival, but the word is pronounced (shō-), as though written *show-*. See show

shillelagh, n., *Irish cudgel*, pronounced (shĭlā′la)

shimmy, n., colloquial and juvenile form of *chemise* (shĭmēz′), and in the name of *the shimmy dance*. The pronunciation (shĭmēz′) reflects the French origin of the word, and (shĭm′ĭ) is an anglicized pronunciation of this word, which has not, however, passed into standard use.

shine, n., slang in the phrase *take a shine to*, take a liking for.

shine, v., *send forth light*, with a past tense and past participle *shone*, when the verb has no object, pronounced (shōn) or (shŏn) When the verb has an object, the past tense and past participle are *shined*, as in *He shined my shoes, After he had shined my shoes*, etc., *He shined things up until they fairly glittered*. This transitive use of shine is colloquial, the more formal word with an object being *polish*.

shingle, n., mildly humorous metaphor for *a small signboard*, especially a lawyer's signboard.

shingles, see measles

shirr, v., *to gather cloth together for a kind of trimming*. Also a noun *shirring*. This word is not current in England, but is in general use in America.

shirty, adj., slang in the sense *angry, quick-tempered*.

**shoat,** n., *a young pig.* The word is not current in England, except locally and dialectally. Its use in America is general and goes back to the early seventeenth century.

**shocking,** adj., colloquial as a general intensive of disapproval, as in *shocking manners,* and used adverbially before *bad,* as in *shocking bad manners,* very bad manners. See **awful**

**shoot,** v., colloquial as an exclamation, *pshaw,* especially in children's English, as in *O shoot, I don't want to go.* Slang in the phrase *shoot one's face,* to speak, express an opinion, *shoot one's lip,* of the same meaning. *To shoot the sun* is nautical English for taking the altitude at noon with a sextant. See **chute, shot**

**shop,** n., in England ordinarily means *a retail store,* in America usually *a large factory where articles are made.* But usage in America is by no means consistent, and *butcher shop, shoe shop, baker shop* are widely current. Recently a tendency has appeared to use the word **shop** instead of *store,* especially for the higher-priced, fashionable kind of store. These sometimes call themselves *shoppes,* like the *beauty shoppes* of the manicurists and hairdressers. The verb *to shop* and the phrase *to go shopping* are generally current in America.

The noun **shop** is sometimes used colloquially in general senses as applying to the place where one works, even when the place is not a shop, as in the phrase *to shut up shop,* to stop work for the day, *all over the shop,* everywhere, and *to talk shop,* to talk about matters of professional or business interest.

**shopkeeper,** n., not a current word in America. In England the word is used of the proprietor of a retail store, often with derogatory implications, as when England is called a nation of shopkeepers. The equivalent term in America is *storekeeper,* but American *storekeeper* can not suggest such deep disgrace as British **shopkeeper.**

**shore,** n., short for *seashore.* In colloquial use *the shore* means the Atlantic littoral as distinguished from *the coast,* the Pacific coast.

The word **shore** is localized in eastern American use in phrases like *shore dinner*, a dinner of sea food, *the Eastern Shore* (in Maryland and Virginia), place names like Shore Acres, Shorehaven, etc.  See **coast**

**short,** see **long**

**shortlived,** adj., *soon dying*, pronounced (-līvd)   So also *longlived*.

**Shoshone,** n., *Indian and geographical name*, pronounced (shŏshō′nĭ)

**shot,** n., colloquial in the phrase *not by a long shot*, a figurative and emphatic negative.

**shot,** adj., colloquial and slang in the sense *intoxicated*, usually in the phrase *half shot*.

**should,** v., and its companion form **would** are the past forms of *shall, will,* and are used in much the same way as *shall, will,* that is, **should** in the first person for simple futurity, **would** in the first, second, and third for desire, volition, etc.  But, like *will,* **would** is often used colloquially in the first person for simple futurity.   In a sentence like *Should you hear of anything, let me know,* the construction is archaic and literary for *If you should hear,* etc.   So also **would** in constructions like *Would I had the wings of a dove,* for *I wish I had,* etc.   See **had, were, shall**

**shout,** v., slang in the phrase *Now you are shouting,* you have said something highly commendable.

**shove,** v., *push,* but less literary than *push.*   Slang in the sense *go,* as in *I guess I'll have to be shoving along,* going.

**shovelboard,** n., *a game,* played with disks of wood and a stick with which to shove them.   Incorrectly *shuffleboard.*

**show,** v., past tense *showed,* past participle *shown,* sometimes *showed.*   An archaic spelling *shew, shewn, shewed* sometimes occurs, especially in England, but the pronunciation is as though written **show,** *shown, showed.*   See **shewbread**

**showing,** n., colloquial for *general appearance, summing up,* as

537

in *The firm made a good showing at the end of the first year of business.* Not current in England in this sense.

**show up,** v., colloquial for *appear, arrive,* as in *He didn't show up until five o'clock.*

**shrink,** v., *recoil, become smaller,* with a past tense *shrank* and a past participle *shrunk, shrunken,* the latter especially in adjective uses.

**shrug,** v., not used alone, but with the word *shoulders* expressed. A sentence like *She shrugged helplessly* is crude stylistically for *She shrugged her shoulders helplessly.* See **sign**

**shuck,** n., a somewhat rustic word for *husk,* as in *corn shucks,* for *corn husks.* Also as a verb, as in *to shuck corn,* for *to husk corn.* But *shucking oysters* is the usual term for removing oysters from the shell. The word *Shucks!* is also a colloquial interjection.

**shuffle off this mortal coil,** trite phrase, from Hamlet's soliloquy, Act. III, Sc. i, but now used only with mild humorous intent.

**shy,** adj., slang for *not well provided with, short of.*

**shy,** v., colloquial in the sense *to throw,* as in *to shy a stone at a dog.* Also a noun, as in *to have a shy at something.*

**shyster,** n., colloquial and slang for *disreputable lawyer.*

**Siasconset,** n., *American place name,* pronounced (skŏn′set), (sīaskŏn′set) being an artificial spelling pronunciation.

**sic,** adv., Latin word, *thus, so,* usually within parentheses and introduced to indicate that a word preceding appeared in the form given in the document from which it was quoted. Pronounced (sĭk)

**sick,** adj., *suffering from illness of any kind.* Not current in this sense in England, where the word usually means *having an inclination to vomit,* in America described as *sick at the stomach.* The English use appears, however, in such colloquialisms as *sick as a horse, sick as a dog,* and in *seasick.* And the American general use appears in such universal English phrases as *sick leave,*

*sick list, sick room, sick bed.* The adjective *sickening* is a colloquial intensive for *distressing, annoying.*

**side,** n., slang in the phrase *to put on side, to have lots of side,* meaning to be proud and haughty.

**sideswipe,** see **sidewipe**

**sidetrack,** v., colloquial and slang for *to deflect, prevent action upon.*
A metaphor from the running of a train into a siding.

**sidewalk,** n., *footpath at the side of a road,* not current in England,
the word *pavement* being the customary term there.

**sideward,** adj., as in *a sideward motion.* This form may also be
an adverb, but usually the adverb is *sidewards,* as in *The boat
moved sidewards.*

**sidewinder,** n., jocose name for a mythical animal with two short
legs on the right side and two long ones on the left, enabling it
to graze on steep hillsides. Slang for *a pacing horse.*

**sidewipe,** v., colloquial term indicating the rubbing or scraping
of one train or automobile by another in passing. The use of
**sidewipe** antedates the invention of the automobile, the earliest
occurrences of the word being found in connection with trains
and railroading. A variant form of the word is *sideswipe,* used
in the same sense as **sidewipe** in connection with automobiles.
Although the form *sideswipe* is later than **sidewipe,** at present
it seems to be the growing form and to be taking the place of
*sidewipe.* See **swipe**

**sieve,** n., *device for sifting,* pronounced (sĭv)

**sight,** n., dialectal and slang in such expressions as *The storm did
a sight of damage, There was a sight of people there, The house was
a sight after the party, Not by a long sight!*

**sign,** v., doubtful idiom in the sense *to make a sign,* as in the following: "but she nursed it now, at least to begin with, in silence,
only signing faintly to his embarrassment, with her grand thick-
braided hair" (Henry James, *Sense of the Past,* p. 9) Just what
she did with her hair is not clear, though probably nothing

more than nod her hair together with her head. Similar literary artificialities are *they chorused*, answered in chorus, *she shrugged*, shrugged her shoulders, *she efforted*, attempted, made an effort.

**signatory,** adj., *signing, consenting,* as in *the signatory powers.* The corresponding noun is *signatary* or *signatory,* preferably the former. See **mandatary**

**signor,** n., Italian word, *a gentleman,* with feminines *signora, signorina,* used in the same ways as the corresponding Spanish forms; see **señor** Pronounced (sēn'yŏr), (sēnyŏr'a), (sēnyŏrē'na)

**silhouette,** n., *outline figure in black,* pronounced (sĭlŏŏĕt')

**silk-stocking,** n., slang for *idle rich person.*

**silvan,** adj., *of the woods,* with a variant *sylvan,* both pronounced (sĭl'van)

**simlin,** n., local, chiefly southern name for *a kind of squash.* Spelled in various ways, *cymlin, cymling, simling, simbling,* etc.

**Simplified Spelling,** see **Spelling Reform**

**simply,** adv., *in a simple way,* but also used as a colloquial intensive, in the sense *really, truly,* as in *I simply don't know what to do, The show was simply grand,* this latter use being low colloquial.

**simultaneous,** adj., *at the same time,* pronounced (sĭmultā'nĭŭs), less commonly (sīmultā'nĭŭs)

**sinecure,** n., *an office without duties,* pronounced (sī'nĭkūr) or (sĭn'ĭkūr)

**sine die,** Latin phrase, *without a day (appointed for a succeeding meeting)* Pronounced (sī'nĭ dī'ē)

**sine qua non,** Latin phrase, *an indispensable condition,* pronounced (sī'nĭ kwā nŏn)

**sing,** n., colloquial for *a meeting for singing.*

**single blessedness,** trite phrase, a rhetorical variation on *unmarried.*

**Sing Sing,** see **Ossining**

**Sinhalese,** see **Cingalese**

**sink,** n., local and dialectal for *a low boggy place.* Also *sink hole.*

**Sinn Fein,** n., *an Irish patriotic movement,* pronounced (shĭn fān)

**sinology,** n., *knowledge of things pertaining to China,* pronounced (sĭnŏl′ojĭ) The term for a person versed in things Chinese is *sinologist* (sĭnŏl′ojĭst) or *sinologue* (sĭn′olŏg)

**Sioux,** n., *Indian and place name,* pronounced (soō), used both as singular and as plural.

**siphon,** n., *a device for drawing water and liquids,* with a less correct variant spelling *syphon,* both pronounced (sī′fon)

**sir,** see **ma'am**

**sirup,** see **syrup**

**sister-in-law,** see **father-in-law**

**sit,** see **set**

**situate,** adj., archaic and legal for *situated,* as in *a house situate at the corner of Fourth and Vine Streets.*

**size,** adj., incorrectly used in constructions like *Not having any complete sets, we had to use different size plates,* for *different sized plates,* or better, *plates of different sizes.*

**size up,** v., colloquial and slang for *estimate, judge,* as in *I sized him up at a glance.*

**skald,** n., *bard, poet,* pronounced (skawld) The word is archaic, poetic, or technical in its modern uses, and not the same word etymologically as the verb *scald.*

**skate,** n., slang for *an old horse.*

**skedaddle,** v., humorous and slang for *to run away ignominiously.*

**skeptic,** n., *a person disposed to doubt,* with related words *skeptical, skepticism.* All have variant spelling with *sc-*, but the pronunciation is always (sk)

**ski,** n., *snowshoe,* pronounced as a Norwegian word, (shē), or anglicized and pronounced (skē) The plural is either **ski** or *skis.* Also used as a verb *to ski,* as in *he skis, he ski'd,* with the apostrophe to distinguish the word from *skid, he has ski'd, he is skiing.*

**skidoo,** v., humorous and slang for *go away, get out.* If all the phrases in the language for this idea were gathered together, they would be many, for example, *get out, vamoose, skedaddle, scoot, slide, slope, sneak, mosey, shove,* and many others.

**skillet,** n., in some localities used for *frying pan.* In England **skillet** may mean a cooking utensil with legs and a long handle, a sense not current in America.

**skin,** v., slang in the sense *to take everything a person has, to get the better of,* as in *He's got you skinned a mile.* Slang also as a noun in the sense *a fraud,* or as an adjective in *skin game,* fraudulent game or action.

**skint,** see **burnt**

**skip,** v., slang for *to abscond.* Also *to skip out.*

**skirt,** n., slang in the sense *woman, girl.*

**skunk,** n., slang for *contemptible person.*

**Skupshtina,** n., Serbian word, *the Serbian parliament,* pronounced (skŏŏpshtē′na)

**sky-pilot,** n., slang for *preacher, clergyman.*

**slacker,** n., slang for *one who evades duty.*

**slake,** v., pronounced (slāk) and current only in the phrase *to slake one's thirst.* This word is a variant of the word *slack,* which may be a noun, as in *Take up the slack,* an adjective, as in *slack times,* or a verb, as in *It is time to slack speed* (also *slacken speed*) Both *slack* and **slake** are used with reference to lime, but *slack* is the usual term, both as a verb, as in *to slack lime,* and as an adjective, as in *slack* or *slacked lime.*

**slam,** n., v., slang in the sense *a bluntly disapproving comment, to comment in this way.*

**slantindicular,** adj., humorous word made on the analogy of *perpendicular.*

**slashes,** n., archaic dialect for *a clearing in the forest,* surviving historically in *the Mill-boy of the Slashes,* a name for Henry Clay.

**slat,** n., slang for *rib.* Also slang for a *thin and angular woman.*

**slate,** v., a kind of office slang in the sense *arrange for, appoint, intend, plan,* and a great variety of similar meanings, as in *The meeting is slated for the first Monday in March, He is slated for an advance in salary.* See **book**

**slather,** v., colloquial and dialectal for *to spread on thick,* both literally and figuratively, as in *to slather on the butter, to slather on the praise.* Probably a corruption of *slaver,* permit saliva to flow from the mouth, beslaver, and figuratively, fawn upon, flatter.

**Slav,** n., *one of the race of the Russians and other Eastern European peoples,* pronounced (slahv) The adjective is *Slavonian* (slavō'-nĭan), *Slavonic* (slavŏn'ĭk), or *Slavic* (slah'vĭk) These words are sometimes spelled *Sclav, Sclavic, Sclavonian, Sclavonic,* but are always pronounced and usually are written as above.

**slay,** v., literary for *kill,* with a past tense *slew* (slōō) and a past participle *slain* (slān)

**sleazy,** adj., colloquial in the sense *not firm in texture,* usually of fabrics. Pronounced (slē'zĭ) or (slā'zĭ)

**sled,** n., with approximately synonymous equivalents in *sleigh* and *sledge.* But a sled is usually a child's sled for coasting, or a heavy frame on runners for dragging loads. A sleigh is usually a light frame on runners for carrying passengers. The term *sledge* is rather literary and general in meaning, covering both *sleigh* and **sled.**

**sleek,** see **slick**

**sleeper,** n., the usual term in America for *a sleeping car.* See **diner** The word **sleeper** also means *railroad tie,* so called perhaps because it lies on the bed of the track. As the name for the *sleeping car* the word **sleeper** is sometimes criticized adversely on the ground that the ending *-er* indicates one who sleeps, not the place where one sleeps. The same objection is made to *diner* for dining car. It is true that the ending *-er* is ordinarily employed to form a noun of agency, but, in spite of any

543

theoretical objections, **sleeper** and *diner* must be accepted as current forms of English in at least good colloquial use. See **broiler, diner, stocker**

**sleep the sleep of the just,** trite phrase, a stylistic and euphemistic variant of *die.*

**sleuth,** n., colloquial for *detective.*

**slew,** see **slue**

**slick,** adj., adv., v., but only in colloquial, verging on low colloquial use, as in *a slick customer, slick as a whistle, slick up,* especially *slick up the hair.* The word is a variant of *sleek,* but *sleek* is used only in the literal sense *plump and glossy.* The words **slick** and *sleek* tend to diverge now into two quite separate words. Thus if one were speaking of a horse, the only appropriate adjective form would be *sleek* to describe his coat, but if one were speaking of smooth ice, one could not say *sleek as glass,* but only *slick as glass.* The difference phonetically between *sleek* (slēk) and **slick** (slĭk) is the same as that between *creek* (krēk) and *crick* (krĭk), dialectal variant of *creek.*

**sling,** v., *to throw,* with a past tense and past participle *slung.*

**slink,** v., *steal away,* with a past tense and a past participle *slunk.* The word *slunk* has a grotesque sound, however, which leads some speakers to avoid it. See **drink**

**slither,** v., colloquial and slang for *to go sliding and bumping,* construed usually with *down,* as in *He came slithering down the stairs and fell in a heap at the bottom step.*

**slithy,** see **chortle**

**slog,** v., *hit hard,* and figuratively, *work hard,* especially in the phrase *slog away.* The word has a variant *slug,* and a related noun *slogger, slugger,* bruiser. All these uses are on the border between colloquial and slang.

**slope,** v., slang in the sense *make off, depart.* See **skidoo**

**slough,** n., v., *a snake's cast skin, to cast off,* pronounced (slŭf)

**slough,** n., *a miry place,* pronounced (slow)  Now current chiefly

in the phrase *Slough of Despond* from *Pilgrim's Progress.* See
**slue**

**sloven,** n., *lazy untidy person,* pronounced (slŭv′n) Slightly
literary. The adjective *slovenly* is general present English.

**slow,** adv., correct both historically and by the test of use in
adverbial constructions like *Go slow, How slow this plant grows,
This clock runs slow.* Theoretical grammarians often replace
all uses of **slow** as adverb by *slowly* on the ground that adverbs
must end in *-ly.* But how about *soon* and many other adverbs
like this which can not end in *-ly?* The rule is entirely artificial,
and adverbs without the ending *-ly* are established beyond
question in good use.

**sloyd,** n., *hand-training through woodwork.* The word is of Swedish origin, pronounced (sloid), and sometimes spelled *slojd,
sloid.*

**slue,** n., local and dialectal word for *marshy ground* or *a shallow
stretch of water.* Also spelled *slew, sloo.* A variant form and
pronunciation of *slough.* A word **slue,** probably of different
etymological origin, is slang for *a large number or quantity,* as
in *a slue of people.* Pronounced (slōō)

**slue,** v., *to slip or skid,* especially *to slue round.* Also spelled *slew.*
The word is somewhat colloquial in flavor, and to some persons
it might even seem to be dialectal.

**slug,** see **slog**

**slumber,** n., v., archaic and literary for *sleep.*

**slump,** v., *to decline, decrease, collapse,* especially with reference to
prices and business activity. The word has passed out of the
realm of slang into that of general colloquial English.

**slut,** n., an archaic word for *slovenly woman,* and formerly even
applied to girls, as in *a pretty slut.* The word still survives in
low colloquial speech as a synonym for *bitch,* but it is avoided
in all senses in cultivated speech as a vulgar word. See **bitch**

**smack,** adv., colloquial in the sense *exactly,* as in *The ball hit him*

545

*smack in the eye.* Other names of sounds are used similarly, for example, *bang, slap.*

**smallpox,** n., *a disease.* Though historically the word *-pox* is a plural of the singular *pock*, it is now no longer felt to be a plural, and is construed as a singular, as in *Smallpox is a loathsome disease.* The spelling *-pox* helps to distinguish the word from *pocks.* So also with *chicken pox.* See **measles, pox**

**smart,** adj., dialectal in the sense *large*, as in *a right smart chunk of a boy.* Fashionable slang in the sense *fashionable*, as in *the smart set, a limousine and a smart chauffeur*, etc. Colloquial in the sense intelligent, as in *a very smart child*, and juvenile colloquial in the sense *fresh, impudent.*

**smarty,** adj., juvenile term of reproach and revilement, *fresh, impudent.*

**smell of,** v., colloquial and dialectal for *smell*, as in *He smelled of the flower and threw it away*, for *He smelled the flower*, etc. See **taste of**

**smelly,** adj., colloquial use for *malodorous, rank.*

**smile,** v., slang as a form of strong asseveration in the phrase *I should smile.*

**smitch,** n., dialectal for *a very small bit or particle.*

**smite,** v., archaic and literary for *strike*, with a past tense *smote* and a past participle *smitten.* The past participle survives in such phrases as *I was much smitten with the idea*, favorably impressed by it, *smitten with consumption*, attacked by consumption.

**smithereens,** n., colloquial and humorous for *small fragments*, pronounced (smĭdherēnz′)

**smithy,** n., *blacksmith's workshop*, pronounced (smĭdh′y)

**smoker,** n., *one who smokes*, or colloquially *that which is smoked*, a cigar, usually *a smoke*, or *a place in which one smokes, a smoking car.* See **sleeper**

**smokestack,** n., *chimney of a steamship*, usually on a river steamer. Smokestacks on ocean liners are more commonly called *funnels.*

**smudge,** n., local and dialectal in the sense *smoky fire to drive mosquitoes away.*

**snack,** n., colloquial use for *light lunch,* and in the phrase *to go snacks,* to go shares.

**snag,** n., colloquial for *unforeseen difficulty,* originally *tree trunk or branch,* dangerous to river navigation.   Hence *to strike a snag.*

**snake,** v., dialectal for *to pull, drag,* as in *to snake logs.*   For *snake* n., see **serpent**

**snake fence,** n., colloquial for *a zigzag rail fence.*

**snakes,** n., slang in the phrase *to have snakes, to see snakes,* for *delirium tremens.*

**snap,** n., slang in the sense *an easy time,* as in *a soft snap.*   Colloquial in the sense *period of cold weather,* as in *a cold snap,* parallel to *spell* for warm weather, as in *a hot spell.*   In some localities, colloquial use also in the sense *bargain.*

**snap,** v., slang in the phrase *snap into it,* a command to move and act energetically.   But also *snap out of it,* come quick, stop doing what you are doing.   See **move**

**snappy,** adj., slang in the sense *quick,* as in *Make it snappy,* Hurry, be energetic.

**snare and a delusion,** trite phrase, applied indiscriminately to all sorts of trivial mishaps and disappointments.

**snare of Cupid,** trite phrase, facetious allusion to love and courtship.

**sneak,** v., *move stealthily,* with a standard past tense *sneaked,* past participle **sneaked,** and a dialectal past tense and past participle *snuk.*   Slang in the sense *take stealthily,* as in *to sneak an apple.*

**snicker,** see **nicker**

**snide,** adj., slang for *clever and swindling,* as in *a snide trick.*

**sniffy,** adj., colloquial use for *disdainful.*

**snigger,** v., *laugh furtively,* with a variant *snicker.*   See **nicker**

**snitch,** v., slang for *steal, abstract surreptitiously,* as in *to snitch a cookie.*

547

**snob,** n., *one who stresses social position unduly.* Originally slang, but now current English.

**snoop,** v., humorous colloquialism for *to spy, to meddle.*

**snooze,** n., humorous colloquialism for *a nap.* The noun *snoozer* is also a humorous colloquialism for *a harmless, queer fellow, a codger.*

**snorter,** n., colloquial for something exceptionally strong or violent, as in *That was a snorter,* a big one, a strong one.

**snot,** n., low colloquial and vulgar for *mucus of the nose.* The polite substitutes are vague words like *mucus* or *discharge.*

**snotty,** adj., low colloquial for *impudent, presumptuous,* especially in the language of children. See **smart, smarty**

**snout,** n., *nose and mouth,* usually of animals. Pronounced (snowt), dialectally (snōōt), as in the low colloquial juvenile phrase *to make snoots at a person,* make faces.

**snuff,** n., slang in the phrase *up to snuff,* not innocent, knowing, perhaps originally of one old enough to take snuff.

**so,** conj., low colloquial and juvenile as the equivalent of *so that,* as in *He started early so he could be home in time for supper,* for *He started early so that,* etc., or *in order to be home,* etc. The word **so** is sometimes used at the beginning of a sentence in the sense *accordingly, consequently,* as in *So it seems we are not to have his company after all,* but the use of **so** beginning every narrative sentence is an unnecessary and monotonous repetition characteristic of crude style, "So then he said . . . . ," "So then she said . . . . ."

When the adverb **so** refers to a preceding statement, care should be taken to make sure that it really does refer to the whole statement. The following sentences say something which they do not mean: *For a number of years the taxicab drivers plied their nefarious trade unmolested. But if they continue to do so today* [i. e., ply their nefarious trade unmolested], *it is under the pains and penalties of law* [which would not be unmolested].

548

**so as,** conj., colloquial and especially characteristic of children's speech, in the sense *in order*, as in *We threw out the bags so as to have more room in the boat*, for *We threw out the bags in order*, etc., or better *To have more room in the boat, we threw out the bags*, or simply *We threw out the bags to have more room*. The use of **so as** is not grammatically incorrect, nor is it unusual to find the construction in literary style. The point is that one should guard against using the construction too frequently or when it is not necessary. See **as to**

**so . . as,** conj., see **as . . as**

**Sobranje,** n., Bulgarian word, *the Bulgarian parliament*, pronounced (sōbrahn′yĕ)

**sobriquet,** n., *nickname*, especially of a singer, dancer, or other public performer. Pronounced (sōbrĭkā′), with a variant *soubriquet* (sōōbrĭkā′)

**sobstuff,** n., slang for *sentimental writing or talk*, especially of a pathetic character.

**soccer,** see **socker**

**social function,** trite phrase, in journalistic style.

**sociology,** n., *study of society*, pronounced (sōsĭŏl′ojĭ), but the adjective is *sociological* (sōsholŏj′ĭkal)

**sock,** v., slang use in the sense *strike, hit*, as in *Sock it to him*, with a noun, *a sock in the eye*, and an adverb, *hit him sock in the eye*, square, slap in the eye. See **smack**

**socker,** n., slang for *Association football*. Also spelled *soccer*. The word is derived from *association* by processes possible only to the youthful football mind. As the word is derived from *association*, the spelling *soccer* is better etymologically than the spelling **socker,** but *soccer* is less in accord with the analogies of English spelling and is less generally used.

**soddened,** adj., *soaked*, as in *her poor little handkerchief was so soddened with tears that it oozed and dripped* (H. G. Wells, *The World of William Clissold*, I, 132) But this is not a general, nor would it ordinarily be considered a correct form of the word. The usual form is *sodden*, which is by origin a past participle of the verb *to seethe*. In the form *sodden*, however, the primary verbal sense has been lost, and the word is now used only as a participial adjective, like *molten*, as participle of *melt*. But since *sodden* is already participial in form, it does not need the *-ed* of *soddened*.

**soi-disant,** adj., French word *self-called, making pretense of,* pronounced (swah dē′zahṅ)

**soirée,** n., *evening reception and entertainment,* but usually only in descriptions written in newspaper style. Pronounced (swahrā′)

**sojourn,** v., *to remain temporarily at a place,* pronounced (sō′jern) ordinarily in America, (sŭj′ern) in England.

**solder,** n., v., *soft fusible metal, to repair or join with solder,* pronounced (sŏd′er) Spelled *sawder* in the colloquial figurative phrase *soft sawder,* flattery, blarney. The *New English Dictionary* records the pronunciations (sŏl′der) and (sō′der), neither of which occurs in America.

**soldier,** v., colloquial and slang in the sense *to work lazily and ineffectively,* as in *to soldier on the job.*

**solemn,** adj., *serious, impressive,* pronounced (sŏl′em) But the verb is *solemnize* (sŏl′emnīz) and the noun is *solemnity* (solĕm′nĭtĭ)

**solemn conclave,** trite phrase, an ambitious commonplace, used in fine writing for any ordinary, everyday kind of meeting.

**solid,** adj., slang in the sense *on good terms, favorably considered,* as in *You must make yourself solid with the boss.*

**so long,** phrase, colloquial interjection at parting, *good-by.*

**solvable,** adj., *susceptible of being solved,* especially of problems, mysteries, etc., with a variant *soluble.* The form *soluble* applies also to substances, but not **solvable,** the proper form of this word as applied to substances being *dissolvable* (dĭzŏlv′abl)

**sombre,** adj., *dark, gloomy,* pronounced (sŏm′ber)

**some,** adj., adv., slang as a general intensive, as in *That is some hat,* a fine hat or remarkable hat; colloquial and dialectal in the sense *somewhat, a little* as in *He is some better today.* See **quite**

**someone,** see **anyone**

**someplace,** adv., colloquial and dialectal for *somewhere.* See **any place**

**somersault,** n., *turn heels over head,* pronounced (sŭm'ersawlt'), with a variant *somerset, summerset* (sŭm'ersĕt') As the word is derived from French *sobresaut,* the form *somerset* is a little closer etymologically to the original than **somersault,** but *somerset* is now regarded as popular and dialectal, and **somersault** as the correct form. The ultimate etymology of the word is Latin *supra,* above, over, and *saltus,* leap, and the *l* in *sault* is a learned restoration from the original Latin form of the word. The form *somer-* is the result of popular etymology through the influence of the English word *summer.* The history of the word presents a strange mixture of confusion and error.

**something,** adv., low colloquial, passing more or less into general colloquial use in constructions like *She behaved something awful, It rained something awful last night, This hat looks something awful,* all in the sense *very badly, severely,* etc.

**sometime,** adj., occasional literary use for former, as in *the sometime president of our organization, sometime fellow of New College.* See **one-time, quondam**

**someway,** adv., rarely used as the equivalent of *somehow.*

**somewheres,** adv., dialectal for *somewhere.*

**son of a gun,** n., low colloquial term of abuse, a euphemistic softening of a still more abusive term.

**sonorous,** adj., *resounding,* pronounced (sōnŏr'us)

**sooner,** n., slang for *fellow, snoozer, codger,* as in *an old sooner.*

**sooner,** adv., low colloquial and dialectal in the sense *rather,* as in *He would sooner starve than work.*

**soot,** n., *a black powder from smoke.*  Pronounced (so͞ot), (so͝ot), and dialectally (sŭt)

**soph,** n., slang abbreviation for *sophomore.*

**soprano,** n., *high-voiced woman singer,* pronounced (soprăn'ō) or (soprah'nō)

**sore,** adj., in colloquial and slang speech, used as a synonym for *angry, annoyed.*

**sorra,** adj., colloquial Irishism for *sorry* as in *Sorra a one did I see,* not a one did I see.

**sort,** n., colloquial in the phrase *of a sort,* as in *He is an artist of a sort,* rather a poor artist, and also in constructions like *He is a pretty good sort,* a pretty good fellow.  Colloquial in the plural in the phrase *out of sorts,* not in good health or good humor.

**sort of,** adv., colloquial and dialectal, as in *He sort of caught his breath and said,* etc., for *He caught his breath slightly and said,* etc.

**sort of a,** see **kind of a**

**S. O. S.,** n., *wireless signal of distress,* not an abbreviation, but an arbitrary group of letters.  Pronounced (ĕs'ō'ĕs')

**so so,** adv., colloquial for *fair, moderately.*

**sotto voce,** Italian phrase, *in a low voice, almost inaudibly,* pronounced (sŏt'ō vō'chä) or as in Italian, (sŏt'tō vō'chä)

**sou,** n., *French coin of small value,* pronounced (so͞o)

**soufflé,** n., *omelette or other dish made light with beaten eggs,* pronounced (so͞oflä')

**sough,** n., v., *the sound made by the wind, to make such a sound.*  Pronounced (sow), but recorded by British authorities also in the pronunciations (sŭf) and (so͝oCH), with the final sound pronounced as in Scotch *loch.*

**sound out,** v., *to make preliminary inquiries,* as in *The minister has been instructed to sound out Great Britain on this question.*  The word *sound* alone, omitting *out,* would adequately express the same meaning, and the simpler phrase would be the better style.  See **up**

**soup,** n., slang in the phrase *in the soup*, in trouble, wrecked, ruined.

**soupçon,** n., French word, *a dash or trace*, pronounced (sōop'sŏn)

**sourdough,** n., slang for *one who has spent one or more winters in Alaska.*

**soused,** adj., slang in the sense *drunk.*  See **pickled**

**Southey,** n., *English poet*, pronounced (sŭdh'ĭ) or (sowdh'ĭ)

**Southland,** n., sentimental for *the South.*

**southron,** n., Scottish usage for *southerner*, that is, an Englishman from the point of view of a Scotchman.

**Southwark,** n., *region of London*, pronounced (sŭdh'ark)

**spa,** n., originally *a watering place in Belgium*, then any watering place or resort.  In New England, *a restaurant*, with the older eighteenth-century pronunciation (spaw) occasionally surviving, although the usual pronunciation is now (spah)

**spacious days of Queen Elizabeth,** trite phrase, a stock phrase of literary criticism.

**spalpeen,** n., Irish dialect for *rascal, youngster.*

**spang,** adv., dialectal in the sense *directly, exactly*, as in *The ball hit the window spang in the center.*  See **smack**

**spank,** v., colloquial for *to punish corporally.*  The adjective *spanking* is slang, as in *a spanking breeze*, a strong and favorable breeze.

**sparrowgrass,** n., dialectal for *asparagus*, being a bit of popular etymologizing.  The abbreviation *grass* pertains to the dialect of the vegetable stand.

**spat,** n., colloquial for *minor quarrel.*

**spay,** v., *castrate*, with a past tense and past participle *spayed.* On the basis of this past form, low colloquial speech has made a present tense *spade*, past tense and past participle *spaded*, as though the word were related to the noun *spade.*

**speak-easy,** n., slang for *place at which intoxicating drinks are sold illegally.*

553

**spec,** n., colloquial and slang abbreviation for *speculation.*

**special,** adj., in some of its uses a synonym of *especial,* in others to be distinguished from *especial.* The words *especial* and **special** have the same meaning when they signify *exceptional in degree, preëminent, particular,* as in *a special occasion* or *an especial occasion, a special friend of mine* or *an especial friend of mine, I take a special pleasure* or *I take an especial pleasure,* etc. But **special** has a special sense, that is, a meaning restricted to it and not shared by *especial,* the meaning *peculiar or individual in kind, not general,* as in *a special privilege, He requires special food, a special edition, a special train.*

**specially,** adv., used in the sense *specifically,* as in *I had this made specially for you,* or *intentionally,* as in *This rule has been specially limited to apply only to the aged.* To be distinguished from *especially,* unusually, exceptionally, as in *I have been especially interested in his later speeches,* which is different from *I have been interested specially in his later speeches,* i. e., have been interested specifically, etc.

**specialty,** n., used interchangeably with *speciality* in the sense *the particular pursuit or product to which one gives attention,* as in *His specialty* or *speciality is speechifying, Custom-made shirts are our specialty, speciality.* But in the sense *distinguishing feature or characteristic of something,* only the form *speciality* is used, as in *The speciality of this coat is its reversible collar.*

**specie,** n., *money in the form of coin,* plural the same, and both pronounced (spē′shē), or very formally (spē′shĭē)

**species,** n., *a class of things,* with a plural the same, and both pronounced (spē′shēz), or very formally (spē′shĭēz) In low colloquial speech a singular *specie* occurs, as in *a specie of bird.*

**speck,** n., dialectal for *bacon.* Formerly common in the whaling industry for the blubber of a whale.

**specs,** n., colloquial for *spectacles.*

**spectator,** n., pronounced (spĕktā′tŏr), not (spĕk′tātor) The word strictly applies only to one who views something, therefore is not a synonym for *audience*, which etymologically refers to persons who hear a performance, etc. One would speak therefore of the *spectators* at a football game, but of the *audience* at a concert.

**speechify,** v., humorous or contemptuous for *to make a speech.* See **argufy**

**speed the parting guest,** trite phrase, by origin a quotation from Pope's *Odyssey*, Book xv, 1. 83.

**speedy,** see **fast**

**spell,** n., colloquial in the sense *period of weather*, as in *a hot spell,* or for *any period of time,* as in *I was in Chicago last winter for a spell, a spell of sickness.* Dialectal as a verb in the sense *to relieve one another by taking turns at work.* See **snap**

**spell,** v., *give the letters of a word*, with a past tense and past participle *spelled* or *spelt.* See **burnt**

**spellbinder,** n., political slang for *eloquent orator.*

**Spelling Reform.** Although spelling reform is a matter that must interest every intelligent student of English, its interest lies rather in the field of theory than in that of practical usage. There are, to be sure, many words which may be spelled in more than one way in the English language, but these are not the words that form the chief concern of the spelling reformers. The endeavor of spelling reforms is to bring about a comprehensive reform of English spelling, not merely to support those spellings which already have the support of more or less general usage, but to introduce new and unauthorized spellings. On the side of theory, much can often be said in favor of the proposed reforms, for even a slight examination of the present system of English spelling shows that it is extremely irregular and uneconomical. However desirable the reforms may be, it must be said nevertheless that, until they have been accepted and have passed more or less into general practice, these reforms are of concern to the theoretical, not to the practical student of English usage.

It is suggested that persons interested in projects of spelling reform should inform themselves of the activities of the two important associations organized for promoting the cause of spelling reform. These are the Simplified Spelling Board and the Simplified Spelling Society. The Simplified Spelling Board was organized January 12, 1906, and has published a number of bulletins and other documents. Its most important publication is a *Handbook of Simplified Spelling*, 1920. Its mailing address is Simplified Spelling Board, 1 Madison Avenue, New York City. The Simplified Spelling Society is the English counterpart to the American Simplified Spelling Board. It likewise has issued many publications, and its address is Simplified Spelling Society, 20 Southampton Street, Bloomsbury Square, London WC 1, England. Both of these organizations welcome correspondence and new members. See also Lounsbury, *English Spelling and Spelling Reform*, 1909.

**Spencer, Herbert,** n., *English philosopher* (1820–1903), not spelled *Spenser*.

**Spenser, Edmund,** n., *English poet* (1552–1599), not spelled *Spencer*.

**spermaceti,** n., *substance in the heads of whales*, pronounced (spermasē'tĭ) or (spermasĕt'ĭ)

**spew,** v., *eject from the mouth, vomit*, with a variant spelling *spue*. The word is archaic or violently rhetorical.

**sphere,** n., *a ball or globe*, pronounced (sfēr), low colloquially (spēr), and so with the initial consonant of the derivatives, *spherical* (sfĕr'ĭkal), *spheroid* (sfē'roid)

**sphinx,** n., *lion with woman's head, unfathomable person*, pronounced (sfĭngks) Written with a capital only when referring to the Sphinx in Egypt.

**spider,** n., local and dialectal for *frying pan*. See **skillet**

**spiffy,** adj., colloquial and dialectal for *smart, spruce.* Also *spiffing.*

**spiflicate,** v., slang and humorous for *punish, chastise.*

**spigot,** n., *plug to which a faucet is attached.* General usage in America, but archaic in England.

**spill,** v., *to cause to flow or fall out,* with a past tense and past participle *spilled* or *spilt.* Slang in the phrase *spill the beans,* do something that causes some plan or endeavor to fail. See **burnt**

**spinach,** n., *a vegetable,* pronounced (spĭn'ĭj) The pronunciation (spĭn'ĭch), through the influence of the spelling, is not current English. Sometimes spelled *spinage.*

**spindrift,** n., *sea spray.* The variant *spoondrift* is no longer in use.

**spinster,** n., *unmarried woman,* usual only as a legal term.

**spirituelle,** adj., French word, *with a look of intelligence and refinement,* pronounced (spĭrĭtüĕl')

**spirt,** see **spurt**

**spit,** n., *spittle.* Also a verb, *to eject spittle or saliva.* The word, both as noun and as verb, is usually avoided as vulgar. For the noun, *spittle* or *saliva* is preferred, and for the verb, some circumlocution. See **saliva, spit,** v. The noun occurs in the colloquial phrase *spit and image,* sometimes incorrectly changed to *spitting image,* meaning *exact likeness.*

**spit,** v., *eject saliva or other matter from the mouth,* with a past tense and past participle *spat,* less frequently *spit,* and low colloquially *spitted.* The word is often avoided as vulgar, the vulgarity of course arising from the action itself, and a more formal expression, *expectorate, eject,* etc., is substituted instead. But if it is necessary to mention the action at all, it would seem that the plain, simple word is the best one to do it with. The phrase *spit it out* is slang for *say what you have to say and be done with it.*

**splendid,** adj., colloquial as a general intensive in approving senses, as in *a splendid dinner, a splendid view,* etc. See **fine, great, wonderful**

557

**splendiferous,** adj., humorous word for *splendid, glorious.*

**splice,** v., *unite*, especially of two pieces of rope; slang in the sense *unite in marriage.*

**split,** v., slang in the sense *betray*, construed with *on*, as in *to split on a confederate.*

**Split Infinitive,** see the **Digest of Grammatical Rules,** §18 (*d*)

**splitting,** adj., colloquial in the sense *violent*, as in *a splitting headache.*

**Spokane,** n., *city in Washington*, pronounced (spōkăn′)

**spoof,** v., slang for *to hoax, to play a joke on*, and also as a noun, *a hoax, a practical joke.*

**spook,** n., humorous word for *ghost*, with an adjective *spooky.*

**spoon,** v., colloquial and slang in the sense *to make love*, with an adjective *spoony.*

**spoonful,** n., *amount a spoon holds*, with a plural *spoonfuls.*

**sport,** n., slang for *good fellow, not a slacker*, as in *Oh, be a sport.*

**sport,** v., slang in the sense *wear*, with the implication ostentatiously, as in *to sport a new hat*, and old slang in the phrase *to sport the oak*, lock the door.

**spot,** v., colloquial and slang in the sense *pick out, distinguish*, as in *I can spot a lawyer every time.*

**spouse,** n., archaic, literary, and sometimes humorous for *bride, wife.*

**spout,** n., slang in the phrase *up the spout*, gone, used up, squandered.   The phrase originally referred to things in pawn, by inference, gone for good.

**spout,** v., colloquial in the sense *orate, talk voluminously*, and perhaps in this sense a corrupt form of *dispute.*

**spread,** n., slang in the sense *a meal*, as in *He treated us to a spread at a lobster palace;* colloquial in the sense *butter, jam, or other material* to be spread on bread.

**spread,** v., slang in the phrase *spread yourself*, behave with unusual generosity or amiability.

**spree,** n., colloquial and slang for *a period of dissipation*, not always reprehensible dissipation.

**spring,** v., colloquial and slang in the sense *to tell unexpectedly*, as in *He sprang this information on me soon after I got home.* But the usage is nevertheless old, and Sir Thomas Browne, *Epistle Dedicatory* to *The Garden of Cyrus* (1658), wrote, "The Field of Knowledge hath been so traced, it is hard to spring anything new."

**springe,** n., archaic werd for *noose*, pronounced (sprĭnj)

**springhalt,** n., *disease in a horse's hind legs*, with a variant form *stringhalt*. The form *stringhalt* is the more general and the more correct etymologically.

**sprint,** n., v., *a fast run, to run fast*, usually for short distances. A word of sporting associations, and, though an old word, widely current only recently in connection with athletic sports.

**sprouts,** n., slang in the sense *discipline*, in the phrase *to put one through a course of sprouts.*

**spry,** adj., *quick, active.* In general use, but ordinarily with a slightly humorous coloring.

**spud,** n., slang and dialectal for *potato*. See **murphy**

**spunk,** n., *courage, spirit, grit.* Generally current as a colloquialism in America, but not in England. Also an adjective *spunky.*

**spurious,** adj., *not genuine*, pronounced (spū′rĭus), not (spōōr′ĭus)

**spurt,** n., v., *a gushing forth, to gush forth*, with a variant *spirt.* The latter spelling is closer to the etymological origins of the word, but the spelling **spurt** is now more general.

**Spuyten Duyvil,** n., *place at the north end of Manhattan Island*, pronounced (spī′tn dī′vl)

**squalor,** n., *griminess, untidiness*, pronounced (skwŏl′or), rarely (skwā′lor) The adjective *squalid* is always (skwŏl′id)

**square,** n., adj., v., colloquial in the sense *honest, candid*, as in *a square deal, a square man, on the square, to square things; requite*, as in *to get square with an enemy; abundant*, as in *a square meal.*

Sinister slang in the sense *bribe*, as in *You will have to square the inspector.*  See **see, straight**

**squash,** see **lemonade**

**squeak,** n., slang in the sense *escape*, as in *That was a close squeak*, a narrow escape.

**squeal,** v., slang in the sense *reveal a secret, confess.*

**squelch,** v., colloquial and slang, meaning *suppress, frown upon.*

**squirm,** v., colloquial, and meaning *to wriggle, writhe.*

**squirrel,** n., *a tree rodent.*  Almost universally pronounced (skwŭr'-el) in America, sometimes (skwĭr'el), (skwĕr'el)  In England usually (skwĭr'el)

**squirt,** n., slang for *insignificant person.*

**stab,** n., slang in the sense *effort, trial,* as in *to make a stab at a thing.*

**stable,** n., primarily *a place in which horses are kept,* but sometimes extended to include buildings for cattle.  See **barn**

**stack,** v., slang in the phrase *stack the cards,* arrange things to secure an unfair advantage.

**staff of life,** trite phrase, a traditional synonym for *bread.*

**stag party,** n., slang for *party or other meeting at which only men are present.*  See **hen party**

**Staked Plain,** see **Llano Estacado**

**stalactite,** n., *a pendent icicle-shaped rocky deposit,* pronounced (stăl'ăktīt) or (stălăk'tīt)

**stalagmite,** n., *cone-shaped deposit on the floor of a cave,* pronounced (stăl'ăgmīt) or (stălăg'mīt)

**stall,** v., generally current in America in the sense *bring to a standstill,* as in *The wagon was stalled in the mud,* or *to stall the engine of an automobile.*

**stamina,** n., originally a plural of Latin *stamen,* but now used as a singular in the sense *power of endurance, strength.*  The singular *stamen,* organ in a flower, has a plural *stamens.*  Pronounced (stăm'ĭna), the singular being (stā'men), its plural (stā'menz)

**stamp, v.,** *to force down with the foot,* pronounced (stămp), dialectally (stŏmp)   See **stomp**

**stanch,** adj., in the sense *firm, loyal;* as a verb in the sense *to stop the flow of,* especially of blood from a wound.   In both uses a variant *staunch* occurs, perhaps more frequently for the adjective than for the verbal use.   Pronounced (stahnch) or (stawnch)   The pronunciation (stănch) is low colloquial.

**stanchion,** n., *post or pillar,* pronounced (stahn′shn) or (stăn′shn)

**stand,** n., colloquial and dialectal in the sense *promising growth,* as in *a good stand of wheat.*   The noun **stand,** meaning *building or site for a business,* as in *business at the old stand,* pertains to the dialect of business.

**stand,** v., slang in the phrases *stand pat,* not to yield from one's position; *stand in with,* receive special consideration from; *stand a person off,* defer paying him his dues; *stand a treat, the drinks,* etc., pay for a treat, etc.; *stand for,* permit, endure. In the sense *endure, tolerate,* as in *I can't stand that person,* the word is colloquial.   See **abide**

**stand-by,** n., colloquial and slang for *resource, something to depend on,* as in *John is my chief stand-by in an emergency.*

**standee,** n., theatrical slang for *one who has to stand at a performance,* the desire of every manager being to have as many standees as possible.

**stand-off,** n., slang for *a draw, a tie,* as in *fight to a stand-off.*

**stand-offish,** adj., colloquial, meaning *distant, stiff.*   See **offish**

**standpoint,** n., in good use as a synonym for *point of view,* though not so general.   It is rejected, however, by some stylists in favor of *point of view,* the latter being the older and more formal phrase.   By origin **standpoint** is a translation of German *Standpunkt,* a word of the same meaning.   See **viewpoint**

**stanza,** see **verse**

**starboard,** n., *right side of a ship,* pronounced (stahr′berd)   See **boatswain**

**start in,** v., colloquial for *begin,* as in *It started in to rain at nine o'clock,* for *It began to rain,* etc.

**state,** v., *to make a statement in a formal way,* but often used when the informal *say* would be better.

**stationery,** n., *writing materials,* to be distinguished from *stationary,* adj., fixed, not moving.

**stature,** n., *height,* literally of the body, figuratively of mental or moral quality. A formal literary word, pronounced (stăt′yer)

**status,** n., *position or rank,* pronounced (stăt′us) or (stā′tus)

**staunch,** see **stanch**

**staysail,** n., *sail on a stay,* pronounced (stā′sl) See **boatswain**

**steal,** n., slang for *theft,* but used chiefly with reference to political corruption, as in *The sale of these street franchises was one of the biggest steals in the history of the city.*

**steed,** n., poetical and literary for *horse.*

**steep,** adj., slang for *excessively costly, extravagant, taxing credulity.*

**steer,** v., slang as applied to persons, as in *I steered him into the dining room as quickly as possible.*

**sterile,** adj., *not capable of producing anything,* pronounced (stĕr′ĭl) or (stĕr′īl) See **-ile**

**stevedore,** n., *worker on the docks,* pronounced (stē′vedōr)

**stick,** n., colloquial in the sense *brandy in tea, coffee,* or any drink laced with spirit; or *a stiff, uninteresting person.*

**stick,** v., slang and colloquial in a variety of phrases, as in *to stick around,* wait, remain, as in *You'd better stick around—we're going to have something to eat pretty soon; stick up,* terrorize at pistol's point, as in *to stick up the town;* or *to place,* as in *Stick it up there on the mantelpiece; stick in,* insert, as in *Stick it in here; stick it,* endure, stand, as in *I can't stick it any longer,* or *stick it out,* endure to the end; *stick it on,* charge high prices; *stick up for,* defend; *stick up to,* oppose, withstand; and in the passive *to be stuck,* on oneself or something or some person, to be enamored of.

**stiff,** n., slang for *a rough, disobliging person,* usually in the phrase *big stiff,* or for *a dead human body.*

**stigma,** n., *mark, stain, brand,* the usual plural being *stigmata* (stĭg′mata), rarely *stigmas* (stĭg′maz)

**stile,** n., *passage over or through a barrier, especially a fence,* to be distinguished from *style,* manner of writing, etc. The word **stile** originally meant a set of steps or other similar device by which one mounted over a fence, but it has been extended to include other means of passing a barrier, for example, to turnstiles.

**stilly,** adv., *in a still or quiet manner.* Though correctly formed, this adverb is very rarely used, the customary adverb being *still,* as in *He lay very still.* An adjective *stilly* occurs rarely in poetry, as in *Oft in the stilly night.* The adverb is pronounced (stĭl′lĭ), the adjective (stĭl′ĭ)

**stimulus,** n., *something calling forth action,* with a plural *stimuli,* pronounced (stĭm′ūlus), (stĭm′ūlī)

**stimy,** n., *a term in golf,* pronounced (stī′mĭ) and occasionally spelled *stymie.*

**sting,** v., slang in the sense *defraud, treat unfairly,* or merely *charge,* as in *He stung me for five dollars,* with or without implication that this was an unfair charge.

**stinger,** n., colloquial for *sharp stroke or blow.*

**stink,** n., v., now avoided as a vulgar word. For the noun, *stench,* is preferred, and for the verb, *to smell,* or elaborate paraphrases like *to emit an odor.* The phrase *stink of money,* be very rich, is slang. The past tense of **stink** is *stank* or *stunk,* the past participle is *stunk.*

**stipend,** n., *regular fixed payment,* as of a pension or salary. Usually with the implication of a payment barely enough to live on. See **honorarium, emolument, salary** Pronounced (stī′pĕnd)

**stirrup,** n., *place for the feet on a saddle,* pronounced (stĭr′up), not (stir′up)

**St. Louis,** n., *city in Missouri,* pronounced (sānt lōō'ĭs) or (sānt lōō'ĭ)

**stocker,** n., technical language of the stockyards for *a steer kept for fattening.* So a *killer* is a steer to be killed, a *canner,* one only good enough for canning. See **diner, sleeper**

**stogy,** n., slang and dialectal for *heavy shoe or boot.* Also the colloquial and commercial name for a long cheap cigar.

**stoke,** v., *feed coals to a fire;* colloquial and slang of persons, *to eat,* usually with the implication of eating abundantly and rapidly.

**stomacher,** n., archaic name for *an ornamental part of a woman's garment,* pronounced (stŭm'acher) It was often richly embroidered, and resembled an elaborate belt front.

**stomp,** v., *to strike with the feet, to press down,* widely current, but only in dialectal speech, as a variant of *stamp.* See **stamp**

**stony,** adv., slang in the phrase *stony broke,* no money left.

**stoop,** n., local and dialectal for *porch,* especially a small porch before the front entry to a house. The word is of Dutch origin and is current chiefly in communities that have come under Dutch influence.

**stop,** v., colloquial and dialectal in the sense *stay, reside,* as in *He is stopping at the station hotel.*

**stopple,** n., a rare variant of *stopper.*

**store,** n., the usual name in America for *any retail establishment,* being thus the equivalent of the British *shop.* In England **store** is not used of smaller establishments, although the larger ones selling a variety of goods are called *stores,* in America *department stores.*

**storekeeper,** n., *a person who conducts a store,* called a shopkeeper in England. See **shopkeeper**

**stork,** n., *a tall wading bird,* colloquially and humorously of the advent of a newly born child, as in *The stork came to our house last week.*

**storm,** v., *rage,* of the weather, and figuratively of persons. In dialectal use **storm** is also used in the sense *rain*, as in *The wind blew last night, but it didn't storm, Is it still storming outside?*

**storthing,** n., Norwegian word, *Norwegian parliament,* pronounced (stŏr′tĭng)

**story,** n., *floor or level of a building,* plural *stories,* as in *a house of three stories.* Commonly spelled *storey, storeys* in England, a spelling which distinguishes *storey* from **story,** *a tale, a legend,* though the two words are so unlike in meaning that one would not often be mistaken for the other with the same spelling for both. For **story,** *tale, legend,* the meaning *lie, falsehood* occurs in children's English.

**stoup,** n., archaic word for *cup, flagon,* pronounced (stō͞op), as in *a stoup of wine.*

**stout,** adj., strictly means *resolute, strong,* but used sometimes euphemistically for *fat, corpulent.* See **fleshy**

**stow,** v., slang in the sense *stop, discontinue,* as in *Stow that yelling.* See **cut**

**straight,** adj., colloquial and slang in the sense *undiluted,* as in *He drinks his whisky straight,* and also in the sense *upright, honest, candid,* as in *There is something not quite straight about this letter.* See **square** The phrase *a straight tip,* positive information, is slang, and *straight away,* at once, is colloquial.

**straitened,** adj., *restricted, limited,* now commonly used only in the phrases *in straitened circumstances, to be straitened for means.* The verb *straiten* is archaic. The word is often misspelled *straightened.*

**strand,** n., literary word for *shore,* no longer current in general use, but persisting as the name of a famous street, *the Strand,* in London.

**strapped,** see **flush**

**strapping,** adj., colloquial for *sturdy, robust.*

**Strasbourg,** n., *a city of Alsace-Lorraine,* now a French city. By a decision of a supplement, published in 1922, the United States

Geographic Board discarded the earlier approved form *Strassburg* and also *Strasburg*, authorizing only **Strasbourg**, the French form of the name. The Permanent Committee on Geographical Names also approves **Strasbourg**.

**stratum**, n., *a term in geology*, with a plural *strata*. Usually pronounced (străt′um), (străt′a), sometimes (strā′tum), (strā′ta)

**straw**, n., colloquial as a contraction of *straw hat*, current especially among the manufacturers and sellers of hats.

**streak**, v., slang in the sense *go rapidly*, *run*, as in *He went streaking it down the avenue*. The phrase *a yellow streak* is colloquial and slang for *not thoroughly reliable or honorable*.

**strength**, n., *power*, *ability*, pronounced (strĕngth) or (strĕngkth), low colloquially (strĕnth) So also *length*.

**strew**, v., a poetic and literary word for *scatter*, with a past tense *strewed*, and a past participle *strewed*, *strewn*. The past participle is now in more general use than the other forms of the word, as in *toys and books strewn about the room*.

**stricken**, v., an archaic form of the past participle of *strike*, surviving only in phrases like *stricken with grief*, *stricken in years*, *the stricken family*, and in the sense *remove* as applied to written records, as in *It was moved that these words be stricken from the record*.

**string**, v., slang in the sense *intentionally mislead as a joke*, and also in the phrase *to string up*, to hang.

**stringhalt**, see **springhalt**

**strychnine**, n., *a drug*, pronounced (strĭk′nĭn) or (strĭk′nīn)

**studding sail**, n., *sail on a ship*, pronounced (stŭn′sl) See **boatswain**

**student**, n., *one engaged in study*, especially in college or in a professional school. The words *pupil*, *scholar* usually apply to younger persons, those in primary, elementary, and high schools, though *student* is also used of high-school pupils. As between *pupil* and *scholar*, *pupil* applies to older and *scholar* to younger

**learners.** The word *scholar* has besides a special sense, *one deeply versed in a learned subject.*

**stuff, v.,** slang in the sense *hoax, mislead,* as in *He's only stuffing you,* telling you tales, and colloquial in the sense *to eat greedily.*

**stuffy,** adj., slang in the sense *angry,* as in *I wonder what makes him so stuffy.*

**stump, v.,** colloquial and slang in the sense *be too much for, confound,* as in *That stumps me. I don't know what it is all about.* As a noun, *stumps,* legs, is slang.

**stunt,** n., slang for *a notable action, a part or turn in an entertainment.* The word is now so generally used that it seems not improbable that it will pass from slang into standard speech. The etymology of the word is not certainly known, but it is probably related to the word *stint,* as in *to do one's stint,* what is assigned to one.

**Stuyvesant,** n., *family and place name,* pronounced (stī′vesant)

**style,** see stile

**Styx,** n., *river in Hades,* pronounced (stĭks)  The equivalent adjective is *Stygian* (stĭj′ĭan)

**suave,** adj., *pleasing, bland,* pronounced (swāv) or (swahv)  The noun *suavity* is pronounced (swăv′ĭtĭ) or (swah′vĭtĭ)

**suaviter in modo, fortiter in re,** Latin phrase, *gently but firmly,* literally, *mildly in manner, firmly in the thing;* pronounced (swā′vĭter ĭn mō′dō, fŏr′tĭter ĭn rē)

**sub,** n., colloquial abbreviation for *substitute,* especially on a baseball or other athletic team.  Also abbreviation for *submarine.*

**subaltern,** n., *a military rank and title,* pronounced (subawl′tern), in England (sŭb′altern)

**sub judice,** Latin phrase, *still under consideration,* pronounced (sŭb jōō′dĭsĭ)

**Subjunctive Mood,** see **Digest of Grammatical Rules,** §20

**subpoena,** n., *a legal writ,* pronounced (subpē′na) or (supē′na), also as a verb, with the same pronunciations.

**sub rosa,** Latin phrase, *confidentially, under pledge of secrecy,* pronounced (sŭb rō′za)

**subsidence,** n., *sinking, settling,* pronounced (sŭbsīd′ens) or (sŭb′sĭdens)

**sub silentio,** Latin phrase, *tacitly, silently,* pronounced (sŭb sĭlĕn′shĭō)

**substitute,** v., *put in place of,* often incorrectly combined with *by,* as in *The special stamp has been substituted by a regular stamp.* The proper phrasing is *substitute for* and *replace by.*

**subtle,** adj., *refined, penetrating, discriminating.* Pronounced (sŭt′l) Older spellings *subtil, subtile* are no longer in use. The derivative forms *subtilize, subtlety, subtly* are pronounced (sŭt′-ĭlīz), (sŭt′ltĭ), (sŭt′lĭ)

**suburb,** n., *outlying region of city,* pronounced (sŭb′urb), low colloquially (sŏŏ′burb) The adjective is *suburban* (subur′ban)

**succès d'estime,** French phrase, *a performance received respectfully but not enthusiastically,* literally, *a success of respect;* pronounced (sŏŏksā′ dĕstēm′)

**succinct,** adj., *brief, concise,* especially as applied to literary style. Pronounced (sŭksĭngkt′)

**succor,** n., v., a literary word meaning *aid, to aid,* pronounced (sŭk′or)

**succulent bivalve,** trite phrase, slightly humorous synonym for *oyster.* See **Polysyllabic Humor**

**such,** adj., colloquial in elliptical exclamatory constructions, as in *We had to wait an hour—such a nuisance!,* and a crude low colloquialism as the equivalent of *same,* as in *All those desiring tickets can procure such by applying at the office.* See **same** Stilted and formalistic in the phrase *as such,* as in *The paper is nonpartisan and will be conducted as such,* in a nonpartisan way, or accordingly.

**such as,** pron., archaic in the sense *all who, those who* or *which,* as in *Such as I have, I give unto thee,* Those that I have, I give unto thee, *Such as are unwilling to stay may leave now*, Those that or who are unwilling, etc.   This use is different from the use of **such as** as a conjunction introducing a concessive clause, as in *You can have them, such as they are*, although they are not very good, this construction being generally current.

**sucker,** n., slang in the sense *gullible person*, as in *Do you take me for a sucker?*

**suction,** v., *to draw out by suction*.   A compact but not unquestionable use.   See **auction**

**Sudan,** n., *region of central Africa*, pronounced (soōdăn′)  The United States Geographic Board rejects a number of variants, including *Soodan* and *Soudan*.

**suffer,** v., *be subjected to*, as in *to suffer from insomnia*.   The word always implies being subjected to some discomfort or disqualification, and therefore it is improperly used in the following: *He appears to imagine that what Frenchmen suffer from is not a sound system of finance but a sufficient sense of national unity.* But Frenchmen could not suffer from a sound system of finance or a sufficient sense of national unity, though they might suffer from the lack of these desirable things.

**sufficient,** n., a formal and literary word meaning *enough*, and sometimes used when better taste calls for the simpler word, as in *"Won't you have some more bread?"   "No, thanks, I've had sufficient,"* better, *"I've had enough."*   Still more artificially pretentious would be *I've had a sufficiency*, at which point the irreverent joker is likely to step in and reduce the phrase to the absurd by saying, *No, thanks, I've had an elegant sufficiency.*

**suffragan,** n., *assistant bishop*, pronounced (sŭf′ragan)

**sugar,** n., colloquial as a very mild euphemistic variation of *pshaw*, or some stronger word, employed as an interjection.

**suggest,** v., *mention, propose*, pronounced (sujĕst′), more formally sometimes (sŭgjĕst′)

569

**suggestio falsi,** Latin phrase, *misrepresentation without direct falsehood*, pronounced (sujĕs'tĭō făl'sī)

**suicide, v.,** *to kill oneself*, avoided by conscientious speakers and writers, who prefer the phrase *commit suicide*. See **suspicion**

**sui generis,** Latin phrase, *individual, like only to itself*, pronounced (sū'ī jĕn'erĭs)  As **sui generis** is singular, it can not be used as a plural phrase.  The sentence *But there are so many of them which are so nearly sui generis that the average man is still unaware of their existence* says literally *But there are so many of them which are so nearly of its own kind*, etc.  As no plural form of **sui generis** is in use, the sentence must be reconstructed to read *But there are so many of them each of which is so nearly sui genersis*, etc.

**sui juris,** Latin phrase, *of full age and capacity*, pronounced (sū'ī jōō'rĭs)

**suite, n.,** *a set of rooms, a piece of music*, pronounced (swēt)  Etymologically the same word as *suit*, as in a *suit of clothes*, but now differentiated from it in meaning, spelling, and pronunciation.

**sum, n.,** colloquial and dialectal for *an arithmetical problem*.

**sumach, n.,** *a kind of shrub*.  Also spelled *sumac*.  Pronounced (sōō'măk), sometimes (shōō'măk)

**summarily,** adv., *directly and expeditiously*, pronounced (sŭm'-arĭlĭ)

**summersault,** see **somersault**

**summons, n., v.,** *official call to appear in court, to serve such a call*.  The noun **summons** is a singular, with a plural *summonses*.  As a verb the word is inflected *I summons, you summons, he summonses, I summonsed*, etc., pronounced (sŭm'onzd)

**sumptuous repast,** trite phrase, in turgid journalistic style.

**sunder, v.,** literary and poetic word for *divide, separate*.

**sundown, n.,** a slightly dialectal term for *sunset*.  See **sun-up**

**sung, v.,** past tense of *sing*, formerly frequently so used, but now almost completely replaced in standard English by *sang*.

**sun-kissed meadows, mountain tops,** etc., trite phrases, characteristic of crudely ambitious literary style.

**sun-up,** n., local and dialectal for *sunrise.* See **sundown**

**superfluous,** adj., *excessive, more than is necessary,* pronounced (sōōper'flōōus), dialectally (sōōperflōō'us)

**supple,** adj., *pliant, flexible,* pronounced (sŭp'l), dialectally (sōō'pl) The adverb is *supply,* pronounced (sŭp'lĭ), or sometimes *supplely,* to distinguish the adverb from the verb *supply* (suplī') But though *supplely* might be written, it would scarcely ever be pronounced.

**supplement,** n., *an addition,* pronounced (sŭp'lĭment) The verb is pronounced (sŭplĭměnt')

**suppose,** v., frequently used introducing a hypothetical clause, as in *Suppose they are not satisfied, what will you do then?* In this construction **suppose** is syntactically an imperative. A variant construction is *supposing,* as in *Supposing they are not satisfied,* etc. Both constructions are in good use, but the construction with **suppose** is grammatically slightly preferable, since *supposing* is a present participle and should not be used without an accompanying noun or pronoun with which it can agree.

**supposititious,** adj., *spurious, substituted for the real,* as in *a supposititious will,* not a genuine one. Pronounced (supŏzitĭsh'us) and often incorrectly given in the form *supposicious* (sŭpozĭsh'us), as though the adjective were formed from the noun *supposition.* In reality the adjective is from a Latin form containing the ending *-ticius,* that is, *suppositicius,* correctly represented in English by the ending *-titious.*

**suppressio veri,** Latin phrase, *a tacit misrepresentation, a silent lie,* pronounced (sŭprĕs'ĭō vē'rī)

**surcease,** n., archaic and poetic for *cessation.*

**sure,** adv., slang and dialectal in the sense *assuredly, undoubtedly, certainly,* as in *"Did you have a good time?" "I sure did."* Often

39                                    571

used low colloquially as a positive *yes*, as in "*Are you going to the game?*" "*Sure.*" Instances of these adverbial uses can be found in Shakspere and other writers, but they are slang nevertheless in their present-day uses because they carry with them the connotation and feeling for slang.

**surety,** n., *certainty,* pronounced (shoor'tĭ), not as a trisyllable. But *nicety* is pronounced (nī'sĭtĭ)

**surrebutter,** n., *a legal term,* pronounced (surrĭbŭt'er), with a complementary term, *surrejoinder* (surrĭjoin'der)

**surreptitious,** adj., a formal and pompous word for *stealthy, underhand,* pronounced (surĕptĭsh'us), often pronounced blunderingly as though the word were *surreptious* (surĕp'shus)

**surtout,** n., *overcoat,* pronounced (sŭrtōō')

**surveillance,** n., *guard, watch,* pronounced (survā'lans)

**susceptible,** adj., construed with *of* in the sense *admitting,* as in *That statement is susceptible of several interpretations,* permits of, admits of several interpretations, but with *to* in the sense *accessible, sensitive to,* as in *I am very susceptible to pain, He is susceptible to kind treatment,* responds, is sensitive to kind treatment. The word may also be used alone in the general sense *impressionable, easily moved,* as in *He is a very susceptible person.*

**suspect,** v., adj., n., as a verb pronounced (suspĕkt'); as an adjective frequently pronounced (sŭs'pĕkt), in the sense *open to suspicion;* as a noun, *a person open to suspicion, suspected person,* perhaps most commonly pronounced (sŭs'pĕkt)

**suspendatur per collum,** Latin phrase, *let him be hanged by the neck,* pronounced (sŭspĕndā'tur per kŏl'um) and abbreviated *sus. per coll.*

**suspenders,** see **galluses**

**suspicion,** v., *to have a suspicion.* Not used by careful stylists as a verb. See **auction**

**sustain,** v., *to bear, endure.* Often used in crudely ambitious writing, as in *John Wild, a plumber's apprentice, sustained a broken right arm yesterday,* for the simpler and better *John Wild, a plumber's apprentice, broke his right arm yesterday,* or *The right arm of John Wild, a plumber's apprentice, was broken yesterday.*

**svelte,** adj., *light and graceful,* especially of a woman's figure; pronounced (svĕlt) A dressmaker's and smart journalistic word.

**swag,** n., slang for *burglar's booty, loot.*

**swagger,** adj., colloquial and slang for *smart, fashionable.*

**swain,** see **admirer**

**swank,** n., slang for *ostentatious manner, showing off.* See **dog**

**swanlike neck,** trite phrase, traditional and conventional literary description.

**swap,** v., colloquial and slang for *to exchange, trade,* also spelled *swop.* The word is old, but it has not outlived its colloquial associations.

**swastika,** n., *a symbol of good luck,* pronounced (swăs′tĭka), not (swahstē′ka)

**swat,** v., slang for *to strike, deliver a blow,* as in *to swat flies.* Also spelled *swot.*

**swear,** v., colloquial in the phrase *swear by,* have great confidence in, as in *I swear by the General Supply Company. They have always treated me fair.*

**sweat,** n., *perspiration.* Often avoided as vulgar, *perspiration* being used instead. The objection of course is not to the word itself, but to the fact that it is a direct and simple term for a physical function, these functions in cultivated speech being ordinarily referred to only by means of euphemistic circumlocutions.

**sweater,** n., *any knit woolen jacket,* worn by women as well as men. Sometimes avoided by women as vulgar, though the word is now unquestionably established in good use. As a substitute for *sweater*, some phrase like *knitted jacket* is occasionally used. The original associations of the word were with gymnastics and sports, but as the name of a garment of general use, the word is no longer limited to these special applications.

**sweet**, adj., general colloquialism as a term of approval, like *pretty*, *nice*, etc., as in *a sweet little house, Doesn't this hat look sweet?*, etc. The word in this sense belongs almost exclusively to the vocabulary of women, though men use the same word ironically, as in *You will have a sweet time putting that machine together again*, a hard time, *He gave him a sweet one on the left ear*, a severe blow. The word is also colloquial use in the phrase *sweet on someone*, in love with.

**sweetmeat**, n., *a bonbon, sugarplum, a piece of candy.* *Sweetmeat*, *bonbon*, and *sugarplum* are not as generally used as *candy* in America. See **candy**

**swell**, adj., n., slang in the sense *fashionable, a fashionable person.*

**swell**, v., with a past participle usually *swollen*, especially when the participle is felt chiefly as a descriptive adjective, as in *His hand is swollen almost twice its natural size*. When the verbal idea is prominent, the form *swelled* is often employed, as in *This door has swelled tight.*

**swig**, n., v., slang in the sense *a drink, to take a drink.*

**swim**, n., slang in the phrase *in the swim*, in the current of things, at home among people of importance.

**swim**, v., *to move oneself forward or backward in the water*. With a past tense *swam* and a past participle *swum*, often used interchangeably in low colloquial but not in standard speech.

**swine**, n., *kind of domestic animal*, with a plural the same. The word is not ordinarily used, however, in general speech, being poetic, literary, legal, and scientific in character. The customary word is *hog* or *pig*. The singular is much less frequently employed than the plural, but as an imprecation the singular is sometimes heard in the phrase *You swine!* See **hog**

**swingletree,** n., *crosspiece for attaching traces to a wagon,* often made by popular etymology into *singletree.*

**swipe,** n., slang in the sense *a blow, stroke.* Also a verb, in the slang sense of *steal, take.*

**Sybil,** n., *a woman's name,* pronounced (sĭb'ĭl), and spelled differently from the common noun *sibyl,* a prophetess.

**sycophant,** n., *obsequious follower,* pronounced (sĭk'ofănt)

**sylphlike form,** trite phrase, in conventional literary descriptions, like *starry eyes, swanlike neck, cherry lips,* etc.

**Symonds,** n., *family name,* pronounced (sĭm'onz)

**Symons,** n., *family name,* pronounced (sĭm'onz)

**sympathy,** n., to be construed with *with* in the sense *fellow feeling,* as in *I have a great deal of sympathy with this movement,* but with *for* in the sense *compassion,* as in *I have a great deal of sympathy for the poor fellow.* The verb *sympathize* is always construed with *with.*

**symphony,** n., *a harmony of sound,* sometimes figuratively extended to a harmony of colors, as in *a symphony in yellow.* Pronounced (sĭm'fonĭ), not (sĭmp'fonĭ)

**syndicate,** n., v., the noun pronounced (sĭn'dĭkĭt), the verb (sĭn'dĭkāt)

**syne,** adv., Scotch dialect for *since,* as in *auld lang syne,* literally *old long since,* the days of long ago. Pronounced (sīn)

**syringe,** n., *a device for squirting liquids,* pronounced (sĭr'ĭnj), less correctly (sĭrĭnj')

**syrup,** n., *thick sweet liquid,* pronounced (sĭr'up), dialectally (sir'up) Also spelled *sirup,* and poetically *syrop, sirop.* On the grounds of simplicity, the spelling *sirup* should be preferred, and this is the general use among chemists. But the spelling **syrup** is nevertheless still the most common form of the word, especially in commercial uses.

**systematize,** v., *reduce to order,* incorrectly *systemize.* So also *systemist* should be *systematist,* and *systemic* should be *system-*

*atic*, unless it refers to the body, as in *systemic disorders*, disorders of the bodily system.

**Széchényi,** n., *noble family name*, pronounced (sā'chĕnyĭ)

# T

**tabby,** n., (1) *a kind of silk cloth*, of a wavy striped texture; (2) *a tabby cat*, (*a*) *one with dark stripes on a gray body*, (*b*) *a female cat*, the opposite of a tom cat; (3) *an old maid*. The word **tabby** as applied to cats seems to be of double origin. As the name for female cat, **tabby** may be an abbreviation of the name *Tabitha*. As the name for a gray striped cat, the term **tabby** applies to both males and females, and this word is probably of the same origin as **tabby** in the sense given under (1), that is, of Arabic origin as the name for a kind of cloth which later was applied to the tabby cat because the tabby cat's fur is marked in a way that resembles the markings of tabby cloth. The use of **tabby** as the name for an old maid is a figurative extension of *tabby cat*, a female cat.

**table-d'hôte,** n., a dinner or meal at a restaurant or hotel in which the several parts from beginning to end are fixed by the management and served to all guests alike at an established price. Pronounced (tahbldōt') The contrasting term is *à la carte*, literally, *according to the card*, a kind of meal of which the parts are ordered separately, and at a price given on the bill of fare, the whole cost of an *à la carte* meal being the sum of the cost of the several dishes ordered. Pronounced (ah lah kahrt')

**taboo,** adj., n., v., a word and custom derived from Polynesia. Less frequently spelled *tabu*. Among the Polynesians, taboo is a religious custom, but as ordinarily used in English the word means a topic of conversation which is avoided by common consent. Pronounced (tăbōō')

**tabula rasa,** Latin phrase, *blank surface ready for writing*, figuratively, *a free hand;* pronounced (tăb'ūla rā'sa)

**taciturn,** adj., *silent, speaking little,* pronounced (tăs'ĭturn), with a noun *taciturnity* (tăsĭtur'nĭtĭ)

**tackle,** n., *rope and pulley for hoisting weights.* Usually pronounced (tăk'l), but sometimes (tā'kl), dialectally (tēkl)

**tackle,** v., colloquial and slang in the sense *undertake, begin,* as in *I have so many letters to answer I hate to tackle them.*

**tacky,** adj., slang and dialectal for *dowdy, shabby.*

**tactile,** adj., *pertaining to the sense of touch,* as in *a tactile impression,* pronounced (tăk'tĭl) or (tăk'tīl) See **-ile** A variant adjective of the same meaning is *tactual* (tăk'tūal)

**taffrail,** n., *rail round the stern of a ship,* with a variant form *tafferel,* closer to the etymological origin of the word, but now less general than **taffrail.** Pronounced (tăf'rĭl) See **boatswain**

**taffy,** n., *a kind of candy.* In England usually called *toffee.* In British use, *Taffy,* a proper noun, is the generic name for a Welshman, like *Paddy* for an Irishman, *Fritz* for a German.

**Tahiti,** n., *place name,* pronounced (tahhē'tĭ), (tahī'tĭ), or (tah'ĭtĭ)

**Tahoe,** n., *lake in California,* pronounced (tah'hō)

**take,** v., colloquial and slang in the phrase *take in,* deceive, mislead, as in *I was completely taken in by his story;* colloquial in the phrase *take stock in,* have confidence in, believe in, usually in the negative, as in *I don't take much stock in such stories;* colloquial, verging on the dialectal, in the phrase *take on,* act violently, as in *He took on like mad,* but *take on,* undertake, as in *He took on too much work,* is only colloquial; colloquial in *take off,* caricature, parody, as in *He can take off a preacher to perfection,* with a corresponding noun *a take-off.*

The sentence *It did not take him much trouble* is unidiomatic, the correct idiom being *It did not cost him much trouble,* or *He did not take much trouble.*

**taking,** adj., colloquial in the sense *attractive,* as in *He has a very taking manner.*

**talcum,** n., *a kind of powder,* pronounced (tăl'kum), not (tawl'kum)

577

The word *talc* is pronounced (tălk), different from *talk* (tawk) because it is a late borrowed word, whereas the verb *talk* is an old native word which has undergone the regular sound change which appears in words like *balk, chalk, walk,* etc.

**talented,** adj., sometimes objected to on the ground that, as there is no verb *talent,* there should be no participial adjective **talented.** Usage, however, has given **talented,** parallel to *gifted,* as in *a talented person,* an established place in the language.

**talisman,** n., *article that brings good luck,* pronounced (tăl′ĭzman)

**talk,** v., slang in the phrase *talk through one's hat,* talk wildly and irresponsibly.

**tall,** adj., colloquial and slang in the sense *exaggerated, high flown,* as in *tall talk, a tall story,* or in the sense *large, big,* as in *a tall order,* a big undertaking.

**Tamalpais,** n., *mountain near San Francisco,* pronounced (tăm′-alpīs)

**tan,** v., slang in the sense *thrash.* Also slang in the phrase *to tan a person's hide,* to give him a tanning.

**tank,** n., slang in the sense *an habitual and copious imbiber of alcoholic beverages.* Also as a verb, especially in the phrase *tank up,* to become intoxicated.

**Tannhäuser,** n., *opera by Wagner,* pronounced (tahn′hoizer)

**tap,** n., the current word in England for what is commonly called *a faucet* in America. But the phrase *on tap* is current in America, as also the verb *to tap,* to draw off liquid from a barrel, etc. The word *faucet* is dialectal in England.

**tap,** v., colloquial in the sense *to repair shoes.* A *heeltap* is a thickness of leather for the making of a heel, by figurative extension, the small quantity of liquid left in a glass after drinking.

**tapis,** n., French word, occurring chiefly in the phrase *on the tapis,* under discussion, on the table. Usually pronounced (tăpē′), but sometimes anglicized to (tăp′ĭs) The meaning of the word **tapis** in modern French is *carpet,* but the French phrase *sur le* *tapis,* on the tapis, does not mean on the floor, as in American parliamentary usage, but *on the tablecloth,* from an older sense of **tapis,** meaning *tapestry,* formerly used as a table covering.

**Tappan Zee,** n., *place in the Hudson River,* pronounced (tăp′ăn zā)

**taps,** n., in United States military usage the signal for *lights out.*

**tarboosh,** n., Arabian word, *a skullcap,* pronounced (tahr′bo͞osh)

**tarnation,** interj., a euphemistic modification of *damnation,* formerly current and traditionally associated with comic New England characters, but now rarely seen and still more rarely heard.

**tarry,** v., *to linger, to remain.* Now archaic and literary, but formerly current colloquially, especially in New England speech.

**tart,** n., means in England what would ordinarily be called *a pie* in America. But in both countries **tart** also means a small piece of pastry with jam or fruit on top. See **pie**

**tassel,** n., *a 'tuft,* on a plant or made with threads. Pronounced (tăs′l), dialectally (taw′sl), and often spelled humorously *tossel* to indicate this pronunciation, as in the name *Farmer Corntossel.*

**taste of,** v., colloquial and dialectal for *taste,* as in *Please taste of this butter and see if you like it.* See **smell of**

**tasty,** adj., dialectal in the sense *pleasant, agreeable,* especially as applied to clothes, as in *a very tasty dresser,* one who dresses in good taste, but also as applied to food, as in *a tasty dinner,* for a good dinner, *a tasty salad,* a well-seasoned salad.

**taube,** n., German word, *kind of aeroplane,* literally, *dove;* pronounced (tow′be) See **Zeitgeist**

**tavern,** n., archaic and literary for what would ordinarily be called *a hotel.* But the word **tavern,** and so also *inn,* has been revived of recent years, especially as names for places of public entertainment along a highway but not in a city.

**taxi,** n., colloquial abbreviation for *taxicab.* Also used as a verb, *to taxi,* with a past tense and past participle *taxi'd,* as in *We taxi'd to the station in ten minutes,* pronounced (tăk′sēd)

**taximeter,** n., *device for indicating the fare in a taxi,* pronounced (tăksĭm′eter)

**Tchaikowsky,** n., *Russian musical composer,* pronounced (chĭkawf′skĭ)

**tea,** n., as the name of a meal, usually designates a light repast in the evening, following dinner at noon. But the customary name for this light evening meal is *supper,* and **tea** ordinarily implies a still lighter meal than supper, a Sunday evening supper. The term **tea** is also used, however, to designate the ceremony, not exactly to be called a meal, known as *five o'clock tea.* This tea is an established custom in all walks of English life, but it flourishes only sporadically in America.

**teach the young idea how to shoot,** trite phrase, from Thomson's *Seasons,* "Spring," l. 1149. Now used only facetiously.

**tea-hound,** n., slang for *man who frequents teas and ladies' company.* Synonyms are *cake-eater, jelly-bean, lounge-lizard.*

**team,** n., in careful use, *two or more beasts of burden harnessed together.* Colloquially, however, the term is sometimes applied to a single horse attached to a wagon, the two together constituting a **team.** The word **team** also applies to a group of persons, as in *a football team,* or a set of workmen may be called a **team.**

**tear,** n., slang synonym of *spree,* as in *to be* or *to go on a tear.*

**tearing,** adj., colloquial in the sense *violent,* as in *a tearing rage, a tearing pace.*

**teat,** n., *nipple.* Now usually only of animals, the word *nipple* being used of women. Pronounced (tēt), dialectally (tĭt)

**technique,** n., *stylistic manner, professional skill,* pronounced (tĕknēk′) A variant form *technic* (tĕk′nĭk) is in less general use.

**Te Deum laudamus,** Latin phrase, *We praise thee, O God,* pronounced (tē dē′um lawdā′mus)

**teem,** v., *to be abundantly supplied with,* as in *This lake teems with fish.* Incorrectly and inaccurately used as equivalent to *be disturbed, agitated,* as in *The fish were so abundant that they made the waters teem, The teeming crowd was difficult to manage.*

**teeny,** adj., dialectal, especially in children's English, for *tiny.* Also *teeny tiny, teeny weeny.* See **tiny**

**teeter,** v., colloquial and dialectal for *to stand unsteadily.* Also in the name of a children's game, *teeter totter.* Probably a variant of *totter.*

**telescope,** n., *device for magnifying the visual impression of objects,* pronounced (tĕl′eskōp), with the derivatives *telescopist* (telĕs′- kopĭst), *telescopic* (tĕleskŏp′ĭc), *telescopy* (telĕs′kopĭ)

**tell,** v., colloquial and low colloquial as the equivalent of *say,* as in *Tell him good-by for me,* for *Say good-by to him for me.*

**tell on,** v., colloquial and children's English for *to inform on, to reveal.*

**temblor,** n., *an earthquake.* The word is Spanish and is current locally in western United States. Sometimes incorrectly given as *tremblor,* by confusion with the English verb *tremble.* Pronounced (tĕmblōr′) The word occurs several times as a place name in California.

**tempest,** n., *violent climatic disturbance,* now archaic or poetical, except in the proverbial phrase *tempest in a teapot.*

**templar,** see **knight templar**

**ten,** numeral, colloquially used as a round number, like *hundred, thousand,* as in *I'd ten times rather stay at home,* much rather.

**tend,** v., *move in a certain direction.* The verb can not take an object, and the sentence *This formality tends them to keep their preaching on a dignified level* must be rephrased to read *This formality leads them,* or *favors a tendency in them,* etc.

The verb **tend** as a shortened form of *attend,* as in *to tend store, to tend school, to tend the baby,* is a low colloquialism. See **mind**

**tender,** v., a somewhat official and formal word, often used when a simpler word would be better, as in *to tender a reception,* for *to give a reception, to tender an offer,* for *to make an offer.*

**tenderfoot,** n., western slang for an Easterner or for any person not hardened to the conditions of rough frontier living.

**tenet,** n., *principle, dogma,* pronounced (tĕn′ĭt), sometimes (tē′nĭt)

**tepid,** adj., *neither hot nor cold,* pronounced (tĕp′id)

**termagant,** n., *a scold,* pronounced (ter′magant), not (ter′majant)

**terminus,** n., *ending place,* especially in the terminology of the railway, with a plural *termini* (ter′mĭnī)

**terminus ad quem,** Latin phrase, *concluding position toward which one's attention is directed,* pronounced (ter′mĭnus ăd kwĕm)

**terminus a quo,** Latin phrase, *starting place in an argument, date,* etc., pronounced (ter′mĭnus ā kwō)

**terra firma,** Latin phrase, *solid earth,* pronounced (tĕr′a fir′ma)

**terra incognito,** Latin phrase, *unknown land,* pronounced (tĕr′a ĭnkŏg′nĭta)

**Terre Haute,** n., *town in Indiana,* pronounced (tĕr′e hōt), less correctly (tĕr′ĭ hŭt)

**terrible,** adj., *that which occasions terror,* but colloquially used as a general intensive of adverse meaning, as in *a terrible night, a terrible distance to walk, a terrible dinner,* often strengthened by adding *perfectly,* as in *a perfectly terrible headache.* See **awful, fearful, fine, great, wonderful**

**tertium quid,** Latin phrase, *something not yes or no, a compromise,* literally, *a third something;* pronounced (ter′shĭum kwĭd)

**tertius gaudens,** Latin phrase, *a third person who profits when two others are at odds,* literally, *a rejoicing third;* pronounced (ter′shĭŭs gaw′dĕnz)

**tetchy,** see **touchy**

**tête-à-tête,** n., French word, literally *head to head,* meaning *two persons dining, talking, etc., intimately;* pronounced (tāt′ahtāt′)

**Texas,** n., *a state of the United States,* pronounced (tĕk′sas), less correctly (tĕk′saz)

**textile,** adj., *pertaining to weaving,* as in *the textile arts.* Pronounced (tĕx'tĭl) or (tĕx'tīl), the former being in accord with the most general tendency in words of this type. See **-ile**

**Thames,** n., *river name in England and America,* pronounced (tĕmz)

**than,** conj., as in *I am taller than he is,* but in low colloquial speech used as a preposition with an objective following, as in *I am taller than him.* The construction *than whom* may be accepted as good English, but sentences in which it occurs can always be improved by rephrasing in simpler syntax, as in *The president, than whom none was more competent to judge of its wisdom, opposed the motion,* but better, *The president, who was the most competent,* etc. See **as**

**Thanks,** n., a much curtailed form of the sentence *I give thanks to you,* like *Good night* for *I give good night to you.* The word **Thanks** as a sentence equivalent is so short as readily to seem curt. It can be used, therefore, only as recognition of relatively slight and trivial favors. The response **Thanks** when a more formal courtesy would be appropriate may convey an ironical meaning or it may express anger and contempt. Varying degrees of formality may be expressed by **Thanks,** *I thank you, Thank you, Thank you very much, Thanks ever so much, Thanks a thousand times,* etc.

**that,** pron., in low colloquial speech used as an adverb, as in *I was that tired,* for *I was so tired, I didn't get that far,* for *I didn't get so far.* So also *this,* as in *He didn't take this much,* for *He didn't take so much* or *as much as this, This much is certain,* for *So much is certain.* The phrase *So that's that* is colloquial use, with the meaning *That's the end of that, That's finished.*

The uses of *this much, that much* are perhaps not all on the same level as the other uses of *this, that* as adverbs. Although sentences like *We had never been this far before, I didn't know it was that high* seem unquestionably low colloquial, similar constructions, like *I will say this much for him, I knew that much before*, are so general that perhaps they must be counted as only colloquial.

The use of **that** as equivalent to *as that in which* is common in incorrect popular style, as in *Editors refer to it in the same scornful manner that a New York reporter talks about the crossroads correspondent of a county-seat weekly; I read it in the same mood that I pored over my geography in the fifth grade.* In both of these sentences, **that** should be replaced by *as that in which.*

**that there,** adj., low colloquial and dialectal, as in *That there fellow has got my hat*, for *That fellow has my hat.* So also *this here.*

**the,** article, used in phrases like *translated from the German* only when the phrase is elliptical for *translated from the German language of the original*, not merely as an equivalent to *translated from German.* Crudely colloquial or dialectal in constructions like *Won't you have some of the beans?*, for *Won't you have some beans?* Archaic and literary in the phrase *to die the death.* The article is occasionally used in constructions like *five dollars the pair, fifty cents the copy* for the more customary *five dollars a pair, fifty cents a copy.* Both constructions are elliptical, and sometimes the construction with **the,** as in *fifty cents the copy*, implies a fuller form, *fifty cents by the single copy*, with the implication of a lower price if one takes more than one copy. But the construction is also used merely as an affected variant of the construction with *a*, especially for the more expensive articles of smart shops.

The article **the** is ordinarily pronounced (dhĭ) before words beginning with a vowel, (dhe) before words beginning with a consonant, and (dhē) only when the word is specially emphasized, as in *I said* the *man, not* a *man.*

**theirselves,** pron., low colloquial for *themselves.*

**them,** pron., low colloquially and dialectally used as a demonstrative adjective, as in *Them boards is too long*, for *Those boards are too long.*

**then,** adv., occasionally in a somewhat artificial literary style used as an adjective, as in *the then Secretary of the Treasury.*

**thence,** adv., *from there.* Now only literary and archaic. The construction *from thence* is pleonastic and incorrect. See **whence**

**there,** adv., low colloquial when added to *that,* as in *That there dog you sold me ran away.* See **here**

**thereabout,** adv., with a variant form *thereabouts.* The two forms are used more or less indistinguishably, though there is some tendency to use *thereabouts* in relation to local position, as in *We camped there or thereabouts,* and **thereabout** for other proximities, as in *A hundred people were present, or thereabout.* But the distinction is not strictly maintained.

**thereby hangs a tale,** trite phrase, already a popular expression in Shakspere's time.

**therefore,** conj., used to express a general relation of consequence or inference, as in *The book was well bound, and therefore has lasted a long time.* The word *therefor* is now rarely used, but when it is used, it has the sense of *for* as a preposition followed by an object, as in *If people ate less, they would be healthier therefor,* for that. In this latter use, both elements of the word would receive a fairly heavy stress, but in **therefore,** conj., only the first element is accented.

**there is,** impersonal verb phrase, often followed in low colloquial speech by a plural noun, as in *There is rich men in this town who don't know how much they own,* for the correct form, *There are rich men,* etc.

**thereof,** phrase, archaic for *of it,* as in *The height thereof was six cubits,* for *Its height* or *The height of it,* etc. So also *whereof* for *of what,* as in *I know whereof I speak,* I know what I am talking about.

**these sort, kind.** The nouns *sort, kind,* being grammatically singular, require a singular form in a preceding adjective pro-

noun, that is, *this* or *that sort, kind*, not *these* or *those sort, kind*.
The use of the plural forms is fairly common, however, in colloquial speech, and in justification it might be said that *sort, kind*
are collective nouns, logically plural, and therefore not unreason-
ably preceded by plural forms of the demonstrative adjective.
This reasoning, nevertheless, can not make *these* or *those sort, kind*
unquestioned good grammatical English.

**thesis,** n., in the sense *essay, proposition* pronounced (thē′sis);
as a term in the scansion of poetry pronounced (thĕs′is), though
sometimes (thē′sis) also in this second sense.

**the table groaned beneath the weight,** etc., trite phrase, in routine
reportorial style.

**they,** pron., colloquial and dialectal as the equivalent of an indefinite pronoun, as in *They don't have street cars in Venice*, for
*Street cars aren't used* or *There are no street cars in Venice*.

**Thibet,** see **Tibet**

**thick,** adj., colloquial and dialectal in the sense *intimate*, as in
the phrases *thick as thieves, thick as two in a bed and three in the
middle.* Slang in the sense *exaggerated, incredible, too much*,
as in *His excuses were a little too thick for anyone to believe,
That's a bit too thick*, of something beyond expectation or reason.

**thicket,** see **coppice**

**thin,** adj., slang in the phrase *too thin*, not credible, obviously
not true, as in *That's too thin.* In the sense *uncomfortable,
unhappy* the use of **thin** is on the border between colloquial
and slang, as in *She is having a pretty thin time of it.* See **thick**

**thing,** n., slang in the phrases *the thing*, the proper or fashionable
thing, *to know a thing or two*, be one who can not be deceived,
*to make a good thing of*, to profit at the expense of.

**things,** n., colloquial for *clothing*, as in *Put on your things and come
down.*

**thinks,** v., rustic and dialectal as a first person in the phrase
*thinks I to myself.*

**this, that, these, those,** pron., colloquially used sometimes like indefinite demonstratives, in a way which indicates a completing relative clause, although no such clause follows, as in *I saw that the book was one of those new thin paper volumes.* Often used in crude narrative, as in *There was this fellow, and he had a wife and two children,* etc. Altogether a use to be avoided in writing and not to be cultivated in speaking. For this as adv., see **that**

**this broad land of ours,** trite phrase, with a sentimental patriotic tinge.

**this too, too solid flesh,** trite phrase, wrested from all semblance to its original use in *Hamlet,* Act I, Sc. ii.

**thither,** adv., archaic and literary for *there, to that place.* In the same class are *hither, hence, thence, unto,* and many similar words which for no apparent reason have become old-fashioned.

**thoro,** adj., occasional variant spelling of *thorough.* Rare examples of the spelling **thoro** can be found at various times within the modern English period, but recently the spelling has become more general because it has been advocated by the supporters of theories of spelling reform. It still remains, however, an exceptional spelling and can be used only by persons who wish to assume the rôle of spelling reformer. See **though, thru,** and **Spelling Reform**

**though,** adv., conj., with a variant spelling *tho,* now established in fairly wide general use as a reformed spelling.

**thought,** n., ordinarily used only of a formulated thought of some significance, as in *The Thoughts of Marcus Aurelius,* a thought weighty with philosophy or reflection. Less correctly used sometimes merely as a synonym for *meaning, intention, purpose,* as in *My thought was that we ought to have our dinner before leaving home.*

**thresh,** v., with a variant spelling *thrash.* The form **thresh** is commonly employed in the literal sense, as of threshing wheat,

40

but *thrash* in transferred senses, as in *to thrash a person*. But the usual pronunciation for both words is (thrăsh), even when the spelling is **thresh**.

**thrice,** adv., archaic and literary for *three times*.

**thrive,** v., *succeed, prosper*, with a past tense *thrived* or *throve* and a past participle *thrived* or *thriven*.

**through,** adv., colloquial and children's English in the sense *done with, finished*, as in *He was not quite through dinner, Are you through with that paper?* See **thru**

**throw,** v., slang in the phrases *throw a fit*, become excited, and *throw down*, refuse, as in *I asked for a raise in pay, but the boss threw me down hard.*

**throw down the glove,** trite phrase, rhetorical variation for *challenge*.

**thru,** prep., a variant spelling of *through*. In recent years the spelling **thru** has been advocated by the supporters of theories of spelling reform, and in consequence it has gained some currency in usage. It is not an old or historical spelling, but a theoretical improvement, that is, a modification of *through* in the interests of simplicity. In spite of this gain, however, the spelling **thru** has not met with a high degree of favor and is not nearly so common as the spelling *tho* for *though* or *thoro* for *thorough*. The reason for this probably is that **thru** has a barbarous look because it ends in the vowel **u**. The only familiar words ending in **u** in English are **you** and **thou**, and, strictly speaking, these words end in **ou**. Other words ending in **u** are exotics, like *gnu, emu*, some French borrowings like *poilu, écru*, etc. The spelling **thru** can be used therefore only by the person who is willing to be known as a somewhat extreme spelling reformer. See **Spelling Reform**

**Thucydides,** n., *Greek historian*, pronounced (thoōsĭd′ĭdēz)

**thug,** n., current in the United States, but not in England, in the sense *ruffian*. Not a slang word, like *roughneck*, nor yet a highly refined word, but one appropriate in color to the object it names.

**thumping,** adj., slang in the sense *big, extraordinary*, as in *a thumping lie, a thumping big turnip*. Also a noun, *a thumper*, a big lie or something else big, a whopper.

**thusly,** adv., facetious for *thus*. The impulse to fashion a humorous form like **thusly** probably arises from the fact that *thus* itself is becoming a somewhat archaic and artificial word.

**thyme,** n., *an herb*, pronounced (tīm)

**Tibet,** n., *a plateau of Central Asia*, not *Thibet*, according to the ruling of the United States Geographic Board.

**tic douloureux,** French phrase, *neuralgia*, pronounced (tēk dōōlōōrö′) If the phrase were anglicized, as indeed it is sometimes, it would be pronounced (tĭk dŏlorōō′)

**tick,** n., slang in the phrase *on tick*, on credit. Apparently an abbreviation of *ticket*.

**ticker,** n., slang for *watch*.

**ticket,** n., slang in the phrase *that's the ticket*, the right thing, the thing wanted.

**ticking,** n., *strong material for making covers for mattresses*, etc., with a variant *tick*, and an older form *ticken*, now usually regarded as dialectal. See **leggings**

**tidal,** adj., *pertaining to tides*. Formerly much criticized as a hybrid, but now fully established in good use. See **al, Hybrids**

**tidings,** n., *news, information*, plural in form and usually construed as a plural, but sometimes also as a singular, like *news*, as in *The glad tidings was received with shouts of joy*. A singular form *tiding* is no longer in use, but neither is the word **tidings** now commonly used. The singular *tiding* is obsolete, and **tidings** is obsolescent, surviving in literary and poetic use, but ordinarily replaced by *news*.

**tidy,** adj., colloquial in the sense *considerable*, as in *a tidy fortune*, enough and to spare, *a tidy little sum*, not small.

**tidy,** v., colloquial for *to make tidy*, especially in the phrase *to tidy up*.

**tiger,** n., slang in the phrase *three cheers and a tiger*, three cheers and a supplementary yell. Also slang in the phrase *to buck the tiger*, to play against the bank, to gamble, and in *blind tiger*, a place where alcoholic liquors are secretly sold.

**tight,** adj., slang in the sense *intoxicated*, also in the sense *stingy*. A *tightwad* is slang for a *stingy person*. The phrase *to sit tight*, not to yield from one's position, is colloquial and on the border of slang. See **close**

**tike,** see **tyke**

**tile,** n., slang in the sense *hat*, especially *a tall silk hat*.

**timber,** n., colloquial in the sense *human material*, as in *We have plenty of good timber for a football team*. The phrase *timber-headed* is slang for *wooden-headed*.

**timbre,** n., French word, *the quality of a voice or other sound*, pronounced (tăm′ber) or (tăṅ′br), the former being a somewhat anglicized, the latter approximately the French pronunciation.

**Timbuktu,** n., *town in Africa*, not *Ten Boctoo, Timbucktoo, Tombouctou, Tombuctoo,* or *Tombuktu*, according to the decision of the United States Geographic Board.

**time,** n., colloquial in the sense *a good time*, as in the phrase *the time of his life*. The phrase *on time*, punctual, is a current colloquialism in the United States, but not in England. The phrases *come to time*, yield, become obedient, and *to get your time*, be discharged from employment, are slang.

**tin,** n., slang in the sense *money*, and as an adjective in *tin hat*, steel helmet, *tin Lizzie*, Ford automobile.

**tiny,** adj., *very small*, with a dialectal variant *teeny*, sometimes combined in colloquial speech into *teeny-tiny*, or in colloquial English **tiny** is supplemented by *little*, as in a *tiny little fellow, a tiny little house*. See **teeny**

**tip,** v., slang in the phrase *tip one off*, give confidential information to, and *tip one the wink*, give one a secret warning. The verb

**tip,** *give a gratuity,* is current English and there is no substitute for it. The word is not dignified, but neither is the custom.

**tire,** n., *rubber part of an automobile wheel,* etc. In England also spelled *tyre,* though Collins, *Authors' and Printers' Dictionary,* an authoritative English work, remarks that though *tyre* is usual in England, **tire** is correct.

**'tis,** verb phrase, a contraction of *it is,* but now only poetic or archaic. But the negative form *'tisn't* still survives colloquially. The form **'tis** was the customary contraction of *it is* well into the eighteenth century, and the form *it's* is therefore relatively recent.

**tissue,** n., *very thin paper, substance of the body,* pronounced (tĭsh'o͞o), (tĭsh'ū), or very formally (tĭs'ū)

**Titian,** n., *Italian artist,* pronounced (tĭsh'n)

**tizzy,** n., British slang for *sixpence.*

**T. N. T.,** n., popular abbreviation for a high explosive, the chemical name of which is trinitrotoluol (trīnītrōtŏl'ūŏl)

**to,** sign of the infinitive, often used in good colloquial speech with the verb unexpressed when it can readily be supplied from the context, as in *He asked me to go with him, but I don't want to.* The preposition **to** after a form of the verb *to be,* as in *Have you ever been to Chicago?,* can be justified only if the verb is understood as a verb of emotion. Better usage would be *Have you ever been in Chicago?* See **be**

**today,** adv., usually written without a hyphen, and so also *tomorrow, tonight.*

**to-do,** n., colloquial variant of *ado,* as in *When the news spread abroad, there was at once a great to-do.*

**toff,** n., British slang for *a gentleman or a person exceptionally well dressed.*

**toffee,** see **taffy**

**tog,** v., slang in the sense *dress elaborately,* especially in the phrase *all togged out.*

591

**together with,** see **along with**

**togs,** n., slang and humorous colloquialism for *clothes.*

**toilet,** see **water-closet**

**tolerably,** adv., dialectal in the sense *moderately,* as in *He's tolerably well off,* neither rich nor poor.

**tomato,** n., *a garden plant and its fruit,* ordinarily pronounced (tomā′tō), less generally (tomah′tō), and dialectally (tomăt′o) The plural is *tomatoes.*

**tommy rot,** see **rot,** n.

**tony,** adj., colloquial and slang for *stylish, fashionable.*

**too,** adv., according to the rule of the grammarians and rhetoricians should not directly modify a past participle, as in *He was too enraged to talk,* for *He was too much enraged to talk, I was too distressed for words,* for *I was too much distressed for words, He was only too pleased to get it,* for *He was only too much* or *too well pleased to get it.* The same rule applies to *very,* as in *They were very pleased to see us,* for *They were very much* or *greatly pleased to see us.* When the past participle is purely adjectival in syntax, it may be modified by the adverbs **too,** *very,* as in *In driving a bargain it is not wise to wear a too pleased expression, He wore a very pleased expression.*
The ground of this criticism is that **too** and *very* are intensifying words, expressing a higher degree of a quality named, and therefore should not be made to modify verbs directly, because verbs name actions, not qualities. From this point of view, the rule is not without justification, but it must be taken as the counsel of perfection, not as an absolute prescription. For certainly a sentence like *He was too enraged to speak* has general good usage on its side, and even *He looked very ashamed* may be heard from cultivated speakers. Such past participles are not merely verbal but also partly adjectival in function.

**too full for utterance,** trite phrase, used facetiously, with literal and metaphorical implications.

**too funny for words,** trite phrase, an easy evasion of the difficulty of telling just how a thing is funny.

**tool,** v., slang in the sense *drive a coach*, etc., and in the phrase *tool the brake*, work the brake on a coach, etc. Also a technical term in ornamental designing.

**toothsome viands,** trite phrase, used in routine reportorial fine style.

**top,** n., slang in the phrase *old top*, old boy, old fellow.

**toper,** n., literary and humorous for *a heavy drinker*.

**topping,** adj., British slang for *very fine, excellent*.

**toreador,** n., *a bullfighter*, pronounced (tŏr′ĭadŏr)

**tortoise,** n., *land and fresh-water hard-shelled reptile*, pronounced (tŏr′tis) See **turtle**

**tosh,** n., British slang for *nonsense*.

**tot,** n., colloquial in the sense *small child, a drink of whisky*, etc.

**tot,** v., colloquial and dialectal for *to add*, as in *to tot up a column of figures*.

**tote,** v., local, colloquial, and dialectal for *to carry*. The word is current chiefly in the South, but it is by no means, as it is sometimes said to be, peculiar to negro English.

**tother,** pron., archaic and humorous for *the other*, as in *to tell the one from tother*, or *the ton from tother* (dhe tŭn frum tŭdh′er), or *to tell tother from which*, to tell one from the other.

**totidem verbis,** Latin phrase, *in so many words, in these exact words*, pronounced (tŏt′ĭdĕm ver′bĭs)

**toties quoties,** Latin phrase, *as often as occasion arises*, pronounced (tō′shĭēz kwō′shĭēz)

**toto caelo,** Latin phrase, *altogether, diametrically*, literally, *by the whole sky;* pronounced (tō′tō sē′lō)

**touch,** v., slang in the sense *to borrow*, as in *to touch a person for five dollars*, and colloquial in the phrase *touch the spot*, be effective, satisfactory. The phrase *to get in touch with* is a trite colloquialism.

**touchy,** adj., *easily angered, inclined to take offense,* in dialect use often pronounced as though written *tetchy.*

**tough,** adj., slang in the sense *depraved, vicious,* as in *a tough lot of boys; bad, distressing,* as in *tough luck;* and as a noun, *a tough,* a ruffian.

**tour,** n., *a journey,* pronounced (tŏŏr), dialectally (towr), with a derivative *tourist* (tŏŏr'ĭst) Also a verb, as in *to tour the country,* with a participial adjective, as in *a touring car,* all with (ōō) as the stressed vowel.

**tournament,** n., *medieval tilting match,* pronounced (tŏŏr'nament) or (tur'nament), with a variant of the same meaning, *tourney,* pronounced (tŏŏr'nā) or (tur'nā)

**tourniquet,** n., *device for stopping the flow of blood,* pronounced (tŏŏr'nĭkĕt), (tur'nĭkĕt), or (tŏŏr'nĭkā), (tur'nĭkā) The last two pronunciations reflect the French origins of the word, the first two being anglicized pronunciations.

**tout court,** French phrase, *informally, brusquely,* pronounced (tōō kŏŏr)

**tout ensemble,** French phrase, *the general effect,* pronounced (tōŏt ahṅsahṅ'bl)

**toward,** adj., *promising, auspicious,* as in *a toward child.* Pronounced (tō'ard) But this use is now archaic, and if it occurs · at all is more likely to occur in the negative compound *untoward,* as in *an untoward experience.* The forms in *-ly, towardly, untowardly,* as in *a towardly child, an untowardly experience,* are more commonly met with than the forms **toward,** *untoward.* See **towards**

**towards,** prep., *in the direction of,* pronounced (tŏrdz), with a variant *toward* (tŏrd) There is no appreciable distinction of meaning between **towards** and *toward,* though the form **towards** is perhaps the one most frequently used colloquially and *toward* in writing. These words may also be pronounced (towŏrd'), (towŏrdz'), but, in spite of the fact that the spelling favors this latter pronunciation, it has not become general and would impress many persons as being dialectal. The word is a good illustration of the arbitrariness of the decisions of usage. For though good use permits and even favors (tŏrd), (tŏrdz) for *toward*, **towards,** it utterly rejects such pronunciations as (băk'ard), (fŏr'ard), (ŭp'ard) for *backward, forward, upward.*

**track,** n., slang in the phrase *make tracks*, go, usually away from some source of danger, discomfort, etc. See **mosey, skidoo, vamose**

**tractor,** see **advisor**

**tradesman,** n., in England the common term for *a shopkeeper;* in America called *a business man* or *a storekeeper.*

**trait,** n., *a feature, characteristic*, pronounced (trāt), but in England frequently pronounced in the French fashion, (trā)

**tram,** n., in England the usual name for *a street car.* In America **tram,** *tramway* usually apply to cars and tracks in a limited way, as they are used, for example, in a shop or factory.

**transact,** v., *carry on, conduct*, pronounced (trănzăkt')

**transcendently,** adv., *in a very high degree, superlatively*, as in *transcendently beautiful.* To be distinguished from *transcendentally*, a philosophic term descriptive of something which exists independently of experience.

**transient,** adj., *not permanent, quickly passing*, pronounced (trăn'zĭent), (trăn'shnt) Also used as a noun, *transient, transients*, not permanent residents, pronounced (trăn'shnt)

**transit,** n., *passage across*, pronounced (trăn'zĭt), and *transition* (trănzĭsh'n), *transitive* (trăn'zĭtĭv), *transitory* (trăn'zĭtorĭ), *translate* (trănzlāt'), and so in other compounds with *trans-* followed by a vowel or a voiced consonant.

**transpire,** v., *to become known.* Often incorrectly used as equivalent to *happen* or *take place*, e. g., *the event which transpired yesterday.* The word is correctly used in the sentence *It transpired finally that the secretary of state had written the letter.* But the word is scarcely a necessity in any sense, and the simpler phrase

*become known* is much to be preferred to the stiff and pedantic
**transpire.**

**Transvaal,** n., *place in southern Africa,* pronounced (trănzvahl′)

**trapes,** v., colloquial for *go about wearily,* as in *trapes around in the
rain.* Sometimes spelled *traipse.* See **mosey, skidoo, vamose**

**traps,** n., colloquial in the sense *belongings,* as in *pack up one's
traps.*

**travail,** n., archaic for *exertion, trouble,* pronounced (trăv′ĭl), therefore slightly different from the verb *travel* (trăv′el)

**traveler,** n., *one making a journey,* with a variant spelling *traveller.*

**trek,** v., slang in the sense *make off, depart, go on one's way.* The
word is by origin Dutch and came into more general use by way
of South Africa during the time of the Boer War. See **trapes**

**tremor,** n., *quivering, thrill,* pronounced (trĕm′or), not (trē′mor)

**trente-et-quarante,** n., French word, name of a game, *rouge-et-noir,*
literally, *thirty and forty;* pronounced (trahṅt ā kărahṅt′‵

**tress,** n., poetic for *lock of hair.*

**trestle,** n., a *support for boards, rails,* etc., pronounced (trĕs′l),
low colloquially (trŭs′l)

**trice,** n., literary in the phrase *in a trice,* at once, immediately.
The word occurs only in this phrase.

**trig,** n., colloquial abbreviation of *trigonometry.* The adjective
*trig,* spruce, neat, is good standard English.

**trim,** v., colloquial in the sense *reprove, thrash,* as in *to trim one
well.* Also used as a participial noun, as in *to give one a good
trimming,* a good thrashing.

**trinitrotoluol,** see **T. N. T.**

**trio,** n., *a set of three,* and also a term in music. Pronounced
(trĭ′ō), not (trī′ō)

**trip the light fantastic toe,** trite phrase, a fancy variation for
*dance,* modified from Milton, *L' Allegro,* ll. 33–34.

**triptych,** n., *altar piece in three panels,* pronounced (trĭp′tĭk)

**triste,** adj., French word, *gloomy, melancholy,* pronounced (trēst)

**troche,** n., *medicated lozenge*, pronounced (trōsh), (trōch), or (trōk), but (trō'kǐ) is "commercial and vulgar," according to the *New English Dictionary*. But a word so infrequently used and so innocent in itself could scarcely become vulgar.

**trolley,** n., colloquial shortening for *trolley car*, also spelled *trolly*. Slang in the phrase *off one's trolley*, fantastic, uninformed.

**Trollope,** n., *English novelist*, pronounced (trŏl'op)

**trot,** n., college slang for *a literal translation*. See **pony**

**troth,** n., archaic in the phrase *in troth*, and literary in the phrase *to plight one's troth*, pledge one's faith.

**troupe,** n., *a group of performers*, pronounced (trōop), and etymologically the same as *troop*, as in *a troop of soldiers*. The spelling *troop* is occasionally used for both senses, but usually **troupe** for the name of a group of professional performers.

**trousers,** n., *man's garment*, construed only as a plural, as in *His trousers were too long*, with no corresponding singular. See **pants** The singular is expressed by the phrase *a pair of trousers*, with a plural *pairs of trousers*. Not spelled *trowsers*.

**trouvaille,** n., French word, *a lucky find or discovery*, pronounced (trōōvā'y)

**trouvère,** n., French word, *medieval French poet*, pronounced (trōōvār')

**trow,** v., archaic for *think*, *believe*, as in *A doughty swordsman, as I trow*, kept alive by Robin Hood and similar stories. Pronounced (trō)

**truck,** n., colloquial in America for *vegetables and all garden products*. Also as adjective in *truck garden*, *truck farmer*.

**trudgen,** n., adj., *a kind of stroke in swimming*, from the name of a person, as in the phrase *trudgen stroke*. Incorrectly *trojan stroke*. Pronounced (trŭj'en)

**true inwardness,** trite phrase, synonym for *hidden meaning*.

**trump,** n., colloquial and slang in the sense *a good fellow, a person to depend on*.

**truth to tell,** phrase, equivalent to a subordinate clause, as in *Truth to tell, the judge himself doubted the evidence,* a literary and formal way of saying what would ordinarily be expressed by *The truth of the matter is* or *If the truth were told,* etc.

**try,** n., colloquial in the sense *attempt,* as in *Have a try at it,* make an attempt.

**try and,** v., colloquial for *try to,* as in *He is likely to try and back out,* for *He is likely to try to back out.* The construction is not infrequently found in good writing of a somewhat informal kind.

**tryst,** n., literary for *engagement, pledge,* pronounced (trĭst)

**tsar,** n., occasional spelling for *czar.*

**Tschaikovsky, P. F.,** n., *Russian musical composer* (1840–1893), pronounced (chīkŏv′skĭ)

**tuberculosis,** see **consumption**

**tuberculous,** adj., *infected by the tubercle bacillus,* and to be distinguished from *tubercular,* according to the decision of the National Tuberculosis Association, the term *tubercular* being used "to describe conditions resembling tubercles, but not caused by the tubercle bacillus." The distinction is useful and should be observed.

**tuberose,** n., *a kind of flower.* Etymologically the word ought to have three syllables, (tū′berōz), but it is commonly understood as though it were a compound of *tube* and *rose* and consequently is ordinarily pronounced (tūb′rōz) The real original of the word is Latin *tuberosa,* provided with tubers.

**tubular,** adj., *like a tube,* pronounced (tū′būlar), not (tŭb′ūlar)

**Tucson,** n., *city in Arizona,* pronounced (tōō′sŏn) or (tōōsŏn′)

**tulle,** n., *material for dresses,* etc., pronounced (tŏŏl) or (tōōl)

**tumultuous applause,** trite phrase, of exhausted vitality as description.

**Tuolumne,** n., *place name in California,* pronounced (tōōŏl′ŭmnĭ)

**tu quoque,** Latin phrase, *a retort in kind,* literally, *thou also;* pronounced (tū kwō′kwĭ)

**turbine,** adj., *a term in mechanics,* pronounced (tur′bĭn), less commonly (tur′bīn)

**Turgenieff, I. S.,** n., *Russian novelist* (1818–1883), pronounced (tōōrgän′yĕf) There are many variations in spelling of this name, but the one given seems to be now the most generally used in English writing.

**turgid,** adj., *swollen,* literally, or figuratively of literary style, pronounced (tur′jĭd)

**Turkey carpet,** n., the common British term for the American *oriental rug.*

**turkey gobbler,** n., colloquial for *turkey cock,* the female being known as a *turkey hen.* Though the same word as the name of the country, as the name of the bird *turkey* is not written with a capital.

**turnip,** n., slang for *watch.*

**turps,** n., workman's colloquial abbreviation for *turpentine.*

**turquoise,** n., *a kind of gem,* pronounced (tur′kwoiz) or (tur′koiz)

**turtle,** n., *dove,* derived from Latin *turtur,* and **tortoise,** derived from modern forms represented by French *tortue,* Spanish *tortuga,* and similar words of the fifteenth and sixteenth centuries. The use of **turtle** alone in the sense *dove* is now archaic, the usual form being *turtle dove.* The form *turkle* for **turtle, tortoise** is dialectal. The word **turtle** is by definition sometimes limited to the sea turtle, the term for land and fresh-water reptiles of this kind being **tortoise.** But this distinction is not carried out in general use, the fresh-water animals being frequently referred to as turtles, and the salt-water as tortoises, as in *tortoise shell.* The word **tortoise,** pronounced (tŏr′tis), is much less generally used than **turtle.**

The phrase *to turn turtle,* applied to boats and automobiles, is slang.

**Tussaud,** n., especially in *Madame Tussaud's,* an exhibition of waxwork figures in London, pronounced (tōōsōz′)

**tussle,** n., v., colloquial for *wrestle, struggle.*

**twaddle,** n., *silly talk or writing,* pronounced (twŏd′l) or (twah′dl)

**twain,** numeral, archaic form of *two.* But the word survives in a few phrases, as in *never these twain shall part,* and in poetry. It also occurs in the name *Mark Twain,* the pen name of S. L. Clemens, literally, *mark two,* from the call of the leadsman in taking the depth of the water on the Mississippi.

**tweezers,** n., *instrument for holding small objects firmly,* construed either as a singular or as a plural. See **scissors** Often referred to as *a pair of tweezers.* A word of similar meaning and also similar form and use is *pliers.*

**twig,** v., colloquial and slang in the sense *observe, note,* as in "*Do you see what that fellow is doing?*" "*Yes, I twig.*"

**two-for,** n., *something sold two for five cents,* especially cigars. A slang abbreviation of *two for* (five cents), pronounced (tŏō′fer)

**tyke,** n., colloquial for *wandering dog of no particular breed,* sometimes extended to apply to a ragged boy. With a variant *tike.*

**typist,** n., *one who operates a typewriting machine.* More generally used in England than in America. In America *typewriter* designates both operator and machine. A stenographer is one who writes shorthand, therefore not necessarily one who uses a typewriter.

**Tyrolese,** adj., *of Tyrol,* pronounced (tĭr′olēz), also *Tyrolian* (tĭrō′lĭan) The noun is Tyrol (tĭrōl′)

**Tzigane,** adj., *pertaining to the Hungarian gipsies,* pronounced (tsĭgahn′)

# U

**u** (ū), the sound of u as in *music.* The question of uncertainty arises mainly in words with *d, t* followed by **u,** as in *duty, tube,* pronounced by some speakers (dū′tĭ), (tūb), by others (dŏō′tĭ), (tŏōb) Academic authority favors the pronunciation (ū) in these words, but practically the pronunciation (ōō) is also widely current in cultivated speech. After *l* as in *delude*, the vowel is almost universally (ōō), that is (dĭlōōd') or (delōōd') Theoretical phoneticians sometimes endeavor to make a distinction between *blew* and *blue*, the former being pronounced (blōō) and the latter (blū) For this distinction, however, there is no justification, either in general custom or in the history of the two words. In normal speech both are pronounced (blōō)

**ugh,** interj., *an expression of disgust, horror,* etc., conventionally written *ugh*, though *uh*, corresponding to the interjection *oh*, would probably be nearer the customary pronunciation. The pronunciation varies a good deal, but a long (ŭ) sound represents it as adequately as a simple phonetic notation is capable of doing. The most expressive parts of the interjection are not phonetic, however, but facial and generally muscular.

**ugly,** adj., colloquial in the sense *quarrelsome, pugnacious, formidable,* as in *an ugly customer, The dog turned ugly.* A verb *uglify* is a humorous counterpart to *beautify.*

**Uhlan,** n., *a kind of soldier,* especially in the German army, pronounced (ōō'lan) or (ū'lan) See **Zeitgeist**

**ukase,** n., *a decree of the Russian government,* pronounced (ūkās')

**ultima ratio,** Latin phrase, *the final argument,* that is, force. Pronounced (ŭl'tĭma rā'shĭō)

**ultima Thule,** Latin phrase, *remote, unknown region,* pronounced (ŭl'tĭma thū'lē)

**ultra vires,** Latin phrase, *beyond one's power, unauthorized,* pronounced (ŭl'tra vī'rēz)

**umbilicus,** n., *navel,* pronounced (ŭmbĭl'ikus) or (ŭmbĭlī'kus) The adjective *umbilical* is likewise pronounced (ŭmbĭl'ikal) or (ŭmbĭlī'kal)

**umbrella,** n., *a rain shade,* pronounced (ŭmbrĕl'a), but with several low colloquial variations, as (ŭmbril'), (ŭmberĕl')

**umlaut,** n., German word, *a change in the quality of a vowel caused* *by a neighboring sound,* pronounced (o͞om′lowt)  Also called *mutation.*  See **ablaut, Zeitgeist**

**'un,** pron., colloquial and humorous for *one,* as in *He's a good 'un.* This pronunciation occurs only when *one* receives a very light stress.

**unbeknown, unbeknownst,** adj., humorous, colloquial, and dialectal for *without the knowledge of,* as in *He did this unbeknownst to me,* without my knowledge.

**unconscionable,** adj., *making extreme or excessive demands.* A slightly humorous word, often used as a general colloquial intensive meaning *long, large, great,* as in *He was an unconscionable time about it, an unconscionable talker, liar,* etc.  Pronounced (ŭnkŏn′shonabl)

**under,** prep., generally current in the phrase *under the circumstances.* Theorists sometimes object to this phrase on logical grounds, for since *circumstances* etymologically means *things surrounding,* one could not well be *under* them. Logic and etymology notwithstanding, *under the circumstances* is good current English.

**underdone,** see **rare**

**understand,** v., *comprehend,* with a past tense and past participle *understood,* the latter with an occasional archaic variant *understanded,* especially in the phrase *a tongue not understanded of the people,* that is, a foreign language.

**uninterested,** adj., *not interested, having no concern, curiosity about.* This word is sometimes confused with *disinterested,* not having expectation of profit or advantage, as *a disinterested witness.* See **interested**

**unique,** adj., *without parallel or equal, only one of a kind.* Inaccurately and loosely used as a synonym for *remarkable, original, entertaining,* as *to present a unique appearance,* a strange appearance, *the society gave a unique entertainment,* unusual or novel entertainment.

**United States,** n., singular as the name of a country, as in *The United States is governed by representatives elected by the people.* If one wished to refer to the states separately, one would say *the states of the United States.* For lack of a better, the form **United States** is also used as an adjective, as in *the United States government, the United States elections,* though the awkwardness of this phrasing is avoided whenever possible by using a prepositional phrase, as in *the government of the United States, the elections in the United States,* etc. See **America, American**

**United States Geographic Board.** This Board is constituted by authority of the government of the United States to pass upon all geographical names that are brought before it, and its decisions "are to be accepted by the departments of Government as the standard authority." The acceptance of others is voluntary, but manifestly advisable. The Board has issued various reports, the most complete being the fifth, 1921, with several later supplementary reports. These reports may be had by addressing the Board at Washington, D. C. Many of the decisions turn on trivial points, as, for example, whether a lighthouse on Lake Champlain shall be known as *Snoddy's Dock* or *Snody Dock,* and are therefore only of local interest and importance. Others, however, are of more general significance, and, of these, representative examples will be found recorded in the present volume.

**universal apathy,** trite phrase, rhetorical newspaper style.

**unless,** conj., often corrupted in children's dialect to something like (lĕs′n), and in the colloquial speech of adults to (lĕs)

**unmoral,** adj., *not concerned with moral distinctions,* and to be distinguished from *immoral,* given to evil practices. The distinction is illustrated in the sentence, *Little children who have not arrived at the age of discretion may be said to be unmoral, rather than immoral.*

**unto,** prep., archaic equivalent of *to*, affected sometimes in literary, oratorical, and poetic style.

**up,** adv., in colloquial style, often appended needlessly to verbs, as in *connect up, cripple up* (*all crippled up*), *divide up, end up, finish up, limber up, open up, polish up, rest up, scratch up, settle up,* etc. Though many of these uses are unquestionably current in good colloquial English, stylistically the particle **up** is only an encumbrance, and care should be taken not to permit one's style to become littered with such unnecessary trifles.

The phrases *all up,* as in *It's all up with him,* no hope for him, and *up to,* as in *What are you up to?,* What concealed purpose, what mischief are you about?, are colloquial; *up to* is colloquial in the sense *incumbent upon, obligatory to,* as in *It's up to you to find the means; up against* is colloquial for *confronting a hard or impossible task,* often with impersonal object, as in *up against it.* See **hard up**

**uplift,** n., *moral elevation or stimulation.* This is a recent word, and though there is nothing unusual in the manner of its formation, being exactly the same in the character of its elements as *income* and many other words, the word is nevertheless avoided by careful speakers and writers, except as it may be used satirically and ironically. The objection to the word is not that it is incorrectly derived, but that it has become a favorite word with a certain class of speakers and writers who designate by it a kind of sentimental and vague moral enthusiasm which would drag down any word that might be used to name it.

**uppers,** n., *upper part of shoes,* and slang in the phrase *on one's uppers,* hard up, from the figure of shoes worn until the soles have disappeared.

**Uppsala,** n., *Swedish place name,* pronounced (ŭp′sahlah)

**up to date,** adj., colloquial and slang for *modern, well equipped and furnished.* As slang, no longer fresh and sparkling, having been replaced by newer terms, *the latest scream, the latest wrinkle,* etc., but, though the phrase has lost its original vivacity, it has not become standard, persisting rather as a kind of shopworn slang.

**upward,** adv., with a variant *upwards.* The word implies a stage beyond that indicated, as in *men of forty years and upwards,* of forty years and more than forty years. The phrase *upwards of a hundred* means a hundred and more, not approaching or nearly a hundred. The word **upward** can also be an adjective, as in *Prices show an upward tendency,* but not *upwards.*

**urban,** adj., *dwelling in or pertaining to a city,* to be distinguished from the adjective *urbane,* polite, courteous, polished, the former pronounced (ur′ban), the latter (urbān′)

**urge,** n., a literary and sometimes facetious synonym for *impulse, desire,* as in *driven by a demonic urge, In the spring, youth feels the urge to poetry.*

**usage,** n., *customary practice,* pronounced (ūz′ĭj), but sometimes also (ūs′ĭj) The analogy of the verb *use* (ūz) supports the first, the analogy of the noun *use* (ūs) supports the second pronunciation.

**use,** n., a colloquial contraction in *It is no use to try,* for *It is of no use to try.* Colloquial as an interjection of discouragement in the phrase *What's the use?* In the sense *custom, practice,* as in *an ancient use of the college,* **use** is literary and archaic.

**used to could,** v., low colloquial and dialectal for *used to be able to do,* as in *I can't see as well as I used to could.*

**usufruct,** n., *right of using,* pronounced (ū′zūfrŭkt) A learned, legal, or pompous word, known to most persons only as an eye-word. The English language is unhappily burdened with many pompous words like this for expressing simple ideas for which simple words are also available.

**usury,** n., *lending of money at excessive rate of interest,* pronounced (ū′zhurĭ), with derivatives *usurer* (ū′zhurer), *usurious* (ūzōō′rĭus)

**ut infra,** Latin phrase, *as below,* pronounced (ŭt ĭn′fra)

605

**uti possidetis,** Latin phrase, *the granting to belligerents of what they have acquired,* literally, *as you possess;* pronounced (ū′tĭ pŏsĭdē′tĭs)

**ut supra,** Latin phrase, *as above,* pronounced (ŭt sū′pra)

**uvula,** n., *part of the palate,* pronounced (ū′vūla), with an adjective *uvular* (ū′vūlar) The plural of **uvula** is *uvulae,* pronounced (ū′vūlē)

**uxorius,** adj., *too much wrapped up in one's wife,* pronounced (ŭksŏr′ĭus) The adjective can be used only in discommendatory senses, as of one who does not exercise moderation in what otherwise might be a virtue.

# V

**V,** n., *five,* slang for *a five-dollar bill.*

**vaccine,** n., *the virus used in vaccination,* pronounced (văk′sĭn) or (văk′sēn)

**vacillate,** v., *waver,* pronounced (văs′ilāt)

**vade mecum,** Latin phrase, *handbook, ready guide,* literally, *go with me.* Pronounced (vā′dĭ mē′kŭm), and often hyphened as one word.

**vae victis,** Latin phrase, *woe to the vanquished,* pronounced (vē vĭk′tĭs)

**vagary,** n., *whim, freak,* pronounced (vagā′rĭ), not (vā′garĭ)

**vagina,** n., *a term in anatomy,* pronounced (vajī′na)

**vale,** n., now only archaic and poetic for *valley.*

**vale,** interj., Latin word, *farewell,* pronounced (vā′lĭ)

**Valenciennes,** n., *a kind of lace,* pronounced (vălensĭĕnz′) or (vălensēnz′) Or it may also be pronounced as the French pronounce it, being by origin the name of a place in France.

**valet,** n., *man who acts as body servant to a man,* pronounced (văl′ĭt), or sometimes as a French word, (vălā′)

**valiant,** adj., *brave, courageous,* but now chiefly literary. See **dauntless**

**valise,** n., old-fashioned word for *an old-fashioned kind of traveling bag,* pronounced (vălēs′)

**Valkyrie,** n., *war maid in Norse mythology,* with a plural the same, *the Valkyrie,* or with the usual ending, *the Valkyries,* pronounced (vălkĭr′ĭ), (vălkĭr′ĭz)

**valse,** n., French form of *waltz,* pronounced (vahls)

**valued,** adj., old-fashioned and formal in business correspondence in phrases like *your valued order.* The word has become old-fashioned in this use perhaps because a simple business transaction calls for simplicity rather than elaborate courtesy.

**vamose,** v., slang for *to depart, make off.* Pronounced (vămos′) and derived from the Spanish word *vamos,* we go. The word has a variant *vamoos,* pronounced (vămōōs′) See **mosey, skidoo**

**vamp,** see **vampire**

**vampire,** n., used figuratively for *a seductive woman.* From this comes the slang verb, *vamp,* to practice the arts of seduction, and the noun *vamp,* one who does this.

**vanilla,** n., *a plant and a flavoring extracted from the fruit of the plant,* pronounced (vanĭl′a), dialectally (vanĕl′a)

**vanquish,** v., literary word for *overcome, conquer.*

**Varangian,** adj., n., especially in the phrase *the Varangian Guard, the Varangians,* the Norse bodyguard of the Byzantine emperors. Pronounced (varăn′jĭan)

**varicose,** adj., *dilated,* especially of a blood vein. Pronounced (văr′ikōs)

**varlet,** n., archaic word for *fellow, rascal,* much used in tales of adventure written in the romantic style.

**varmint,** n., colloquial and dialectal for *a troublesome mischievous child or boy.* Obsolete name also for small predatory animals, being a corruption of *vermin.*

**varsity,** n., colloquial and college slang for *university.*

**vase,** n., *a vessel for holding flowers and other articles,* pronounced (vās), (vāz), or (vahz) The pronunciation (vās) is by far the most general, and the pronunciation (vahz) begins now to seem a little affected.

**vast assembly, multitude, throng,** trite phrases, used so often they have lost all descriptive power.

**vaudeville,** n., *a kind of entertaining performance,* pronounced (vōd'vĭl) or (vō'devĭl) Low colloquially (vaw'devĭl), though this pronunciation, a natural anglicization, is widespread, and perhaps should be characterized only as general colloquial.

**vaunt,** v., literary for *boast.*

**Veda,** n., *the Veda* or *the Vedas,* sacred books written in Sanskrit, pronounced (vā'da), (vā'daz)

**vehement,** adj., *vigorous, violent,* pronounced (vē'ĭment), dialectally (vēhē'ment)

**vehicle,** n., *wagon, carriage,* etc., pronounced (vē'ĭkl), dialectally (vē'hĭkl) The adjective is *vehicular* (vēhĭc'ūlar)

**Velazquez, D. de Silva,** n., *Spanish painter* (1599–1660), pronounced (vĕlahth'kĕth) Sometimes spelled less correctly *Velasquez.*

**veldt,** n., *open country in Africa,* pronounced (fĕlt)

**velours,** n., *velvet,* from the French word of the same form. Pronounced (velōōr'), and often written *velour.*

**velvet,** n., slang for *easy-going, not exacting,* as in *His new job was all velvet for him.*

**venal,** adj., *corruptible, purchasable,* to be distinguished from *venial,* pardonable, trivial, as in *a venial offense,* a pardonable fault or offense, *a venal official,* a corrupt official.

**venery,** n., archaic word meaning *hunting,* pronounced (vĕn'erĭ) Also archaic is the word **venery,** of the same spelling and pronunciation but different etymological origin, in the sense *venereal indulgence.*

**venison,** n., *the flesh of deer,* pronounced (vĕn'izon) or (vĕn'zon)

**ventre à terre,** French phrase, *as rapidly as possible,* literally, *with belly to the earth;* pronounced (vahṅ'trahtār')

**verandah,** n., *porch*, also spelled *veranda*.  Now a somewhat old-fashioned word.  See **piazza**

**verbal,** adj., *pertaining to words*, as in *a verbal correction*, a correction in wording.  Strictly the word should be distinguished from *oral*, spoken, but in colloquial use **verbal** is often employed in the sense of *oral*.  See **literal, oral**

**verbatim,** adv., *word for word*.  Especially in the phrase *verbatim et literatim*, word for word and letter for letter.  Pronounced (verbā′tĭm), (lĭterā′tĭm)  Not to be confused in meaning with *verbal*.

**verbena,** n., *a kind of flower*, pronounced (verbē′na), dialectally often (verbēn′ya)

**verbum sat sapienti,** Latin phrase, *a word to the wise is sufficient*, pronounced (ver′bum săt săpĭĕn′tĭ), and abbreviated *verb. sap.*

**verdigris,** n., *green incrustation on copper*, pronounced (ver′dĭgrĭs), colloquially often (ver′dĭgrēs)  The second element of the word is not related etymologically to the noun *grease*, but comes ultimately from the proper noun *Greece*.  It seems probable that the colloquial pronunciation will prevail in this word.  See **ambergris**

**verein,** n., German word, *association*, as in *Turnverein*, gymnastic association, and other compounds.  Pronounced (fĕrīn′)  On the capitalization of German words, see **Zeitgeist**

**verily,** adv., archaic and literary for *in truth, indeed*.

**veritable avalanche, shower,** etc., trite phrases, especially in exaggerated epistolary style.

**vermicelli,** n., *paste of flour made into fine threads*, pronounced (vermĭsĕl′ĭ) or (vermĭchĕl′ĭ)

**vermouth,** n., *a liqueur*.  The word is derived from German *wermuth*, and is sometimes spelled *vermuth*.  It is pronounced (vermōōth′) or, after the German fashion, (vār′mōōt)

**Versailles,** n., *French palace and place*, pronounced (versālz′) or as a French word.

**versatile,** adj., *adapting oneself easily to new tasks or situations,* pronounced (ver′satĭl) or (ver′satīl)   See -ile

**verse,** n., (1) *a line in a metrical composition;* (2) *a set of these constituting a group,* also known as a stanza, as in *a song in three verses.*   The use of **verse** in this second sense is sometimes reprehended and *stanza* is prescribed as the proper term for a set of verses.   This is undoubtedly the more careful and the more literary usage, but **verse** in the sense *stanza* is so generally customary that it must be accepted as passable usage.   In references to hymns, for example, **verse** is the prevailing term for *stanza,* as in *Let us sing the first, second, and third verses.*   In the sense *line,* **verse** is limited to technical literary usage.

**vers libre,** French phrase, *free verse,* that is, not following strictly defined metrical rules.   Pronounced (vär lē′br)   The phrase resists anglicization because it belongs to the sophisticated speech of literary criticism.

**versus,** prep., Latin word, *against,* pronounced (ver′sus) and abbreviated *v.* or *vs.*

**vertebra,** n., *one of the segments of the backbone,* pronounced (ver′-tebra), with a plural *vertebrae* (ver′tebrē)   See **alumna**

**vertigo,** n., *dizziness,* pronounced (vertī′gō) according to the older and formal authorities, but actually, in present use, commonly pronounced (ver′tĭgō)

**verve,** n., literary word for *brilliance, vitality,* pronounced (värv)

**very,** see **too**

**vest,** n., the usual term in America for *man's garment worn under the coat.*   In England known as *a waistcoat,* (wās′kōt), (wĕs′kĭt), the term **vest** in England being used in this sense only in Shakspere's English.   Also used as the name for a woman's undergarment.   See **waistcoat**

**vet,** n., slang abbreviation for *veteran* or for *veterinary.*

**veteran,** n., *one who has had long service,* especially in war.   From the meaning it is therefore pleonastic to speak of *an old veteran.*

In recent use, however, it has become increasingly customary to speak of any person who has served in a war that has come to an end as a veteran, whether he has served long or not, as in *the veterans of the Spanish-American War*. In this use **veteran** would merely mean one who had formerly been a soldier.

**via,** prep., *by way of, passing through,* a Latin word, but ordinarily anglicized and pronounced (vīa) Sometimes written **viâ** to indicate that the word is an ablative case.

**vial,** see **phial**

**via media,** Latin phrase, *a middle course between extremes,* pronounced (vī′a mē′dĭa) Not written **viâ** because in this construction **via** is a nominative. See **via**

**viands,** n., archaic and literary for *foods served at a meal.*

**vicar,** n., *a parish priest.* In England **vicar** and *rector* do not have the same meaning, but the distinction between the two words is technical and calls for special examination on the part of anyone to whom the words are strange.

**vice,** prep., Latin word, *in place of,* pronounced (vī′sĭ) In print, *vice* as a Latin word would be distinguished from the noun **vice** by the use of italic type for the Latin word.

**vice versa,** Latin phrase, *the other way round, just the opposite,* pronounced (vī′sĭ ver′sa)

**vichy,** n., *a kind of table water,* pronounced (vĭsh′ĭ)

**victuals,** n., *articles of food,* pronounced (vĭt′lz) The word is now rarely used, and when it is used, it has an archaic or depreciatory coloring. It is construed as a plural, though there is no corresponding singular *victual.*

**vicuna,** n., *South American animal and the wool it yields.* Also spelled *vicuña, vicugna,* and in this spelling pronounced (vĭko͞on′-ya), but usually anglicized in pronunciation to (vĭko͞o′na)

**vide,** v., Latin word, *see,* as reference to a passage in a book, etc. Pronounced (vī′dĭ) and abbreviated *v.*

**videlicet,** adv., Latin word, *namely, that is to say,* introducing an

611

explanatory word or group of words. Pronounced (vĭdē′lĭsĕt) See **viz.**

**vie,** v., *compete as a rival.* Rarely used in spoken English, but overused in newspaper style. See **ban, pact**

**vi et armis,** Latin phrase, *by armed force,* pronounced (vī ĕt ahr′mĭs)

**viewpoint,** n., *point of view.* The word **viewpoint** is in good general use, but it is rejected by some stylists in favor of *point of view.* The compound **viewpoint** is recent, probably made on the analogy of *standpoint.* The objection to both **viewpoint** and *standpoint* is that they seem crudely economical as compared with the more formal phrase *point of view.* See **standpoint**

**view with alarm,** trite phrase, used so often that it no longer excites alarm.

**vignette,** n., *a kind of drawing for illustration, a short literary sketch,* pronounced (vēnyĕt′)

**villain,** n., *wicked person,* pronounced (vĭl′an), low colloquially often (vĭl′yan) The adjective *villainous* (vĭl′anus) is used as a colloquial intensive in generally adverse significance, as in *villainous tea, weather, music,* etc., and it has a variant spelling *villanous.* So also *villainy* has a variant *villany.* To be distinguished from the word *villein* (vĭl′ĭn), a feudal tenant owing menial service to an overlord.

**villegiatura,** n., Italian word, *period of residence in the country,* pronounced (vĭlājahtōō′rah)

**vingt-et-un,** n., French word, *name of a game,* literally, *twenty and one,* pronounced (vănt ā ŭn)

**vin ordinaire,** French phrase, *the wine that is served with the dinner in French restaurants,* pronounced (văn ŏrdĭnār′)

**Viola,** n., *woman's name,* variously pronounced as (vīō′la), (vī′ōla), (vĭ′ōla), (vĭō′la), (vē′ōla), (vēō′la), etc.

**violoncello,** n., *bass violin,* pronounced (vĭolŏnchĕl′ō), but usually employed in the abbreviated form *cello.* See **cello**

**virago,** n., *fierce or scolding woman,* with a plural *viragos,* pronounced (vĭrā′gō), (vĭrā′gōz)

**Virgil,** n., *Latin poet* (70-19 B. C.)  The Latin form of the name
is *Vergilius*, and in English the form *Vergil* is sometimes used,
though **Virgil** is much more general.

**virginibus puerisque,** Latin phrase, *for boys and girls, suitable for
boys and girls*, pronounced (virjĭn'ĭbŭs pūerĭs'kwĭ)

**virile,** adj., *masculine, vigorous*, pronounced (vĭr'ĭl), (vī'rĭl), or
(vĭr'īl) (vī'rīl)  See -ile  The noun is *virility* (vĭrĭl'ĭtĭ)

**virulent,** adj., *powerful, malignant*, pronounced (vĭr'ōōlent), not
(vĭr'ūlent)

**virus,** n., *poison*, pronounced (vī'rus)

**visage,** n., literary word for *face, countenance*, pronounced (vĭz'ĭj)

**vis-à-vis,** adv., French word, *facing each other*, pronounced (vē'-
zahvē')

**viscount,** n., *a title of nobility*, pronounced (vī'kownt), with a
feminine *viscountess* (vī'kowntes)

**viscous,** adj., *thick but fluid*, pronounced (vĭs'kus), with a variant
of the same meaning, *viscid*, pronounced (vĭs'ĭd)

**visé,** n., *endorsement on a passport*, pronounced (vē'zā)  A variant
of the same meaning is *visa* (vē'zah)

**visor,** n., *part of a helmet*, pronounced (vī'zor), with a variant
spelling *vizor*, and a variant form of the same meaning, *visard*,
*vizard*, (vĭz'ard)

**visual,** adj., *pertaining to sight*, pronounced (vĭzh'ūal), less commonly (vĭz'ūal)

**vitamin,** n., *an element in foods*, with a variant form *vitamine*,
and two corresponding pronunciations, (vī'tamĭn) and (vī'tamīn)
The form **vitamin** is generally preferred in scientific use.

**vitiate,** v., *make ineffective*, pronounced (vĭsh'ĭāt)

**viva,** an exclamation, Italian word, *Long live*, followed by the
name of the person applauded.  Pronounced (vē'vah)  The
equivalent French exclamation is *vive*, pronounced (vēv), and
the equivalent Latin is *vivat*, pronounced (vī'văt)

**vivandier,** n., French word, *man who sells provisions to French* *troops*, pronounced (vēvahn'dïä), with corresponding feminine *vivandière*, pronounced (vēvahndïär')

**viva voce,** Latin phrase, *spoken,* literally, *with the living voice;* pronounced (vī'va vō'sï)

**viz.,** adv., abbreviation of the Latin word *videlicet,* that is to say. When the abbreviation **viz.** appears in a passage which is being read or spoken, it is usually spoken as *namely,* as in *There shall be three officers, viz., a president, a secretary, and a treasurer,* spoken as *There shall be three officers, namely,* etc.   See **videlicet**

**voice like a bell,** trite phrase, commonplace description, of the same kind as *eyes like stars.*

**Volapuk,** n., *an artificial international language,* pronounced (vŏl'apo͝ok)

**vol-au-vent,** n., French word, *a kind of raised pie,* pronounced (vŏl ō vahn)

**volcano,** n., *eruptive mountain,* pronounced (vŏlkā'nō), not (vŏlkah'nō)   Plural *volcanoes.*

**volkslied,** n., German word, *a song of the people,* pronounced vŏlks'lēd)   See **Zeitgeist**

**volte-face,** n., French word, *complete reversal of position in an opinion or argument,* pronounced (vŏlt fahs)

**voodoo,** see **hoodoo**

**vortex,** n., *whirlpool,* with a plural *vortices* (vŏr'tïsēz), or an anglicized plural *vortexes* (vŏr'tĕksez)

**Vosges,** n., *mountains in France,* pronounced (vōzh)

**vote,** v., colloquial in the sense *pronounce, acknowledge to be,* as in *The picnic was voted a success,* was acknowledged to have been a success, and in the sense *propose,* as in *I vote for tennis,* propose we play tennis.

**vox humana,** Latin phrase, *the human voice, an organ stop,* pronounced (vŏks hūmā'na)

**vox populi, vox dei,** Latin phrase, *the voice of the people is the voice of God,* pronounced (vŏks pŏp'ūlī, vŏks dē'ï)

# W

**Wabash,** n., *river and college in Indiana,* pronounced (waw'băsh)

**Waco,** n., *place in Texas,* pronounced (wā'kō)

**wad,** n., slang in the sense *roll of bank notes, money in general.* Slang also in *tightwad,* a stingy person.

**wade into,** v., slang for *to scold, reprimand.*

**wager,** v., *to bet,* but now a somewhat literary and archaic word. Also used as a noun, *a bet.* See **bet**

**wages,** n., commonly used only in the plural, and construed with a plural verb, as in *Wages were good then.* The singular *wage* is literary and learned, as in *a living wage,* not the word of the man who works for wages. Sometimes, however, **wages** is construed as a singular, as in *The wages of sin is death.* See **emolument, salary, stipend**

**Wagner,** n., *German musical composer,* usually pronounced (vahg'-ner) As an Americanized name, **Wagner** is pronounced (wăg'-ner)

**wagon,** n., *a wheeled vehicle,* often spelled *waggon* in England.

**wain,** n., poetic name for *wagon.*

**waistcoat,** n., ordinarily called *vest* in America, the word **waistcoat** being more general in England. Pronounced (wās'kōt) or (wĕs'kĭt) See **vest**

**wait,** v., *defer, delay,* as in *to wait dinner for someone,* old and still current, but not very general usage.

**waive,** v., *not to insist on,* to be distinguished from *wave,* to move back and forth.

**wake,** v., now ordinarily used only as a transitive verb, as in *I waked him at five o'clock,* but formerly, and still in literary use, also as an intransitive, as in *Whether I wake or sleep.* The usual construction in this latter sense is now *to be awake, Whether I am awake or asleep.* But **wake** is still in use as an intransitive when followed by *up,* as in *I wake up at five o'clock.* See **awake**

**waken,** see **awake**

**wale,** n., *a stripe on the body from a stroke.* Also a verb *to wale*, to whip, and a participial noun, as in *to get a waling.* The noun **wale** has a less frequent variant *weal.* These words are sometimes incorrectly spelled *whale, whaling.*

**walk,** v., slang in the sense *to thrash*, as in *He took off his coat and walked right into it,* or *to consume, eat up,* as in *Here's your dinner. Walk into it.*

**wallop,** v., slang for *to thrash*, as in *He walloped him in one round,* and also as an adjective *walloping*, big, as in *a walloping lie.*

**Waltham,** n., *place name in Massachusetts,* pronounced (wŏl'thăm)

**Walton, Izaak,** n., *English writer* (1593–1683), not *Isaac.*

**want,** v., dialectal followed directly by a clause, as in *I want you should be happy,* for *I want you to be happy.* Colloquial and dialectal also in the sense *ought, should,* as in *You want to keep your eyes open in the city or you will be taken in.* The constructions *want in, off, out* are dialectal with the verb of motion omitted, as in *I want off here,* for *I want to get off here, The cat wants in,* for *The cat wants to come in.*

**wanting,** adj., colloquial in the sense *mentally deficient, feeble-minded.*

**Wardour,** n., *name of a street in London,* pronounced (wŏr'der), like *Warder.*

**warm,** adj., slang in senses similar to the slang uses of *hot.* See **hot**

**warn,** v., construed with *of* or *against*, as in *We warned him of* or *against the danger.*

**Warwick,** n., *place in England,* pronounced (wŏr'ĭk)

**was,** v., low colloquial use for standard *were*, with singular pronoun *you*, e. g., *I didn't know you was here.* In the condition contrary to fact, e. g., *If I was you, If I were you,* usage is divided; the former construction is doubtfully permissible, but the latter is unquestionable. The construction *you was* was formerly good English, and numerous examples of it will be found in the writings of standard authors of the eighteenth cen-

**tury.** These of course provide no justification for the present use of *you was*, a construction which occurs now neither in good spoken nor in good written English.

**Wasatch,** n., *western mountain range*, pronounced (waw'săch)

**washstand,** n., *a kind of table at which one washes*, often called also *a washing stand*. Compounds like **washstand** for *washing stand*, *cookstove* for *cooking stove* have often been criticized, but long and extensive use has made them good English.

**washwoman,** n., a current equivalent word for *washerwoman*, the latter being the more common term in England, and sometimes theoretically preferred as being the more correctly formed etymologically. But compounds of verbs and nouns like **wash-woman** are normal in English, as in *workman*, man who works, *hoptoad*, toad that hops, though they are not very numerous.

**wassail,** n., archaic word for *drinking combined with feasting*, pronounced (wah'sl), (wŏs'l), or (wăs'l) From the Anglo-Saxon phrase *wes hal*, be hale, equivalent to the modern *May you live long and prosper*.

**water-closet,** n., avoided in polite conversation and replaced by some euphemistic substitute, such as *bathroom, toilet, convenience, W. C., comfort station*.

**watery grave,** trite phrase, rhetorical variation for *to drown*.

**Waukegan,** n., *place name*, pronounced (wawkē'gan)

**Waukesha,** n., *place name*, pronounced (waw'keshaw)

**wax,** v., archaic word for *increase, grow*, still used occasionally as a facetious word in the phrases *wax wroth, wax fat*.

**wax bean,** n., *yellow podded bean*, called *butter bean* in England. In America *butter bean* is the name for a kind of Lima bean.

**way,** n., in the phrase *under way*, of ships just after they are in motion, that is, on their way. Incorrectly given sometimes as *weigh*, as though the phrase had something to do with the weighing of the anchor.

**way,** n., *distance*, as in *I will go a little way with you, Christmas* *is a long way off.* Colloquial in this form, but dialectal in the form *ways*, as in *He rode a little ways with us.*

**W. C.,** see **water-closet**

**weapon,** n., *instrument for attack or defense,* pronounced (wĕp′n), dialectally (wē′pn)

**weave,** v., *interlace threads to make a cloth,* and figuratively, *arrange the elements of a plot to make a story.* The figurative sense has been so constantly and unnecessarily employed that any writer with a literary conscience would now avoid it.

**wed,** v., archaic and newspaper literary synonym for *marry,* especially in headlines, as in *Popular young couple wed in Grace M. E. Church.* As an adjective the participle *wedded* is still in use in a few phrases, as in *wedded love, wedded bliss, wedded life,* but in these also the word is a bit archaic.

**ween,** v., archaic for *think, believe.*

**weep,** v., archaic, literary, and facetious for *cry, shed tears.*

**wee small hours,** trite phrase, affected synonym for the early hours of the morning, that is, the hours immediately after twelve.

**Weihaiwei,** n., *Polynesian place name,* pronounced (wā′hī′wā′)

**weir,** n., *dam,* with a variant but less common spelling *wear,* both pronounced (wēr)

**weird,** adj., slang in the sense *remarkable, unusual, striking.* The standard meaning of the word is *supernatural, unearthly.*

**welkin,** n., literary and poetic word for *sky.*

**well,** see **say**

**we'll,** see **I'll**

**Welsh,** adj., *of Wales,* with a variant but less general spelling *Welch.* As a family name the spelling *Welch* survives extensively.

**welsher,** n., *one who evades his responsibility in a joint undertaking,* originally one who departs without paying a racing debt. Also spelled *welcher,* but less generally, with a verb *to welsh, welch.*

**Wemyss,** n., *family name,* pronounced (wēmz)

**wench,** n., archaic and humorous word for *girl, woman.*

**wend one's way,** trite phrase, a literary echo.

**were,** v., literary and archaic introducing a subordinate clause, as in *Were I to tell you all of it, you would not believe me,* for *If I were to tell you,* etc. See **had, should, would** Ordinarily pronounced (wer), sometimes (wĕr), especially in England. Another artificial literary use of **were** is that which gives it the value of *would be,* as in *It were idle to deny that his efforts have failed.*

**Wesleyan,** adj., *of the sect of Wesley,* pronounced (wĕs′lĭan) or (wĕz′lĭan)

**we-uns,** pron., dialectal variant of the nominative plural pronoun of the first person, *we.* The form *you-uns* for *you* also occurs dialectally. See **you all**

**wh** (wh), as in *wheat.* In American English the custom is to pronounce **wh** as (wh), especially in a stressed word or syllable, as in *wheat* (whēt), *white* (whīt), *while* (whīl), etc., and the pronunciation of these words as (wēt), (wīt), (wīl), etc., is usually regarded as dialectal and incorrect. In England the pronunciation of **wh** as (w) is more general and is regarded with more favor, some English phoneticians going so far as to commend it as the only correct pronunciation, at the same time characterizing the pronunciation of **wh** as (wh) as dialectal.

**wharf,** n., *place at which ships load and unload.* With a plural *wharves,* sometimes *wharfs.*

**what,** pron., crude and low colloquial as an elliptical sentence of interrogation by itself. It is better English to use a full sentence, *What do you want?, What did you say?, What was that?,* or some similar amplification. For *but what,* see **but that** In British smart slang, **what** is used as an exclamation, as in *Fine day, what!, A handsome girl, what!* etc.

**whatever,** pron., low colloquial as equivalent to the interrogative *what,* as in *Whatever does he want?, Whatever reason had he for* *making such a statement?* The correct use of **whatever** is as an indefinite, as in *He took whatever he wanted.* See **however, whyever**

**what . . . for,** pron., colloquial but good idiom in the construction *What do you do that for?*, for *Why do you do that?* Or colloquial also when spoken together in asking a question, as in *"Please turn round." "What for?"*

**what not,** pron., literary, at end of a list of things, meaning *et cetera, all sorts of things,* as in *The room was filled with broken-down chairs, cracked mirrors, discarded clothing, and what not.*

**what with,** prep., literary style in constructions like *What with the rain and the mud, we could make only fifteen miles an hour.* The more usual construction would be *because of, on account of.*

**what-you-may-call-it,** phrase, colloquial substitute for a specific term. See **contraption, gadget**

**wheel,** n., colloquial for *bicycle.* See **bike**

**wheeze,** n., slang for *a joke,* especially one interpolated in his lines by an actor.

**whence,** adv., conj., pron., archaic and literary for *from where, from which,* etc. The construction *from whence* is pleonastic and incorrect. See **thence**

**where,** adv., sometimes used like a relative pronoun, as in *This is the house where Grant was born.* Perhaps this construction might be permitted in sentences with *place* as the antecedent, as in *This is the place where I lost my pocketbook,* but otherwise it is both inexact grammatically and crude stylistically. The sentence above should be *This is the house in which Grant was born.* Constructions like *No one knew from where it had come, No one knew where it had come from* are good English, *from where* being a conjunctive adverb.

The addition of *at, to,* in the use of **where** as an interrogative, is dialectal, as in *Where is he at?, Where has he gone to?,* for *Where is he?, Where has he gone?*

The use of **where** as a synonym for *that* is crude and low colloquial, as in *I saw in the paper the other day where a man had been killed by being bitten by a bee*, for *I saw in the paper the other day that*, etc.

**whereabouts**, n., adv., colloquial, as in *I know nothing of his whereabouts*, i. e., where he is; *Whereabouts is he?*, i. e., Approximately where is he? The form *whereabout* is no longer in use.

**whereof**, see **thereof**

**wherever**, adv., low colloquial as an equivalent of *where*, as in *Wherever have you been?* See **whatever**

**which**, pron., not now used to refer to persons, as in the archaic *Our Father which art in Heaven*. The usual pronouns referring to persons are *who, whom, that*, as in *This is the man who* or *that spoke to me, This is the man to whom I spoke*. Persons in groups may be referred to by **which**, as in *The legislature, which had been in session since June, now dispersed*. The use of **which** introducing a parenthetic clause is colloquial and dialectal, though sometimes carried over into a highly colloquial literary style, as in *If he is elected, which he won't be, he will make a good president*. See **and which**

**while**, conj., in good English used as a conjunction in the sense *during, although, whereas*, but in crude style often used as the equivalent of *and*, as in *One was red, another was yellow, while a third was green*. In the sense *although*, **while** is somewhat crude stylistically, and *While he made a success of business, he was known chiefly as a writer* would be better *Although he made a success*, etc. So also **whilst**

**whilst**, adv., archaic form of *while*.

**whit**, n., archaic and literary in phrases like *not a whit, never a whit*, etc., for *not at all, never at all, not a bit, never a bit*, etc.

**white**, adv., colloquial in the sense *fairly, generously*, as in *He has always treated me white*.

**whither**, adv., archaic and literary for *where, to what place*.

**Whitsunday,** n., *seventh Sunday after Easter,* pronounced (whĭt'-sundĭ)

**whoever's,** pron., low colloquial for *whosever, whosesoever,* as in *I don't know whose hat this was, but whoever's it was, it is mine now,* for *whosever it was,* or *whosesoever it was.* See **else**

**whole,** n., *entire amount.* Though **whole** when it names a sum of single objects logically contains a plural idea in it, nevertheless grammatically it is treated as a singular. In the two sentences following, however, it is treated as a plural: *The whole of the anti-Fascist organizations have been broken up by decree. All the opposition papers have been suspended indefinitely,* and *the whole of the 'Aventine' deputies — Communist, Socialist, Republican, Catholic — Popular, and Democratic; in a word, the whole of the existing Parliamentary Opposition — have been unseated.* Undoubtedly the person who wrote these sentences knew what he was doing, and perhaps he was a little proud of having used **whole** as a plural. He could put up a pretty defense of his use on the ground of the logically plural content of **whole.** Nevertheless his usage remains conscious and theoretical, and that is the chief objection to it. The prevailing usage in the language takes **whole** as a singular collective noun, and as this is just as defensible logically as it is to take it as a plural, there is no reason why the general custom should not be followed.

**whom,** pron., objective case of *who,* but often incorrectly used by inexperienced writers, as in *But if for any reason you prefer to have me write to those whom you think would be interested, I shall be glad to do so.* The syntax here requires *who* as the subject of *would be interested,* the words *you think* being parenthetic. In colloquial speech, however, *who* is often used in constructions grammatically requiring **whom,** as in *Who do you mean?, Who do you think he meant?* These uses are so general that they have acquired good standing as permissible colloquialisms.

**whopper,** n., slang in the sense *something big, remarkable, a lie,* as in *Oh, what a whopper!,* what a lie.   See **thumping**

**whortleberry,** n., a variant name for *huckleberry, bilberry,* pronounced (whur'tĭbĕrĭ)   See **huckleberry**

**who's,** phrase, contracted form of *who is,* written with an apostrophe, as *whose,* possessive case of *who,* is not.

**whose,** pron., possessive case of *who,* and according to the rule of many grammarians not to be used when the antecedent is an inanimate object.   Thus one would not say *The house, whose roof had fallen in,* etc., but *The house, the roof of which had fallen in,* etc.   But though many speakers and writers would avoid a construction like this, in which the antecedent is a simple concrete object like *house, tree, stone,* etc., nevertheless the rule that the antecedent of **whose** must always be a person is by no means strictly observed.   In a sentence like *These were long-standing objections whose weight had not been diminished by the fact that they had been long neglected,* the use of **whose** is both good idiom and good style.   It may be pointed out that historically **whose** corresponds to both the masculine and the neuter genitive of the pronoun in Anglo-Saxon, and that **whose** has always been freely used as the possessive of neuters.   The systematic substitution of *of which* for **whose** when the antecedent is not a person is a mark of formal and theoretical, not of natural style.   In the sentence *His income came not from the "Herald," whose circulation was always small, and whose advertising was comparatively negligible,* the word **whose** could be replaced in its two occurrences only at the expense of making the sentence stiff and pedantic.

**why,** see **say**

**whyever,** adv., low colloquial as the equivalent of *why,* as in *Whyever did you do that?*   When the words are separated, as in *Why did you ever do that?,* the construction may perhaps pass as a colloquialism, but even colloquially it would be better usage to omit *ever*.  See **however, whatever**

**Wichita,** n., *city in Kansas,* pronounced (wĭch'ĭtaw)

**Wiclif,** see **Wycliffe**

**widow woman,** n., low colloquial and dialectal for *widow* and sometimes affected as a bit of dubious humor.

**wield,** v., *have control or command of,* but now chiefly literary, as in the phrase *wield a trenchant pen.*

**wight,** n., archaic and humorous word for *person,* as in the phrase *luckless wight.*

**Wilhelmstrasse,** n., German word, *the place of the German Foreign Office,* pronounced (vĭl'hĕlmstrah'se)

**Wilkes-Barre,** n., *a city in Pennsylvania,* not *Wilkes Barre* or *Wilkesbarre,* according to the decision of the United States Geographic Board.  The name was made by combining the names of two men, *Wilkes* and *Barre,* and therefore both elements should be capitalized.  Pronounced (wĭlks'bär'ĭ)

**will,** see **shall**

**Willamette,** n., *name of a river,* pronounced (wĭlăm'et)

**willowy form, grace,** trite phrases, from old-fashioned stock descriptions.

**wily,** adj., *crafty,* pronounced (wī'lĭ), not (wĭl'ĭ)

**wind,** n., *strong current of air,* pronounced (wĭnd), but in poetry sometimes (wīnd)  Slang in the phrase *raise the wind,* raise the money.

**window,** n., *opening for light and air,* pronounced (wĭn'dō), low colloquially (wĭn'do), (wĭn'der)  See **piano**

**win out,** see **lose out**

**wipe,** v., slang in the sense *aim a blow at,* especially a long sweeping blow, and in the phrase *wipe the floor with,* defeat utterly.  See **sideswipe**

**wire,** n., v., colloquial for *telegram, to telegraph.*  Slang in the phrase *a live wire,* an energetic, active person.

**wise,** adj., slang in the phrase *put one wise,* give information to, especially confidential information.

**wish,** v., dialectal for *care for* or *want, desire,* as in *Do you wish* or *wish for cream in your coffee?,* *General Harney did not wish the office.*

**wishy-washy,** adj., colloquial term for *feeble and insipid.*

**wistaria,** n., *a flowering plant,* pronounced (wĭstā′rĭa), incorrectly (wĭstĭr′ĭa)

**witch-hazel,** n., *kind of shrub,* with a variant spelling *wych-hazel,* both pronounced (wĭch hā′zel)

**with,** prep., dialectal for *by,* as in *kicked with a horse, stung with a bee,* for *kicked by a horse, stung by a bee.*

**withal,** adv., archaic for *besides,* as in *a sturdy fellow and cunning withal;* also archaic as a preposition as in *I know not what we shall buy our bread withal.* Pronounced (wĭdhawl′)

**without,** prep., dialectal as a conjunction *unless,* as in *He won't come without you give your consent,* for *He won't come unless,* etc.

**witness,** v., strictly a formal word, usually with legal implications; therefore not to be loosely used merely in the sense *see, attend,* as in *No one should fail to witness the performance of Hamlet at the Strand.*

**wizened,** adj., *shriveled, dry and wrinkled,* pronounced (wĭz′nd), with variants of the same use and meaning, *wizen* (wĭz′n), *weasen* (wē′zn)

**woman's,** n., used as a general descriptive possessive, as in *the woman's rights movement, Vassar is a woman's college.* The plural is used only when the meaning is specific, *women's rights,* that is, the rights of women, *women's colleges,* colleges for women, *women's department,* department for women, *women's wear,* clothing for women.

**womenfolk,** see **menfolk**

**wonder,** v., *to feel astonishment,* but in colloquial English *to be mildly curious,* as in *I wonder if it will rain today.*

**wonderful,** adj., *exceptional, very remarkable.*  Used colloquially as a general adjective of approval, especially by women, as a synonym for *fine, good, amusing, entertaining,* etc.  See **elegant, fine, grand, great, nice**

**wood,** n., *a forest.*  The word may be either a singular **wood** or a plural *woods,* and it is construed accordingly with a singular or plural verb.

**Woolwich,** n., *town in England,* pronounced (wŏŏl′ĭj)

**wop,** n., disparaging slang word for *an Italian,* especially for the unassimilated Italian.  See **dago, ginny**

**word,** see **last word**

**words are inadequate, fail me,** trite phrases, an easy way of evading a difficulty.

**work,** v., colloquial and slang in the sense *manipulate something out of a person,* as in *Do you think you can work the boss for a vacation?*  The past tense and past participle of **work** is usually *worked,* but an archaic form *wrought* survives in a few uses: (1) with reference to metals, as in *wrought iron, The design was wrought in brass, He wrought it out on the anvil,* hammered it out; (2) in figurative senses, as in *This belief has wrought much evil, He was wrought into the highest pitch of excitement, The miserable creature wrought on my feelings until I became miserable.*

**works,** n., *factory, shop,* usually construed as a plural, as in *The works were not running,* but sometimes as a singular, as in *At the edge of the town stands a large gas-works.*

**worsen,** v., *to become worse.*  Occasional examples of this use occur, but it is much too rare to be counted customary good English.

**worsted,** n., *a kind of cloth,* pronounced (wŏŏs′ted), not (wŏŏs′terd)

**worst way,** adv., colloquial and slang in constructions like *I want to go to the game the worst way,* very much.  The phrase *The worst kind* is used in the same way.  The adverb *worse* is sometimes used alone as a colloquial and low colloquial intensive, as in *I want to see you worse than I can tell*, for standard *I want to see you more than I can tell*.

**worth,** adj., slang in constructions like *He struck out for all he was worth*, He struck out with all his strength.

**worth,** v., archaic word for *befall*, especially in the phrase *woe worth the day*, curses on the day.

**worth-while,** adj., *rewarding, profitable*, as in *a worth-while book*, book worth reading, *worth-while pictures*, not frivolous. A literary use, not very frequent, and not characteristic of the best literary style.

**would,** see **should**

**wound,** n., v., *an injury, to inflict an injury*, pronounced (wōōnd) Formerly also in good use (wownd), but this latter pronunciation is now only low colloquial and dialectal.

**wrack,** see **rack**

**wrath,** n., *anger*, pronounced (răth), sometimes (rahth) in America, but (rawth) in England. But the word is now current only as a literary, poetic, or facetious term. An adjective *wrathy* (răth′ĭ) has the color of slang. See **wroth**

**wreak,** v., archaic and literary for *bring into effect*, especially in the phrases *wreak one's will, wreak vengeance upon*.

**wrestle,** v., *to struggle*, pronounced (rĕs′l), dialectally (răs′l)

**wrinkle,** n., slang in the sense *nicety of fashion*, as in *This tie is the latest wrinkle*.

**write,** v., colloquial and commercial when followed only by a personal pronoun, as in *If I hear anything further, I will write you*. It would be better style to say *I will write to you* or *I will let you know*. It is of course correct to say *I wrote you a letter, I will write you a letter*, etc., in which *letter* is the direct object and *you* the indirect object of **write**. The objection is only to the use of *you* after **write** without a direct object.

**writer,** n., often used to escape employing the pronoun of the first person, as in *The writer was not at the office when your letter* *arrived.* It is better to say simply *I was not,* etc. A cumbersome evasion is never as good as a simple direct statement.

**write-up,** n., colloquial, verging on low colloquial, in the sense *account, description,* as in *The paper had a write-up of the dance.*

**wroth,** adj., archaic and literary for *angry,* pronounced (rawth) or (rōth)

**Wycliffe,** n., *early English theologian,* pronounced (wĭk′lĭf) and also written *Wiclif.*

**Wyoming,** n., *name of a state,* pronounced (wīō′mĭng), less correctly (wī′ōmĭng)

# X

**Xanthippe,** n., *Greek proper name,* pronounced (zăntĭp′ĭ) The word is sometimes generalized in meaning to designate any shrewish wife, from the name of the wife of Socrates, reputed to have been a termagant.

**Xavier,** n., especially in the name St. Francis Xavier, pronounced (zăv′ĭer) or (zā′vĭer)

**Xenia,** n., *place name,* pronounced (zēn′ya), (zē′nĭa)

**Xenophon,** n., *Greek historian,* pronounced (zĕn′ofon)

**Xerxes,** n., *Persian king,* pronounced (zerk′sēz)

**xylophone,** n., *a musical instrument,* pronounced (zĭl′ofōn) or (zī′lofōn)

# Y

**Y,** n., colloquial abbreviation of *Y. M.* or *Y. W. C. A.,* Young Men's or Young Women's Christian Association, usually referred to in this abbreviation as *the Y.*

**-y,** suffix, when added to nouns forms an adjective often expressing a slight degree or disagreeable aspect of the idea indicated by the noun, as in *a woody flavor, watery potatoes, a sugary manner, a Frenchy look, a summery feeling, a greeny yellow.* See **-ish**

**-y, -ie,** suffix, added as a diminutive to short words, as in *cooky, birdie,* always with sympathetic implications. Though **-y** and **-ie** have the same general value, they are not interchangeable; thus one would write *doggie,* but never *pussie,* and one would write *laddie,* but not *sonnie, Johnnie,* the conventional forms of these words being *pussy, sonny, Johnny.* The word *girlie* is an endearing diminutive, but *girly* means *unpleasantly like a girl.* The spelling **-y** occurs much more frequently than **-ie** in words of this type, and, other things being equal, it is the spelling one would ordinarily employ in using a new word in this fashion. If a noun ends in *e* and one wishes to make a diminutive of it by adding **-y,** the final *e* must remain; as in *horsey,* diminutive of *horse,* as distinguished from *horsy,* pertaining to horses, or one might speak of a baby's *wee little nosey,* not *nosy.* But better forms would be *horsie, nosie.*

**yahoo,** n., a word invented by Swift designating a degraded being (see *Gulliver's Travels,* Part IV) Now extended in colloquial use to mean any rough, unkempt person. Pronounced (yā'hōō)

**yank,** v., colloquial for *jerk, pull.* Also a noun, *a jerk, a pull.*

**Yank,** n., colloquial and scornful abbreviation of *Yankee.*

**Yankee,** n., a Northerner as distinguished from a Southerner; or a New Englander as distinguished from a native of other regions of America; or, in British use, any American. In general in European use **Yankee** is equivalent to *American,* the finer shades of the American feeling for the use of the word being naturally beyond the ken of the European. The word **Yankee** sometimes has a contemptuous color, as in the phrase *a Yankee trick.* Various explanations for the origin of this word have been brought forward, but none has been definitely proved. The word came into general use at the time of the American Revolution.

**yataghan,** n., Turkish word, *a Turkish sword,* pronounced (yăt'agăn)

**ye,** pron., archaic form of the second personal pronoun plural, surviving in poetic and formal pulpit style, but ordinarily replaced by *you.* Historically **ye** is only a nominative, the objective being *you,* and a careful student of speech, if he used the form at all, would use it only as a nominative. Numerous examples will be found, however, of an undiscriminated use of **ye** as subject or object.

**yᵉ,** definite article, *the.* An archaic form occasionally revived in modern names, as in *Yᵉ Shippe Tavern.* The word is pronounced like *the,* not like *ye,* the letter *y* in *yᵉ* being merely a printer's substitution of a familiar letter for an older runic symbol for *th* which did not commonly appear in founts of type.

**yeast,** n., *for fermenting materials for bread,* pronounced (yēst), dialectally (ēst)

**Yeats,** n., *family name,* pronounced (yāts) as the name of the Irish poet, but some families pronounce it (yēts)

**yelk,** see **yolk**

**yellow,** adj., colloquial and slang in the sense *unscrupulous, unprincipled,* as in *yellow journalism, a yellow streak.* Pronounced (yĕl'ō), low colloquially (yĕl'o), (yăl'o), this last pronunciation being the one commonly written *yaller* in dialect stories.

**yellow-hammer,** n., *a kind of bird,* with a variant *yellow-ammer,* etymologically more correct, but not current in general use.

**yes,** adv., as direct answer to a question, often softened by the addition of some form of address to avoid seeming too abrupt. See **ma'am, sir** Thus children are taught to answer *Yes, Mother, No, Mother,* or *Yes, Miss White, No, Miss White.* But such forms of address scarcely find a place in adult speech, or if used there, seem scornful rather than respectful.

**Yid,** n., colloquial for *Jew,* especially German Jew.

**yolk,** n., *yellow part of an egg,* pronounced (yōk) A variant *yelk* (yĕlk) is much less commonly used.

**yon,** adv., archaic and dialectal for *yonder*.

**Yosemite,** n., *valley in California*, pronounced (yōsĕm'ĭtĭ)

**you,** pron., frequently used informally as an indefinite pronoun, as in *When you enter the room, the first thing you see is an enormous mirror.* More formally this would be *When one enters the room, the first thing one sees*, etc., or *On entering the room, one sees first,* etc. See **one**

**you all,** pron., local colloquialism in the South for the plural *you*. The question is much debated whether **you all** is ever used in the South as a singular pronoun, and the general opinion is that it is not, that **you all** implies always either a plural or a collective idea. In southern usage, **you all** is not limited to dialectal or uneducated speech, but is generally heard both in cultivated and in uncultivated circles. See **we-uns**

**Youghiogheny,** n., *place name*, pronounced (yŏkogā'nĭ)

**youngster,** n., colloquial for *youth, boy*.

**your esteemed, honored, valued favor,** trite phrases, in the old-fashioned formal style of business correspondence. See **valued**

**Ypsilanti,** n., *city in Michigan*, pronounced (ĭpsĭlăn'tĭ)

**yrs,** pron., to be avoided as abbreviation of *yours* at the closing of a letter, *yrs truly* being on about the same level as *gents* as an abbreviation.

**Yugoslavia,** n., *kingdom of the Serbs, Croats, and Slovenes*, pronounced (ūgōslah'vĭa) The adjective is *Yugoslav* (ūgōslahv') The United States Geographic Board rejects the variants *Jugo-Slavia, Jugoslavia, Yougoslavia, Yugo-Slav,* and *Yugo-Slavia.* The Permanent Committee on Geographical Names also approves **Yugoslavia**

# Z

**Zealand,** n., an island belonging to Denmark, but *Zeeland*, a province in the Netherlands. These are the spellings approved by the United States Geographic Board.

**Zeitgeist,** n., German word, *the spirit of the times,* literally, *time-spirit;* pronounced (zīt'gīst)   All nouns in German, common as well as proper, begin with capitals, and consequently in carrying this word over into English, and similarly with other borrowed nouns, the German custom is sometimes retained and the word is printed with a capital.   Ordinarily, however, German words used in English are treated like English words and begin with small letters.

**zemstvo,** n., Russian word, a *political division in Russia,* pronounced (zĕmst'vō)

**zenana,** n., Persian word, *women's quarters in an East Indian house,* pronounced (zenah'na)

**zenith,** n., *the sky directly above, the point of highest development,* pronounced (zē'nĭth) or (zĕn'ĭth)

**Zeppelin,** n., *kind of airship,* from the name of a person, Count Zeppelin, pronounced (zĕp'elin) or as a German word.

**Zeus,** n., *a Greek god,* pronounced (zōōs)

**zip,** n., colloquial and slang in the sense *energy, force.*

**zollverein,** n., German word, *union of states with common customs tax,* pronounced (tsŏl'fĕrīn)   See **Zeitgeist**

**zoo,** n., colloquial for *zoological garden.*

**zoology,** n., *a branch of science,* pronounced (zōŏl'ojĭ), not (zōōŏl'-ojĭ)

**Zoroaster,** n., *Persian religious teacher,* pronounced (zō'rōăs'ter)

**zouave,** n., *kind of soldier,* pronounced (zōōahv')

**zwieback,** n., *toasted bread,* German word, pronounced (tswē'bahk), incorrectly (tswī'bahk)   See **Zeitgeist**

# THE APPENDIX

## I. DIGEST OF GRAMMATICAL RULES

### CONTENTS

§19. Tense
   (*a*) Present Tense
   (*b*) Present Tense in Questions
   (*c*) Permanent Truths
   (*d*) Continued Action
   (*e*) Historical Present
   (*f*) Completed Action

§19. Tense (*continued*)
   (*g*) Perfect Infinitive
   (*h*) Past Conditional
   (*i*) Perfect Conditional

§20. Mood
   (*a*) Subjunctive Mood
   (*b*) Imperative Mood

## §1. Parts of speech

The part of speech of a word in English is determined by its function and its use in its context, not by its form. Any word which is used as subject or object of a verb, as predicate nominative, or as object of a preposition is a **noun.** Any word which is used as a predicate expressing an action or state of being is a **verb.** Any word which limits or modifies a noun is an **adjective.** Any word which modifies an adjective, a verb, or another word of its own kind is an **adverb.** **Pronouns** are substitutes for nouns. **Prepositions** are known by the fact that they indicate relationship and may be followed by a pronoun in the objective case. **Conjunctions** are known by their use as connectives joining words, phrases, or clauses.

## §2. Verbs from nouns

Verbs are freely made from nouns in English, as in *to curtain the windows, to seat the guests, to water the flowers, to motor to town, to paper a room, to leaf a book, to table a motion, to pipe the water.* It does not follow, however, that every noun may be used as a verb. One might speak of *curtaining windows,* but scarcely of *shading windows,* that is, providing them with window shades. In all instances the proprieties of actual speech must govern use. Yet even the construction *to shade windows* might be used in the technical speech of one whose business it is to attach shades to windows.

### §3. Nouns from verbs

Nouns from verbs are more likely to have the color of colloquial or low colloquial speech than verbs from nouns. Examples from colloquial English are *a try*, from *to try*, *a go* (an agreement), from *to go*, *a steal*, from *to steal*, *a run*, from *to run*, *a meet* (an athletic meet), from *to meet*, *a combine*, from *to combine*, *an invite*, from *to invite*. But numerous examples also occur in standard English, as in *a walk*, from *to walk*, *a drive* (as in a carriage, but also a concerted plan of action), from *to drive*, *a sail* (a short voyage in a boat), from *to sail*, *a cut* (an incision), from *to cut*, *a lift*, from *to lift*.

### §4. Adjectives and adverbs

Whether a word is an adjective or an adverb can be determined only by observing the function of the word. The statement that adverbs end in *-ly* is too broad, since many adjectives end in *-ly*, as in *a kindly thought, a manly fellow, a surly official, a daily paper, a likely story, a cleanly habit, a goodly number, a sickly smile;* and many adverbs do not end in *-ly*, as in *The blows fell thick and fast; Hit hard; Work hard; Go easy; He laughed loud and long; Go slow; Go fast.* Practical usage, however, exhibits clear tendencies, as follows:

(*a*) To make adjectives freely from nouns by adding *-ly* to the noun, as in *manly, womanly, scholarly, queenly, earthly, stately.*

(*b*) To make adverbs freely from adjectives by adding *-ly* to the adjective, as in *fairly, boldly, heavily, sternly, easily, slowly, swiftly.* But the ending *-ly* can not be forced upon all words in adverb function. *Go slow* is just as good as *Go slowly*, and uses like *Hit hard, to strike something hard, to turn quick as a wink, to run as swift as the wind*, are the only ones possible. Some adjectives with the ending *-ly* may be either adjectives or adverbs, as in *Kindly words must be kindly meant.* On the other hand, to use a noun with the ending -*ly* as an adverb is likely to be felt as incongruous; constructions like *He behaved manly; She behaved womanly* are not generally acceptable English. But certain nouns with the ending -*ly* are regularly employed as adverbs, as *daily, monthly, yearly*, and most speakers and writers would accept *He behaved very friendly* or *He cowardly withdrew at the first sign of danger* as good idiom. Here as ever the final test must be current practice. Forms with -*lily* for adverbs, such as *friendlily, cowardlily, manlily*, are no longer in use and are avoided as awkward.

## §5. Noun adjectives

Nouns are sometimes used with the function of adjectives, as in *the total energy production of the body, the total heat production of the body, the digestion products of protein, the prevention of tissue breakdown*, etc. Phrases like *energy production, heat production, digestion products, tissue breakdown* come very near to being compound words. This usage is specially frequent in scientific writing, and, though it is a growing usage, the general employment of it would be avoided by most persons interested in cultivating a literary style.

## §6. Adjectives after *to be*

The modifying predicate word after a form of the verb *to be* or after verbs expressing the idea of *seeming, appearing, becoming* is an adjective, not an adverb. The predicate words in the following sentences are adjectives: *He is well, good, right; He seems well, ill; He feels well, bad, sick; He looks well, bad, sick; It looks clean; He seems bright and cheerful; The room became dark; The leaves turned yellow.*

The word *well* may be either an adjective, *He is well*, or an adverb, *He speaks well*, but *good* is only an adjective. Constructions like *He writes good* occur only in low colloquial English.

The word *badly* is only an adverb, and *He looks badly* is not as correct English as *He looks bad.* See **good, bad, well, fine, nicely, poorly** in the body of the book.

## §7. Adverbs as adjectives

The use of a word prevailingly adverbial as an adjective is either artificially literary, as in *the once owner of this mansion, the above passage,* or colloquial and low colloquial in tone, as in *the off horse, the down train, the under dog, the upper hand, a through ticket.*

## §8. Conjunctions as prepositions

The test of a word as a preposition is its ability to take an object after it. By this test, *than* is not a preposition, for constructions like *I am taller than him* (for *I am taller than he,* or *than he is*) are not good current English. The construction *than whom,* as in *The district attorney, than whom no one was more competent to judge of the merits of the case, decided in favor of the defendant,* has a certain degree of literary currency, but is now avoided by careful writers. It is cumbersome and has become shopworn through long-continued discussion and criticism. See **but.**

## §9. Prepositions as conjunctions

The word *like* is current in unquestioned use as a preposition, as in *He rows like a professional,* but *like* as a conjunction, as in *I felt like I had stolen something,* for *I felt as though I had stolen something,* is ordinarily condemned by rhetoricians and grammarians, though it occurs occasionally in certain forms of local cultivated speech.

The use of *without, except* as conjunctions, as in *You can't get in without, except you have a ticket,* for *unless you have a ticket,* is low colloquial.

## §10. Adverbs as relative pronouns

The adverbs *when, where* are sometimes used, both in speaking and in writing, as equivalents of relative conjunctional phrases, as in *This is the place where he was born; This is a time when all men must help*, for *This is a time in which all men must help*. This usage may be permissible when the antecedent is a word like *time* or *place*, which readily takes adverb modifiers, but much less so when the antecedent is a noun naming a concrete object, for example, *house*, as in *This is the house where he was born*. This sentence in correct style would have to be *This is the house in which he was born* or *This is the house he was born in*

## §11. Impersonal pronouns

(a) *One*. As an impersonal pronoun, *one* is slightly literary in tone. According to rule, the impersonal *one* can be referred to only by a form of the same word, as in *One can not buy a ticket direct to one's destination*, not *One can not buy a ticket direct to his destination*. If the correct form seems somewhat stilted, the best way to improve it is to change the impersonal to a personal subject, as in *A traveler can not buy a ticket direct to his destination*.

(b) *You*. As an impersonal, *you* is more colloquial than *one*, as in *You can not buy a ticket direct to your destination*, i.e., *you* in general. This is appropriate only in informal spoken English.

(c) *They*. The impersonal use of *they* verges on the low colloquial, as in *They don't seem to have any street cars in this town*.

(d) *It*. The use of *it* referring vaguely to some person is low colloquial, as in *In the paper this morning it tells about a man who lost his memory for twenty years*.

(e) *Editorial "we."* The plural *we* is used only when it refers to several persons as antecedents, as in an editorial which supposedly refers to the editorial staff of a paper. Except perhaps by royalty, it is not used to refer to a single person.

### §12. Reflexive pronouns

The reflexive pronouns are used for emphasis, not merely as equivalents of the personal pronouns. The sentence *A friend and myself were walking down the street the other day* should be *A friend and I*, etc. The use of *self* as in *Will you please reserve accommodations for my wife and self* is low colloquial, and in better style should be *Will you please reserve accommodations for my wife and me*.

### §13. Relative pronouns

The relatives *who, whose, whom* refer to living objects, especially persons. The relatives *which, that* ordinarily refer to inanimate objects and the lower creatures, as in *This is not the horse that I bargained for*. The choice between *which* and *that* depends mainly upon stylistic considerations, such as variety and euphony.

### §14. Complements with *when, where*

A clause used as a predicate complement can not be introduced by an adverbial conjunction, as in *Treason is when a man commits a crime against his country; The first chapter is where he is shipwrecked*. Such sentences must be recast, e.g., *Treason is criminal action against one's country; The first chapter tells the story of his shipwreck*. The adverbs *when, where* can introduce subordinate clauses only when the clauses are adverbial modifiers, as in *He came when we least expected him; He landed where he had intended to land*.

### §15. Gender

(*a*) *Antecedents of distributive pronouns.* Distributive pronouns like *each, every, either, neither, any*, etc., take *his* as the pronoun referring to them, even when the distributives apply both to males and females, as in *There was a long line of women and children, and each in passing took his share of food in silence*.

*(b) Common gender.* No pronoun indicating common gender in the singular exists in English. Instead the forms of the masculine, *he, his, him,* are generally used, e.g., *Neither parent was willing to assume his share of the blame for their son's behavior; Not a man, woman, or child would show his ticket; Everybody is charitable if you give him the right opportunity.* When strict verbal accuracy is necessary, both pronouns must be used, i.e., *his or her, him or her,* etc. A plural pronoun is sometimes incorrectly used to evade the logical difficulty of the singular, e.g., *Not a man, woman, or child would show their ticket.*

*(c) Gender in professional names.* The custom now is to use the simpler and shorter, that is, the masculine form, for the name of a professional person when two forms are available, unless for some reason the idea of sex requires to be specially stressed. Thus the words *artist, author, chairman, doctor, singer,* and many others apply indifferently to men or women. In a few words, however, custom preserves the distinctively feminine forms, as in *actress, headmistress, saleslady, saleswoman.*

## §16. Case

*(a) Pronouns after "to be."* A pronoun after a form of the verb *to be* is in the nominative case, and so also is a noun according to the customary nomenclature of grammar, though nouns have nothing distinctive in form to indicate this. The correct grammatical forms are *It is* or *was I, he, she, we, they.* Colloquial English often has *It is* or *was me,* less often *It is or was him, her, us, them,* but none of these forms has been universally accepted in good spoken or written English and all are open to a certain degree of objection.

Before and after the infinitive *to be* in a dependent clause, the pronouns are objective, as in *He took me to be him.* Sentences like *It seems to be he* take the subject form of the pronoun after *to be* because the pronoun completes the meaning of the impersonal subject *it*. The pronoun after the verbal noun *being* takes the form of the object, as in *The notion of its being me never entered their heads*. If sentences like those discussed in this paragraph seem unnatural, the corrective is rephrasing in such a way as to avoid awkwardness. Every sentence grammatically possible is not necessarily stylistically commendable.

(*b*) *Ungrammatical objectives*. In colloquial and low colloquial speech the phrase *between you and I* is current, but correct English always requires the form of the objective for the objective case, that is, *between you and me*.

In correct English *than* and *as* are not prepositions, therefore can not be followed by an objective case, unless the objective can be construed by supplying an ellipsis in the clause containing *than* or *as*, as in *I like him better than* (*I like*) *her; He told them as well as* (*he told*) *me the most remarkable story*.

In colloquial English, especially in questions, the form *who* is used for an objective, as in *Who do you mean?* Though not strictly grammatical, this has passed into current spoken use and may be accepted on the colloquial level.

(*c*) *Possessives*. Ordinarily the use of the possessive case of nouns is limited to nouns naming living things, or to personified inanimate objects, as in *a dog's tail, a man's wages, the nation's greatness* (a kind of weak personification). But constructions like *the house's roof, the tree's leaves* are not current idiom. To the rule as thus given, however, there are numerous exceptions, as in *a day's work, a quarter's worth, an hour's distance, a stone's throw, a flower's fragrance*, etc. In all these exceptions it will be observed that the idea conveyed is not simply of possession, but a more complicated relationship between the possessive and the word it modifies.

(*d*) *Forms of the possessives*. The possessives of singular nouns are formed by adding the apostrophe and *s* to the nominative, as in *the boy's hat;* of plural possessives by adding only the apostrophe after the *s* of the plural, as in *the boys' hats.* The possessives of nouns that have no ending in the plural are made in the same way as the possessives of those that do, as in *The sheeps' tails were so long that they dragged them on the ground.*

The possessives of pronouns take no apostrophe, as in *its, ours, yours, theirs.* The form *it's* stands only for *it is.* The combination of *one* and *self* as pronoun takes the form *oneself,* and *one's self* can be written only when *self* is a noun and *one's* a possessive modifier. Thus one would write, *It is not advisable to indulge oneself too much,* and one might write, *One's self is ordinarily more important to one than any other person's self.*

(*e*) *Nouns ending in "s."* Nouns ending in *s,* like *Dickens, Howells,* form their possessives by adding only the apostrophe, as in *Dickens' works, Howells' characters,* or by adding the apostrophe and *s,* as in *Dickens's works, Howells's characters.* The latter is the more formal usage and might be written or printed, even when it would not be spoken. Nouns ending in *ss* form their possessives in the same way, as in *This is the boss's day off.*

(*f*) *Possessives in titles.* Sometimes in titles, on letterheads, and on signs, the apostrophe of a possessive is omitted, as in *Teachers College, Womans Suffrage Headquarters, Mens Department.* The omission of the apostrophe often improves the appearance of the printing in titles, signs, etc., and what determines its omission is therefore not grammar but the effectiveness of the design. So also in names like *Pikes Peak,* in which *Pikes* is no longer felt as a possessive, the apostrophe may be omitted.

(*g*) *Possessives before gerunds.* A noun or pronoun modifying a gerund is by rule in the possessive case, as in *We rejoiced at our candidate's being elected president; We rejoiced at his being elected president.* But this rule frequently fails of observance, both in written and in spoken English. It is most likely to be observed when the word before the gerund names a person, but constructions like the following are not infrequent: *The needles of the Alps have resulted from the cover being pushed off; There is no such thing as a language becoming corrupt.* Even when the word before the gerund names a person, some good writers do not use the possessive, as in *Joanna could not bear the notion of her husband going to sea* (Hardy, *To Please His Wife*).

Awkward combinations with gerunds should be rephrased. The sentence *His work may bear the impress of another mind without he himself or his reader being once conscious of imitation* should be recast to read, *His work may bear the impress of another mind without his being or his reader's being once conscious of imitation.*

(*h*) *Possessives with antecedents.* A possessive is not used as the antecedent of a pronoun. The sentence *In the mayor's report, he recommends the reduction of taxes* should read, *In his report, the mayor recommends the reduction of taxes.* The sentence *It was their misfortune who had invested their money in this way* should be *It was the misfortune of those who,* etc.

## §17. Agreement

(*a*) *Subject and verb.* A verb agrees in number with its subject, not with its predicate.

Wrong: The worst element in the crowd are the foreigners.
Wrong: The battleships of a country is its chief defense.
Right: The worst element in the crowd is the foreigners.
Right: The battleships of a country are its chief defense.

If the sentence *The worst element in the crowd is the foreigners* seems awkward, it must be corrected by rephrasing, e.g., *The worst element in the crowd is the foreign element,* or *The foreigners are the worst element in the crowd.*

(b) *Compound subjects.* Two or more singular subjects connected by *or, nor* take a singular verb, as in *A horse or a dog is always a good companion; Neither the driver nor the automobile was injured.*

Two or more subjects connected by *and* take a plural verb, as in *The house and the barn were insured.* But two nouns forming a compound subject naming the same person or thing take a singular verb, as in *Their friend and protector was thus suddenly taken from them.*

Two subject nouns so closely related in meaning as to make a single thought sometimes take a singular verb, as in *The shouting and the tumult dies* (Kipling, *The Recessional*).

(c) *Singular subject with modifiers.* The subject remains singular, consequently also the verb, when the subject is followed by a phrase like *accompanied by, together with, with, as well as, including, in addition to, no less than*, as in *The boy, accompanied by his father, was about to take the train; The house, with the barn, costs five thousand dollars; The daughter, as well as the sons, was still in school.*

(d) *Distributive pronouns.* The pronouns *each, every, either, neither, any, anyone, everyone, someone, somebody, everybody, nobody, no one*, etc., are singular and are followed by singular, not plural, verbs, and are referred to by singular pronouns.

Wrong: Every man in the room take their seats at the sound of the bell.

Right: Every man in the room takes his seat at the sound of the bell.

Wrong: Are either of you going to town?
Right: Is either of you going to town?

Wrong: No one must vote out of their turn.
Right: No one must vote out of his turn.

Although by origin it is a compound of *no* and *one*, the word *none* is nevertheless commonly used as a plural, as in *None of the books were lost.* It can also be used as a singular, but for the singular the more usual form is *not one*, as in *Not one of the books was lost.*

(*e*) *Intervening words.* A verb must agree with its subject, not with some intervening word which happens to stand closer to the verb. *Every statement in these pamphlets have been verified* is wrong and should read, *Every statement in these pamphlets has been verified,* or *All the statements in these pamphlets have been verified.*

(*f*) *Discordant subjects.* When a sentence contains two or more subjects differing in number or person connected by *or, nor,* the rule generally given is that the verb agrees in number or person with the nearest subject. According to this rule, one would say, *Neither the captain nor the soldiers know this region,* but *Neither the soldiers nor the captain knows this region.* Or one would say, *Either you or I am right; Neither I nor you are right.* But the rule does not produce satisfactory English. In all cases in which the subjects are discordant, it is better to recast the sentence so that each subject has its appropriate verb, as in *Either you are right or I am; Neither of us is right; The captain does not know this region and neither do the soldiers.*

(*g*) *Collective nouns.* Collective nouns take either a singular or a plural verb according as the idea of the noun is thought of as a whole or disjunctively, that is, in its separate parts. One may say, therefore, *The jury was out one hour,* but also *The jury were much divided in their opinions.*

(*h*) *These* and *those kind; these* and *those sort.* The words *kind* and *sort* are sometimes thought of as collective nouns and thus preceded by a plural demonstrative and followed by a plural verb, as in *These kind of people are always getting into trouble.* Though much can be said for such constructions from the point of view of logic and something from the point of view of use, careful speakers and writers nevertheless prefer to use *kind* and *sort* as singulars.

(*i*) *Names of sciences.* Certain names of sciences or names for general activities, *physics, ethics, dynamics, acoustics, athletics,* etc., though plural in form, take a singular verb when they refer to the science or activity as a whole. Thus we say, *Physics is a useful study; Acoustics is the science of sound; Athletics is a necessary part of college life.* But when *physics, acoustics,* etc., are used to indicate the physical or acoustic properties of some object, they are plurals and take plural verbs, as in *The acoustics of this room are not very good.* So also *athletics* may be a plural when it means athletic activities, as in *The athletics of the college are in good condition.*

(*j*) *Quantity and number.* Sums of numbers and quantities, and multiples, when they are thought of as forming a single idea, take a singular verb, as in *Two and two* (i.e., the single amount of two and two) *is four; A pint and a quart* (i.e., this total quantity) *makes three pints; Eight times six* (i.e., the amount) *is forty-eight.* It is possible, though not quite so natural, to think of these ideas disjunctively, in which case the verbs would be plural.

(*k*) *Fractions.* Fractions and words like *rest, remnant, remainder, number* take a singular verb when they refer to a quantity or amount thought of as a whole, as in *Two-thirds of the food was eaten the first day; Part of the crowd was dispersed, and the remainder was taken into custody.* They take a plural verb when the word or the fraction is thought of in its component parts, as in *Some went away and the rest were easily pacified; Of the total receipts, three-eighths were allotted to me and five-eighths to my partner.*

A construction like *the average of 0.58 grams of glucose per 1.0 gram of protein* is incorrect and must be changed to *the average of 0.58 of a gram of glucose per 1.0 gram of protein.*

## §18. Modifiers

(a) *Unattached modifiers.* A modifying word or phrase must be used in such a way as to make clear the syntactical relationships of the word or phrase to the part of the sentence which it modifies. Thus a present participle should not be used without a word to which it may be attached, as in *Examining the box, the money was found untouched.* This sentence would be correctly phrased, *Examining the box, we found the money untouched.* But this rule is not invariably observed even by good writers, as in *Thence, looking up and however far, each fir stands separate against the sky no bigger than an eyelash* (Stevenson, *Silverado Squatters*). In colloquial English a participle is sometimes used loosely, as in *Speaking off-hand, this does not seem to be a well-considered proposal.* But this is merely a colloquial ellipsis for *Speaking off-hand, I would say that,* etc.

(b) *Gerund phrases.* When a gerund phrase begins a sentence, its grammatical relationships to what follows must be made clear.

Wrong: After waiting for two hours, the secretary said the doctor was out.

Right: After waiting for two hours, I learned from the secretary that the doctor was out.

(c) *Suspended syntax.* To separate the words of a close syntactical group by an intrusive phrase produces an awkward and disturbing effect, as in *each of the by no means small cabins; to most even decently well-read persons; The newly appointed minister (to he had forgotten where) cultivated a fine habit* (Henry James, *Tragic Muse*, II, 696). Such awkwardness can always be avoided by rephrasing.

(d) *Split infinitive.* The split infinitive is a form of suspended syntax. Ordinarily the infinitive and its sign *to* form a close syntactical group, and to insert any words between *to* and the infinitive is contrary to the history of the construction and to present conservative theory. In practice, however, the theory is not always observed, and some good writers permit themselves the liberty of placing an adverbial modifier between *to* and the infinitive on the ground of clearness and emphasis, as in *the important thing to be here observed; It is the function of the judges to watchfully observe the developing moral thought,* etc. But the thought in these sentences could be as well expressed without splitting the infinitive, with the added gain that the taste of no one would be offended.

(*e*) *Omissions.* Omission of words from a phrase is permissible only when the ellipsis does not result in a syntactical discord or a logical absurdity. If it does, the omission must be supplied, and often the sentence must be recast to avoid awkwardness.

Wrong: He is older and quite as experienced as his brother.
Right: He is older than his brother and quite as experienced.
Awkward: He is older than and quite as experienced as his brother.

Wrong: Japan has not and will not make any such demand.
Right: Japan has not made and will not make any such demand.

Wrong: He is as old and more experienced than his partner.
Right: He is as old as his partner and more experienced.
Awkward: He is as old as and more experienced than his partner.

Wrong: He was one of the greatest, if not the greatest president, we have had.
Right: He was one of the greatest presidents we have had, if not the greatest.

Wrong: He said only what others have and are saying.
Right: He said only what others have said and are saying.

Right, but awkward: He was troubled by, at the same time that he was pleased with, the result of the conference.

Better: He was troubled by the result of the conference and at the same time pleased with it.

Wrong: While still a boy of ten, Mr. Thompson took his son to Europe.

Right: While his son was still a boy of ten, Mr. Thompson took him to Europe.

The sentence *Neither you nor I* (*am, are, is*) *right* is a case of suspended syntax, since *you* and *I* can not be followed by the same verb. The awkwardness can be avoided only by rephrasing, as in *Neither of us is right, Neither you are right, nor am I* (awkward).

(*f*) *Nouns in sequence.* When two or more nouns in a series name different objects, but might be mistaken for nouns naming the same object, uncertainty is avoided by repeating the article, possessive adjective, or demonstrative pronoun before each.

Wrong: He is under great obligations to his present and former employer (correct only if the reference is to one person).

Right: He is under great obligations to his present and to his former employer (correct because the reference is to two different persons).

Wrong: The president, secretary, and treasurer served for three years (wrong, unless one person held the three offices).

Right: The president, the secretary, and the treasurer served for three years, *or* The president, the secretary, and the treasurer each served for three years.

## §19. Tense

(*a*) *Present tense.* The common use of the simple present is to express habitual or continued action, as in *He takes a bath every morning; He takes his bath almost as a religious ceremony.*

For specific action proceeding and taking place in present time, the form used is the so-called progressive present, as in *He is taking his bath; I think* (continued action) *he is taking his bath; I am thinking* (specific present action) *of taking a bath.*

Both the simple and the progressive present forms may be used with future meaning, as in *He leaves at four o'clock today; He is leaving at four o'clock today.* For other forms of the future, see **shall** and **will** in the body of the book.

(*b*) *Present tense in questions.* In questions habitual or continued action is expressed by a verb phrase with *do,* as in *Does he take a bath every morning? Do you think* (continued action) *he is taking his bath?*

Specific action proceeding and taking place in the present is expressed in questions by the usual progressive present forms, as in *Is he taking his bath? Are you thinking of taking a bath?*

(*c*) *Permanent truths.* Facts permanently true, or so conceived, are expressed in the present tense, even when the statement is contained in a subordinate clause dependent on a main clause with a verb in the past tense, as in *Columbus was convinced that the earth is round, though many of his contemporaries believed that it is flat.*

(*d*) *Continued action.* Action begun in the past and continuing in the present is expressed by the present tense, even in subordinate clauses dependent on main clauses with verbs in the past tense, as in *They testified that they write every week to their clients, giving them all necessary information.*

(*e*) *Historical present.* As a somewhat artificial literary device, the forms of the present tense are sometimes used of past events in narration to produce the effect of vivid action, as in *Caesar then assembles his whole army and delivers to them the following eloquent address.* Good writers use this device very sparingly.

(*f*) *Completed action.* Action completed in the past is expressed by the present perfect tense in a subordinate clause when the verb of the main clause is in the present tense, as in *They say they have repeatedly written to him.*

A continued action completed in the past is expressed by the past tense in a subordinate clause when the verb of the main clause is in the past tense, as in *They testified that while the company was being formed they wrote to their clients frequently.*

A specific action completed in the past is expressed by the past perfect tense in a subordinate clause when the verb of the main clause is in the past tense, as in *They testified that they had written to him while the company was being formed.*

(*g*) *Perfect infinitive.* The perfect infinitive expresses action completed before the action of the principal verb, as in *I believe him to have been completely unaware of what he was doing.* Otherwise the present infinitive is used, as in *I believed him to be completely unaware of what he was doing* (both past time), or *I believe him to be completely unaware of what he is doing* (both present time).

(*h*) *Past conditional.* A past tense is used with present meaning in a conditional clause contrary to fact, as in *If I knew where he is, I would tell you.* To express the past condition contrary to fact, the past perfect is used, *If I had known where he was, I should have told you.*

(*i*) *Perfect conditional.* The present perfect conditional tense in a dependent clause expresses action completed before the action of the principal verb, as in *I believe that they would have done this if they had known the facts.* Otherwise the tense of the verb of the conditional clause is the same as the tense of the verb of the main clause, as in *I believe they will do this if they know the facts.*

See also **Sequence of Tenses,** page 528.

## §20. Mood

(*a*) *Subjunctive mood.* The subjunctive mood in present English is restricted almost entirely to the condition contrary to fact, as in *If he were commander-in-chief, there is no question what he would do.*

In literary style a concession or supposition is sometimes expressed by the subjunctive, as in *Were I to do that, I should never regain my self-respect; If I were to do that,* etc., but the more usual form for expressing this idea would be, *If I did that, I should never regain my self-respect.*

In literary style sometimes a high degree of doubt is expressed by the subjunctive, as in *If climate be an important element in the formation of national character, then character ceases to be entirely a subjective creation.*

In colloquial speech, even in the condition contrary to fact, the forms of the subjunctive appear frequently only when the subject of the verb is a personal pronoun, *I, you, he, she, we, they.* But in these constructions also, colloquial speech ordinarily has the indicative, as in *If he was here, he would tell us what to do; Tottering as if he was about to fall (New York Times); I wish I was in your place.* These uses are now so general that they must be accepted as at least good colloquial English.

The subjunctive is employed most frequently, when it is employed at all, in forms of the verb *to be.* With other verbs, the subjunctive has a distinctly literary, often artificial color, as in *If he believe honestly, a believer will readily make converts.* But the more natural phrasing would be *If he believes honestly,* etc.

(b) *Imperative mood.* The imperative commonly expresses a command, but the forms of the imperative sometimes express a condition, as in *Do that and you will suffer for it; Waste your money and you will end your days in the poorhouse,* for *If you do that,* etc., *If you waste,* etc.

A mild imperative may take the form of a question, as in *Will you hand me that book,* pronounced with falling inflection.

In military use an officer may issue a command to a subordinate officer in the form of a future, as in *You will take these letters and deliver them at headquarters.*

## II. PUNCTUATION

The customary marks of punctuation in English are:

1. Question Mark       ?
2. Exclamation Point     !
3. Period               .
4. Colon                :
5. Semicolon         ;
6. Comma           ,
7. Apostrophe        '
8. Quotation Marks     " " ' '
9. Parentheses        ( )
10. Brackets          [ ]
11. Hyphen          -
12. Dash            —

The uses of these will be described in the order in which they have been given.

### §1. Question mark

The question mark is used at the end of an interrogative sentence, as in *What time will you be there?*

A question inserted parenthetically in the body of another sentence does not usually take a question mark after it, as in *The difference between these two totals, may I explain, is not nearly so great as the figures indicate.*

A sentence interrogatory in form which is only slightly interrogatory in meaning may end with a period instead of a question mark, as in *Will you please send all the articles on this list to the address at the head of this letter.* Or a sentence interrogatory in form may be exclamatory in meaning, as in *What could we do!*

The adding of a question mark within parentheses after a word or phrase to indicate that the idea expressed by the word or phrase is dubious is a crude device which experienced writers do not employ. One would not write, *In introducing the speaker, the chairman delivered an eloquent (?) address*, even if one thought the address was not eloquent.

## §2. Exclamation Point

(*a*) The exclamation point is used at the end of an exclamatory sentence, as in *What a time we had!*

But sometimes when the exclamatory sentence is long and therefore becomes only mildly exclamatory by the time the end is reached, the exclamation point is not used, as in *What a difference it would make if it should turn out that after all he was not the only surviving heir.*

Sometimes a simple declaratory sentence is made exclamatory by ending it with an exclamation point, as in *It was then just three o'clock!* The evident intention of such a sentence is that it shall be pronounced in an ejaculatory manner, but good writers are chary of calling in punctuation as an aid to determine the manner of speaking of their sentences. It is a safe rule to use the exclamation point as sparingly as possible.

(*b*) An interjectory word is followed by an exclamation point when it is an independent sentence element, as in *Oh! There is one thing more I want to say*, or *Hark! The trumpet call sounds loud and clear.* But when the exclamatory word is a closely joined part of a sentence, it is not followed by an exclamation point, as in *O for a lodge in some vast wilderness*, or *Pshaw, I knew it would turn out that way.*

## §3. Period

(*a*) The period or full stop marks the end of a declaratory or imperative sentence, as in *The voyage had already lasted two years. Don't wait for me.*

(*b*) Abbreviations also end with a period, as in *J. G. Whittier was born in Haverhill, Mass., on Dec. 17, 1807.*

When an abbreviation is made by dropping out a portion of the middle of a word, some writers prefer not to end it with a period, as in *hrs* for *hours, cwt* for *hundredweight*. But the more usual custom is to end such abbreviations with a period, as in *Va., Vt., Ky.,* for *Virginia, Vermont, Kentucky*. When an abbreviation stands at the end of a sentence, only one period is used, as in *He was born in Louisville, Ky.*

(*c*) A group of periods, usually three in number, is sometimes used within a sentence or at the end of a sentence to indicate a pause which is supposed to be unusually heavy with meaning. These are called **Suspension Periods**. This habit was satirized by Don Marquis in the *New York Evening Sun* as follows:

> Whenever you see . . . three little dots . . . such as these . . . in the stuff of a modern versifier . . . even in our stuff . . . it means that the writer . . . is trying to suggest something rather . . . well, elusive, if you get what we mean . . . and the reason he suggests it instead of expressing it . . . is . . . very often . . . because it is an almost idea . . . instead of a real idea.

(*d*) In a passage of quotation, suspension periods are used to indicate that a part of the quoted passage has been omitted, as in *"Liberty will have another feather in her cap . . . The ensuing winter [1789] will be the commencement of a Golden Age"* was the glowing prophecy of an enthusiastic Boston journal (Beveridge, *Life of John Marshall*, II, 5, quoted in Summey, *Modern Punctuation*, p. 163).

## §4. Colon

The colon is now commonly used only to mark a pause at the end of a clause followed by a quotation, as in *Above the door were inscribed these words: "All ye who enter here, leave hope behind"*; or at the beginning of a list, as in *The names of those present are as follows: John Smith, Henry Brown*, etc.

"The colon gives the impression of saying to the reader, 'Look closely; important matter coming!' In the great majority of cases introductory matter, save before a quotation or list, is better pointed with period than with colon. The period is lighter and less formal" (Summey, *Modern Punctuation*, p. 66).

## §5. Semicolon

(*a*) The semicolon indicates a pause not quite as complete as that indicated by a period or a colon. It is used chiefly in sentences made up of several parts each of which might be an independent sentence, but which are so closely related that to separate them completely by periods and capitalization would produce a disjointed, choppy effect. The semicolon is a compromise punctuation. It separates the parts of such a sentence, but does not make completely independent elements of them. The following is an illustration:

In advance of the storm, you may often see the clouds grow; the condensation of the moisture into vapor is a visible process; slender, spiculae-like clouds expand, deepen, and lengthen; in the rear of the low pressure, the reverse process, or the wasting of the clouds, may be witnessed.

The whole process here described is viewed as one, and the semicolons, linking the several sentences yet separating them, are more appropriate than a punctuation with periods would be.

(*b*) The semicolon is also used in the punctuation of a group of coordinate phrases, as follows:

The topics before the conference are the following: (1) the powers and purpose of a world court; (2) the manner of organization of a league of nations; (3) the kind of authority such a league may exercise.

This sentence might also be punctuated as follows:

The topics before the conference are the following:

(1) The powers and purpose of a world court.
(2) The manner of organization of a league of nations.
(3) The kind of authority such a league may exercise.

The phrases of a series, as in the passage as first given, might also be punctuated by commas; but the comma is more appropriate in a rapid grouping of words or very short phrases, the semicolon in a formal enumeration, especially in one in which the parts are distinguished by numerals

## §6. Comma

The comma is the most generally used of all forms of punctuation. It occurs only within the body of a sentence, and it indicates a briefer pause than the semicolon or any of the terminal marks of punctuation. The important uses of the comma are as follows:

(*a*) To separate coordinate words in a series, as in *The bag contained a hammer, a saw, a short crowbar, and some nails.* Some writers omit the comma before the *and* connecting the last two members of a series.

(*b*) To separate the coordinate sentence elements in a compound sentence, as in *He stopped at the corner, dismounted, and examined the ground carefully.*

On the use of the semicolon in groups of phrases and clauses, see under semicolon.

(*c*) To separate the main from the subordinate elements in a complex sentence, as in *If you will give me your address, I shall be glad to send you some copies.* Subordinate relative clauses are of two kinds, demonstrative (also called restrictive) and descriptive (also called nonrestrictive). The demonstrative relative clause, which limits its antecedent by making it specific, is not separated from the main clause by a comma, as in *The building which stood at the corner of Fourth and Elm has been torn down* (i.e., that particular building). The descriptive relative clause adds a further detail with respect to the antecedent, and it is separated from the main clause by commas, as in *The building, which stood at the corner of Fourth and Elm, has been torn down* (i.e., the building already specified, concerning which the further fact of its situation is now given).

(*d*) To separate an appositional word or phrase from its context, as in *Philadelphia, the City of Brotherly Love, lies between New York and Baltimore.*

(*e*) To set off an adjective phrase which follows the noun it modifies, as in *The book, handsomely bound and illustrated, was formally presented at a banquet.*

(*f*) To set off participial modifying clauses and parenthetic elements in the sentence, as follows:

(*1*) *The boat, turning a point suddenly, ran into a sunken log.*
(*2*) *The automobile, if it could be called by such a dignified name, was held together by straps, wires, and bits of string.*

A prepositional phrase is not usually set off by commas unless it is desirable to detach the prepositional phrase from its context for purposes of emphasis. Thus one might write, *This dwelling, with the surrounding land, must be sold, with or without the owner's consent;* but ordinarily the prepositional phrases would call for no punctuation, as in *He lay in bed for the greater part of the morning.*

When logical clearness requires it, a prepositional phrase must be followed by a comma, as in *In his dealings with Henry, Brown had always been generous.* Without the comma, the reader's tendency would be to make *Henry Brown* one name.

So also when an object is transposed to a position before the verb, for the sake of logical clearness it is followed by a comma, as in *That, John would never admit; The evil man does, man cannot undo.* Punctuation, however, does not relieve this construction of its awkwardness.

(*g*) To set off general qualifying words like *however, also, nevertheless,* as in *This was not, however, his first venture in business.* The use of commas emphasizes the qualifying word, but in a rapid and colloquial passage this emphasis may be avoided by omitting the commas, as in *He was nevertheless very much disturbed; He felt however that he ought not to take the money.*

(*h*) To separate the quoted part from the narrative part in a passage of dialogue, as follows:

*"You may go now," said the bandit, "but don't look back."*

(*i*) To separate numbers and letters in a series, as in *The letters a, e, i, o, u stand for vowels; The winning numbers were 18, 24, 48, and 96.* The numbers in dates are also separated by commas, as in *Oct. 12, 1492.*

## §7. Apostrophe

(*a*) The apostrophe indicates the possessive case, in the singular, as in *The ship's sails were white*, and in the plural, as in *The ships' sails were white.*

See also **Possessives,** §16 in the Digest of Grammatical Rules.

(*b*) The omission of one or more letters in a contracted word is indicated by the apostrophe, as in *These boards won't do; they don't match the others.* So also in literary words, such as *e'er* for *ever, ne'er* for *never,* etc.

(*c*) The plurals of figures and letters take the apostrophe, as in *He took out all the 3's, 5's, and 8's from the deck; He never crosses his t's or dots his i's.*

### §8. Quotation Marks

Quotation marks are of two kinds, double " " and single ' '.

(*a*) Double quotation marks are used to separate a word or a group of words introduced as a direct quotation from the context in which it appears, as in *The words,* "*The quality of mercy is not strained,*" *are from The Merchant of Venice.* Some writers treat all titles like quotations and inclose them within quotation marks, as in *He is playing Shylock in* "*The Merchant of Venice.*" Most writers, however, prefer to indicate titles more simply, as by italics, as in: He is playing Shylock in *The Merchant of Venice;* or best of all merely by capitalization, as in: He is playing Shylock in The Merchant of Venice.

If a quoted passage contains more than one paragraph the quotation marks are repeated at the beginning of each paragraph, but no quotation marks appear at the end of any paragraph of the quotation except the last.

(*b*) Single quotation marks are most generally used to indicate a quotation within a quotation, as in *His concluding words were,* "*The world and the world courts may cry 'Peace! Peace!' but there is no peace.*"

Single quotation marks are sometimes used when a writer wants to use a word, for example, a slang word, but also wants to indicate that he does not assume full responsibility for the word, as in *The hat she wore was a 'lid' of extraordinary magnificence.*

### §9. Parentheses

(*a*) Parentheses are used to inclose letters or numbers marking the divisions and subdivisions of a subject, as at the beginning of this sentence. But the parentheses may of course be omitted, and often are with numerals, especially Roman numerals.

(*b*) Parentheses are used to inclose a bibliographical or other reference embodied in the text, as in *The author then returns to his main subject (p. 287), and treats it in fuller detail.* This punctuation would be avoided in literary style.

(*c*) Parentheses are sometimes used to inclose words which are inserted as general comment or explanation more or less independently of the rest of the sentence, as in *My country estate (if I ever have one) must border on the ocean.* In general this punctuation should be sparingly used. In most instances commas will serve as well as parentheses.

### §10. Brackets

Brackets are used to inclose explanatory insertions made in the body of a text by author, editor, or printer, as in *These petty princes [i.e., of the house of Hanover] were regarded with much disfavor by the older aristocracy.* This punctuation is permissible only in learned or technical writing.

### §11. Hyphen

(*a*) The commonest use of the hyphen is to separate the parts of a compound word which by means of the hyphen are exhibited as not completely fused into a single word. "Just what shall be hyphened has to be decided arbitrarily in part, because dictionaries and style books do not agree" (Summey, *Modern Punctuation*, p. 175).

"According to careful American practice," says Summey, p. 176, "the important classes of expressions which regularly or usually take the compounding hyphen are (1) compounds with *self* . . . [as in *self-control, self-taught*], (2) compound numerals like *twenty-six*, (3) prepositional-phrase compounds like *son-in-law*, (4) adjectival compounds of words naming colors (*silver-gray tone*), (5) expressions in which the hyphen is necessary to clearness, as in *re-creation* (remaking), which without the hyphen might be confused with *recreation*, and (6) certain compounds beginning with *ex, pre, pro, ultra, quasi* (*ex-governor, pre-Shakespearean, pro-German, quasi-compliment*).   Miscellaneous words usually hyphened include *party-colored, great-grandson* and similar words of relationship in the fourth generation, and often words with *fellow*—except *fellowship* [*fellow-countryman, fellow-feeling*, etc.]."

Words like *hero-worship, man-eater, property-holder*, in which the first element stands in a kind of object relation to the second (one who worships a hero, a tiger that eats men, one who holds property), are usually hyphened, unless the word is a very common and familiar word, like *taxpayer, bookseller, lawnmower*, etc. Opinion will naturally differ as to just when a word becomes very common and familiar, but the best rule is to use a hyphen only when it seems necessary.   Many similar phrases are best written as two words, for example, *tax collector, newspaper editor, garbage consumer, etc.*

(*b*) Hyphens are used to make casual compounds, like the *Yale-Harvard football game*, sometimes of a humorous character, as in *We had a sort of dinner-supper meal*. Such compounds are frequent in scientific writing, as in *foot-pound, kilowat-hour*, etc., though these combinations are often written as two separate words without a hyphen.

(*c*) The words *today, tonight, tomorrow* are not usually hyphened, though some printers and writers prefer to hyphen them.

(*d*) The hyphen is sometimes a convenience in the formation of a compound adjective, as in a *direct-circuit current, large-scale production, a better-babies campaign, an apple-tree borer*.

(*e*) The hyphen is used to indicate the division of a polysyllabic word which has to be broken at the end of a line of printing or writing.

(*f*) Some special examples and illustrations of the use of the hyphen are given in the following list.

**Ante, anti, extra, bi, tri,** and other compositional elements
should be combined with the second element as one word,
as in *antediluvian, antislavery, extrajudicial, biennial,* except
when writing them so would produce an awkward combination, as in *ante-election prophecies, anti-imperial, semi-inde-
pendent,* etc., and when the second element is a proper noun,
as in *anti-Semitic, pro-Darwinian,* etc. The best general
rule, so far as there is one, is to use the hyphen only when the
two elements of the compound are distinctly and separately
felt, but to write as one word when they are not. Compounds
with **co** are rarely written with a hyphen, but usually as one
word, as in *cooperate, coincidence, coefficient, coordinate,* etc.
Some writers employ the dieresis in words like *coöperate,
coördinate,* to indicate that the two letters are pronounced
separately.

**By and by** and **by the by** are written without hyphens.

**Ever, never** are written without hyphens in phrases like *a never
ending sermon, your ever grateful friend, this ever memorable
occasion, this never to be forgotten moment,* etc. Words like
*everready, neverbreak* are of course special formations.

**Fellow** before a noun is written as a separate word, as in *fellow
members, fellow citizens, fellow creature, fellow countryman.*
A hyphen is used in *fellow-feeling,* and *fellowship* is always
written as one word. But some writers prefer to hyphenate
*fellow-countryman.*

**Fold** is written as one word in *twofold, fourfold, hundredfold,* etc.

**Good-by** is written with a hyphen, but *good day, good night* as
two separate words.

**Half** is written with a hyphen when it forms a compound with
an adjective, as in *a half-forgotten memory, a half-hearted consent, a half-breed dog,* etc. The word *halfwitted,* however, is
usually written without a hyphen.

**Like** is written as one word in words like *manlike*, *childlike*, *womanlike*, but compounds like *bell-like*, *ball-like* are written with a hyphen to prevent the awkwardness of having three letters of the same kind coming together.

**Master** is written as a separate word in *master builder*, *master mason*, *master mariner*, etc., but *masterkey* and *masterpiece* are written as one word.

**Mid** is not hyphened in familiar words, like *midsummer*, *midday*, *midnight*, *midshipman*, *midland*, *midway*, etc., but a hyphen may be used in occasional compounds, such as *mid-air*, *mid-ocean*, though some writers prefer to write these as separate words, *mid air*, *mid ocean*, *mid career*, *mid channel*.

**Near by** may be written as two words, or as one, *nearby*. (See p. 404.)

**Non** is ordinarily not hyphened, as in *nonconductor*, *nonresistance*, *noncombatant*, etc. But some writers prefer to separate the parts of such compounds by a hyphen.

**Northwest** and other points of the compass, like *northeast*, *southwest*, etc., are written as one word, but *north-northwest*, etc., are hyphened.

**Nowadays** is not hyphened or written as separate words.

**Room** takes no hyphen in *ballroom*, *bathroom*, *bedroom*, *classroom*, *hallroom*, *workroom*. But *breakfast room*, *dining room*, *dressing room*, *sitting room*, *sleeping room* are written as two words. The words *drawing-room*, *reception-room* would usually be written with a hyphen.

**School** is written with a hyphen in *school-teacher*, *school-teaching*, but as a separate word in *school board*, *school children*, *school days*, *school studies*, and other combinations which are felt not to be closely compounded. But *schoolbook*, *schoolboy*, *schoolhouse*, *schoolroom*, and many similar close compounds are written as one word.

**Self** is followed by a hyphen in *self-absorbed, self-contained, self-reliant, self-respect, self-starter*, etc. But *selfsame* is written as one word.

**Un, under, in** are not followed by hyphens, as in *undesirable, understatement, indestructible*, etc.

### §12. Dash

In form the dash is a prolonged hyphen. The uses of the dash are as follows:

(*a*) To indicate a broken or interrupted sentence structure, as in *"Could you tell me—"* I asked. *"To be sure,"* the stranger replied before I could finish.

(*b*) To indicate an emphatic conclusion or addition within a sentence, as in *The solution came to me as I walked away—the house had been moved bodily from its foundations.*

(*c*) To indicate an emphatic parenthesis, as in *This manufacturing plant—the largest in the world—is conducted entirely by the workmen.* Ordinarily, parentheses, or merely commas, would be used in a sentence like this.

(*d*) To connect two numbers with the implication of the inclusion of the numbers between, as in *the years 1914–1918, the series 10808–12786.*

(*e*) To veil the form of a word which for some reason it is desirable not to print as a whole, as in *Mr. B——g* for *Mr. Browning*, *the d——l, d——n*, or *d——*.

(*f*) The dash is sometimes employed in combination with the colon, less frequently with the period and the comma. In most of these uses the dash could be omitted without loss. The salutation of a letter is sometimes given in the form *My dear Mr. Brown:—*, or more informally with the dash alone, as in *My dear Mr. Brown—*

## III.  CAPITALIZATION

**§1.** Capitalize the first word of every sentence.

(*a*) But a short parenthetic sentence within the body of another sentence need not be capitalized, as in *He came to Rome (he had never been there before) with a great doubt and hesitation in his mind.* Constructions like this, however, should be only sparingly used.

(*b*) A word or phrase standing by itself as a kind of sentence equivalent is capitalized, as in *All right, Very well, Yes, No, Never, Why?, Good!, Fine!*

(*c*) In quotations, a sentence which is quoted as a whole begins with a capital, as in *You say in your letter, "We are quite unable to see the reason for your complaint."* Stated indirectly the quoted sentence would not be capitalized, as in *You say in your letter that you are quite unable to see the reason for our complaint.*

(*d*) A declarative sentence which propounds a direct question has a capital both at the beginning of the sentence and at the beginning of the question, as in *What I want to know is, Will this bill reduce taxes?*

**§2.** Capitalize the first word of every line of poetry. This is the conventional rule, though occasionally modern free verse poets pay no more heed to this convention than to others.

**§3.** Capitalize all proper nouns and adjectives.

(*a*) This includes all Christian and family names, and all modifications of these names when the modifications are used as the designations of persons, as in nicknames, *Tom, Jack, Scotty, Betty, Junior, Shorty.* Personifications are capitalized, as in *He worshiped the god Success.*

(*b*) Capitalize any epithet which stands for the name of a person, as *the Iron Chancellor, the Plumed Knight,* or which regularly accompanies the name of a person, as in *William the Conqueror, Charles the Bold.*

(*c*) Nouns originally proper nouns or proper adjectives which are no longer felt to be proper are not capitalized, as *arab* (a street arab), *japan* (a kind of varnish), *morocco* (a kind of leather) *bologna* (a kind of sausage), *champagne* (a kind of wine), *volt, ampere, paris green, manila paper, pasteurized milk, quixotic* (from Don Quixote).

(*d*) Capitalize all titles, whether in their full or abbreviated forms, preceding a name, as in *General (or Gen.) Grant, President Lincoln, Col. White, Admiral Farragut, Dr. Holt, Professor Long, President Coolidge, Rear-Admiral Burns, ex-President Roosevelt, Chief Justice Taft.* The titles of address, *Mr., Mrs., Miss, Master, Messrs., Madam,* are always capitalized. The word *sir* is capitalized only in titles of nobility or in the salutation of a letter.

Titles are not capitalized, however, when they do not form a part of a person's name as used in address but are merely descriptive of his rank, as *W. H. Taft, chief justice of the Supreme Court, A. B. Long, professor of botany, Thomas Becket, archbishop of Canterbury.*

(*e*) Capitalize the titles or names of offices when they stand in place of the names of persons, as in *the President*, the *Secretary of the Treasury, Mr. President, Your Honor, His Majesty, the Pope, the King.*

(*f*) Capitalize the names of institutions, organizations, and buildings when they are used to refer definitely to a particular institution, organization, or building, as in *the Smithsonian Institution, the Bureau of Ethnology, the Chamber of Commerce, the Republican Party, the Post Office, the Armory, Grand Central Depot, the Supreme Court, Congress, the House of Representatives, the Senate, the Legislature, Yale University, the Holland House, the Manhattan Hotel, Methodist Church, Quakers, Catholic Church.*

(*g*) Capitalize the names of nations, tribes, races, as *Indian, Japanese, Chinese, Jew, American, Slav, Bohemian, Armenian, Turk.* The word *negro* is capitalized by some writers and printers; by others it is written with a small letter. The distinction is sometimes made that when *negro* refers to a negro or to negroes as members of a race, the word should be capitalized, as in *The Negro has made astonishing advances in civilization*, but when it refers merely to a person, it should be written with a small letter, as in *The watchman was an old and rheumatic negro.* But the distinction seems artificial, and no similar distinction is made in other words of this kind, as in *Chinese, Japanese, Jew*, etc. Since the word is not a recognized race name, on the whole it seems better to write *negro* always with a small letter, as one would write *white man.* The word *gypsy* is not capitalized.

(*h*) Capitalize the proper names for places, cities, continents, states, streets, rivers, bays, lakes, oceans, mountains, public squares, docks, piers, wharves, and all places known by an accepted and established designation, as in *Chicago, Africa, Idaho, Clark Street, Herald Square, Delaware River, Atlantic Ocean, Great South Bay, the Singer Building, the Plaza Hotel, Pikes Peak, Great Salt Lake, Yale University* (capitalized both as the name of a place and as the name of an institution). An accompanying word, like *street, river, county, state, college, university*, which forms part of the name of a place is capitalized, as in *Main Street, Green River, Westchester County, Beloit College, Columbia University, Union City, New York State.* Such words are not capitalized, however, when they are not parts of the established names of the places to which they refer, as in *Westchester is a county of New York State; He lived in the city of Chicago.*

The nicknames of places are capitalized in the same way as their formal names, as in *the Windy City, the Hub, the City of Brotherly Love, the Buckeye State, Hoosier State*, etc.

Capitalize also the names for national flags, as in *the Stars and Stripes, the Red, White, and Blue, Old Glory, the Tricolor.*

(*i*) Capitalize *North, East, South, West, Southwest,* etc., when the words refer to specific regions, but not when they indicate direction in a general way. Thus one would write, *The cities of the East are larger than the cities of the West,* but *Columbus sailed west with his three ships.*

The adjectives *northern, eastern, southern, western,* etc., are not usually capitalized, even when they refer to specific localities, as in *They entertained us with true southern hospitality.*

(*j*) Capitalize the names of the days of the week, of the months, and of holidays and festivals, like *Labor Day, Thanksgiving, the Fourth of July,* etc., but the names of the seasons are not usually capitalized unless they are personified.

(*k*) Capitalize the names of the Deity, of Jesus Christ, of the Trinity, as in *Father, Son, and Holy Ghost,* of the Virgin Mary, and so also the names of exalted religious persons in other than the Christian religion, as in *Buddha, the Great Spirit,* etc.

Some persons capitalize all pronouns which have God or Christ as antecedents, as in *Christ shed His blood for the sins of mankind,* but ordinarily such pronouns would not be capitalized.

(*l*) Capitalize the names of important historical events, periods, movements, enactments, treaties, etc., as in *the Norman Conquest, the Stone Age, the Woman's Suffrage Movement, the Emancipation Proclamation, the Treaty of Versailles,* etc.

Capitalize *Constitution* when the word refers to the Constitution of the United States, but not when it refers to a state constitution or the constitution of some private organization.

(*m*) Capitalize the first word and all important words in a title, as in *The Decline and Fall of the Roman Empire, The Rime of the Ancient Mariner, The Ring of the Nibelungs, A Midsummer Night's Dream.*

The articles *the, a, an* at the beginning of titles may be treated as integral parts of the titles and thus capitalized, as in the examples above, or they may be regarded as not forming necessary parts of the titles and consequently may be written with small letters, as in: I have been reading the *Decline and Fall of the Roman Empire* by Gibbon.

(*n*) Capitalize the names of the planets, stars, and constellations, as in *Jupiter, the Milky Way, the Southern Cross*, etc., but *sun, moon,* and *earth* are not capitalized unless they are personified.

(*o*) Capitalize the abbreviations *A.D., B.C., A.U.C.,* but ordinarily *a.m., p.m.* are not capitalized. The abbreviation *No.* (number) is almost always capitalized.

(*p*) Capitalize the pronoun *I* and the interjection *O*, but capitalize *Oh* only at the beginning of a sentence.

(*q*) In drawing up a formal document, capitalize such words as *Whereas, Resolved* at the headings of the several sections, and capitalize also the beginning word of each of the sections following the words *Whereas, Resolved*, etc.


After all the rules have been given, it must be added that capitalization is to a considerable degree a matter of taste and of varying traditional custom on the part of different publishers. The best guide to capitalization is to take some reputable publication of the kind one is interested in and follow it as a model. The same may be said of punctuation.


## IV. CUSTOMARY ABBREVIATIONS

### §1. Days of the week

| Mon. | Tu. | Wed. | Th. | Fr. | Sat. | Sun. |
|------|-----|------|-----|-----|------|------|

## §2. Months of the year

March, April, May, June, and July are usually not abbreviated. The abbreviations for the other months are:

Jan.    Feb.    Aug.    Sept.    Oct.    Nov.    Dec.

## §3. Names of states and possessions of the U. S. (United States), U. S. A. (United States of America)

Alaska, Guam, Hawaii, Idaho, Iowa, Ohio, Samoa, and Utah are usually not abbreviated. The abbreviations for the other states and possessions are:

| | | | |
|---|---|---|---|
| Ala. | Alabama | N. D. | North Dakota |
| Ariz. | Arizona | Neb. | Nebraska |
| Ark. | Arkansas | Nev. | Nevada |
| Calif. | California | N. H. | New Hampshire |
| Colo. | Colorado | N. J. | New Jersey |
| Conn. | Connecticut | N. M. | New Mexico |
| D. C. | District of Columbia | N. Y. | New York |
| Del. | Delaware | Okla. | Oklahoma |
| Fla. | Florida | Ore. | Oregon |
| Ga. | Georgia | Pa. | Pennsylvania |
| Ill. | Illinois | P. I. | Philippine Islands |
| Ind. | Indiana | P. R. | Porto Rico |
| Kan. | Kansas | R. I. | Rhode Island |
| Ky. | Kentucky | S. C. | South Carolina |
| La. | Louisiana | S. D. | South Dakota |
| Mass. | Massachusetts | Tenn. | Tennessee |
| Md. | Maryland | Tex. | Texas |
| Me. | Maine | Va. | Virginia |
| Mich. | Michigan | V. I. | Virgin Islands |
| Minn. | Minnesota | Vt. | Vermont |
| Miss. | Mississippi | Wash. | Washington |
| Mo. | Missouri | Wis. | Wisconsin |
| Mont. | Montana | W. Va. | West Virginia |
| N. C. | North Carolina | Wyo. | Wyoming |

## §4. Abbreviations in general use

| | |
|---|---|
| A. A. A. | American Automobile Association |
| A. A. U. W. | American Association of University Women |
| A. B. | able-bodied seaman |
| A. B. *or* B. A. | Bachelor of Arts (Latin *Artium Baccalaureus*) |
| abbr. | abbreviation |
| abl. | ablative |
| Abp. | Archbishop |
| A. C. | Before Christ (Latin *ante Christum*) |
| acc. | accusative |
| A. D. | in the year of our Lord (Latin *anno Domini*) |
| ad. fin. | toward the end (Latin *ad finem*) |
| ad. inf. | to infinity (Latin *ad infinitum*) |
| ad init. | at the beginning (Latin *ad initium*) |
| adj. | adjective |
| Adjt. | Adjutant |
| ad lib. | as far or as much as desired (Latin *ad libitum*) |
| Adm. | Admiral |
| adm. *or* admr. | administrator |
| adv. | adverb |
| advt. *or* ad. | advertisement |
| ae., *or* aet., *or* aetat. | of the age, aged (Latin *aetatis*) |
| A. E. F. | American Expeditionary Force |
| Aen. | *Aeneid* |
| A. H. | in the year of the Hegira (Latin *anno Hegirae*) |
| A. L. A. | American Library Association |
| A. M. *or* M. A. | Master of Arts (Latin *artium magister*) |
| a. m. *or* A. M. | before noon (Latin *ante meridiem*) |
| anon. | anonymous |
| app. | appendix |
| arith. | arithmetic |
| A. S. | Anglo-Saxon |

| | |
|---|---|
| A. U. C. | from the founding of Rome (Latin *ab urbe condita*) |
| A. V. | Authorized Version |
| A. Y. L. | Shakspere's *As You Like It* |
| A. & C. | Shakspere's *Antony and Cleopatra* |
| b. | born |
| B. A. | *see* A. B. |
| Bart. | Baronet |
| bbl., *plural* bbls. | barrel, barrels |
| B. C. | Before Christ; British Columbia |
| B. C. L. | Bachelor of Civil Law |
| B. D. | Bachelor of Divinity |
| Beds. | Bedfordshire |
| B. Mus. *or* Mus. B. | Bachelor of Music |
| Bp. | Bishop |
| Bros. | Brothers |
| B. S. *or* B. Sc. | Bachelor of Science |
| Bucks. | Buckinghamshire |
| B. V. M. | the Blessed Virgin Mary |
| C. | Centigrade |
| c. | cent, cents; century; chapter; circa (*also* ca.) |
| Cambs. | Cambridgeshire |
| Can. | Canada |
| Cantab. | Cantabrigian, of Cambridge |
| Cap. | chapter (Latin *caput*) |
| cap. *or* caps. | capital letters |
| Capt. | Captain |
| Card. | Cardinal |
| CC. | chapters |
| C. E. | Civil Engineer |
| Cent. | Centigrade |
| cf. | compare (Latin *confer*) |
| ch. *or* chap. | chapter |
| Chas. | Charles |

| | |
|---|---|
| Ches. | Cheshire |
| Co. | Company; County |
| %o | care of |
| C. O. D. *or* c. o. d. | cash on delivery |
| Col. | Colonel; *Colossians* |
| Coll. | College |
| colloq. | colloquial |
| con. | against (Latin *contra*) |
| conj. | conjugation; conjunction |
| Coop. | Cooperative |
| cor. | corner |
| Cor. | *Corinthians;* Shakspere's *Coriolanus* |
| cp. | compare |
| c. p. | candle power; chemically pure |
| C. P. A. | Certified Public Accountant |
| Cr. | Creditor |
| cres. | crescendo |
| cwt. | hundredweight |
| Cymb. | Shakspere's *Cymbeline* |
| d. | penny, pence (Latin *denarius*); died |
| d. *or* D. | remove, delete (Latin *dele*) |
| D. A. R. | Daughter(s) of the American Revolution |
| dat. | dative |
| D. C. | from the beginning (Italian *da capo*) |
| D. C. L. | Doctor of Civil Law |
| D. D. | Doctor of Divinity |
| D. D. S. | Doctor of Dental Surgery |
| deg. | degree |
| Dept. | Department |
| Deut. | *Deuteronomy* |
| D. G. | by God's grace (Latin *Dei gratia*) |
| dial. | dialect; dialogue |
| dim. | diminuendo, with decreasing force |
| D. N. B. | *Dictionary of National Biography* |
| do. | ditto |

| | |
|---|---|
| dol. | dollar(s) |
| doz. | dozen |
| Dr. | Debtor; Doctor |
| dram. pers. | the persons in a play (Latin *dramatis personae*) |
| D. S. C. | Distinguished Service Cross |
| D. V. | God willing (Latin *Deo volente*) |
| E. | East |
| Eccles. | *Ecclesiastes* |
| ed. | edition; editor |
| Ed. | Edward |
| Edm. | Edmund |
| E. E. T. S. | Early English Text Society |
| e. g. | for example (Latin *exempli gratia*) |
| Eph. | *Ephesians* |
| esp. | especially |
| Esq. | Esquire |
| et al. | and others (Latin *et alii*) |
| etc. | and so forth (Latin *et cetera*) |
| et seq. *or* et seqq. | and what follows (Latin *et sequentia*) |
| etym. | etymology |
| Exod. | *Exodus* |
| Ezek. | *Ezekiel* |
| 8vo | octavo |
| f. *or* ff. | following |
| F. *or* Fahr. | Fahrenheit |
| fcap. *or* fcp. | foolscap |
| fem. | feminine |
| ff. | very loud (Italian *fortissimo*) |
| fid. def. | defender of the faith (Latin *fidei defensor*) |
| fig. | figure |
| flor. | flourished (Latin *floruit*) |
| f. o. b. | free on board |
| fol. | folio |
| fr. | franc(s) |
| Fr. | French |

| | |
|---|---|
| Fred. | Frederick |
| Frl. | Miss (German *Fräulein*) |
| F. R. S. | Fellow of the Royal Society |
| ft. | foot, feet |
| 4to | quarto |
| gal. | gallon(s) |
| Gal. | *Galatians* |
| G. A. R. | Grand Army of the Republic |
| gen. | general; genitive |
| Gen. | General; *Genesis* |
| Geo. | George |
| geog. | geography |
| geol. | geology |
| geom. | geometry |
| Gk. *or* Gr. | Greek |
| Glam. | Glamorganshire |
| Glos. | Gloucestershire |
| G. O. M. | Grand Old Man |
| G. O. P. | Grand Old Party |
| Gov. | Governor |
| h. | hour(s) |
| Hab. | *Habakkuk* |
| Haml. | Shakspere's *Hamlet* |
| Hants. | Hampshire |
| H. B. M. | His *or* Her Britannic Majesty |
| H. C. | House of Commons |
| Heb. | *Hebrews* |
| Herts. | Hertfordshire |
| hhd. | hogshead |
| H. L. | House of Lords |
| H. M. | His *or* Her Majesty |
| H. M. A. | H. M.'s airship |
| H. M. S. | H. M.'s ship |
| Hon. | Honorable |
| Hon. Sec. | Honorary Secretary |

| | |
|---|---|
| Hos. | *Hosea* |
| h. p. | horsepower |
| H. Q. | Headquarters |
| hr(s). | hour(s) |
| H. R. H. | His *or* Her Royal Highness |
| Hunts. | Huntingdonshire |
| ib. *or* ibid. | in the same place (Latin *ibidem*) |
| id. | the same (Latin *idem*) |
| i. e. | that is (Latin *id est*) |
| I H S | Jesus |
| in. | inch(es) |
| inc. | incorporated |
| incl. | inclusive |
| incog. | incognito |
| ind(ic). | indicative |
| indecl. | indeclinable |
| inf(in). | infinitive |
| I. N. R. I. | Jesus of Nazareth, King of the Jews (Latin *Jesus Nazarenus Rex Judaeorum*) |
| inst. | instant, in the present month |
| Is. | *Isaiah;* Island |
| It. | Italian |
| ital. | italics |
| I. W. | Isle of Wight |
| I. W. W. | Industrial Workers of the World |
| Jas. | James |
| J. D. | Doctor of Laws (Latin *Jurum Doctor*) |
| Jer. | *Jeremiah* |
| Jno. | John |
| Jon. | Jonathan |
| Jos. | Joseph |
| Josh. | *Joshua* |
| J. P. | Justice of the peace |
| Jr. | Junior |
| Judg. | *Judges* |

| | |
|---|---|
| K. C. | King's Counsel |
| K. G. | Knight of the Garter |
| K. L. | Shakspere's *King Lear* |
| Knt. *or* Kt. | Knight |
| K. of C. | Knights of Columbus |
| Lancs. | Lancashire |
| lat. | latitude |
| lb(s). | pound(s) (Latin *libra, librae*) |
| l. c. | lower case (i. e., small letter), in the place quoted (Latin *loco citato*) |
| Ld. | Limited |
| Leics. | Leicestershire |
| Lev. | *Leviticus* |
| L. H. D. | Doctor of the Humanities (Latin *Literarum Humanarum Doctor*) |
| Lieut. | Lieutenant |
| Lincs. | Lincolnshire |
| Linn. | Linnaeus |
| Lit(t). D. | Doctor of Letters (Latin *Literarum Doctor*) |
| ll. | lines |
| LL. B. | Bachelor of Laws (Latin *Legum Baccalaureus*) |
| LL. D. | Doctor of Laws (Latin *Legum Doctor*) |
| L. L. L. | Shakspere's *Love's Labor's Lost* |
| loc. cit. | in the place quoted (Latin *loco citato*) |
| long. | longitude |
| loq. | speaks (Latin *loquitur*) |
| Lt. | Lieutenant |
| Ltd. | Limited |
| LXX | Septuagint |
| m. *or* M. | noon (Latin *meridies,* |
| M. | French *Monsieur*, Mr.  *See* MM. |
| M. | thousand (Latin *Mille*) |
| M. A. | Master of Arts |
| Macb. | Shakspere's *Macbeth* |
| Maj. | Major |

| | |
|---|---|
| Man. | Manitoba |
| masc. | masculine |
| math. | mathematics |
| Matt. | *Matthew* |
| M. B. | Bachelor of Medicine (Latin *Medicinae Baccalaureus*) |
| M. C. | Member of Congress |
| M. D. | Doctor of Medicine (Latin *Medicinae Doctor*) |
| M. E. | Middle English; Mechanical Engineer; Mining Engineer; Methodist Episcopal |
| memo. | memorandum |
| M. for M. | Shakspere's *Measure for Measure* |
| Mgr. | Manager; Monseigneur; Monsignor |
| M. L. A. | Modern Language Association |
| Mlle. | French *Mademoiselle*, Miss |
| Mlles. | French *Mesdemoiselles*, Misses |
| MM. | French *Messieurs*, Sirs |
| Mme. | French *Madame* |
| Mmes. | French *Mesdames* |
| M. N. D. | Shakspere's *Midsummer Night's Dream* |
| M. of V. | Shakspere's *Merchant of Venice* |
| M. P. | Member of Parliament |
| MS. *or* ms. | manuscript |
| MSS. *or* mss. | manuscripts |
| Mus. B. *or* Mus. Bac. | Bachelor of Music |
| Mus. D. *or* Mus. Doc. | Doctor of Music |
| M. W. W. | Shakespere's *Merry Wives of Windsor* |
| Mx. | Middlesex |
| myth. | mythology |
| N. | North |
| n. b. *or* N. B. | note well (Latin *nota bene*) |
| N. B. | New Brunswick |
| n. d. | no date |
| N. E. A. | National Education Association |

| | |
|---|---|
| N. E. D. | *New English Dictionary* (also called *Oxford English Dictionary*) |
| nem. con. | no one objecting (Latin *nemine contradicente*) |
| nem. dis. | no one dissenting (Latin *nemine dissentiente*) |
| neut. | neuter |
| N. F. | Newfoundland |
| Nº *or* No. | number (Latin *numero*) |
| nom. | nominative |
| noncom. | noncommissioned officer |
| non seq. | it does not follow (Latin *non sequitur*) |
| Northants. | Northamptonshire |
| Northumb. | Northumberland |
| Nᵒˢ *or* Nos. | numbers |
| Notts. | Nottinghamshire |
| N. P. | Notary Public |
| n. p. or d. | no place or date |
| N. S. | New Style; Nova Scotia |
| N. S. P. C. A. | National Society for the Prevention of Cruelty to Animals |
| N. S. W. | New South Wales |
| N. T. | New Testament |
| Num. | *Numbers* |
| ob. | died (Latin *obiit*) |
| obj. | object |
| obs. | obsolete |
| oct. | octavo |
| O. E. | Old English |
| O. E. D. | *Oxford English Dictionary.* *See* N. E. D. |
| O. F. | Old French |
| O. K. | all correct |
| O. N. | Old Norse |
| Ont. | Ontario |
| op. | work (Latin *opus*) |
| op. cit. | the work cited (Latin *opus citatum*) |
| opt. | optative |

| | |
|---|---|
| O. S. | Old Style |
| O. S. A. | of the Order of St. Augustine |
| O. S. B. | of the Order of St. Benedict |
| O. S. D. | of the Order of St. Dominic |
| O. S. F. | of the Order of St. Francis |
| O. T. | Old Testament |
| Oth. | Shakspere's *Othello* |
| Oxon. | of Oxford; Oxfordshire |
| oz. | ounce(s) |
| p., pp. | page, pages |
| p. c. | per cent |
| P. C. G. N. | Permanent Committee on Geographical Names for British Official Use[1] |
| pd. | paid |
| Ph. B. | Bachelor of Philosophy (Latin *Philosophiae Baccalaureus* |
| Ph. D. | Doctor of Philosophy (Latin *Philosophiae Doctor*) |
| Phil. | *Philippians* |
| Philem. | *Philemon* |
| philol. | philology |
| phr. | phrase |
| pl. | plural |
| p. m. *or* P. M. | afternoon (Latin *post meridiem*) |
| P. M. | Postmaster |
| P. O. | Post Office |
| P. P. C. *or* <br> p. p. c. | to take leave, to say good-by (French *pour prendre congé*) |
| pr. | pair |
| pred. | predicate |
| Prof. | Professor |
| pron. | pronoun |
| pro tem. | for the time being (Latin *pro tempore*) |
| Prov. | *Proverbs* |

[1] The publications of this committee may be procured from the Royal Geographical Society, London, England.

| | |
|---|---|
| prox. | next, in next month (Latin *proximo*) |
| P. S. | postscript |
| Ps. | *Psalms* |
| pseud. | pseudonym |
| pt. | pint |
| q. or qy. | query, question |
| Q. C. | Queen's Counsel |
| Q. E. D. | which was to be demonstrated (Latin *quod erat demonstrandum*) |
| qt. | quart(s) |
| quant. suf. *or* quantum suff. | as much as suffices (Latin *quantum sufficit*) |
| quot. | quotation |
| q. v. | which see (Latin *quod vide*) |
| R. C. | Roman Catholic |
| recd. | received |
| ref. | reference |
| regt. | regiment |
| rel. pron. | relative pronoun |
| Rev. | *Revelations;* Reverend |
| Revd. | Reverend |
| R. F. D. | Rural Free Delivery |
| R. I. P. | May he, she, or they rest in peace (Latin *Requiesca(n)t in pace*) |
| R. M. S. | Royal Mail Steamer |
| R. N. | Royal Navy |
| Robt. | Robert |
| rom. | roman type |
| Rom. | *Romans* |
| R. R. | Railroad |
| r. s. v. p. *or* R. S. V. P. | Please answer (French *répondez s'il vous plaît*) |
| Rt. Hon. | Right Honorable |
| Rt. Rev. | Right Reverend |
| R. & J. | Shakspere's *Romeo and Juliet* |

| | |
|---|---|
| Ry. | Railway |
| S. | South; Saint |
| S. A. | South Africa; Salvation Army |
| Salop., Shrops. | Shropshire |
| Sam. | *Samuel* |
| S. A. R. | Sons of the American Revolution |
| sc. | namely (Latin *scilicet*); scene; carved (Latin *sculpsit*) |
| scil. | namely (Latin *scilicet*) |
| sculps. | carved (Latin *sculpsit*) |
| sec. | second |
| Sec. | Secretary |
| sen. *or* senr. | senior |
| seq(q). | *see* et seq(q). |
| Sergt. | Sergeant |
| sh. | shilling |
| Shak. | Shakspere |
| sing. | singular |
| S. J. | Society of Jesus |
| Skr. | Sanskrit |
| S. O. S. | wireless signal of distress |
| S. P. C. K. | Society for Promoting Christian Knowledge |
| S. P. E. | Society for Pure English |
| S. P. G. | Society for the Propagation of the Gospel |
| sp. gr. | specific gravity |
| S. P. Q. R. | the Roman Senate and People (Latin *senatus populusque Romanus*) |
| sq. | square |
| Sr. | Senior |
| S. S. | Steamship |
| SS. | Saints |
| st. *or* St. | Street |
| St. | Saint |
| Staffs. | Staffordshire |
| S. T. D. | Doctor of Sacred Theology (Latin *Sacrosanctae Theologiae Doctor*) |

| | |
|---|---|
| stg. | sterling |
| S. T. P. | Professor of Sacred Theology (Latin *Sacrosanctae Theologiae Professor*) |
| subj. | subject; subjunctive |
| sup. | above (Latin *supra*) |
| superl. | superlative |
| Supt. | Superintendent |
| s. v. | under that word (Latin *sub voce*) |
| syn. | synonym |
| 6to | sexto |
| 16mo | sextodecimo |
| temp. | in the period of (Latin *tempore*) |
| Temp. | Shakspere's *Tempest* |
| T. G. V. | Shakspere's *Two Gentlemen of Verona* |
| Thess. | *Thessalonians* |
| Thos. | Thomas |
| Tim. | *Timothy* |
| Tit. | *Titus* |
| T. N. | Shakspere's *Twelfth Night* |
| T. N. T. | trinitrotoluol |
| T. of A. | Shakspere's *Timon of Athens* |
| tr. | transpose |
| trans. | transitive |
| Treas. | Treasurer |
| trig. | trigonometry |
| T. & C. | Shakspere's *Troilus and Cressida* |
| 12mo | duodecimo |
| u. c. | capital, upper case |
| ult. | last month (Latin *ultimo*) |
| U. P. | United Presbyterian |
| v., *plural* vv. | verb; verse |
| v. *or* vid. | see (Latin *vide*) |
| Ven. | Venerable |
| verb. sap. *or* verb. sat. sap. | a word to the wise is sufficient (Latin *verbum sapienti*) *See* p. 609. |

| | |
|---|---|
| viz. | namely (Latin *videlicet*) |
| voc. | vocative |
| vol. | volume |
| vs. | against (Latin *versus*) |
| v. s. | see above (Latin *vide supra*) |
| V. S. | Veterinary Surgeon |
| Vulg. | Vulgate |
| W. | West |
| w. c. | water-closet |
| W. C. T. U. | Women's Christian Temperance Union |
| w. f. | wrong fount or font (of type) |
| Wilts. | Wiltshire |
| Wm. | William |
| Worcs. | Worcestershire |
| wt. | weight |
| W. T. | Shakspere's *Winter's Tale* |
| Xmas | Christmas |
| Xt | Christ |
| Xtian | Christian |
| yd., yds. | yard, yards |
| yᵉ | the |
| Y. M. C. A. | Young Men's Christian Association |
| Y. M. H. A. | Young Men's Hebrew Association |
| Yorks. | Yorkshire |
| Y. W. C. A. | Young Women's Christian Association |
| Y. W. H. A. | Young Women's Hebrew Association |
| Zech. | *Zechariah* |
| Zeph. | *Zephaniah* |
| Zool. | Zoology |

## §5. Rules for Abbreviations

(*a*) The extent to which abbreviations are employed depends very much on the style of writing. In a formal literary style no abbreviations are used, except conventional forms of address, like *Mr., Mrs.;* honorary titles after names, like *Esq., D.D.; B.C.* and *A. D.* with dates; sometimes *No.* with numerals. Either the form *Saint John* or *St. John* may be used. Titles preceding names are customarily written in full in formal style, as in *General Hooker, Governor Smith, Professor Brown,* or *General John Hooker, Governor Wm. Smith, Professor H. E. Brown.* See **Honorable, Reverend** in the body of the book.

The names of days, months, countries, states, cities, and other political divisions, streets, railroads, and all similar terms are written in full in formal style.

Abbreviations like *a. m., p. m., i. e., e. g., viz., &,* etc., are avoided in formal literary style, and the corresponding full phrases are used instead.

Such words as *avenue, boulevard, street, building, railroad, mountains, manufacturing, company, corporation, university,* and others forming parts of names are always written in full in connected formal discourse.

Names of railroads, steamboat lines, business firms, magazines, and other publications are written in full in formal style.

In informal style, abbreviations may be used to an extent which can be determined only by the degree of informality of the writing and the taste of the writer.

In technical writing, including technical business correspondence, lists, footnotes, bibliographies, time tables, etc., abbreviations are employed freely. Good form requires, however, that the use of them in a given piece of writing or a given document shall be consistent.

(*b*) An abbreviation is followed by a period. But some authorities distinguish two kinds of abbreviations, those in which the abbreviation ends with the final letter of the word abbreviated, as in *Ky.* for *Kentucky*, and those in which the final letter of the abbreviation is not the same as the final letter of the word, as in *Mo.* for *Missouri*. Abbreviations of the first type are sometimes printed and written without a period, as in *Ky*, and only abbreviations of the second type with a period. The distinction seems unimportant, however, the significant thing about an abbreviation being that it is such, not the specific manner of its formation. It seems better, therefore, to follow a general rule and to end all abbreviations with periods. As exceptions to this rule, some writers regularly omit the period after *Mr*, *Mrs*, and *Dr*. So also in technical writing, as after *MS*, *per cent*, the period is occasionally omitted in certain frequently recurring abbreviations.

The word *Miss* is not an abbreviation, therefore takes no period. Likewise the forms of the ordinals *1st, 2d, 2nd, 3d, 3rd, 4th, 5th*, etc., are not abbreviations and do not take periods.

(*c*) Capitalize an abbreviation when the word for which it stands would be capitalized if written in full.

(*d*) References to passages in books, plays, and the Bible may be given as follows:

| | | |
|---|---|---|
| p. 48 | *for* | page 48 |
| pp. 45–48 | *for* | pages 45 to 48 |
| Vol. I, p. 18, *or* I, 18 | *for* | Volume one, page 18 |
| Cap. IV, *or* Ch. IV, *or* Chap. IV, *or* chap. iv | *for* | Chapter four |
| T. G. V. I, III, 84, *or* T. G. V., Act I, Sc. III, 1. 84 | *for* | { *Two Gentlemen of Verona*, Act I, Scene III, line 84 |
| 2 Cor. I, 3–8, *or* II Cor. I, 3–8, *or* II Cor. I: 3–8 | *for* | { *Second Corinthians*, Chapter one, verses 3 to 8 |

(*e*) Dates should be given in the simplest possible form, as for example:

May 20, 1924
November 18, 1925 *or* Nov. 18, 1925

The letters *st*, *nd*, *d*, *rd*, or *th* after the number giving the day of the month should not be used.

Terms like 3/6/21 or 3-6-21 are not to be recommended, for if the first two numbers are both below twelve, it is impossible to tell which refers to the day and which to the month. The date 3/6/21 might mean March 6, 1921, or June 3, 1921.

(*f*) In formal connected discourse numbers are always written in full, except large exact numbers, for example, 148,641, which would be cumbersome if written out. In lists, reports, commercial and technical writing, figures are used for both large and small numbers. Sums of money and the hours of the day are frequently expressed by figures in informal style, as in *The repairs cost $12.86; We left at 9:30 a. m.*, but such phrasing would be avoided in formal style.

(*g*) A number should be expressed both in figures and in words only in legal or business documents in which one form is necessary as a check on the other, as in *Please pay the bearer $14.50 (fourteen dollars and fifty cents)*.

(*h*) A sentence should not begin with a figure, but the number should be spelled out or the sentence should be recast to begin in some other way.